W9-BQW-286

LEGENDARY GUITARS

OFF
PATENTED

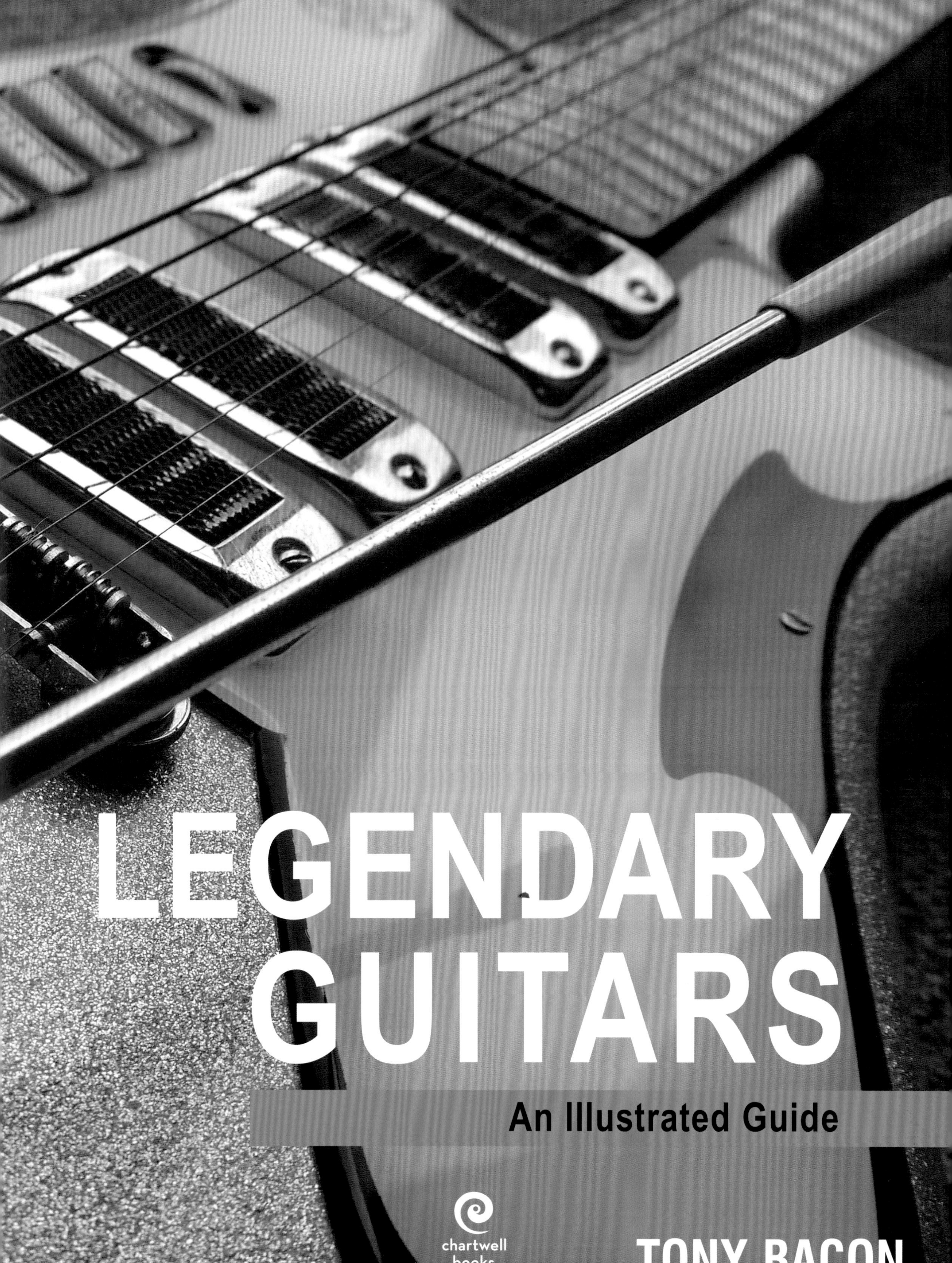

LEGENDARY GUITARS

An Illustrated Guide

chartwell books

TONY BACON

Brimming with creative inspiration, how-to projects, and useful information to enrich your everyday life, quarto.com is a favorite destination for those pursuing their interests and passions.

This edition published in 2022 by Chartwell Books,
an imprint of The Quarto Group
142 West 36th Street, 4th Floor
New York, NY 10018 USA
T (212) 779-4972 **F** (212) 779-6058
www.Quarto.com

Chartwell titles are also available at discount for retail, wholesale, promotional, and bulk purchase. For details, contact the Special Sales Manager by email at specialsales@quarto.com or by mail at The Quarto Group, Attn: Special Sales Manager, 100 Cummings Center Suite 265D, Beverly, MA 01915, USA.

10 9 8 7 6 5 4 3 2 1

ISBN: 978-0-7858-4131-9

Printed in China

Contents

"People are getting tired of sitting in front of a television set. They want to get together and entertain themselves, and there's no better instrument than a guitar for building a convivial atmosphere."

SIDNEY KATZ, PRESIDENT, THE HARMONY COMPANY, 1959

background

The first commercial electric guitars, which began to appear in the 30s, were acoustic guitars with added pickups and controls. This was a natural move on the part of guitar makers, who were used to taking something already in existence and modifying it to better suit the prevailing musical requirements.

The demand for electric guitars came from guitarists who found it increasingly difficult to compete with and even match the volume of the instruments all around them—bigger drum kits, blaring horns, banjos and mandolins, and so on. They wanted a solution, and amplification provided the means to that end.

The acoustic guitar had been around for some time. By the early 16th century, it had the shape and style that we would recognize today as a guitar, and from the earliest years of its existence, guitarists and designers tried to increase its volume and cutting power, for example by grouping strings together and increasing their number.

Later moves that helped to boost volume, power, and tonal versatility included the wide adoption of steel strings in the early decades of the 20th century. Martin in Pennsylvania used X-shape bracing for flattop acoustics and added a dreadnought body design with thick waist and wide, squared shoulders. In the early 20s, Lloyd Loar developed the archtop guitar at Gibson in Michigan with the L-5 model, which had f-holes and a neck-strengthening truss-rod. Gibson, Epiphone, and others developed this idea in the USA. Later in the 20s, National in Los Angeles came up with the resonator guitar, an instrument with a metal body that had metal resonator discs inside, which acted like mechanical loudspeakers to spread the brash sound of the guitar. But there was still some frustration at the limitations a hollow body placed on the electric guitar.

GIBSON ES-150
THIS EXAMPLE: ***1938***
The ES-150 was Gibson's first Spanish electric guitar, introduced in 1936 as the firm began to focus on guitars following its early emphasis on mandolins and then banjos, which until the early 30s had been the most popular stringed instruments.

Epiphone's Electar brand on a 1937 catalogue cover.

EPIPHONE ZEPHYR
THIS EXAMPLE: ***1941***
The Zephyr was typical of the non-cutaway electric guitars that the New York City maker Epiphone began to produce from the 30s, at first with the brandname Electar.

This 1942 Gibson catalogue reflects the range of the firm's products.

GIBSON ES-300
THIS EXAMPLE: ***1941***
The most expensive pre-war Gibson electric, the shortlived ES-300 had an unusually large pickup cover so that it could be angled to accentuate bass and treble tones.

"THE SONORA"

The enchantment of dreamy Mexico and rare romance of old Spain are deeply entwined into the mellow rich tone of this unusual electric guitar.

Strikingly beautiful, the appeal of this sparkling electrical instrument affords all that professional brilliance so essential to the paid artist.

The "wasp-waist" slenderness of the graceful "free-action" neck will amaze you with its adaptability for high speed technique.

The "Sonora's" exclusive "tandem" individual pick-up units afford rippling free power without the sacrifice of tonal fidelity. The thrilling depth and fullness of the bell clear electrical reproduction has won the favor of the keenest of critics. A Truly Vital Spanish Guitar Tone!

No. 175 Sonora Electric Spanish Guitar & cord . . $175.00
No. 5D Case—3 ply—Basket Weave—Curly Plush . $28.00
Mated Amplifiers—See pages 31 and 33

Radiant Blonde **"Natural" finish** available on special order—No Extra Charge.

The first two-pickup electric, National's Sonora of 1939.

George Beauchamp and some colleagues at National in Los Angeles developed a working magnetic pickup in the early 30s. To test the pickup, they built a one-off wooden guitar, nicknamed the Frying Pan for the look of its small round body and long neck. Beauchamp and Paul Barth joined Adolph Rickenbacker, who ran a local tool-and-die firm, to put these ideas into production. They formed a new company and in 1932 began manufacturing cast aluminum Frying Pan electric lap-steel guitars, each fitted with Beauchamp's "horseshoe" electro-magnetic pickup.

These Electro-brand Frying Pan steels were the first electric guitars in general production with a string-driven electro-magnetic pickup. Around 1934, the brandname was changed to Rickenbacker Electro (sometimes spelled "Rickenbacher"). Gibson's first electric guitar was the E-150, introduced at the end of 1935, also with an aluminum body, although both Rickenbacker Electro and Gibson soon became aware of the shortcomings of that material and switched to wood, with Gibson subtly renaming its model as the EH-150.

George Beauchamp wrote in the 1934 patent application for his early electrics that the body "may be" hollow, mainly so it could be "light in weight," but added that "in some instances it may be desirable to make the body solid." The following year, he developed new steel and Spanish electrics for Rickenbacker Electro with almost-solid Bakelite bodies, in effect the first solidbody electric guitars. Another early Spanish solidbody electric was the Slingerland Songster 401, introduced around 1936, probably the first electric guitar with a solid wooden body. Of greater importance was a guitar Paul Bigsby made for Merle Travis in California in 1948. Bigsby made it from solid maple with a through-neck design, routing out the rear to reduce weight and locate components. It was closer to our modern idea of a solidbody electric guitar than anything that had gone before.

RICKENBACKER ELECTRO SPANISH
THIS EXAMPLE: ***1936***
Introduced in 1935, Electro's Spanish model with its "horseshoe" pickup was the first solidbody electric guitar, although its Bakelite body had small pockets inside to reduce weight.

Electro catalogue of 1932 with aluminum-body "Frying Pan" lap-steel.

STANDARD OF THE WORLD

SLINGERLAND
ELECTRICALLY AMPLIFIED GUITARS

Style No. 400
Hawaiian

Style No. 401
Spanish

Complete with Amplifier
Price $135.00

This amplified guitar preserves the mellow and rich intonation of the traditionally beautiful Hawaiian instrument. Tones amplified a thousand-fold through the entire gamut of dynamics without distortion. It is indeed the Wonder instrument of electrical amplification—in modern design, presentation, and superb tonal qualities. This instrument comes complete with specially constructed 5-tube, 8-watt amplifier of airline style with two plug outlets. Instrument standard equipped with volume and tone controls (amplifier with volume control). Each instrument may be purchased with Kant-Krack tailored, plush-lined, case at a slightly additional cost.

No. 400—Hawaiian Amplified Guitar .... $ 75.00
No. 401—Spanish Amplified Guitar .... $ 75.00
Kant-Krack, plush-lined case to fit .... $ 15.00
Slingerland Amplifier .... $ 60.00
Complete Outfit, including all cases $150.00

The Slingerland 401 Spanish (1936 catalogue) with solid wooden body.

BIGSBY MERLE TRAVIS
THIS EXAMPLE: ***1948***
A significant early solidbody electric instrument custom built by Paul Bigsby for the guitarist Merle Travis, and one that inspired contemporary makers, not least Leo Fender.

GIBSON ELECTRIC HAWAIIAN GUITARS

EH-150 **NEW** MODEL

INSTRUMENT

Highly figured curly maple
Hand rubbed lustrous finish with sunburst on top, back and neck
White ivoroid binding on top of body and around fingerboard
Rosewood fingerboard with 29 inlaid frets—nearly 4½ octaves
Special pearl position inlays arranged to tell positions at all times
Tone control (independent of tone control on amplifier)
Volume control (independent of volume control on amplifier)
Special pick-up unit with finest cobalt magnets made
Easy adjustment for pick-up unit
Body size — 13½" long, 9" wide, 1⅞" deep

INSTRUMENT CASE

Heavy Faultless construction, form fitting — green flannel lining — covered with Aeroplane cloth to match amplifier.

AMPLIFIER

Six tubes—five metal and one glass
Four stage amplification
Two instrument sockets
One microphone socket
One socket for additional "Echo" speaker
Volume control for instruments
Volume control for microphone
Tone control for bass or normal tone
On-off ruby signal lamp
Easily accessible fuse
Waterproof Aeroplane cloth covering
Removable back
Finest ten inch Ultrasonic High Fidelity Reproducer
Fifteen watt output
Waterproof slip cover

CORDS

The finest shielded cords made
Strong nickel shielded plugs complete with spring cord protectors
15 foot instrument cord and 10 foot amplifier cord

PRICES

Complete outfit with 6-string guitar, case, amplifier and cords	$150.00
Complete outfit with 7 string guitar, case, amplifier and cords	155.00
Amplifier only	70.00
Instrument only (6-string) with cord	70.00
Instrument only (7-string) with cord	75.00
Instrument case	10.00

Write for information about Amplifiers made for AC-DC Current.

Gibson's hollowbody electric steel, the EH-150, in a 1936 catalogue.

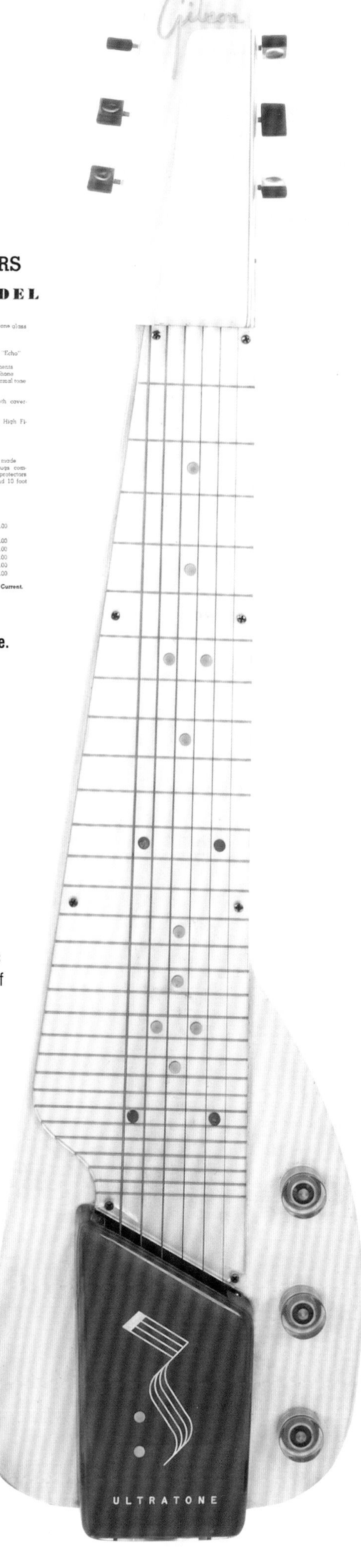

GIBSON ULTRATONE
THIS EXAMPLE: ***1949***
This remarkably modernistic electric lap-steel, made from an artful mix of enameled wood and plastics, was created for Gibson in 1946 by an independent design firm.

"The 50s created the teenager, the teenager demanded pop music, and pop music's shiniest icon was the electric guitar."

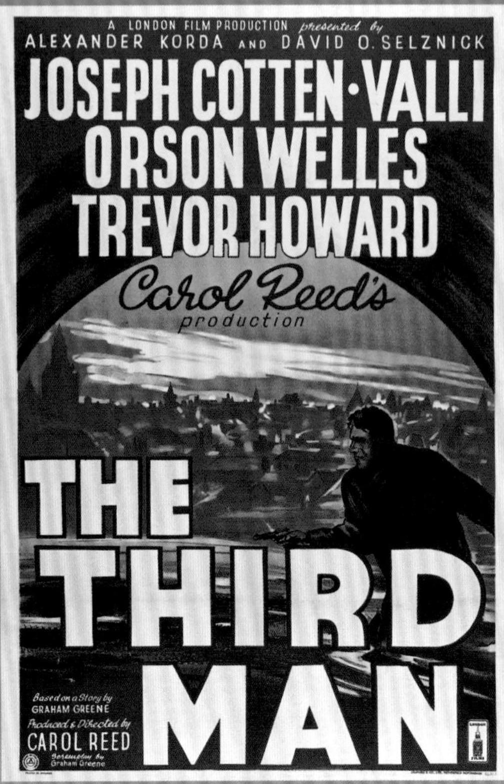
A LONDON FILM PRODUCTION presented by
ALEXANDER KORDA AND DAVID O. SELZNICK
JOSEPH COTTEN · VALLI
ORSON WELLES
TREVOR HOWARD
Carol Reed's production
THE THIRD MAN
Based on a Story by GRAHAM GREENE
Produced & Directed by CAROL REED
Screenplay by Graham Greene

*hallicrafters
FIRST in precision TV!
16-Inch Console
When you turn on this beautiful console, you'll thrill to television's clearest picture…a spectacular performance! Hallicrafters sensational DYNAMIC TUNER with the "Precision Printed Circuit" is the answer. See it before you buy!
• Rectangular Black Tube
• Exclusive "Silver Vortex" Antenna
hallicrafters
CHICAGO 24, ILLINOIS
WORLD'S LEADING MANUFACTURER OF Precision RADIO & TELEVISION

The NEW SOUND!
Capitol
LES PAUL
BRAZIL
HIP-BILLY BOOGIE
SWISS WOODPECKER
CARAVAN
LOVER
THE MAN ON THE FLYING TRAPEZE
BY THE LIGHT OF THE SILVERY MOON
WHAT IS THIS THING CALLED LOVE

- **THE KOREAN WAR** starts in June when North Korean troops invade South Korea. The United Nations supports South Korea, China enters on the North Korean side, and the fighting escalates.

- **GEORGE BERNARD SHAW**, the Irish dramatist best known for *Pygmalion*, dies aged 94.

- **TELEVISION** viewing matches radio listening in New York City for the first time. In 1946, the US had six stations; by the end of 1950, there are over a hundred.

1950

- **THE THIRD MAN THEME** from the 1949 film is released by zither player Anton Karas and sells four million copies during 1950, proving that catchy instrumental records can become big pop hits.

- **HIT RECORDS** include Nat King Cole's 'Mona Lisa,' which wins this year's Academy Award for best song. Patti Page's 'Tennessee Waltz' is a number one smash, outselling the rival version by Les Paul, who releases his debut collection *The New Sound*.

- **DECCA** issues the first LPs on to the UK market. Columbia in the US had issued the first 33⅓ rpm ten-inch and twelve-inch LPs in 1948, and RCA Victor the first 45rpm seven-inch EP records in 1949. LPs followed in Russia and France (1951), Germany (1952), and Spain and Denmark (1953).

From humble beginnings in California, Fender was to become one of the most radical and successful guitar manufacturers of the 50s and 60s, shaking up the industry with boldly styled mass-produced solidbody electric guitars, and in the process changing the way in which guitars were produced, marketed, and played.

Leo Fender's earliest production guitars were electric lap-steels. At first, in the mid 40s, he made these with his partner Doc Kauffman under the K&F brand. Soon, Kauffman left and Leo changed the name of his company to the Fender Electric Instrument Co, which continued to produce electric steels and a modest line of small amplifiers through into the 50s.

Leo's modest firm, based in Fullerton in Orange County, California, began to consider the possibility of a new type of instrument, a solidbody electric Spanish guitar. Fender wanted to make a solidbody not only for musical reasons but also because it would be easier to produce. The company's first solidbody guitar was introduced in 1950, briefly called the Esquire, then the Broadcaster (and a little later, as we shall see, the Telecaster).

Meanwhile, other makers continued to develop the archtop hollowbody electric. Epiphone in New York City, for example, was making some models with three pickups and multiple controls, emphasizing the exciting sonic potential of the electric guitar.

Fender's Broadcaster, the first commercially available solidbody electric guitar, turned the electric instrument into a factory-made product, stripped down to its essentials, built from easily assembled parts, and produced at a relatively affordable price. Fender's methods made for easier, more consistent production, and a different sound. Not for Fender the fat, warm Epiphone-style jazz tone. Instead, the Broadcaster and its descendants had a clearer, sustained sound that was something like a cross between the clean tone of an acoustic guitar and the cutting sound of Fender's existing electric lap-steels.

ORIGINAL **FENDER BROADCASTER**
THIS EXAMPLE: ***1950***
The Broadcaster is historically important as the world's first commercial solidbody electric guitar, and it came to exemplify Fender's relatively simple screw-together construction process.

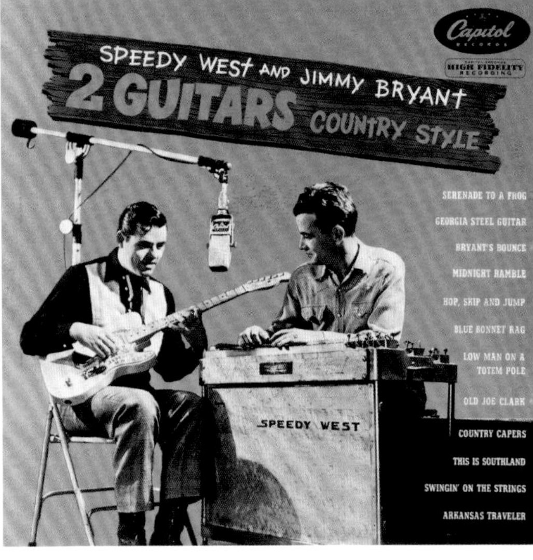

Jimmy Bryant, an early Fender player, pictured (left) on a 1954 album.

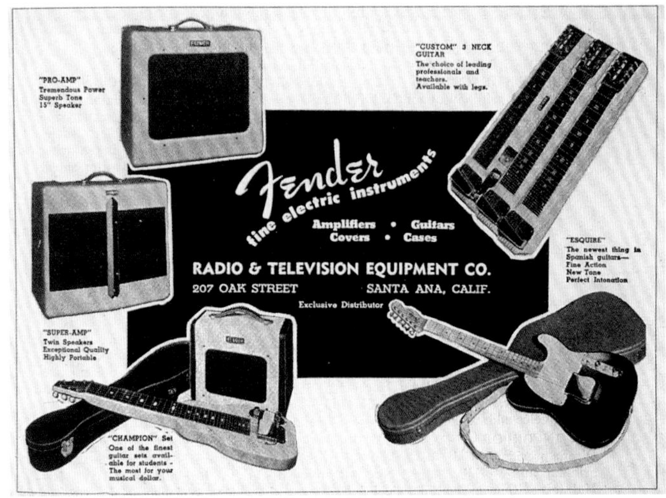

Fender's first solidbody electric appears in early Esquire guise in this 1950 ad.

ORIGINAL **EPIPHONE ZEPHYR EMPEROR REGENT**
THIS EXAMPLE: ***1954***
This impressive hollowbody electric had a pair of volume and tone controls plus a panel of six pushbuttons to select different combinations of its three Epiphone "New York" pickups.

Epiphone's 1954 catalogue cover features the Zephyr Emperor Regent.

Fender ad of 1949 for the Champion steel-and-amp set.

Epiphone 2009 ad with Nick Colionne and electric hollowbodys.

FENDER LEO FENDER BROADCASTER *2000*
Marking the 50th anniversary of the Broadcaster in 2000, Fender's Custom Shop produced this model in a limited edition of 50. It has Leo Fender's signature on the headstock in place of the regular Fender logo.

1001
SIGNET
J. D. SALINGER
The Catcher in the Rye
This unusual book may shock you, will make you laugh, and may break your heart—but you will never forget it
A SIGNET BOOK

DELL
I Love Lucy comics
Still 10¢
Lucy makes it hot for Ricky when she discovers Ricky's old flame.

ALAN FREED
PRESENTS
THE BIG BEAT

- **DJ ALAN FREED** begins his R&B radio show out of Cleveland, Ohio. During the next few years, he starts to describe the music he plays as rock'n'roll.

- **I LOVE LUCY**, the definitive 50s TV sitcom, starts a nine-year run with Lucille Ball as Lucy Ricardo and Desi Arnaz as Ricky the hard-pressed hubby.

- **WINSTON CHURCHILL** (Conservative) replaces Clement Attlee (Labour) as Prime Minister in the UK, where post-war austerity fades a little as the Festival Of Britain is opened by King George VI in London.

1951

- **J.D. SALINGER's** *Catcher In The Rye* is published. It is the story of Holden Caulfield, who sums up forever how oh-so-lonely it is to be an adolescent.

- **ARMISTICE** negotiations, which become prolonged, open in Korea in July. Elsewhere, King Abdullah I of Jordan is assassinated, and Libya becomes an independent kingdom.

- **LES PAUL** & Mary Ford achieve their first number one hit with 'How High The Moon,' full of Paul's multi-layered recording techniques. He tops the Best Guitarist list in the readers poll for jazz magazine *Down Beat* and will win again for the following two years.

1951

During 1951, Fender changed the name of its original two-pickup solidbody electric, the Broadcaster, which by now had a single-pickup companion model, the Esquire. The Gretsch company of New York City asked Fender to stop using the Broadcaster model name, because it was using "Broadkaster" for some drums (and had earlier used the name for a few banjos and guitars). Fender complied and coined a new name: Telecaster. In the meantime, workers at Fender simply snipped the old Broadcaster name from the headstock decals, creating a future collectable, the so-called Nocaster.

The new Telecaster name was on headstocks of the two-pickup guitar by April 1951, and at last Fender's still-new solidbody electric had a permanent name. The Fender Telecasters and Fender Esquires of the early 50s could be identified when later compared to subsequent models by their fretted maple neck and lacquered black fiber pickguard fixed with five screws—and so collectors have nicknamed them "black-guard" Teles and Esquires.

The controls in the first few years were idiosyncratic. The knob nearest the bridge was for volume; the rear one was a blend control. The selector switch in the rear position delivered both pickups, with the rear knob controlling the amount of neck-pickup sound blended into the bridge-pickup sound. The selector in the other two positions delivered neck-pickup only with two preset tones: in the middle position a "natural" tone and in the front position a more bassy tone. The rear knob did not function in those two settings.

The Fender Telecaster is still in production today, notable among many others things as the longest-running electric guitar model. Back in the early 50s, business began to pick up for Fender as news of the Telecaster and Esquire spread and as the firm's salesmen began persuading store owners to stock the new solidbody instruments.

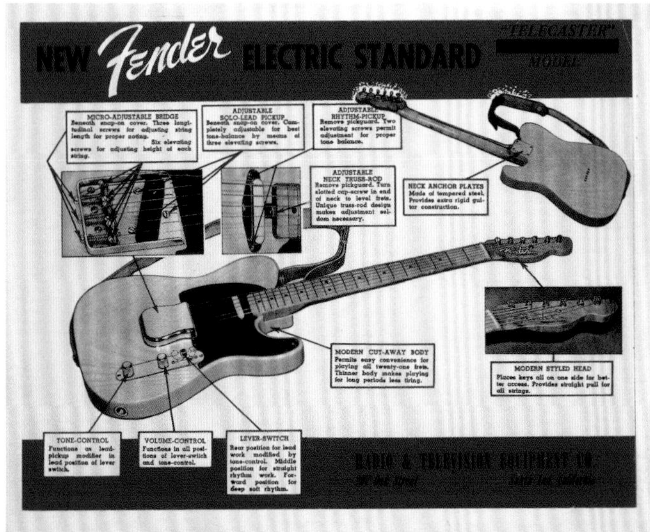

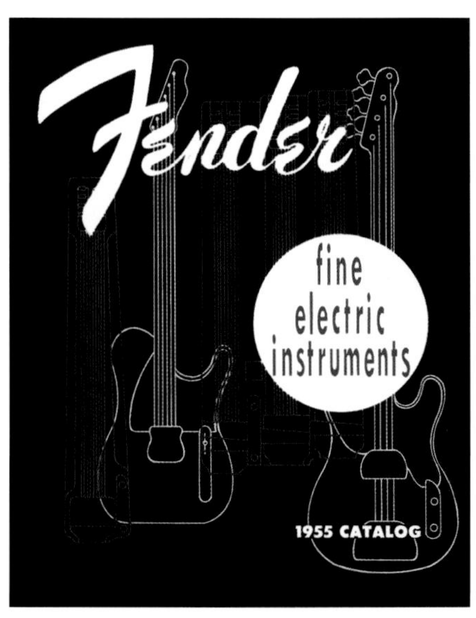

LEFT: **A 1952 ad lists the single-pickup Esquire and dual-pickup Telecaster.**

CENTER: **Fender promo sheet from 1951 detailing the renamed Telecaster.**

RIGHT: **1955 catalogue cover featuring a stylized Telecaster.**

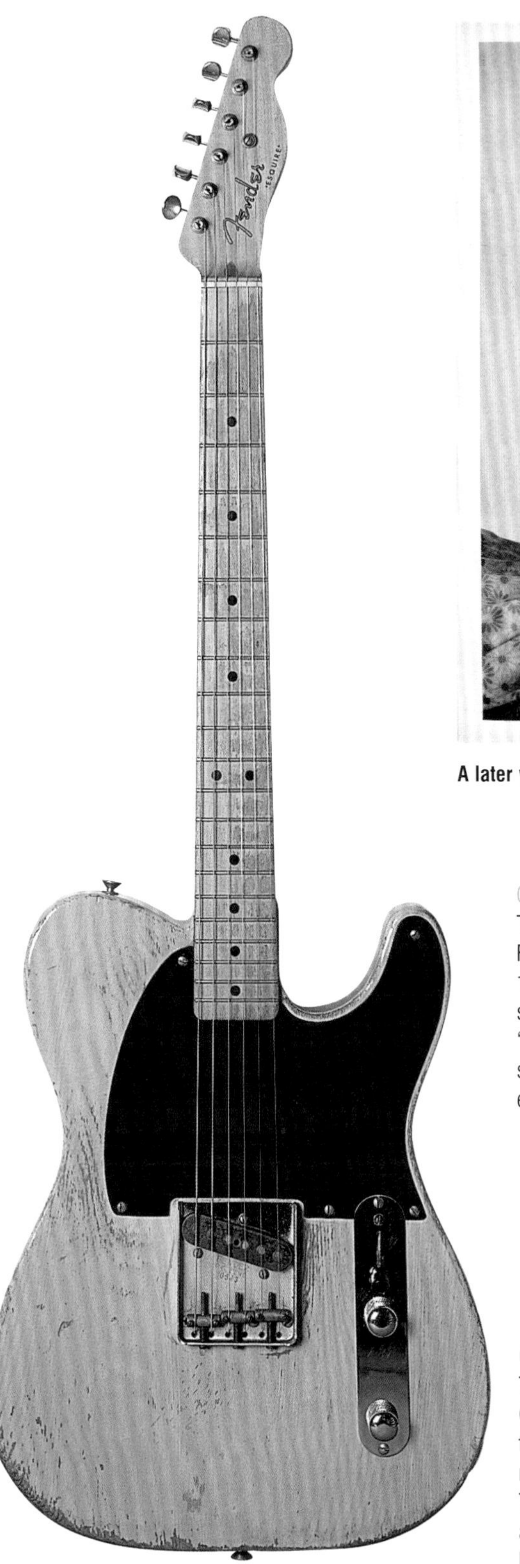

A later white-guard Tele features in Fender's 1959 ad.

ORIGINAL **FENDER ESQUIRE**
THIS EXAMPLE: ***1953***
Fender first used the Esquire name in 1950 for the earliest incarnation of its solidbody electric, but early in 1951 "Esquire" became the name for the single-pickup model, which it has been ever since.

ORIGINAL **FENDER "NOCASTER"**
THIS EXAMPLE: ***1951***
Gretsch complained about prior use of the name Broadkaster, so Fender renamed its two-pickup solidbody the Telecaster. In the meantime, the guitar appeared briefly with only the Fender logo on the headstock, a rare variant later nicknamed the Nocaster.

ORIGINAL **FENDER TELECASTER**
THIS EXAMPLE: ***1953***
Here is the newly named Telecaster in its classic '51–'54 style, with black pickguard and a fretted maple neck. The body was made of ash, and the neck was fixed to it with four machine screws. It was simple and very effective.

An early attempt at a vintage reissue 50s-style Telecaster in a 1982 catalogue.

Fender grew successfully as the 50s gave way to the 60s and on into more recent decades. The company has weathered two major changes of ownership. The first occurred in 1965, when the mighty CBS corporation snapped up Fender for $15 million, and the second 20 years later when CBS sold out to a group headed by the existing management. During these years of change, Fender has consistently looked to its original classic designs for outright copies as well as to draw inspiration for new and not-so-new interpretations and re-imaginings of the solidbody electric guitars—which in the meantime have become prime music-industry standards.

The original Telecaster of the early 50s, with its black pickguard and fretted maple neck, is now recognized as an iconic Tele look, much admired and desired by many collectors and players. During the 80s, Fender started to get serious about making reissue models. The intention was to re-create with keen accuracy the look and feel of original instruments, and the results at first showed varying degrees of fidelity. As time went on, Fender's research managed to improve the period-correctness of these and other reissues, in parallel with a strongly growing interest from collectors (and in some cases hugely increased values) for the original instruments, which for some time had been known as vintage guitars.

Meanwhile, Fender established a Custom Shop in the mid 80s at the firm's factory in Corona, California. The original intention was that a small team of workers there would build one-offs and special orders for professional players. That has continued—customers have included everyone from Bob Dylan to John Mayer—but the Shop has gradually moved to enjoy a much wider role in Fender's expanding business.

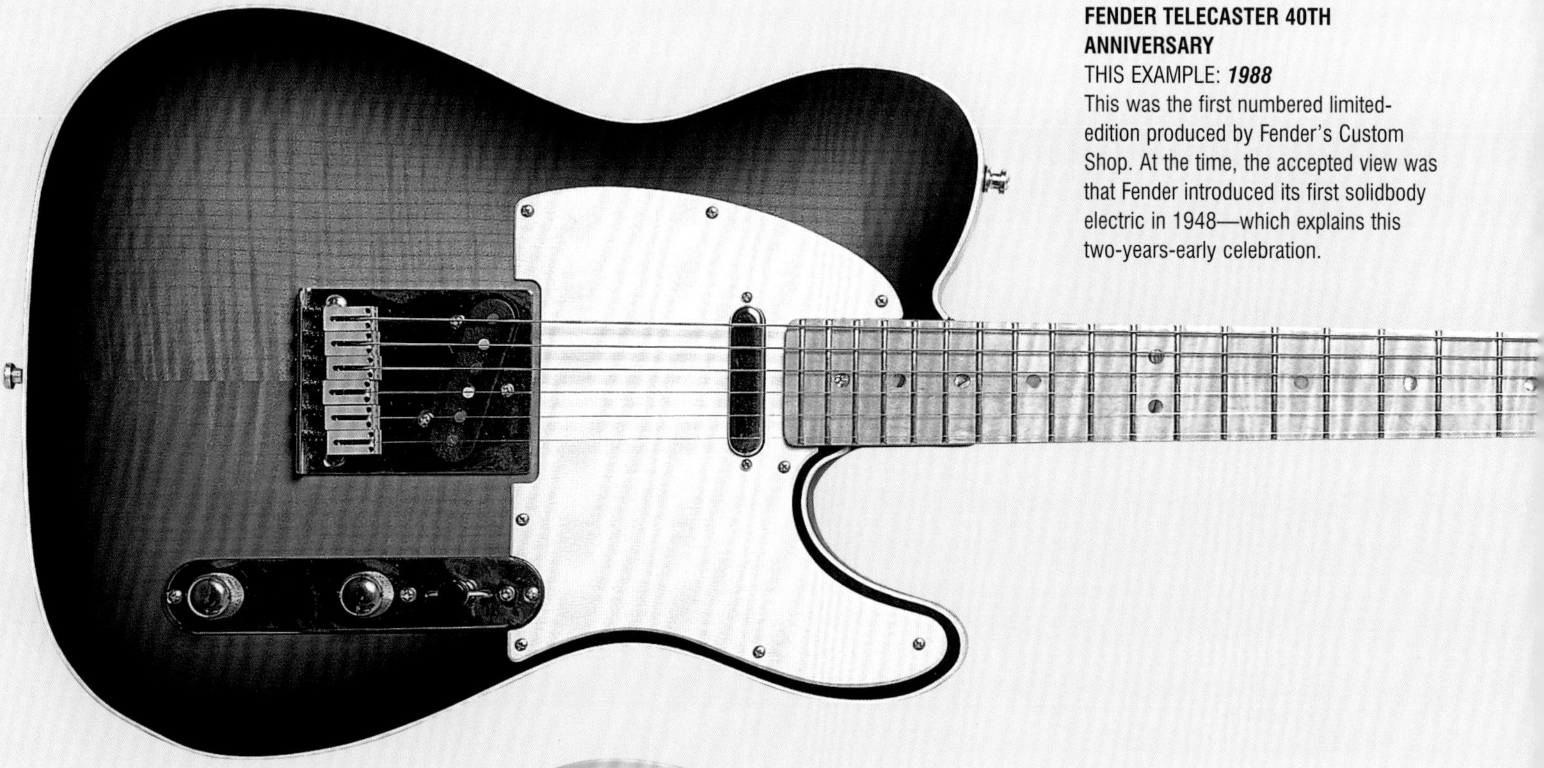

FENDER TELECASTER 40TH ANNIVERSARY
THIS EXAMPLE: ***1988***
This was the first numbered limited-edition produced by Fender's Custom Shop. At the time, the accepted view was that Fender introduced its first solidbody electric in 1948—which explains this two-years-early celebration.

FENDER AMERICAN ORIGINAL 50s TELECASTER
THIS EXAMPLE: ***2018***
The American Original series offered at the time of writing the latest incarnations of Fender's vintage re-creations. It combined what the company called period-correct authenticity with modern playability and performance.

FENDER 50s TELECASTER
THIS EXAMPLE: ***1997***
During the 90s, Fender made this mid-price 50s-style Tele in Japan, and later at its factory in Mexico, to provide the black-guard and maple-neck look of the original.

Jeff Beck's original Esquire re-created in 2007 in the Custom Shop with aged finish.

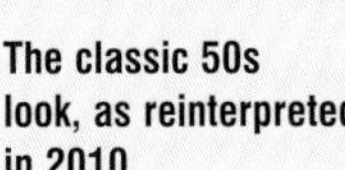

The classic 50s look, as reinterpreted in 2010.

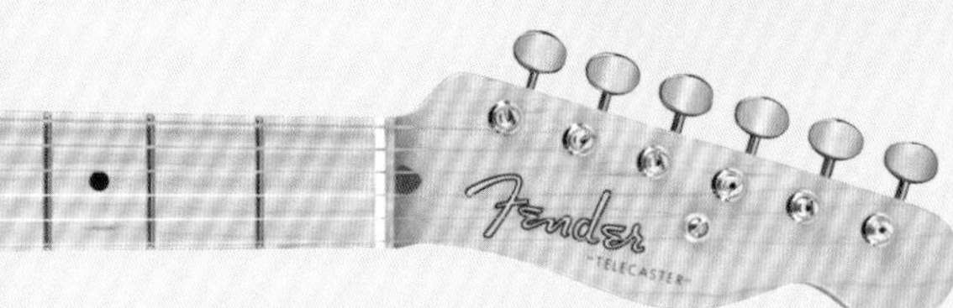

FENDER '51 NOCASTER RELIC
THIS EXAMPLE: ***2006***
Another of Fender's Custom Shop models, the '51 Nocaster reproduced the original's clipped Fender-logo-only on the headstock. It was offered in various levels of the Shop's aged finishes: the example shown has the heavily-worn Relic level.

1951

Gibson led the way in the early 50s with the development of the hollowbody electric guitar, and three important instruments from that period are illustrated here. The Super 400CES (cutaway electric Spanish) was Gibson's top-of-the-line electric when it was launched in 1951, and at nearly 3 ½ inches deep and 18 inches wide, it was also the biggest. The guitar was based on the company's existing 400C acoustic archtop (C for cutaway), but with a slightly thicker top and stronger internal bracing underneath intended to help prevent feedback. Hollowbody electrics can suffer from feedback if a player manages to turn up the amplifier too loud; it wasn't until the 60s that some players discovered feedback could be encouraged and exploited for musical use.

The 400CES at first had a pair of Gibson's P-90 pickups, in combination with the classic control layout of a volume and tone per pickup and a three-way selector switch offering each pickup individually or both together. The 400's P-90s were soon replaced by Alnico types and, later in the 50s, by Gibson's humbuckers.

A little before Gibson issued that 400CES electric version of the 400C in 1951, the firm had combined elements of its acoustic L-5C and electric ES-5 models to create the L-5CES, another high-end electric hollowbody archtop. Like the 400, the L-5CES had a traditional carved spruce top, a carved maple back, and maple sides. The two new models underlined Gibson's belief in the potential of hollowbody electric instruments for professional guitarists.

The ES-175 had first appeared at the every end of the 40s and over the years would become a bestselling hollowbody electric for Gibson, with notable approval among jazz guitarists. Its sharp cutaway was unique on a Gibson guitar for some years, and the 175 popularized the use of a pressed, laminated maple-and-basswood body, which many felt contributed to its bright tone.

ORIGINAL **GIBSON SUPER 400CESN**
THIS EXAMPLE: ***1952***
This 400CESN (N for natural finish) has the visual hallmarks of a high-end Gibson, including gold-plated metalwork, split-block fingerboard inlays, split-diamond headstock motif, and marble-effect pickguard.

ORIGINAL **GIBSON ES-175D**
THIS EXAMPLE: ***1953***
Gibson introduced its single-pickup ES-175 model in 1949, and in '51 it began to offer a transitional model with two pickups that two years later officially became the ES-175D (the D stands for double pickups).

Gibson's 1951 ad for the L-5CES, "leading in tone, response and beauty."

FOR FAST FINGERING, SHORT SCALE LENGTH, LOW ACTION

Acclaimed by artists as the finest instrument in its price class, the ES-175 is extremely light and features a special fingerboard length for very fast playing. The Florentine design of this Gibson Electric Spanish Cutaway model aids the player in reaching all frets with ease and at the same time offers a unique, attractive appearance.

- Positive electronic pickup by use of individually adjustable Alnico No. 5 magnets.
- Tone and volume controls conveniently mounted for fast action.
- Powerful electronic response faithfully reproduced.
- Gibson Adjustable Truss Rod neck construction.
- Artistically designed and beautifully finished.
- Heavily plated, decorative metal fittings.
- Body dimensions—16¼" wide and 20¼" long.

ES-175 *Electric Spanish Cutaway Guitar, Regular Sunburst Finish.*

ES-175N *Electric Spanish Cutaway Guitar, Natural Finish.*

Cases for Above Instruments
514 *Faultless* 103 *Challenge* 515 *Plush*

TWO BUILT-IN PICKUPS A HIGHLIGHT OF THIS GIBSON

This special model of the popular ES-175 is equipped with two built-in pickups and a three position toggle switch which activates either or both pickups. The ES-175 D is extremely lightweight and features a special fingerboard length for very fast playing. This beautiful instrument, with its Florentine cutaway design, is available in the Natural Finish (as shown) or the Gibson Golden Sunburst Finish.

- Tone and volume controls for the two pickups are separate and can be pre-set.
- Individually adjustable Alnico No. 5 magnets give true tone balance.
- Gibson Adjustable Truss Rod neck construction.
- Body size: 16¼" wide and 20¼" long.
- Metal fittings are heavily plated.

ES-175 D Electric Spanish Cutaway Guitar—Golden Sunburst Finish

ES-175 DN Electric Spanish Cutaway Guitar—Natural Finish

Cases for Above Instruments
515 Plush *514 Faultless* *103 Challenge*

ES-175DN

1956 catalogue page showing single and double-pickup versions of the 175.

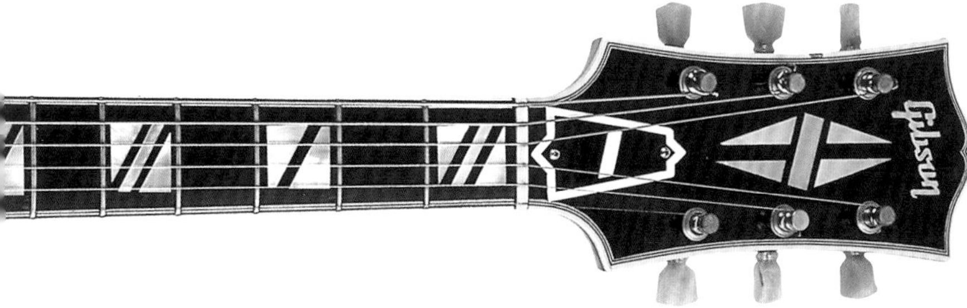

ORIGINAL **GIBSON L-5CES**
THIS EXAMPLE: ***1951***
Like many of the Gibson hollowbody electrics of this period, the L-5CES had a rounded shape to the cutaway (Gibson called it a Venetian cutaway), although in 1960 this was changed to a sharp cutaway (which Gibson called a Florentine cutaway).

A natural-finish 175 in Gibson's 1999 catalogue.

Gibson introduced various hollowbody electrics during the period from the 30s to the 50s, and these models have seen mixed fortunes in more recent years. They have often been overshadowed by the company's more popular solidbody and semi-solid instruments. The ES-175D has fared relatively well in the decades since its launch, and it has managed to maintain its strong popularity among jazz players. It has even had the chance to broaden its appeal enough to attract the occasional discerning rock guitarist. The single-pickup version of the 175 was dropped by Gibson in the early 70s, but the two-pickup 175D has earned a relatively steady place in the company's line through the years.

Both the Super 400CES and the L-5CES have remained at or near the top of Gibson's catalogue of hollowbody electrics, and mostly they have been produced with the rounded (Venetian) cutaway style, which was the way the instrument was designed in its original form in the early 50s, only changing to a sharp (Florentine) cutaway for the duration of the 60s. Occasionally, Gibson has marked a significant date in these models' histories with special editions, such as when it celebrated the 50th anniversary of the introduction in the 30s of the acoustic Super 400.

One of the best known jazz guitarists drawn to Gibson's L-5CES was Wes Montgomery, who started on a 175 but soon moved up to the higher-end model. Later, Gibson made custom models specially for Montgomery based on the L-5CES but with only a single pickup, positioned at the neck—which seemed to suit his distinctive thumb-picking style—and a necessarily simpler control layout with just two knobs and no switch. Gibson reintroduced this same non-standard design in 1993 for its Wes Montgomery signature model, a specialist guitar that it offered at first in sunburst or wine red finish.

GIBSON SUPER 400CES 50th ANNIVERSARY
THIS EXAMPLE: ***1984***
Around ten 400CES guitars were made with "50th Anniversary" at the 19th fret, marking the date of the original acoustic Super 400. The guitars also marked the imminent closure of Gibson's longstanding factory in Kalamazoo, Michigan, in September 1984.

GIBSON WES MONTGOMERY
THIS EXAMPLE: ***1997***
This was an unusual single-pickup version of the L-5CES, reflecting a design originally devised for the great jazz guitarist Wes Montgomery.

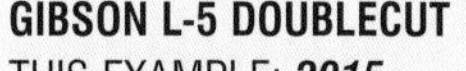
A 1973 strings ad with Roy Clark digging in to his L-5CES.

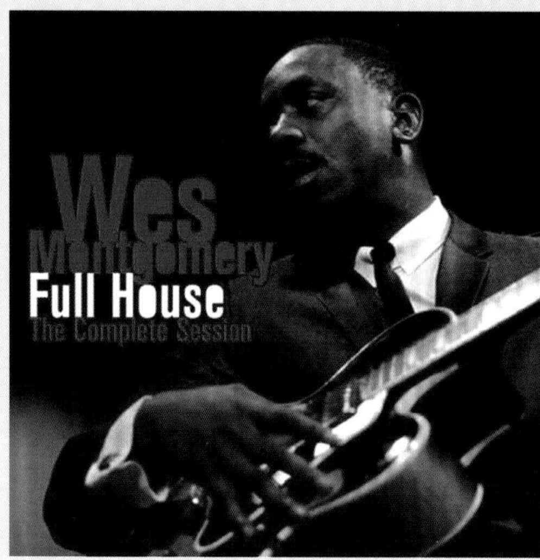

Wes Montgomery with a single-pickup L-5CES on a 2012 CD compilation.

GIBSON L-5 DOUBLECUT
THIS EXAMPLE: ***2015***
The Custom Shop's L-5 Doublecut first appeared in 2015 and seemed like a mashup of several models. Its medium-depth ES-330-like double-cutaway hollow body had the switch positioned like an ES-175 and the general appointments of an L-5CES.

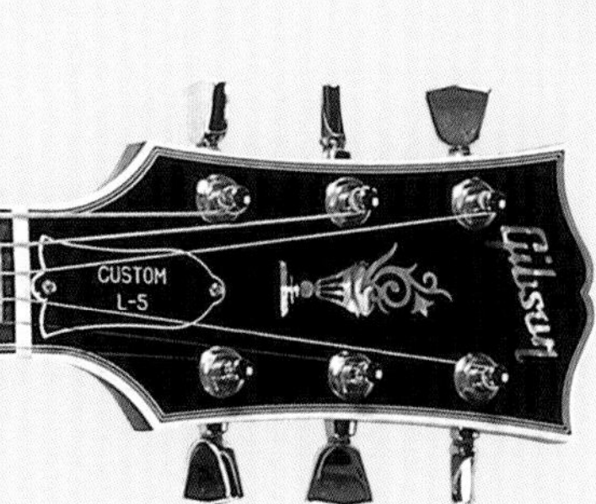

GIBSON ES-175DN
THIS EXAMPLE: ***2015***
Today's incarnation of the 175D, seen here in natural finish, derives from the classic humbucker-equipped period of the model, which began in 1957, and also has the T-and-zigzag tailpiece introduced around the same time.

OKeh
Trade Mark Reg. U. S. Pat. Off. Marcas Registradas • Made in U. S. A. Pats. Pending
6840
(CO 46970)
CRY
- Kohlman -
Vocal
JOHNNIE RAY
and The Four Lads
with Orchestral Acc.

COMET
The New World Airliner
Comets have already flown
22,000 hours — nearly ten million
miles — in air-line service
They are now clocking 150,000 miles a week
DE HAVILLAND
of GREAT BRITAIN

XV
OLYMPIA
HELSINKI
1952

- **KING GEORGE VI** dies at Sandringham, England, while Princess Elizabeth is away on a Commonwealth tour. The new Queen takes up residence at Buckingham Palace three months later.
- **JOHNNIE RAY** is the first white singer in the US to hit both pop and R&B charts, with 'Cry,' and this heralds the erosion of music's racial barriers.
- **MR. POTATO HEAD** becomes the first children's toy to be advertised on television.

1952

- **THE FIRST** detonation of a hydrogen bomb—many times more powerful than an atom bomb—takes place at Eniwetok Atoll in the Pacific Ocean by the US. The first accident at a nuclear reactor occurs at Chalk River, Canada, without apparent casualties.
- **THE GAMES** of the XV Olympiad, or Summer Olympics, are held at Helsinki, Finland.
- **THE WORLD's** first fare-paying jet airliner passenger is Alex Henshaw of Mablethorpe, England, who travels on a BOAC Comet on its first commercial flight, BA113, from London to Johannesburg in May with thirty-five other passengers.

1952

Not long after Fender's new solidbody electrics were released, Gibson signed up Les Paul, the best-known guitarist in America, to help sell Gibson's own take on the solidbody phenomenon. By the time of the endorsement deal in the early 50s, Les Paul had modified several guitars in an attempt to get closer to the kind of electric instrument he wanted and the tones he sought—and also, more importantly for Gibson, he had become famous. Paul played on a Bing Crosby hit, and then he was signed to Capitol Records. That led to Les Paul's first hit, 'Lover,' in 1948, where he used home-recording techniques to create multiple guitar sounds. Next, he teamed with a singing partner, Mary Ford, and the pair hit number one in 1951 with 'High How The Moon.'

Gibson had kept an eye on the upstart Leo Fender, whose company's solidbody guitars were gaining in popularity. Gibson had to compete, and it decided to make its own electric solidbody. The company's boss, Ted McCarty, contacted Les Paul and struck a deal for the famous guitarist to endorse the company's new solidbody electric, introduced in 1952 as the Les Paul Model. Gibson described it as a "unique and exciting innovation in the fretted instrument field."

At first, many of the other leading US guitar makers were surprised that the conservative Gibson could indulge in this new-fangled solidbody style, which was seen by some companies as a fad or as a kind of second-class instrument.

The new Les Paul Model's solid body cleverly combined a carved maple top, drawing on Gibson's craft heritage, with a mahogany base, a sandwich that united the darker tonality of mahogany with the brighter "edge" of maple. And the distinctive colored finish soon led to a suitable nickname for this type of Les Paul: the Goldtop.

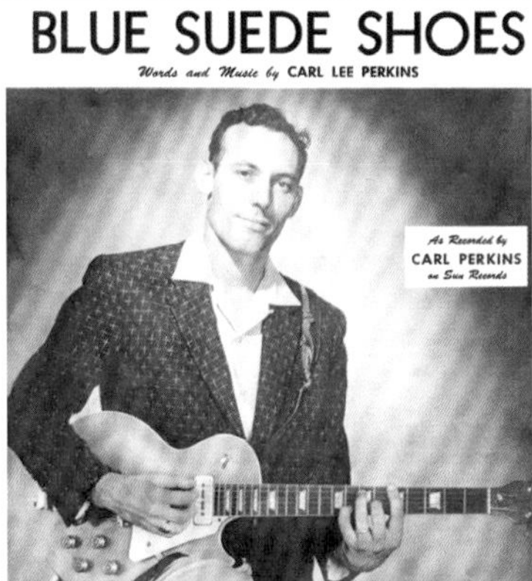

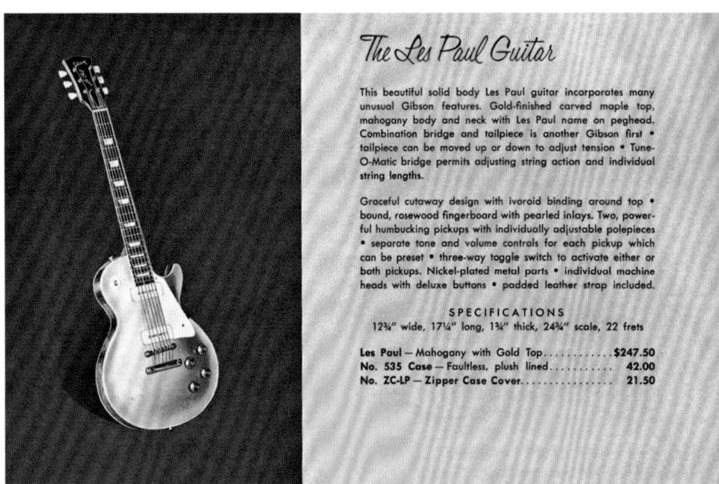

The Les Paul Guitar

This beautiful solid body Les Paul guitar incorporates many unusual Gibson features. Gold-finished carved maple top, mahogany body and neck with Les Paul name on peghead. Combination bridge and tailpiece is another Gibson first • tailpiece can be moved up or down to adjust tension • Tune-O-Matic bridge permits adjusting string action and individual string lengths.

Graceful cutaway design with ivoroid binding around top • bound, rosewood fingerboard with pearled inlays. Two, powerful humbucking pickups with individually adjustable polepieces • separate tone and volume controls for each pickup which can be preset • three-way toggle switch to activate either or both pickups. Nickel-plated metal parts • individual machine heads with deluxe buttons • padded leather strap included.

SPECIFICATIONS
12¾" wide, 17¼" long, 1¾" thick, 24¾" scale, 22 frets

Les Paul — Mahogany with Gold Top **$247.50**
No. 535 Case — Faultless, plush lined **42.00**
No. ZC-LP — Zipper Case Cover **21.50**

LEFT: **Carl Perkins with his original Les Paul Model.**

CENTER: **A change to the Les Paul in 1955 resulted in a separate Tune-o-matic bridge plus tailpiece.**

RIGHT: **Les Paul himself features in this 1952 ad.**

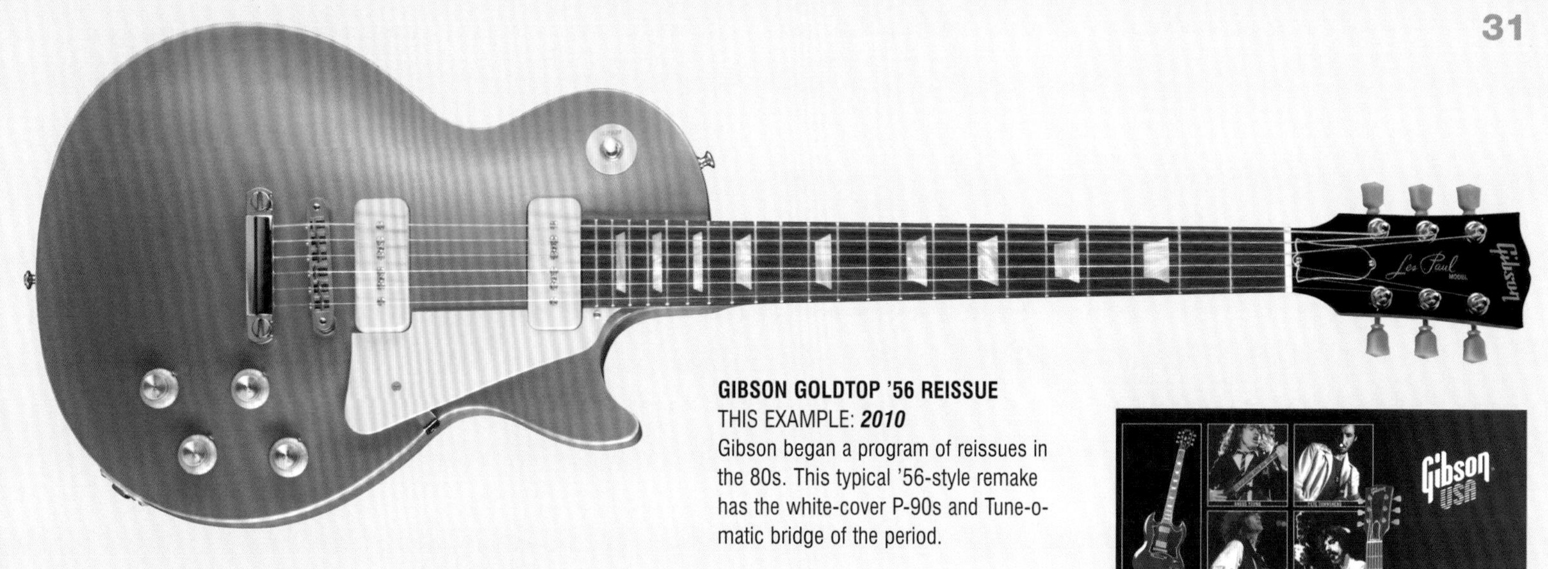

GIBSON GOLDTOP '56 REISSUE
THIS EXAMPLE: ***2010***
Gibson began a program of reissues in the 80s. This typical '56-style remake has the white-cover P-90s and Tune-o-matic bridge of the period.

Gibson introduces its new Les Paul Model in 1952.

A gallery of Gibson stars frame a '56 Reissue in this 2004 ad.

ORIGINAL **GIBSON LES PAUL MODEL**
THIS EXAMPLE: ***1955***
The original trapeze unit of the Goldtop was replaced with a simpler bar bridge/tailpiece during 1953, when Gibson also increased the angle at which the neck meets the body, all designed to improve playability and intonation.

ORIGINAL **GIBSON LES PAUL MODEL**
THIS EXAMPLE: ***1953***
Gibson's first solidbody electric, launched in 1952, was endorsed by Les Paul. This first type has a long "trapeze" bridge/tailpiece and white-cover P-90 pickups.

Les Paul and Mary Ford

THE GIBSON LES PAUL GUITAR

THE POPULAR "LES PAUL" SOLID BODY

The famed "Les Paul tones" can now become a reality for all guitar players with this beautiful, solid body Les Paul guitar, incorporating many unusual Gibson features. Striking in appearance with its gold-finished, carved maple top, mahogany body and neck, the Les Paul name is in gold script on the peghead of this model.

A unique, new feature is the metal combination bridge and tailpiece, with the strings making contact on top of the bridge and adjustable both horizontally and vertically. This new style bridge and tailpiece enables the player to dampen the tone with the heel of the picking hand for muffled "Les Paul tones."

- Two pickups have separate tone and volume controls.
- Three position toggle switch activates either or both pickups.
- Tone can be pre-set to any desired quality and change from one pickup to another can be accomplished by a flip of the toggle switch.
- No dead notes—clear, sustaining tones in all positions with the 22 fret finger-board.
- No buildup of synthetic tones or feed back.
- Body size—length, 17 ¼", width 12 ¾"; scale length, 24 ¾".
- Gibson Adjustable Truss Rod neck construction.
- Padded leather strap included.

Les Paul Solid Body Electric Spanish Cutaway Guitar
Case: 535 Faultless

The new bridge/tailpiece seen in a 50s catalogue.

1952

Paul A. Bigsby worked in Downey, California, and we met him earlier in the Background section thanks to the remarkable solidbody electric guitar that he made for Merle Travis. Bigsby was a private maker who built instruments for individual musicians—today we'd call him a custom or boutique builder—and at first he made only electric steel guitars. Following the Travis guitar, he also began to make more Spanish-style electrics. (At the time, the term Spanish was used for the regular type of guitar, as opposed to the steel or Hawaiian type, which was usually played on the guitarist's lap or on a stand.)

Among the Spanish electrics that Bigsby made was the first solidbody double-neck guitar, built in 1952 for the renowned Nashville studio guitarist Grady Martin, who worked with everyone from Marty Robbins to Patsy Cline. Martin ordered his Bigsby double-neck with a regular six-string neck and a five-string mandolin neck. Double-neck guitars are intended to help a guitarist on-stage who wants to change quickly between two different kinds of instrument. There is of course a disadvantage of the weight and relative awkwardness of the bigger double-neck, but the idea did catch on with other makers, as we'll see. For Bigsby, used to making double and triple-neck steels, it must have seemed a logical step. It was also in 1952 that Bigsby applied for a patent for his True Vibrato, the device for which most guitarists will know his name.

Meanwhile, Gibson offered a new hollowbody ES model in the same gold color that the company would use for its new solidbody Les Paul guitars. The ES-295 was in fact an ES-175 with all-gold finish, trapeze tailpiece, and two white-cover P-90 pickups. The unpopular model was dropped the following year, only to be revived in more recent years.

A crowd of Gibson stars from the 1952 catalogue.

ORIGINAL **BIGSBY DOUBLE-NECK**
THIS EXAMPLE: ***1952***
The first electric solidbody double-neck guitar, this was (clearly) built for country sessionman Grady Martin by Paul A. Bigsby in California. It has an early version of the vibrato unit that made Bigsby's name.

1952

Introduced in 1952 as an enhanced ES-175, the ES-295's Cadillac gold look soon found its way into the hands of some of the young rock and roll stars of the early 1950s. Scotty Moore rocked Elvis Presley's first recordings with the ES-295 while other artists used this instrument to express their rock-a-billy message. Today's ES-295 carries on this tradition with a significant enhancement. Replacing the original trapeze tailpiece with a tune-o-matic avoids the intonation problems of the early ES-295s. Vibrato capabilities are also possible with the custom built Bigsby tailpiece. Finished off with the original gold paint used by Gibson in the 1950s, this guitar is a natural for any modern player's catalogue.

ES-295 *Antique Gold*

Pickups	Two P-90 single coil
Controls	Two volume, two tone, 3-way switch
Hardware	Gold
Scale /Nut width	24 ¾" / 1 11/16"
Fingerboard/Inlay	Rosewood, 20 fret / Parallelogram
Binding	Body / Neck
Bridge/Tailpiece	ABR-1 Tune-o-matic / Bigsby
Materials	Maple body, Maple neck
Finish	Antique Gold

1994 promo for an early revival of the ES-295.

GIBSON 1952 ES-295
THIS EXAMPLE: ***2013***
A faithful re-creation of the original P-90-equipped ES-295, including its clear pickguard with flower motifs and what Gibson calls split-parallelogram fingerboard inlays.

ORIGINAL **GIBSON ES-295**
THIS EXAMPLE: ***1953***
Gibson's gold-finish hollowbody ES-295, introduced in 1952, came with P-90 pickups, although briefly, from 1957, it was fitted with the company's new humbucking pickups until the model's demise the following year.

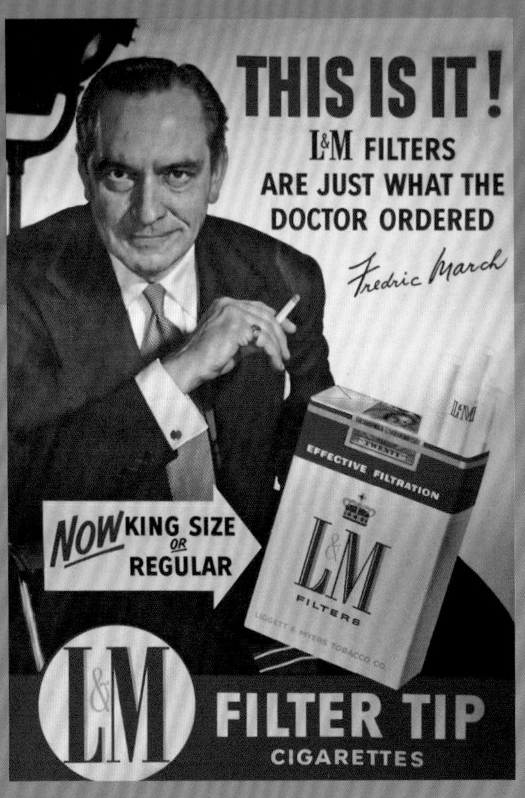
THIS IS IT!
L&M FILTERS
ARE JUST WHAT THE
DOCTOR ORDERED
Fredric March
NOW KING SIZE OR REGULAR
EFFECTIVE FILTRATION
L&M
FILTERS
L&M
FILTER TIP
CIGARETTES

Brighten your Summer
WITH A COLOR STYLED
Portable
GE

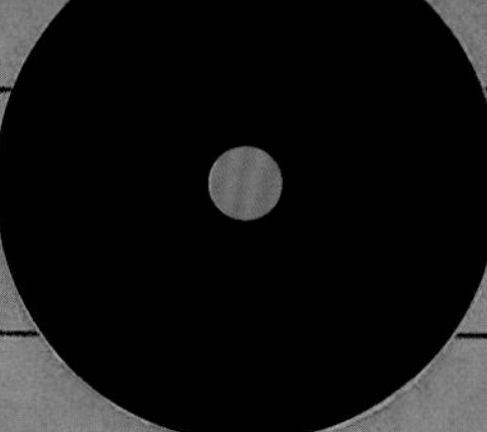
Essex
RECORDS
EASTWICK MUSIC
BMI
E-321-A
Mfg. By
Palda Record Co.
Phila., Penna.
CRAZY MAN, CRAZY
(Bill Haley)
BILL HALEY
With
HALEY'S COMETS
321

- **JAMES BOND** debuts in Ian Fleming's first novel, *Casino Royale*... but not in Simone De Beauvoir's seminal feminist work *The Second Sex*, translated to English this year.
- **CRAZY MAN CRAZY** by Bill Haley & His Comets is arguably the first hit rock'n'roll record, reaching number 12 in May.
- **CIGARETTE SMOKING** and its link to lung cancer is reported as "beyond reasonable doubt." Meanwhile, L&M still advertise their cigarettes as "just what the doctor ordered."

1953

- **PORTABLE RADIOS** keep folks up to date with news such as Republican Dwight D. Eisenhower's inauguration as 34th US president, the end of the Korean War, the conquest of Mount Everest, and Queen Elizabeth II's coronation.
- **JUKEBOX** favorites include Willie Mae Thornton's 'Hound Dog,' an early take on country rock with a rip-roaring guitar solo by Pete Lewis of Johnny Otis's band. The Leiber & Stoller song will later provide a big hit for Elvis Presley.
- **DIED:** Django Reinhardt, Dylan Thomas, Joseph Stalin. Born: Alex Lifeson, Mike Oldfield, Robert Cray.

ORIGINAL **GRETSCH COUNTRY CLUB 6196**
THIS EXAMPLE: ***1956***
This model, introduced in 1953 to sit at the top of Gretsch's hollowbody line, had a pair of the firm's DynaSonic single-coil pickups. One finish option was the gleaming Cadillac green seen on this Club.

GRETSCH SOLID BODY TWIN PICKUP ELECTRIC GUITARS

A revelation of electronic perfection, notable for solid tone projection, wonderfully sustained, with infinite variety of tonal coloring. Twin Gretsch-Dynasonic built-in pickups, played singly or together at a touch of the fingertip switch, range from rich solo voice to commanding brilliance as you choose. Adjustable permanent magnet for each string assures perfect tonal balance. The slim, fast-playing Gretsch 'Miracle Neck' joining at the 16th fret, and the deep cutaway of the body, combine to open up the full fingerboard for fast, easy playing in any position. Small compact body (13¼" wide) in beautiful modern finishes; individual machines with slip-proof metal buttons; adjustable variable saddle bridge gives individual tuning for each string. Strings are flat-wound Gretsch "Electromatic" — soft-pressure, smooth as silk. Complete with solid leather shoulder strap. (For cases, see Page 16). Offered in four models, each one a triumph of modernistic beauty and musical performance.

GRETSCH "DUO-JET", a beauty in black, mahogany and polished chrome. For speed, flexibility and tonal qualities this guitar and its three fellow models top the solid body field.
PX6128—Gretsch "Duo-Jet" Solid Body Electric Guitar **$255.00**

GRETSCH "SILVER JET" (not illustrated.) For unequalled spotlight sparkle. Mahogany body and neck; flashing silver sparkle top; chrome plated metal parts.
PX6129—Gretsch "Silver Jet" Solid Body Guitar **$255.00**

GRETSCH "ROUND-UP"—Masculine beauty in real Western finish. Tooled leather shoulder strap and body binding; gold plated metal parts.
PX6130—Gretsch "Round-Up" Solid Body Guitar **$325.00**

GRETSCH "JET FIRE BIRD" for the progressive guitarist. Two-tone with polished ebony finished body and neck contrasting with brilliant Oriental red top. Metal parts polished chrome plate.
PX6131—Gretsch "Jet Fire Bird" Solid Body Guitar **$255.00**

GRETSCH "JET FIRE BIRD" **$255.00** | GRETSCH "DUO JET" **$255.00** | GRETSCH "ROUND-UP" **$325.00**

Three early Gretsch semi-solids in a 1955 catalogue.

ORIGINAL **GRETSCH COUNTRY CLUB 6196**
THIS EXAMPLE: ***1955***
The Country Club was officially offered in natural, sunburst, or Cadillac green, but this two-tone gray finish was less common. Both Clubs pictured have "hump-top" fingerboard inlays, which replaced the model's original block markers around 1955.

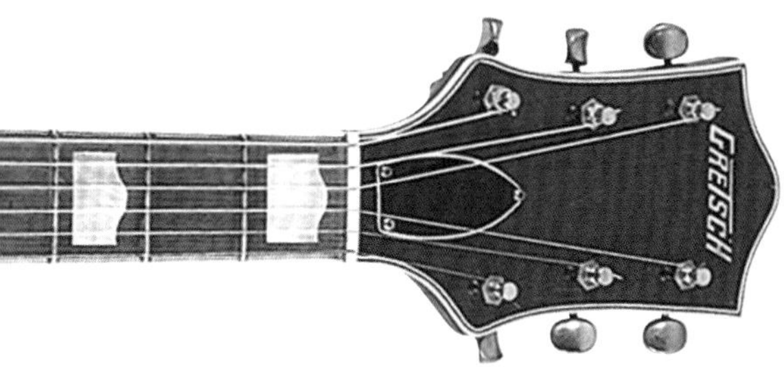

Friedrich Gretsch, a German immigrant, established the Fred Gretsch Manufacturing Co. in 1883 when he left Houdlett, a small maker of banjos and drums in New York City, to set up there on his own. Soon, Gretsch was selling a line of drums, banjos, tambourines, and novelty toy instruments from his firm's humble HQ in Brooklyn. When Friedrich died suddenly in 1895, his son Fred took over the business, and by 1900 he had added mandolins to the company's product lines.

In 1916, Fred saw construction completed of the large ten-story Gretsch Building close to the Brooklyn side of the Williamsburg Bridge that crossed the East River to Manhattan. By the early 20s, Gretsch could advertise a big, flourishing line of instruments, mostly with Rex or 20th Century brands and including banjos, mandolins, guitars, violins, band instruments, drums, accordions, harmonicas, and accessories.

As the guitar became more popular compared to the banjo at the end of the 20s and into the 30s, the company started to use Gretsch-American (in 1927) and then simply Gretsch (1931) as the brandname for its acoustic guitars. Following the end of World War II, Gretsch began to shift from its role as primarily a distributor and manufacturer of instruments for other companies to an emphasis on the Gretsch brand. In the late 40s, still based in New York City, the firm introduced Gretsch drums, and by 1950 it had established Gretsch acoustic and electric guitars. Jimmie Webster, a musician and piano tuner, came on board to promote and develop the new guitars.

Among Gretsch's early new electrics were the hollowbody Country Club, a development of the Electro II model, and the Duo Jet, with its unusual semi-solid body. From the start, Gretsch made a mark with colorful finish options, including an impressive "Cadillac green" for the Club.

Studio guitarist Billy Mure with a Country Club in 1954.

Jimmy Cannady praises a Country Club in this 1956 ad.

ORIGINAL **GRETSCH DUO JET 6128**
THIS EXAMPLE: ***1953***
A first-year Duo Jet, Gretsch's first "solidbody" electric. In fact, its body was made semi-solid with internal pockets, setting it apart from recent solidbody guitars such as Fender's Telecaster and Gibson's Les Paul.

D.H. Baldwin, an Ohio-based instrument firm, bought the Gretsch company in 1967 for around $4 million. Baldwin, best known for pianos and organs, had its eye on the guitars, of course, as well as Gretsch's popular drums. However, the deal did not bring the kind of returns that Baldwin had in mind. Change was in the air, and in 1970, Baldwin decided to move the Gretsch factory out of the decades-old site in Brooklyn and relocate operations well over a thousand miles away at Booneville, Arkansas, where Baldwin had a number of other plants. Few of the old Gretsch workers made the move, and production at the new site struggled for a while.

By the early 70s, Baldwin had contracted out manufacture of Gretsch products to the factory manager at Booneville, Bill Hagner, an arrangement that lasted until 1978. The last Gretsch guitars of this era were manufactured around 1980, and sales stopped some three years later. Baldwin went bankrupt in 1983, one of its managers bought the music portion of the business, and in January 1985, the ex-Baldwin man sold Gretsch to another Fred Gretsch. This Fred Gretsch was a nephew of one of the original Gretsches and the son of Bill Gretsch, who ran the company from 1942 until his premature death six years later. The "new" Fred Gretsch continues to run the Gretsch business today, from 2003 in an alliance with Fender.

Since that teaming with Fender, Gretsch guitars have been improved and updated, while often maintaining the vintage vibe that so many fans of the brand find appealing. A series of reissues and old-look instruments has followed, alongside newer ideas and instruments, and Gretsch seems even healthier now than it was back in its heyday in the 50s and 60s.

GRETSCH DUO JET 6128T-1957
THIS EXAMPLE: ***1995***
A revived Gretsch began to produce guitars again in the mid 80s, and this Duo Jet is typical of the early Japanese-made instruments from that period.

GRETSCH CLIFF GALLUP SIGNATURE DUO JET 6128-CLFG
THIS EXAMPLE: ***2017***
Cliff Gallup used a Duo Jet on a remarkable series of cameo solos with Gene Vincent's Blue Caps on 50s cuts such as 'Be Bop A Lula' and 'Race With The Devil,' and this recent model re-creates Gallup's guitar.

GRETSCH VINTAGE SELECT EDITION '59 COUNTRY CLUB 6196T-59
THIS EXAMPLE: ***2016***
New for 2016 was Gretsch's Vintage Select Edition, a series of re-created oldies that the company said were "inspired by the pivotal and prolific years of Gretsch's 50s and early 60s golden age."

Cadillac green Country Clubs in a 2006 promo, with or without Bigsby.

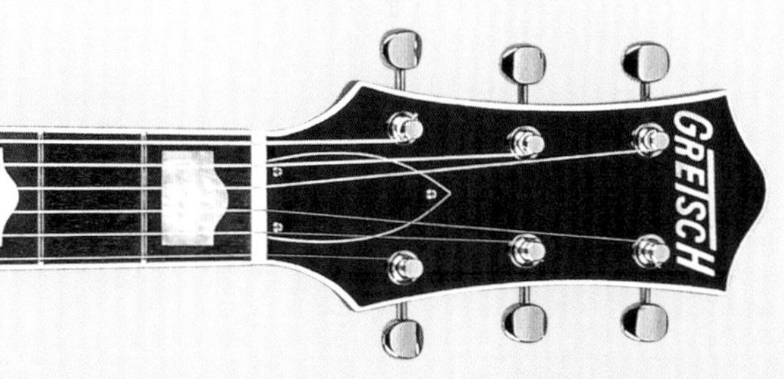

2012 catalogue for a guitar modeled on George Harrison's early-Beatles Duo Jet.

GRETSCH COUNTRY CLUB 7576
THIS EXAMPLE: ***1979***
This was the final version of the Country Club, made during the dying days of Gretsch. The brand had been sold to Baldwin in 1967, and production ground to a halt around 1980.

The Guild company started business in 1952, set up in New York City by Alfred Dronge and George Mann. They hired a team that consisted primarily of ex-Epiphone workers who had decided they did not want to make the move to Epiphone's new home in Philadelphia. Guild would itself move from New York in 1956, to Hoboken, New Jersey, and would be best known throughout the 50s for high quality archtop guitars. During the 60s, the firm's flattop acoustics would also be well regarded by many players.

The origins of Kay date back to 1890 and a company called Groehsl, which by 1921 had become known as Stromberg-Voisinet, and by the mid 20s, Henry Kay Kuhrmeyer was the main influence on the company's strategies. Kuhrmeyer expanded Stromberg-Voisinet during the latter half of the 20s, also taking on contract work for Montgomery Ward and Regal among others, and in 1931 the name of the company was changed to Kay Musical Instruments, with headquarters on Walnut Street in Chicago. Kuhrmeyer would eventually sell Kay in 1955 to a group of investors that included Sidney Katz, who had been a manager at the other big Chicago company of the time, Harmony. There were exceptions, but Kay was known primarily for mid-priced student-grade instruments.

Harmony in Chicago was in something of a transition during the 50s between its pre-war success, which had been substantial, and its coming success in the mid 60s, which would be staggering. Aside from building guitars for mail-order operations such as Sears, Harmony offered everything from bargain flattops with stenciled cowboy graphics and basic little Stratotones to quality electric archtops and other models of professional caliber. A report on Harmony's 60th anniversary in 1952 claimed that the company produced more than half of all the fretted instruments made in the United States.

Jazz guitarist Johnny Smith with a Guild X-550, 1955.

ORIGINAL **GUILD STUART X-550**
THIS EXAMPLE: ***1953***
The X-550 and its partnering sunburst X-500 were top of Guild's line of electric archtops when introduced in 1953. Note the Epiphone-like fingerboard markers that reveal the previous employer of some of Guild's workforce.

1955 Guild catalogue including the small Aristocrat, a hollowbody without f-holes.

moderately priced
spanish electrics…

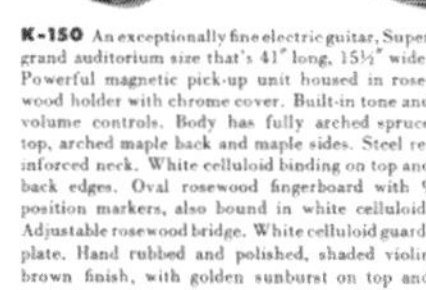

K-125 Solid body Spanish electric guitar. Small, compact, easy to play. Full professional 25¾" scale, yet instrument is only 37" long, body 10½" wide. Select hardwood body. Oval fingerboard with heavy frets and four position markers. High fidelity magnetic pick-up unit with built-in tone and volume controls plus a "Hi-Low" selector switch that enables player to instantaneously switch from the rhythm bass tone to the high solo treble tones. Price, complete with neck cord and brackets, without amplifier **$49.50 (A)**
No. 220-73 Carrying case for K-125. $6 (A)

K-150 An exceptionally fine electric guitar, Super grand auditorium size that's 41" long, 15½" wide. Powerful magnetic pick-up unit housed in rosewood holder with chrome cover. Built-in tone and volume controls. Body has fully arched spruce top, arched maple back and maple sides. Steel reinforced neck. White celluloid binding on top and back edges. Oval rosewood fingerboard with 9 position markers, also bound in white celluloid. Adjustable rosewood bridge. White celluloid guard-plate. Hand rubbed and polished, shaded violin brown finish, with golden sunburst on top and back. Price without amplifier .... **$60 (A)**

K-151 A large master size cut-away "electric" with full 17" body, specially designed to produce a clear, rich tone. Deluxe type pick-up unit is small, compact and powerful, with individual adjustments for each string. Cover of unit is bright chrome. "Quick change" built-in tone and volume controls. Cord is detachable. Body has fully arched spruce top and curly maple back. Curly maple sides. Metal reinforced slenderized hard maple neck. Top and back edges are bound with white celluloid. Extra black and white celluloid inlay on top edge. Oval rosewood fingerboard has 9 large dots, heavy professional frets, and is bound in white celluloid. Deluxe patent heads have built-in covers. Rosewood bridge is adjustable. Guard-plate, heavy white celluloid. Hand rubbed and polished. Dark brown shaded finish golden sunburst top and back. Flat wire wound strings. Without amplifier .... **$92.50 (A)**

Three Kay electrics in a 1953 catalogue.

ORIGINAL **HARMONY STRATOTONE H44**
THIS EXAMPLE: ***1953***
The H44 marked Harmony's entry into the world of solidbody electrics, quickly following the pioneering models from Fender and Gibson.

The Kay factory in the early 50s.

Harmony's H62 model stars on the 1954 catalogue cover.

ORIGINAL **KAY THIN TWIN K161**
THIS EXAMPLE: ***1954***
The name came from the Thin body and Twin pickups, and the body had an unusual construction, with parallel wooden braces inside the otherwise hollow body running from neck to end-block.

Following the establishment of Guild as a classy player in the world of hollowbody electrics during the 50s and 60s, the company continued to be known primarily for its flattop acoustic guitars. In 1966, Guild was bought by Avnet, an electronics company that at the same time acquired the Goya brandname, and production was shifted a few years later from Guild's home in Hoboken, New Jersey, to a new factory in Westerly, Rhode Island, overlapping with Hoboken until 1971.

Guild's electric lines were focused on solidbody models, and while hollows continued to appear they never quite matched the wider appeal of models by Gibson, Epiphone, or Gretsch. After changes of ownership in the 80s, Guild was sold to Fender in 1995, an opportunity for Fender to improve its position in the flattop acoustic market. The archtop maker Bob Benedetto helped to revive some archtop models, starting in 2000, but Guild's electric production ceased some years later. A new Custom Shop, opened in 2013, offered a few high-end archtops, including the A-150 Savoy, but the following year Fender sold Guild to Cordoba Music Group. The new owner provided some stability after Guild's rocky recent history, and models have included a number of hollowbody electrics.

The Kay brandname was sold to AR Musical Enterprises of Indiana in 1980, starting a new era of beginners' electrics. In 2010, guitar maker Roger Fritz came on board, and he helped with the introduction of several reissues of classic Kay models, including the Thin Twin.

Eastwood was founded by Mike Robinson in Toronto, Canada, in 2001 with the intention of re-creating desirable models from the past and improving the playability where necessary. In the process, Eastwood helped refine the retro trend, offering some models with the old Airline brand, recalling several of the heritage instruments that we'll be visiting in this book.

Guild's slogan from a 2015 catalogue.

A 2018 ad for Eastwood's retro Airline brand.

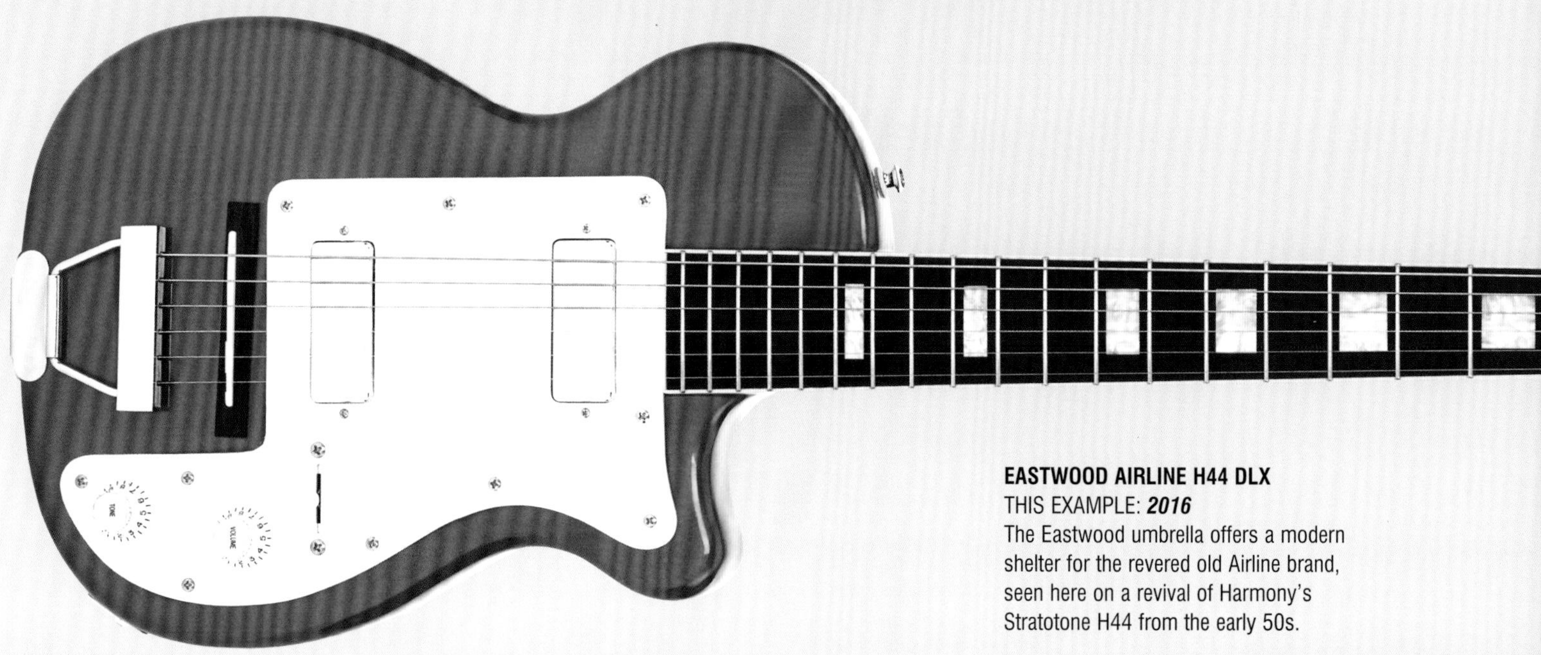

EASTWOOD AIRLINE H44 DLX
THIS EXAMPLE: ***2016***
The Eastwood umbrella offers a modern shelter for the revered old Airline brand, seen here on a revival of Harmony's Stratotone H44 from the early 50s.

GUILD MANHATTAN X-175
THIS EXAMPLE: ***2017***
A few hollowbody electrics such as this X-175 appeared alongside solidbody models in the revived electric lines offered by Cordoba, which acquired Guild from Fender in 2014.

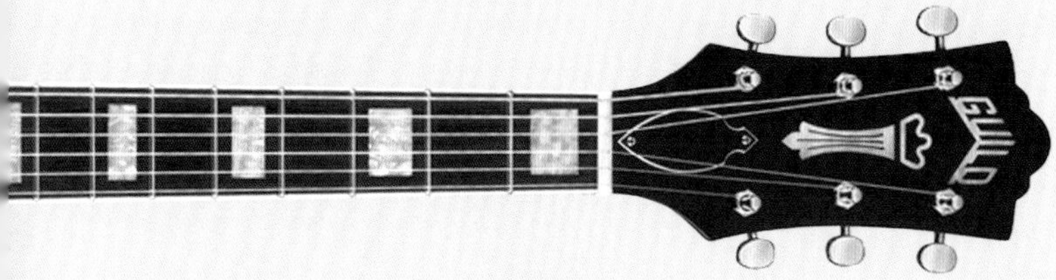

Kay means Kool on this 2009 catalogue cover.

1978 ad for Guild's hollowbody X-500.

KAY THIN TWIN
THESE EXAMPLES: ***2008***
In its modern incarnation, Kay offers a line of beginner guitars, but also several reissues devised by guitar maker Roger Fritz and including the Thin Twin, shown here in three finish options.

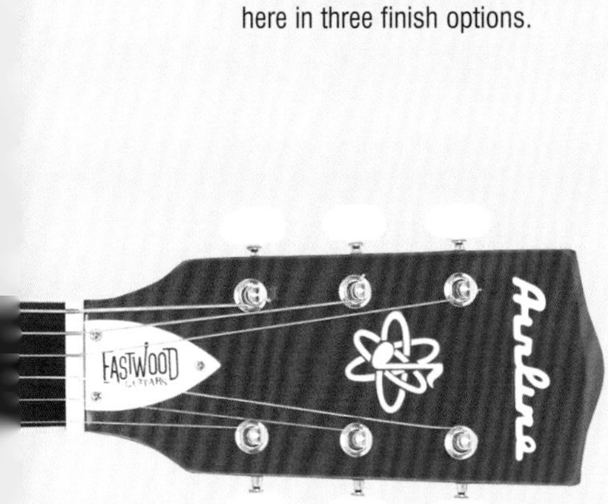

CHICAGO • SAN FRANCISCO
THE VISTA-DOME
California Zephyr

FUSSBALL-WELTMEISTERSCHAFT 1954, 16. JUNI - 4. JULI
COUPE
JULES RIMET
MARY Long
OFFIZIELLES PROGRAMM / PROGRAMME OFFICIEL

Vee-Jay RECORDS
Conrad Music
53-112
BMI
Vocal
GOODNITE, SWEETHEART, GOODNITE
(Carter-Hudson)
SPANIELS
Rythm Acc.
VJ-107

- **RIGHT-WING** Republican Senator Joseph McCarthy is discredited by the US Senate. A wave of anti-communist hysteria, blacklists, and McCarthy's investigations committee were unleashed after his unsubstantiated claim in 1950 that the State Department was infiltrated by "known communists."

- **DESPITE** containing just six percent of the world's population, the US has 34 percent of its railways, 58 percent of the telephones, and 60 percent of the cars.

1954

- **TRANSISTOR RADIOS** are introduced, made by Texas Instruments for the Regency brand.

- **DOO-WOP** heaven as The Spaniels make 'Goodnite Sweetheart, Goodnite' and The Penguins record 'Earth Angel.' Meanwhile, Elvis Presley makes his first commercial recordings.

- **IN THE UK**, food rationing officially ends, celebrated by a bonfire of ration books in London. In the US, the term "fast food" is coming into use.

- **WEST GERMANY** wins the soccer World Cup, beating favorites Hungary 3–2. Roger Gilbert Bannister, a 25-year-old British medical student, runs the first sub-four-minute mile.

1954

Following on from the introduction of the Telecaster, Fender's next move was to create something more stylish, and the result a few years later came in the shape of the Stratocaster. This was a beautiful three-pickup solidbody with a clever vibrato system and a pleasing curvaceous design. The Strat went on to became an industry standard and fired the music of players as diverse as Buddy Holly and Jimi Hendrix.

Fender made working samples of its new model early in 1954. Following the first advertisements and press for the guitar in April and May, the firm started sporadic production around May, June, and July. The firm's sales manager, Don Randall, told dealers that he expected shipments to begin on May 15, and the factory boss, Forrest White, recalled later that the first run of a hundred Strats came in October. It was Randall who named the new Fender model. His inspiration came from the dawning space age, and as a keen pilot he was probably aware that Boeing's jet bomber, the B-47, was called a Stratojet. There was also Pontiac's sleek Strato-Streak car, and Randall, who attended all the musical instrument trade shows for Fender, would surely have seen Harmony's recent Stratotone models.

Randall set the price for the new Stratocaster at $249.50 ($229.50 for a version without vibrato) at the head of Fender's solidbody list, with the Telecaster at $189.50 and the Precision Bass, launched in 1951, at $199.50. Gibson's Les Paul Model (Goldtop) listed at $225 while Gretsch's Duo Jet was pitched a touch higher at $230. When it was launched in 1954, the Stratocaster looked like no other guitar around. As we shall see, over the ensuing decades it would become one of the most popular and one of the most desired electric guitar designs of all time.

ORIGINAL **FENDER STRATOCASTER**
THIS EXAMPLE: ***1956***
Fender's Stratocaster first appeared in 1954, its sleek lines and contoured body a shocking and futuristic departure from convention. Its distinctive looks, crisp sounds, and easy playability soon turned it into a bestseller.

Strat, Twin Amp, and cool cat in a 1955 ad.

Buddy Merrill appeared regularly with a Strat on Lawrence Welk's 50s TV show.

Fender's first ad for the "comfort contoured" Stratocaster.

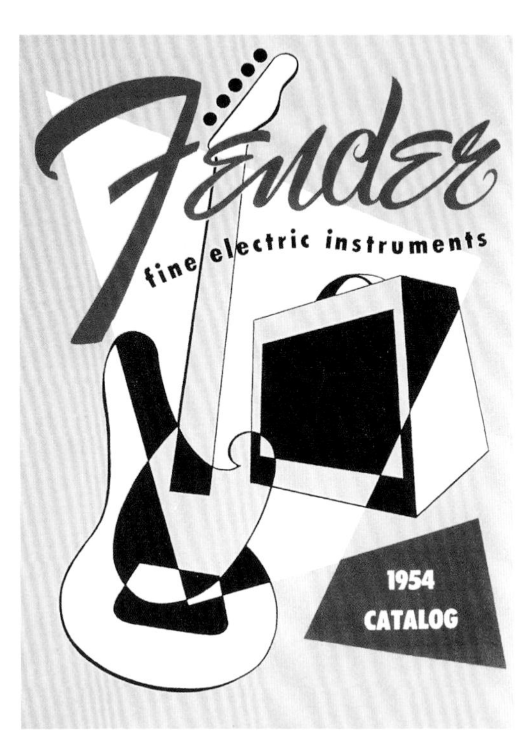

A stylized Strat on the 1954 catalogue cover.

An early logo of the Fender Sales company.

ORIGINAL **FENDER STRATOCASTER**

THIS EXAMPLE: ***1958***

This natural "blond" finished Strat with gold-plated metalwork, announced in 1957, was later nicknamed the Mary Kaye for the musician who appeared with one in Fender promotional material.

The particular look of a 50s Stratocaster has become an iconic image among collectors and players who have an affinity for this classic period of Fender history. The most obvious feature of the Strat's 50s look was the distinctive pale-color wood of the fingerboard. In fact, there was no separate fingerboard, but instead the playing surface was simply the top of the maple neck, with frets fitted directly into it. As we shall see, that would change in 1959, when Fender shifted some of the Strat's standard features to include a separate rosewood fingerboard—and that had an equally distinctive darker color. Fender has marked a number of anniversaries of the 50s-style Strat through the years, mostly linked to its year of introduction in 1954, and a couple of interesting examples are illustrated here.

Fender popularized the idea of the relic'd guitar in 1995, and soon other makers were continuing or starting with the idea of new guitars with aged finishes, stained fingerboards, and tarnished hardware. In 1998, Fender's US Custom Shop established three styles of re-creations to create its Time Machine series. The Relic style had aged knocks and the look of heavy wear, as if the guitar had been out on the road for a generation or so. The Closet Classic style was made to look as if it had been bought new many, many years ago, played a few times, and then stuck in a closet. And the N.O.S. style (New Old Stock) was like an instrument bought brand new back in the day and then put straight into a time machine that transported it to the present day. Fender's Mexico factory introduced its own more affordable take on the idea with a number of Road Worn models, which were first offered for sale in 2009.

FENDER RELIC 50s STRATOCASTER
THIS EXAMPLE: ***1997***
An early example of the aged models that Fender's Custom Shop introduced in 1995, this one with the heavily knocked-about finish known as Relic.

FENDER 50th ANNIVERSARY GOLDEN STRATOCASTER
THIS EXAMPLE: ***2004***
Fender pulled out the stops for the golden anniversary of the Strat in 2004 with several special-edition guitars, including this model from the Mexico factory with its fitting gold theme.

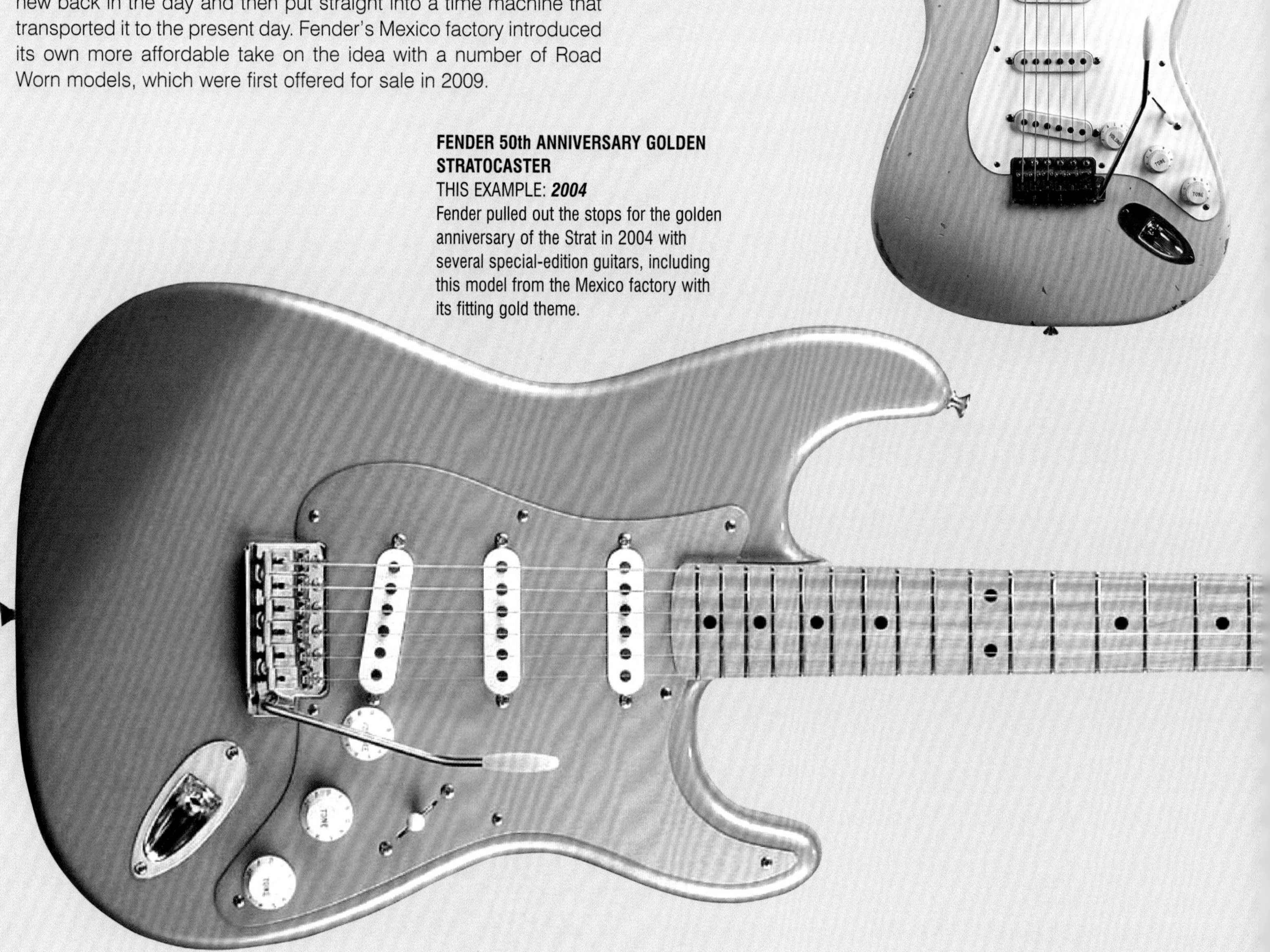

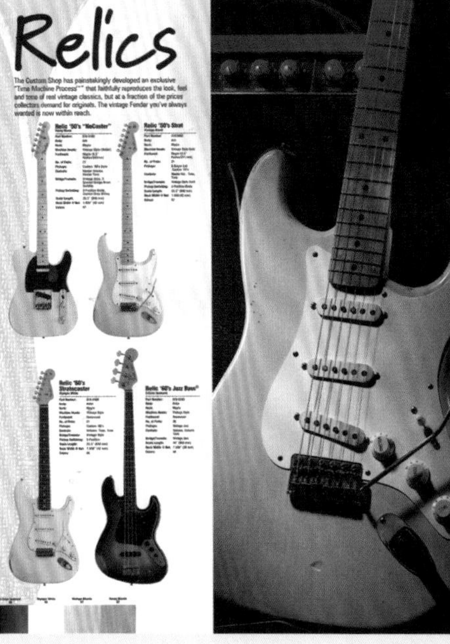

Custom Shop 1996 ad for its aged Time Machine series.

FENDER ROAD WORN 50s STRAT
THIS EXAMPLE: ***2010***
Fender's Mexico factory, established in 1987, offered its own version of aged new guitars with the Road Worn series, which was introduced by the company in 2009.

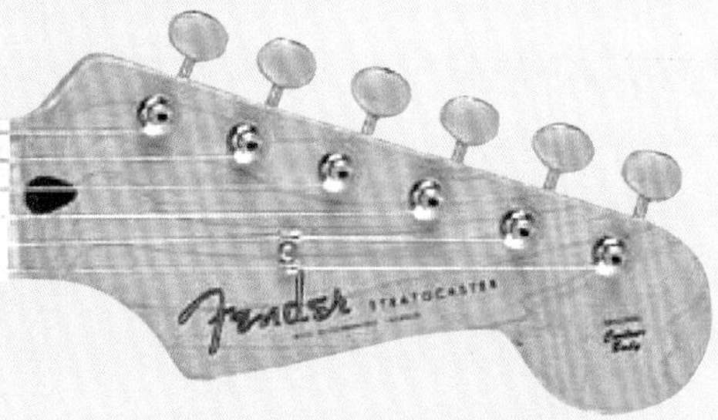

FENDER 25th ANNIVERSARY STRATOCASTER
THIS EXAMPLE: ***1979***
Fender's first attempt to celebrate its own history came with this birthday guitar, but it had few stylistic links to the original instrument from 1954.

Fender's debt to the earliest style of Stratocaster that arrived in the 50s is reflected in the number of models it has introduced in more recent years that draw on the classic features. The company's first blatant reissue of instruments that attempted to be as period-correct as possible came in 1983 with the launch of the '57 Stratocaster and its partnering model, the '62 Stratocaster. The clue was in the names, with the '57 model aping the maple-neck look of a vintage original. The difference came in the price. In the early 80s, an original '57 Strat might have set you back around $3,000, whereas this new Vintage series '57 was marked up with a list price of $995. Since that debut, Fender has worked hard on the retro reissue side of its business to get closer and closer to the look, feel, and playability of its revered oldies.

The first signature or artist Stratocaster produced by Fender was the Eric Clapton model. Clapton had discovered that his faithful old Strat, which he called Blackie, was coming to the end of its useful life, and he began talking about a modern replacement. Fender delivered prototypes to Clapton in 1986 while he was recording his *August* album in Los Angeles, and the final design eventually went on sale to the public in 1988 as the Eric Clapton Stratocaster.

Fender had demonstrated to Clapton that Lace Sensor pickups and a midrange-boosting active circuit could deliver the "compressed" sound he described as his aim. The production model also had a blocked-off vintage-style vibrato unit, carefully duplicating that feature of Clapton's favored set-up. He never used vibrato, but disliked the sound of "hardtail" (non-vibrato) Strats. Clapton retired Blackie around this time and soon began playing his new signature models. Many other signature-model Strats have followed since then.

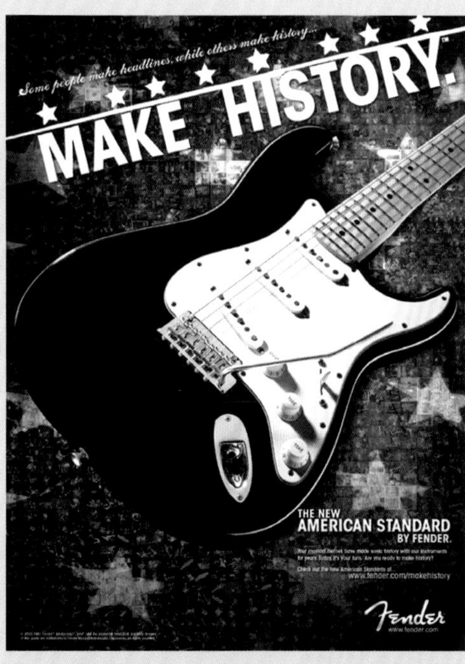

LEFT: **Eric Clapton with signature Strat in a 1998 ad.**

CENTER: **Strat history as seen in 2012.**

RIGHT: **Nineteen-Fifty-New means vintage today in a 2018 ad.**

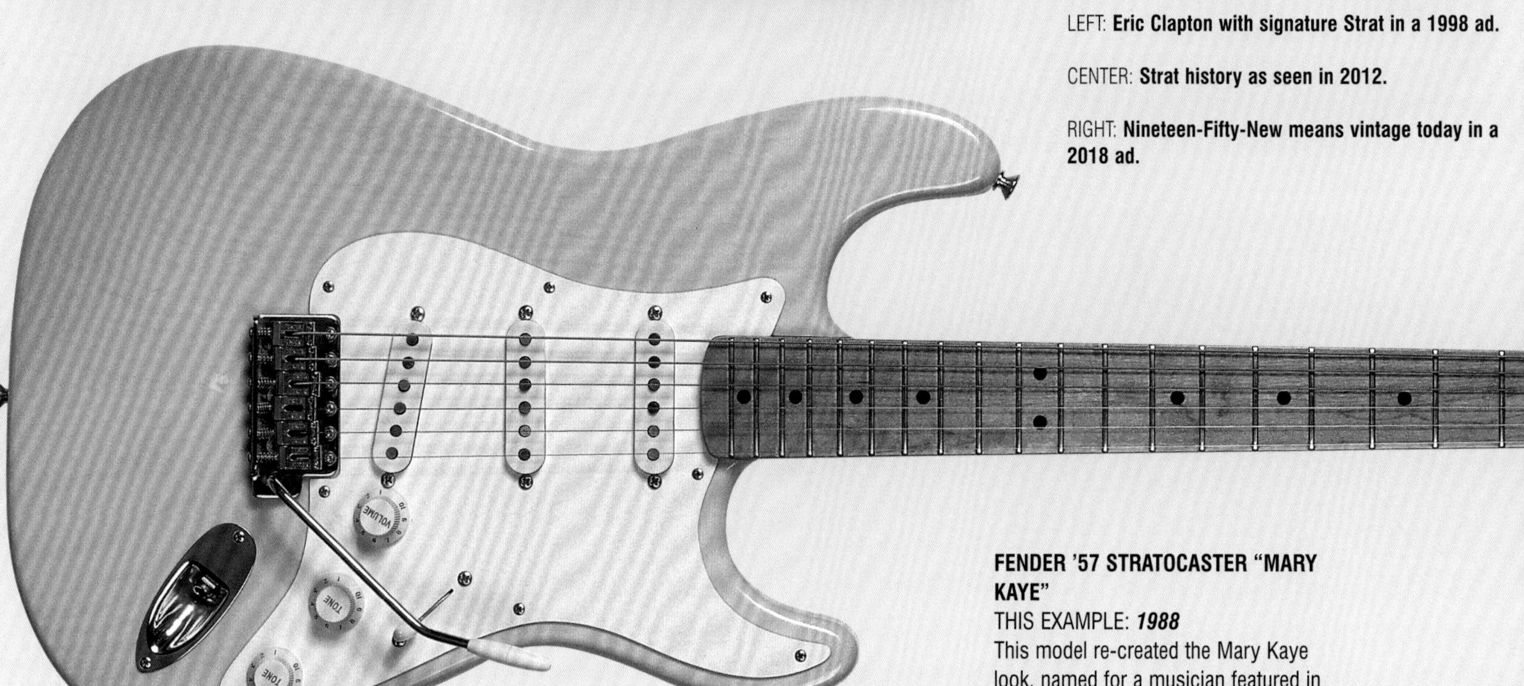

FENDER '57 STRATOCASTER "MARY KAYE"

THIS EXAMPLE: ***1988***

This model re-created the Mary Kaye look, named for a musician featured in 50s Fender ads playing a Strat with a blond finish and gold-plated metalwork.

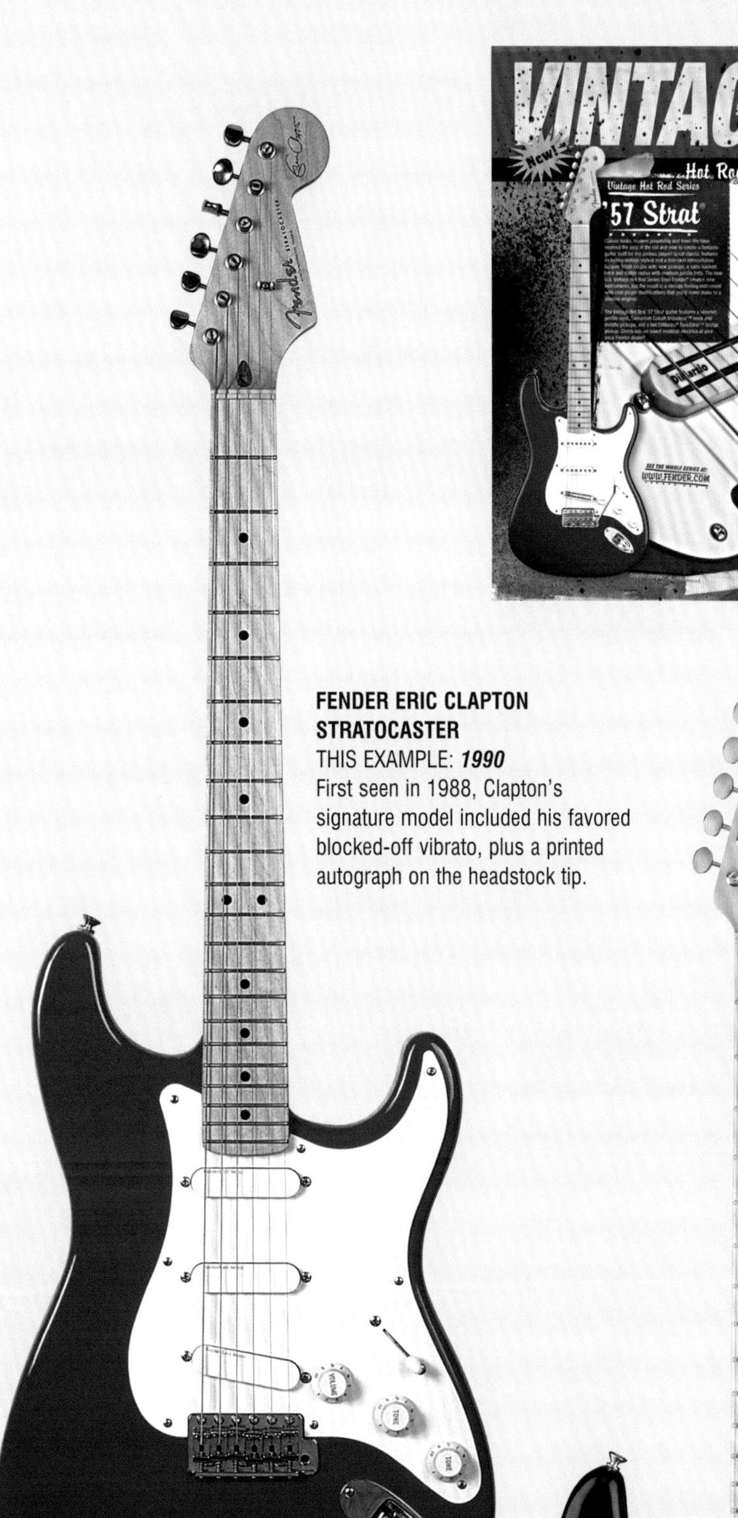

The Vintage Hot Rod '57 Strat in 2007 mixing new and old.

FENDER ERIC CLAPTON STRATOCASTER
THIS EXAMPLE: ***1990***
First seen in 1988, Clapton's signature model included his favored blocked-off vibrato, plus a printed autograph on the headstock tip.

FENDER '54 STRATOCASTER FMT
THIS EXAMPLE: ***1996***
For this Custom Shop model introduced in 1995, Fender followed the general spec of a 1954-style Strat but added gold-plated metalwork plus a figured maple top (FMT) of the type seen on contemporary PRS instruments.

FENDER AMERICAN ORIGINAL 50s STRATOCASTER
THIS EXAMPLE: ***2018***
At the time of writing, the new American Original series included the latest example of Fender's continuing quest to create a period-faithful 50s-style Stratocaster.

Like many guitar makers, Gibson's working method once a single model proved popular was to build a series around it. We've seen how the Les Paul Model—which we know today as the Goldtop—was the first of Gibson's solidbody models, introduced in 1952. Two years later, with some satisfactory sales of that model under its belt, Gibson introduced two new Les Pauls to create some options for guitarists interested in the new style of instrument. One was the Les Paul Custom, which was an upscale model above the Goldtop; the other was the Les Paul Junior (for more on the Junior, see the following pages), which was a budget model below the Goldtop.

The Les Paul Custom had an all-mahogany body, rather than the maple–mahogany mix of the Goldtop. The new model was promoted in later catalogues as "the fretless wonder" because of its low, flat fretwire, different to the wire used on other Les Pauls at the time. For some players, it seemed to help them play more speedily. In addition to its conventional P-90 pickup at the bridge, the Custom featured a new style of pickup at the neck, soon known as the Alnico. It was also the first Les Paul model with the company's Tune-o-matic bridge, used in conjunction with a separate bar-shaped tailpiece. This offered for the first time on a Gibson the opportunity to individually adjust the length of each string, which improved tuning accuracy. From 1955, the Tune-o-matic became a feature of the Goldtop model as well.

Guild, meanwhile, added new models to its hollowbody electric line, including the two-pickup X-400 and M-75 Aristocrat, and the three-pickup X-600. A few years later, Guild moved its factory from New York City to Hoboken, New Jersey

ORIGINAL **GUILD STRATFORD X-350**
THIS EXAMPLE: ***1954***
The X-350 reflected the experience of Guild's ex-Epiphone workers, with a notable similarity to the Epiphone Zephyr Emperor Regent in its layout of pickups and controls.

Red Newmark and Roberta Sherwood try a Guild X-350, 1959.

ORIGINAL **GIBSON LES PAUL CUSTOM**
THIS EXAMPLE: ***1954***
Introduced in '54, the Custom was Gibson's lavish reply to the popularity of the original Goldtop, with a luxurious black finish, gold-plated metalwork, and fancier inlays.

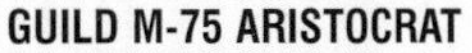

GUILD M-75 ARISTOCRAT
THIS EXAMPLE: ***2017***
Guild's classic small-body M-75 hollowbody electric was one of the vintage models re-created by Cordoba, which acquired the Guild brand in 2014.

GIBSON LES PAUL CUSTOM 1954
THIS EXAMPLE: ***2008***
Gibson's quest for reissue accuracy has focused heavily on the various Les Paul models through the decades, as seen on this luscious re-creation of a 50s Custom.

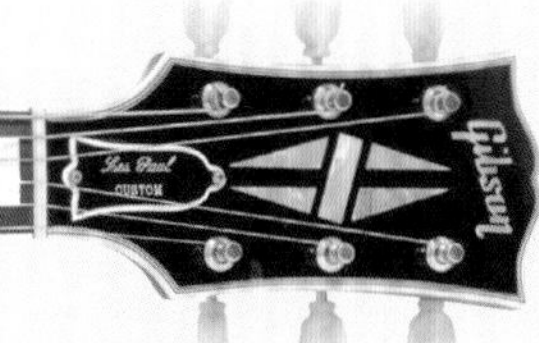

2004 Gibson Custom Shop catalogue with figured-top Les Paul Custom.

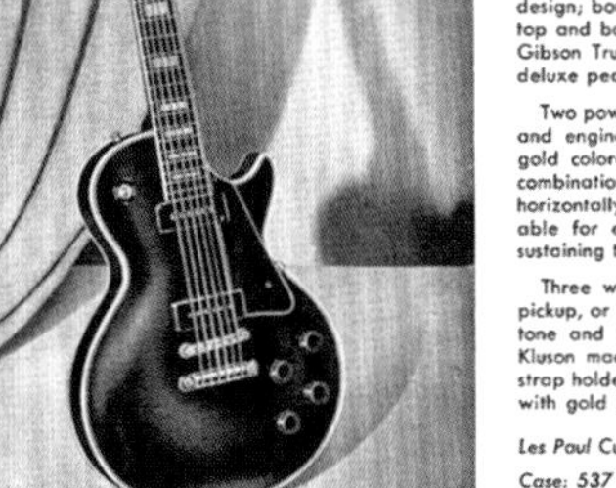

"THE FRETLESS WONDER"
LES PAUL CUSTOM GUITAR

Here is the ultimate in a solid body Gibson Electric Spanish Guitar . . . players rave about its extremely low smooth frets and playing action, call it the "Fretless Wonder." Features clear, resonant and sparkling tone, with widest range of tone colorings.

Solid Honduras Mahogany body with carved top, size 17¼" long, 12¾" wide, 1¾" thick with graceful cutaway design; bound with alternating white and black strips on top and bottom of body. Mahogany neck, with exclusive Gibson Truss Rod neck construction; ebony fingerboard; deluxe pearl inlays.

Two powerful magnetic type pickups specially designed and engineered for this model; individually adjustable gold colored magnets, gold plated polepieces. Double combination Bridge and Tailpiece . . . adjustable both horizontally and vertically, Tune-O-Matic bridge, adjustable for each string length. This combination provides sustaining tone quality and precision adjustment.

Three way toggle switch selects either front or back pickup, or both simultaneously; each pickup has separate tone and volume controls; finest individual gold-plated Kluson machine heads; gold plated metal end pin and strap holder. Finished in solid Ebony color for rich contrast with gold plated fittings. Padded leather strap included.

Les Paul Custom Guitar

Case: 537 Faultless

Les Paul Custom in Gibson's 1956 catalogue.

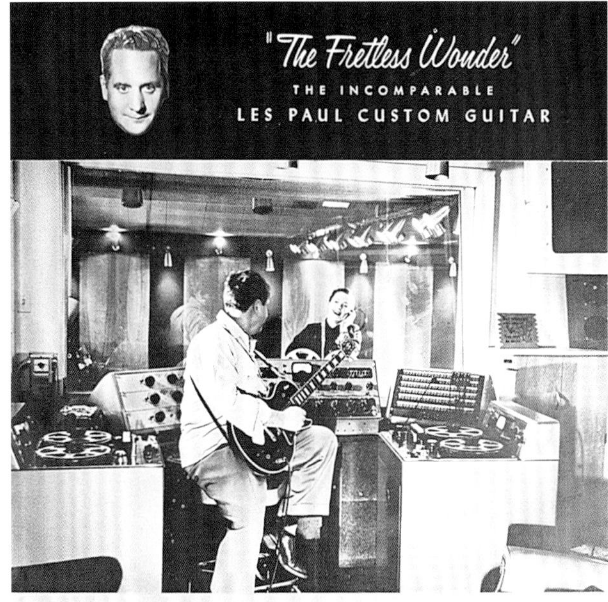

Les Paul & Mary Ford recording at home with the new Custom, 1955.

As the 50s progressed, several of the big-name guitar manufacturers would add to their lines of electric guitars as they began to better understand what players wanted and what their factories were capable of producing. In many ways this was new and uncharted territory, and while some companies made sure to tread carefully, others marched out into the widening world of solidbody electrics with renewed optimism and flair.

In a mark of confidence in this new style of electric guitar, in 1954 Gibson added two new models alongside its original solidbody Les Paul Goldtop, which it had first sold two years earlier. We have just met the high-end Les Paul Custom (see the previous pages), and the second new model was the Les Paul Junior.

The budget Junior was designed for and aimed at beginners, and it did not pretend to be anything other than a cheaper guitar. The outline shape was the same as the Goldtop and Custom, but the most obvious difference was a flat-top solid mahogany body and a single P-90 pickup, simple controls, and plain dot-shaped fingerboard markers. Gibson's September 1954 pricelist showed the Les Paul Custom at $325 and the Les Paul Junior at $99.50, with the Goldtop at $225.

Gretsch, too, added two new models in 1954 to partner the semi-solidbody Duo Jet that it had introduced the previous year, the country-flavored Round Up and the sparkle-finished Silver Jet. Gretsch aimed the Round Up squarely at the rising number of country players, adorning the guitar with unrelenting Western decoration, including a big "G" for Gretsch actually branded into the front of the Western orange-finish body. Gretsch described the Round Up as having "masculine beauty." Also unsubtle was the Silver Jet, effectively a Duo Jet with a body front finished in silver-sparkle wrap borrowed from Gretsch's drum department.

Les Paul Junior Guitar

The trim, neat appearance, easy playing action, and unusual brilliant tones of the Les Paul Jr. Guitar, together with its unbelievable low, popular price, have made it Gibson's best selling electric solid body instrument. Gibson quality throughout, coupled with top performance, have earned for it tremendous popularity with students and advanced players alike. Golden Sunburst finish on top with dark brown mahogany color on back, rim and neck.

Graceful cutaway design • slender mahogany neck with Gibson Adjustable Truss Rod • rosewood fingerboard with pearl dot inlays. Powerful pickup located near bridge for clarity of tonal response • individually adjustable polepieces to balance each string • separate tone and volume controls • bright nickel-plated metal parts, quality machine heads • new metal combination bridge and tailpiece, adjustable horizontally and vertically • padded leather strap included.

SPECIFICATIONS

12¾" wide, 17¼" long, 1¾" thick, 24¾" scale, 22 frets

Les Paul Jr.—Sunburst Finish $120.00
No. 115 Case—Durabilt construction 13.50

ORIGINAL **GIBSON LES PAUL JUNIOR**
THIS EXAMPLE: ***1956***
Launched in 1954, the budget Junior had Gibson's traditional brown-to-yellow sunburst and the wrapover stopbar bridge/tailpiece of the contemporary Goldtop.

Les Paul Junior profiled in the 1958 Gibson catalogue.

ORIGINAL **GRETSCH SILVER JET 6129**
THIS EXAMPLE: ***1956***
The flamboyant Silver Jet was introduced in 1954 alongside the Round Up, aimed at country players, and the existing Duo Jet, Gretsch's original semi-solid electric.

Thumbs Carlille shows off Gretsch's "Western-style" Round Up, 1954.

GIBSON LES PAUL JUNIOR 1958
THIS EXAMPLE: ***2010***
Gibson's Les Paul Juniors may have started life at the bottom of the 50s pricelist, but soon they were praised as great little rock'n'roll workhorses, and many reissues have appeared.

Retro-style 2008 catalogue page for the Gretsch Silver Jet.

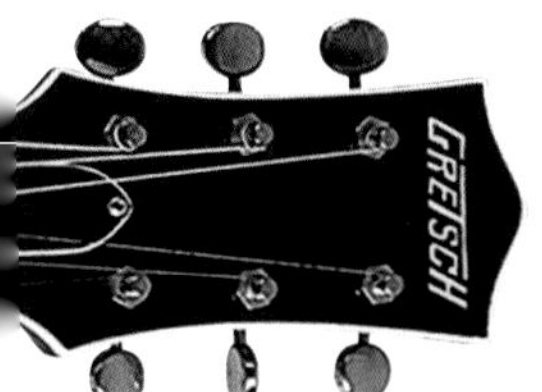

GRETSCH '57 SILVER JET 6129T-1957
THIS EXAMPLE: ***2018***
This recent reissue of an early-style Silver Jet reproduces the original's single-coil DeArmond-made DynaSonic pickups and Melita bridge, plus an optional Bigsby vibrato.

Walt Disney's
Disneyland
The Happiest Place On Earth
OPENING & DEDICATION CEREMONY
2:30PM SUNDAY
JULY 17TH, 1955
"To all who come to this happy place, Welcome. Disneyland is your land."
Main Street USA
ADVENTURELAND
Frontierland
TOMORROWLAND

The star sensation of 'East of Eden'
JAMES DEAN
IN
"REBEL WITHOUT A CAUSE"
WARNER BROS'. CHALLENGING DRAMA OF TODAY'S JUVENILE VIOLENCE!
CINEMASCOPE AND WARNERCOLOR
NATALIE WOOD · SAL MINEO · JIM BACKUS · ANN DORAN · COREY ALLEN · WILLIAM HOPPER · STEWART STERN
DAVID WEISBART · NICHOLAS RAY

PHIL SILVERS
Starring as
SGT. BILKO
10¢
FEB. NO. 11
APPROVED BY THE COMICS CODE AUTHORITY
SUPERMAN DC NATIONAL COMICS
CBS

- **ROSA PARKS**, a black passenger on a bus in Montgomery, Alabama, defies a segregated seating rule when she refuses to give up her seat to a white person. Martin Luther King takes part in the year-long Montgomery bus boycott, which leads to the nullification of the bus-segregation laws and helps establish King as leader of the US civil rights movement.

- **JAMES DEAN** is killed in a car wreck; earlier in the year he'd appeared in "chicken run" smash scenes in *Rebel Without A Cause*. Meanwhile, a disaster at the Le Mans road race in France kills 83 onlookers and one driver.

1955

- **DISNEYLAND** is opened in Anaheim, Los Angeles. Walt Disney originally planned to call it Mickey Mouse Park.

- **PHIL SILVERS** debuts on US TV as Sgt Bilko. Commercial TV stations start broadcasting in the UK alongside the BBC; the first British TV ad is for toothpaste.

- **CHARLIE PARKER** and Albert Einstein die. "Einstein's famous equation linking mass and energy pointed the way to the fission of uranium, and so to Hiroshima and Nagasaki," a newspaper obituary says.

- **CHUCK BERRY** and Bo Diddley cut their debut records, on Chess and Checker. Bill Haley's 'Rock Around The Clock' is number one in the US and UK after it is featured in the movie *Blackboard Jungle*.

Gibson was always looking to refine its hollowbody electrics to suit the way players wanted to use them. This was the case for all makers. The company that failed to listen to musicians would soon find their instruments falling out of favor. But Gibson was more attuned than most to the criticisms heard at the gig and in the studio thanks to its long history of closeness with danceband and jazz guitarists.

The ES-5 was among the first three-pickup guitars when Gibson introduced it in 1949. But players struggled to get the most from its control layout of three volume knobs and one master tone. In 1955, the model was reconfigured and given a new name that hinted at its new control scheme: the ES-5 Switchmaster. Mirroring the regular layout for two-pickup guitars, the model now had a volume and tone control for each pickup, making for six knobs in all, and where the master tone knob had been on the ES-5's cutaway, the Switchmaster had a new four-way selector switch that offered each pickup in turn or all three together.

Gibson decided that the deep body of its hollowbody electrics put off some players, and also this year launched the Byrdland (calling on help from guitarists Billy Byrd and Hank Garland), the ES-350T, and the ES-225T. They had slimmer bodies that aimed for sleek comfort. Gibson called this style "thin" but most people call it "thinline," a term Gibson itself didn't use until the 70s. The body on many of Gibson's hollow electrics was about three-and-a-half inches deep, but these new thinlines were around two inches deep. They combined the lean vibe of Gibson's recent solidbody electrics with dependable hollowbody tradition. The Byrdland and 350T had a shorter scale-length and a slimmer neck, too, contributing to the easier and more playable feel of the new guitars.

ORIGINAL **GIBSON ES-5 SWITCHMASTER**
THIS EXAMPLE: ***1955***
A redesigned ES-5, the Switchmaster had a more logical layout of controls, with a volume and tone per pickup plus a four-way switch that gave bridge, middle, or neck pickup, or all three at once.

ORIGINAL **GIBSON BYRDLAND**
THIS EXAMPLE: ***1957***
Something like a thinline L-5CES, the Byrdland had the ES-350T's shorter, narrower neck that was intended to provide an easier, playable feel for some guitarists.

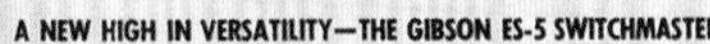

ES-350T—"ARTIST APPROVED" FOR SOLO OR BACKGROUND WORK

The Gibson ES-350T Cutaway Electric Spanish Guitar has a reduced depth of body, a smaller, more streamlined neck and a shorter scale length—all requested features of the leading guitarists. A wide choice of tonal effects, plus the beauty of appearance of the ES-350T hold promise of popularity for another fine Gibson instrument . . . highlighted as always by craftsmanship and quality, by performance and dependability.

"Artist Approved" Features of the ES-350T:

- Comfortable playing, easier, less tiring pick action with the body size: 17" wide, 21" long and 2¼" deep.
- Faster and easier left hand fingering with the smaller, streamlined neck: 22 fret rosewood fingerboard, 23½" scale length.
- Clear, brilliant solos or full, mellow backgrounds with regulated dual pickup amplification.
- Powerful Gibson pickups with Alnico magnets and individually adjustable polepieces for better tone balance.
- Separate tone and volume controls for each pickup, can be preset to any desired quality or volume.
- Three position toggle switch on treble side activates either or both pickups.
- Kluson deluxe individual enclosed machine-heads.
- Gibson Tune-O-Matic Bridge for greater sustaining power and accurate pitch adjustment on each string.
- Streamlined calibrated control knobs, easier to read, set to any desired position.
- Gibson Adjustable Truss Rod Neck construction joined to body at 14th fret.
- Figured curly maple body and neck, finished with Gibson Golden Sunburst or selected Natural Finishes, accented by ivoroid binding on body, fingerboard and peghead.

ES-350T—Electric Spanish Cutaway Guitar—Golden Sunburst Finish
ES-350TN—Electric Spanish Cutaway Guitar—Natural Finish
No. 603—Faultless Plush-lined Case

LEFT: **Billy Byrd + Hank Garland = Byrdland, 1956 ad.**

CENTER: **Nat King Cole's guitarist John Collins with the earlier ES-5, 1954.**

RIGHT: **ES-350T in Gibson's 1956 catalogue.**

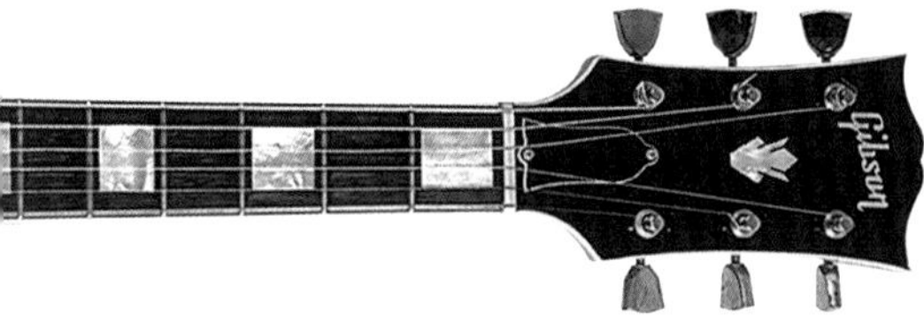

A NEW HIGH IN VERSATILITY—THE GIBSON ES-5 SWITCHMASTER

An increased range of performance, quality and playability, wonderful tone and beautiful appearance—all these features are destined to make the ES-5 Switchmaster a favorite among discriminating guitarists. This attractive Electric Cutaway Spanish Guitar is of highly figured curly maple with multiple binding, bound rosewood fingerboard with large block mother-of-pearl inlays.

Special Features of the Switchmaster are:

- Three separately controlled pickups with Alnico magnets for the greatest range of tone qualities . . . from crisp, brilliant trebles to deep, rich basses.
- **Six Controls**—separate tone and volume control for each of the three pickups, permitting presetting of each.
- **Four way toggle switch** to activate each of the three pickups separately or all three simultaneously. At the "all on" position, by regulating volume controls, each pickup can be activated separately, any combination of two together, or all three.
- Gibson Tune-O-Matic Bridge for greater sustaining power and perfect tuning accuracy for each string.
- Gibson Adjustable Truss Rod Neck Construction joined to body at the 14th fret.
- Body size: 17" wide and 21" long.
- Individual gold plated enclosed Kluson machine-heads with Keystone buttons.
- Available in beautiful Natural Finish or the famous Gibson Golden Sunburst.

Switchmaster ES-5 Electric Spanish Cutaway Guitar—Golden Sunburst Finish
Switchmaster ES-5N Electric Spanish Cutaway Guitar—Natural Finish
No. 600 Faultless Plush-lined Case   No. 606 Faultless, Flannel-lined Case

ES-5 Switchmaster in the 1956 catalogue.

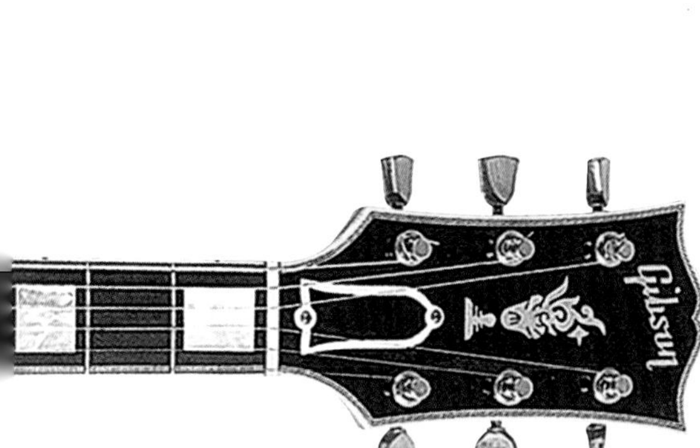

ORIGINAL **GIBSON ES-350T**
THIS EXAMPLE: ***1957***
Along with the Byrdland and ES-225T, the 350T had Gibson's new thinline body, a slimmer take on its existing deep-body style. Chuck Berry understood the appeal, using one for many of his classic cuts and gigs.

A reissued Byrdland, 1999 catalogue.

Gibson's thinline style of hollowbody electric guitars began with three instruments that were launched in 1955, namely the Byrdland, the ES-350T, and the ES-225T. They prompted a number of other slim, comfortable hollow electrics from the company in the following decades—and one of those original models, at least, lasted for some time in Gibson's lines.

The Byrdland reflected some of the changes that Gibson introduced across many of its models as time went on, including in 1957 a shift from the original P-90 single-coil pickups to a pair of the company's new twin-coil humbuckers, and then in 1960 a change from the original rounded cutaway shape (Gibson called it "Venetian") to a pointed shape ("Florentine") that lasted to the end of the 60s, when the rounded shape returned. The Byrdland remained on Gibson pricelists into the late 80s, when it was dropped until a limited run in 1993 and then a return to the line in '98 as a Custom Shop model, where it still resided at the time of writing.

The ES-350T followed the Byrdland's change of pickups and cutaway shape, but the model was dropped in the early 60s until reintroduced for about four years from 1977. Since then, it has popped in and out of the line on several occasions, and it was last seen on a pricelist in 1999. The ES-225T lasted only three years or so after its introduction in 1955.

Meanwhile, the ES-5 Switchmaster was also among the full-body hollowbody electric models that followed Gibson's across-the-board changes made to pickups and to the shape of the cutaway. The Switchmaster's original run was relatively brief, ending in the early 60s, but this was followed by its reintroduction in 1996 and (at the time of writing) a final showing on a Gibson pricelist in 2014.

GIBSON ES-5 SWITCHMASTER
THIS EXAMPLE: ***1996***
The Switchmaster was first reissued in 1996 as part of the Custom Shop's Historic Collection, after an absence since the early 60s. As well as the expected sunburst and natural finishes, it was also offered in this transparent wine red.

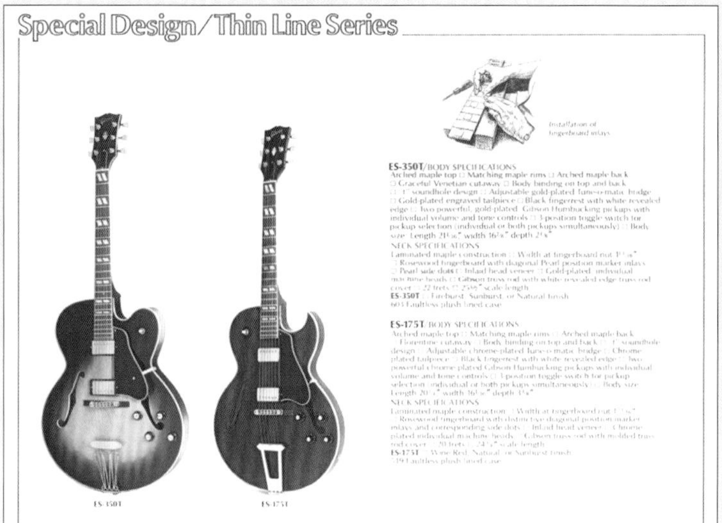

An ES-350T alongside a 175 in Gibson's 1978 catalogue.

GIBSON ES-5 SWITCHMASTER
THIS EXAMPLE: ***2002***
Made at Gibson's Custom Shop in Nashville, this example of the reissued Switchmaster has a vintage sunburst finish highlighting some attractively figured maple.

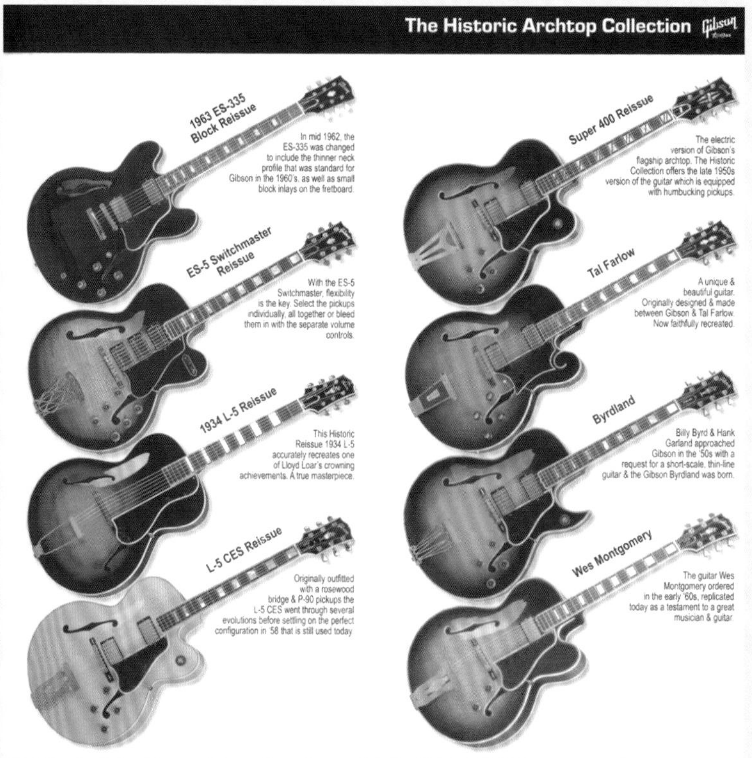

The Historic Archtop Collection

1963 ES-335 Block Reissue
In mid 1962, the ES-335 was changed to include the thinner neck profile that was standard for Gibson in the 1960's, as well as small block inlays on the fretboard.

ES-5 Switchmaster Reissue
With the ES-5 Switchmaster, flexibility is the key. Select the pickups individually, all together or bleed them in with the separate volume controls.

1934 L-5 Reissue
This Historic Reissue 1934 L-5 accurately recreates one of Lloyd Loar's crowning achievements. A true masterpiece.

L-5 CES Reissue
Originally outfitted with a rosewood bridge & P-90 pickups the L-5 CES went through several evolutions before settling on the perfect configuration in '58 that is still used today.

Super 400 Reissue
The electric version of Gibson's flagship archtop. The Historic Collection offers the late 1950s version of the guitar which is equipped with humbucking pickups.

Tal Farlow
A unique & beautiful guitar. Originally designed & made between Gibson & Tal Farlow. Now faithfully recreated.

Byrdland
Billy Byrd & Hank Garland approached Gibson in the '50s with a request for a short-scale, thin-line guitar & the Gibson Byrdland was born.

Wes Montgomery
The guitar Wes Montgomery ordered in the early '60s, replicated today as a testament to a great musician & guitar.

Byrdland and Switchmaster among the archtops, 2006.

GIBSON BYRDLAND FLORENTINE
THIS EXAMPLE: ***2016***
Gibson reintroduced this 50s model in 1998 as a Custom Shop guitar, either as the Byrdland, with rounded cutaway shape, or as the Byrdland Florentine, with pointed cutaway.

Les Paul, Mary Ford, and Gibson on television, 1957.

Gibson's '56 promo shot of a Les Paul TV in the classroom.

The Les Paul Special

The Les Paul Special combines tone, versatility, slender neck and low, fast action with a moderate price • solid Honduras mahogany body and neck finished in highly polished, limed finish • black Royalite pickguard and unit covers • nickel-plated metal parts.

Graceful cutaway design • Gibson Adjustable Truss Rod neck • bound, rosewood fingerboard with sparkling pearl dot inlays. Two, powerful pickups with individually adjustable polepieces to balance each string • separate tone and volume controls for each pickup which can be preset • three-way toggle switch to activate either or both pickups; unique combination metal bridge and tailpiece, adjustable horizontally and vertically; enclosed individual machine heads; and padded, adjustable leather strap.

SPECIFICATIONS
12¾" wide, 17¼" long, 1¾" thick, 24¾" scale, 22 frets

Les Paul Special – Limed Mahogany Finish $179.50
No. 535 Case – Faultless, plush lined 42.00
No. 115 Case – Durabilt 13.50

Les Paul TV in the '58 catalogue.

ORIGINAL **GIBSON LES PAUL SPECIAL**
THIS EXAMPLE: ***1955***
The two-pickup single-cutaway Les Paul Special had a "limed mahogany" finish, the same as that of the single-pickup Les Paul TV model.

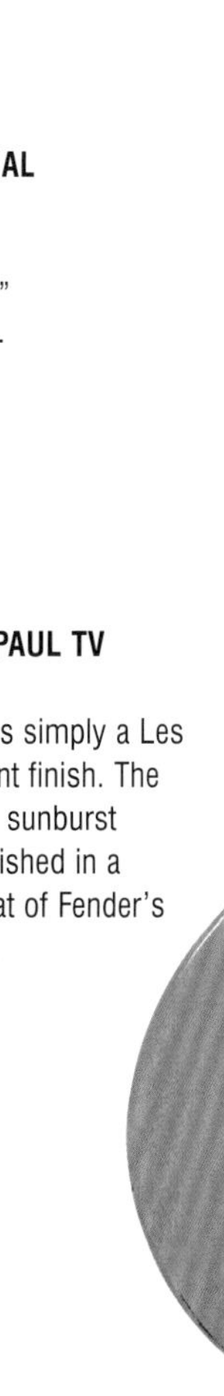

ORIGINAL **GIBSON LES PAUL TV**
THIS EXAMPLE: ***1956***
Gibson's Les Paul TV was simply a Les Paul Junior with a different finish. The Junior came (for now) in sunburst finish, but the TV was finished in a beige color, not unlike that of Fender's contemporary Telecaster.

Gibson added two more models to its growing Les Paul solidbody line in 1955, the Les Paul TV and the Les Paul Special. Both were versions of the budget Junior introduced the previous year. The TV came in a different finish; the Special added an extra pickup.

Gibson used various descriptions for the finish of the TV, calling it "natural," "limed oak," or "limed mahogany." The surviving Les Paul TVs of the 50s do reveal a variety of colors, with earlier examples tending to a beige-like hue, while later ones are often distinctly yellow. As for the TV name, one theory suggests the budget model's pale color was designed to stand out on black-and-white television screens. That seems unlikely, because pro players appearing on television would surely opt for a high-end model. Or perhaps "TV" was an unsubtle reference to the competing blond-colored Telecaster made by Fender?

The TV name was more likely coined to cash in on Les Paul's regular appearances at the time on television, on *The Les Paul & Mary Ford Show*. Les and Mary signed a three-year contract in 1953 for two million dollars for the show, a sponsored daily spot for a toothpaste company. Gibson may have reasoned that if you had seen Les Paul on TV, you might go and buy his TV guitar.

The Les Paul Special, also new in 1955, was a Junior with a second P-90 pickup at the neck, in addition to the existing bridge pickup, and of course it was given a suitable complement of controls and a pickup switch. At first, the Special was finished in the same beige color as the new TV—although the Special was never called a TV, which still confuses some collectors—but a cherry red option would be added with the move to a double-cutaway body in '59.

> *Les Paul TV Model*
>
> Designed to emphasize the latest in modern appearance with beautiful limed-mahogany finish and incorporating unusual quality, features and performance at a popular price. Its easy, low playing action, slender neck, and clear sustaining tone make it a favorite with students and advanced players.
>
> Graceful cutaway design • slender mahogany neck with Gibson Adjustable Truss Rod • rosewood fingerboard with pearl dot inlays. Powerful pickup located near bridge for clarity of tonal response • individually adjustable polepieces to balance each string • separate tone and volume controls • bright nickel-plated metal parts, quality machine heads • new metal combination bridge and tailpiece, adjustable horizontally and vertically • padded leather strap included.
>
> SPECIFICATIONS
> 12¾" wide, 17¼" long, 1¾" thick, 24¾" scale, 22 frets
>
> Les Paul TV – Limed Mahogany Finish $132.50
> No. 535 Case – Faultless, plush lined 42.00
> No. 115 Case – Durabilt 13.50

A Les Paul Special II is part of this Epiphone starter-pack in a 2013 ad.

EPIPHONE LES PAUL JUNIOR
THIS EXAMPLE: ***2012***
Gibson has owned the Epiphone brand since 1957 and today uses it on a number of budget Gibson-like models, including this recent Indonesian-made Les Paul Junior.

GIBSON LES PAUL SPECIAL
THIS EXAMPLE: ***1991***
A reissue of the Les Paul Special from the early 90s in heritage cherry, offered by Gibson at the time alongside tobacco sunburst and TV yellow.

1955

Other makers began to notice the success Gibson had with its Les Paul models. This idea of a signature guitar, named for a famous musician, went beyond the type of advertising used by Gretsch and others that simply highlighted the use of this or that model from the company's line by particular players. Gretsch decided it needed its own Les Paul, a well-known player whose name it could put on an instrument to attract untapped interest to its guitars. Gretsch's Jimmie Webster came up with Chet Atkins.

Atkins's career had developed quickly, and he played many sessions, including hits for Elvis Presley and The Everly Brothers, but it was the instrumental gems made under his own name – from 'Main Street Breakdown' to 'Yakety Axe' – that had guitarists rushing to try his multi-line picking style. His records helped define the new potential of the electric guitar, mixing keen skills, clever effects, and studio tricks to open up an exciting world of possibilities.

Jimmie Webster at Gretsch put together a prototype to show Atkins, and as with Les Paul and Gibson, the guitarist had little input to the original design of his signature model. Gretsch reckoned his country leanings excused its re-use of the Western decoration from the Round Up model. Atkins had reservations about the steer's head on the headstock, cacti and steers on the inlays, and a G-brand on the body. But he gave in because he wanted a signature guitar, just like Les Paul.

Gretsch introduced two Chet Atkins models in 1955. The Solid Body was a Jet-style semi-solid, while the Hollow Body became for a short while Atkins's exclusive instrument, and it has gone on to become one of the most revered of Gretsch's original models. It's usually known simply by its Gretsch model number, the 6120.

ORIGINAL **GRETSCH PROTOTYPE**
THIS EXAMPLE: ***1954***
Gretsch sent a first prototype to Chet Atkins based on the company's earlier Streamliner model, and then this trial guitar, which was fitted with the Bigsby vibrato Atkins wanted and which would be retained on the production version.

ORIGINAL **GRETSCH CHET ATKINS SOLID BODY 6121**
THIS EXAMPLE: ***1955***
The 6121 was the semi-solid companion to the 6120, but it was never as popular, and it sat awkwardly in Gretsch's line alongside the similar Round Up model. It was gone by the early 60s.

Gretsch Spotlight

Sal Salvador, his Gretsch and his group a hit with Birdland customers

Sal Salvador and his Gretsch Guitar

YOU'LL LIKE "Autumn in New York" the way Sal Salvador and his group play it at Birdland and on the new Capitol Album, "Sal Salvador Quartet." (Also features two originals—"Salutation" and "Nothin' to Do.") Sal finds his unique styling sounds better on a Gretsch guitar. "My Gretsch produces a full, rich sustaining sound in every register," says Sal. Finds the famous Gretsch "Miracle Neck" comfortable to play—praises Gretsch's tone, too. Try a Gretsch guitar yourself. Send for your FREE Gretsch guitar catalog. Describes the Electromatic Cutaway Guitar Sal plays. At the same time, ask for your *free* autographed photo of Sal. Address: FRED. GRETSCH, Dept. M1255, 60 Broadway, Brooklyn 11, N. Y.

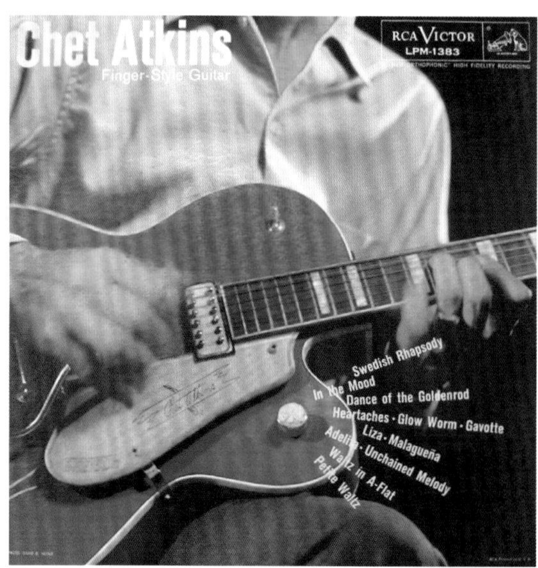

LEFT: **Gretsch's established links were with jazzmen like Sal Salvador, as in this 1955 ad.**

CENTER: **Atkins in a rare pose with a 6121, which he hardly used, in an ad from '55.**

RIGHT: **Experimental sealed-top 6120 on a 1956 album cover.**

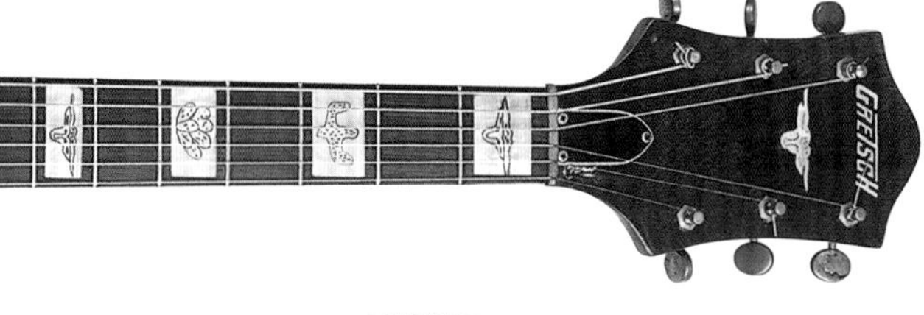

ORIGINAL **GRETSCH CHET ATKINS HOLLOW BODY 6120**
THIS EXAMPLE: ***1955***
The 6120 had a hollow body and two single-coil pickups. Chet Atkins disliked the country-style decoration, and gradually Gretsch would remove it during the coming years.

CHET ATKINS with his thumb pick and his four fingers plays in his inimitable 'modern-country' style to produce a tone that delights the listener. It's so tasteful, so melodic, so enhanced by Chet's own clever improvisations! Every Chet Atkins appearance, whether in person or on T-V (you should see and hear his reception at Grand Ol' Opry!) and every new album he cuts for RCA Victor, wins new admirers to swell the vast army of Chet Atkins fans.

CHET ATKINS ELECTRIC GUITARS by GRETSCH

Chet Atkins' own ideas combine with Gretsch 'know how' to produce these two truly distinctive guitars. For real country-style tone, for exceptional playing convenience and comfort, and for regular he-man good looks, it's mighty hard to match them—*anywhere*! In both models you find every one of these important construction features:

- Deep cut-away bodies for easy fingering of the entire scale;
- Twin, built-in Gretsch Dynasonic pickups (no others come even close for sensitivity, fidelity, and power) with five controls, including two-way, finger-tip switch to cut out either pickup or combine them—*instantly*;
- Built-in Vibrato tailpiece for exciting tonal effects; single tones or full chords sustain with beautiful tremolo under manipulation of the lever;
- Metal bridge saddle and nut, perfect for real cowboy and country-style tone;
- Special thin-gauge strings;
- Chet Atkins-designed shorter scale;
- Oval rosewood fingerboard with pearl positions engraved in Western motifs, on fast-playing Gretsch 'Miracle Neck';
- Individual machines with slip-proof metal buttons;
- Metal parts heavily gold plated.

CHET ATKINS SOLID BODY GUITAR

Compact 13½" body and neck of selected brown mahogany, hand polished finish. The slim 'Miracle Neck' joining at the 16th fret and the deep cutaway help you get those highs in brilliant fashion. Western style decorations including carved saddle leather body binding and shoulder strap. For ultra-fine tone projection and sustaining power, this is your guitar! (Illustration "A")

PX6121—Chet Atkins Solid Body Electric Guitar $385.00

CHET ATKINS HOLLOW BODY GUITAR

Conventional style but a little narrower (15½") and a little thinner (2¾") to give you that Gretsch new look, new feel, new playing comfort. Body and neck are choice curly maple finished Western-style in amber-red, highly polished by hand. The neck joins at the 14th fret. Complete with carved saddle leather shoulder strap. Here's a wonderful combination of mellow tone with brilliance when you want it! (Illustration "B")

PX6120—Chet Atkins Hollow Body Electric Guitar $385.00

(See Page 16 for Chet Atkins Guitar Cases.)

Chet Atkins 6120 and 6121 in the Gretsch catalogue for 1955.

Beyond Chet Atkins himself—who would switch to the Gretsch Country Gentleman model when it was introduced in 1958—a number of other famous guitarists have sensed the appeal of the Hollow Body 6120. Brian Setzer and The Stray Cats personified the rockabilly revival of the early 80s, and Setzer chose a Hollow Body, his favored guitar since he bought his first 50s 6120 in the 70s. In 1993, Gretsch officially recognized his importance by issuing a Brian Setzer model. A second Setzer line, the stripped-down fancy-finish Hot Rods, first appeared in 1999, but it wasn't until Gretsch's alliance with Fender in 2003 that Setzer got everything he wanted for them, such as the internal bracing that Gretsch had used from the late 50s into the early 60s, designed to reduce feedback and improve tone.

Eddie Cochran was a talented, accomplished guitarist who started out as a session player and made some classic 50s solo singles, including 'Summertime Blues,' although his talents were wide-ranging. His music was a mix of rockabilly, country, and blues, and at its heart was his '55 Gretsch 6120, on which he replaced the neck pickup with a meatier Gibson P-90. Sadly, his career was cut short when he was killed, just 21 years old, in a car crash while on tour in Britain in 1960. Gretsch first offered a Cochran-model 6120 in 2010.

Meanwhile, Duane Eddy cut a string of hits based on his deceptively simple instrumental style, forever identified with the word twang. His twangy tone came as he played melodies on the bass strings of his 6120 and used the pitchbending potential of the guitar's Bigsby vibrato, his amplifier's tremolo, and the studio's echo facilities. The result was hits like 'Rebel Rouser' and 'Peter Gunn.' Gretsch introduced Eddy-signature 6120s in 1997 and 2012.

GRETSCH BRIAN SETZER HOT ROD 6120SH
THIS EXAMPLE: ***2018***
Simplicity rules for the Hot Rod signature models of rockabilly star Brian Setzer, with straightforward controls (just volume and selector) and an eye-catching selection of car-crazy colors.

GRETSCH EDDIE COCHRAN SIGNATURE HOLLOW BODY 6120
THIS EXAMPLE: ***2013***
Following a Custom Shop aged model in 2010, this Eddie Cochran signature model also has the P-90 neck pickup and distinctive pickguard that identified Cochran's original 6120.

GRETSCH '59 CHET ATKINS SOLID BODY 6121-1959
THIS EXAMPLE: ***2011***
This latest remake of an original-style 6121 semi-solid Chet Atkins model was introduced in 2007, following Gretsch's alliance with Fender four years earlier that saw many models improved and, in the case of reissues, made more accurate.

Gretsch promotes its budget Electromatic brand in 2018 with a 6120-influenced 5420.

1998 ad for Duane Eddy and his first signature 6120.

GRETSCH VINTAGE SELECT EDITION '55 CHET ATKINS HOLLOW BODY 6120T-55
THIS EXAMPLE: ***2017***
At the time of writing this was the latest Gretsch model to strive for the tone and feel and playability of an original mid-50s Chet Atkins 6120, complete with period-correct features and details.

1955

GRETSCH "WHITE FALCON"
TWIN PICKUP ELECTRIC GUITAR

(A) Cost was never considered in the planning of this guitar. We were building an instrument for the artist-player whose calibre justifies and demands the utmost in striking beauty, luxurious styling, and peak tonal performance and who is willing to pay the price. This beauty is 17" body width and in the new thin model that's so comfortable to play. It is finished in gleaming white with gold sparkle binding on F-holes, body edges and fingerboard. Choicest spruce top and maple for the body and neck; finest Madagascar ebony fingerboard with pearl positions, engraved and inlaid in gold. Unique handmade tailpiece of tasteful modern design. Grover precision 16-to-1 ratio machines for hair-line tuning. Twin Gretsch-Dynasonic pickups with five Gretsch controls to make them even more effective. All metal parts heavily plated in 24-K gold. The finest guitar we know how to make—and what a beauty!

PX6136—Gretsch "White Falcon" Electric Guitar **$600.00**

What a beauty! The Falcon's '55 catalogue entry.

ORIGINAL **GRETSCH CONVERTIBLE 6199**
THIS EXAMPLE: ***1957***
The Convertible, with its floating pickup and controls, was offered in one of Gretsch's two-tone finishes of the period, here with lotus ivory (cream) front and copper mist (brown) back and pickguard.

ORIGINAL **GRETSCH WHITE FALCON 6136**
THIS EXAMPLE: ***1959***
Gretsch made some small modifications to the White Falcon during the 50s, including a shift of its headstock logo, a move to humbucking FilterTron pickups, and the use of "thumbnail" fingerboard markers.

A White Falcon among the colorful cover stars of Gretsch's 1955 catalogue.

Not content with the coup of attracting Chet Atkins to Gretsch, Jimmie Webster worked on a new idea for a guitar that would become Gretsch's top-of-the-line model. Gretsch first sold the White Falcon in 1955, and it was an impressive instrument. The big body came with a gleaming white finish, and there were gold sparkle decorations on the "winged" headstock. Metalwork was gold-plated, including the fancy Grover Imperial tuners and the stylish new "Cadillac" tailpiece. The new "hump-top" fingerboard markers had suitably bird-related engravings, and the gold-colored pickguard featured a flying falcon that seemed as if it were about to land on the nearby Gretsch logo.

"Cost was never considered in the planning of this guitar," Gretsch said in its '55 catalogue. "An instrument for the artist-player whose caliber justifies and demands the utmost in striking beauty, luxurious styling, and peak tonal performance, and who is willing to pay the price." The new Falcon listed at $600, well above the next highest, the Country Club at $400. Gibson's most expensive hollowbody electric in 1955 was its $690 Super 400CESN, but that was by comparison a sedate natural-finish product from the relatively conservative Gibson. Gretsch meanwhile said the idiosyncratic White Falcon was "the finest guitar we know how to make—and what a beauty!"

Gretsch sneaked out another new guitar in 1955, the Convertible. Its name alluded to its role as an acoustic archtop guitar "converted" for electric playing, which was not uncommon during this period. The Convertible's pickup and controls floated on the pickguard (although the pickup's poles extended into the body), and Gretsch said this "prevented the combination of electric and acoustic properties." Jazz guitarist Sal Salvador became closely linked with the Convertible, and toward the end of the 50s Gretsch renamed it the Sal Salvador model.

ORIGINAL **GRETSCH WHITE FALCON 6136**
THIS EXAMPLE: ***1956***
The luxurious white finish and gold-colored decoration of Gretsch's impressive new White Falcon model, introduced in 1955, marked it out as one of the most striking electric guitars of the era.

Studio guitarist Mary Osborne with her White Falcon, 1956.

Gretsch first tried the idea of reissuing an earlier type of one of its hollowbody models in 1975, when it introduced an "old style" White Falcon. It was at this time that the idea of vintage had begun to take hold among some guitarists, the notion that somehow, old guitars might be better than those the big manufacturers were producing at the time.

The 70s Falcon reissue drew on the original style of the 50s model, at least as far as its single-cutaway body and Filter'Tron-style humbuckers. That was in contrast to the double-cutaway look of Gretsch's existing hollowbody electrics of the time. But it was nothing like the detailed period-correct reissues that would follow in later years. For now, it was significant only as a first step for Gretsch toward a realization that interest was growing in the look and sound of several of its older models.

For the Falcon, a proper attempt at a reissue of a 50s single-cut model did not come until 1989, and only with the alliance between Gretsch and Fender in 2003 did the brand appear fully serious about attending to many of the all-important details. An unusual twist on the original look of the Falcon came with the introduction of various Black Falcon models, first seen in 1992 and in both single and double-cutaway styles.

Well known players of the 50s-style White Falcon included Stephen Stills, who was best known for his work during the 70s in Crosby Stills Nash & Young, a band where he and Neil Young often pulled out a fine-looking Gretsch. A signature Stills Falcon was introduced in 2000. And Billy Duffy used a 70s single-cut Falcon as The Cult found fame in the following decade. Gretsch issued his signature model in 2013.

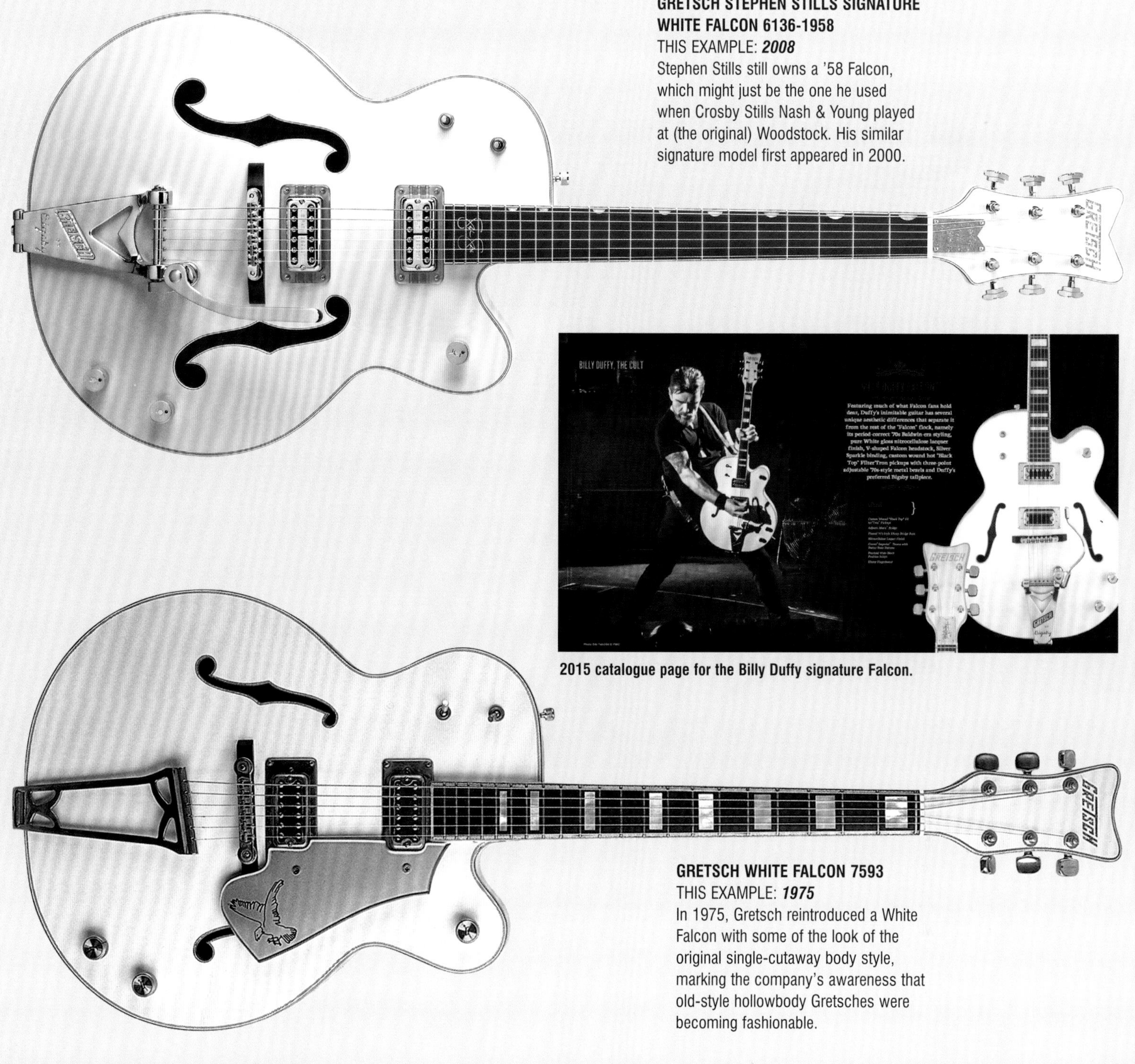

GRETSCH STEPHEN STILLS SIGNATURE WHITE FALCON 6136-1958
THIS EXAMPLE: ***2008***
Stephen Stills still owns a '58 Falcon, which might just be the one he used when Crosby Stills Nash & Young played at (the original) Woodstock. His similar signature model first appeared in 2000.

2015 catalogue page for the Billy Duffy signature Falcon.

GRETSCH WHITE FALCON 7593
THIS EXAMPLE: ***1975***
In 1975, Gretsch reintroduced a White Falcon with some of the look of the original single-cutaway body style, marking the company's awareness that old-style hollowbody Gretsches were becoming fashionable.

Single-cutaway White Falcon on the 1975 catalogue cover.

GRETSCH WHITE FALCON 6136CST
THIS EXAMPLE: ***2011***
Gretsch's US Custom Shop was under way by 2004, and this high-end 50s-style Falcon re-creation was among the many instruments it has offered since.

GRETSCH BLACK FALCON 7593
THIS EXAMPLE: ***2001***
Gretsch called the Black Falcon "a scorcher just like its brother." It was a sort of reversed White Falcon, and a variation, the Silver Falcon, had a black body with chrome rather than gold-plated metalwork.

Hofner guitars were first made in Germany in the 20s, although the Karl Höfner company had been making instruments since its foundation in Schönbach in the 1880s. Hofner electrics appeared in the early 50s, a few years after the company moved south-west to its new HQ in Bubenreuth. These electrics were widely used by up-and-coming guitarists in Britain in the 50s, where import controls restricted the availability of American guitars.

Following the end of World War II, Britain controlled US imports to try to improve the nation's poor financial position, and from that time, new American guitars were rarely seen in UK music shops. Broader restrictions announced in 1951 applied mainly to food and manufactured goods, including records and several categories of instruments, such as guitars. The restrictions were eventually lifted during 1959, but in the meantime the Selmer company in London began to import Hofner guitars, most of which were made or modified to Selmer's specifications, and they proved popular.

Hofner's Club guitars were staples of the growing beat-group scene in Britain, played by guitar-mad youths such as John Lennon and David Gilmour. Other Hofners were seen in the hands of early UK guitar stars like Bert Weedon and Tommy Steele. The Clubs were basic hollowbody electrics with small single-cutaway bodies and no f-holes, available at first from 1955 as the single-pickup Club 40 and two-pickup Club 50.

Meanwhile in America, Gretsch added yet another finish variation to its semi-solid models, naming it the Jet Fire Bird and describing it as "for the progressive guitarist" and with a "brilliant Oriental red top." The new guitar completed Gretsch's Jet line, which now consisted of the black Duo Jet (listing at $290), the red Jet Fire Bird ($300), the Silver Jet ($310), and the "Western finish" Round Up ($350).

A new model designed specifically for electrical work. The body is built on "semi-acoustic" principles which give the tone a round character not found in solid instruments. The shape and fretting of the neck is designed to facilitate modern rapid chord and single string passages. Bridge adjustable for height and tuning compensation. Nickel silver frets, screw cog machines and reinforced plated tailpiece. One built-in Hofner Super-unit with tone and volume control. Complete with amplifier lead.

No. 389 Club 40 32 gns.

A similar model to the Club 40 but fitted with two Hofner Super-units—each with tone and volume controls, and on/off switches. The "feel" of the specially designed necks must be experienced; the section is cut down to minimum width and strings are set close to the rosewood fingerboard in which buzz-free frets are carefully bedded down over their entire length. The body is gracefully cut away to give easy control of the extreme top register. The two units offer a wide range of tonal effects. Complete with amplifier lead.

No. 390 Club 50 39 gns.

8

Hofner Club 40 and Club 50 in Selmer's 1957 catalogue.

ORIGINAL **HOFNER CLUB 40**
THIS EXAMPLE: ***1956***
Hofner's Club electrics, made in Germany and introduced in Britain by Selmer in 1955, were especially popular through the decade at a time when guitar imports to the UK from the United States were restricted.

GRETSCH JET FIREBIRD 6131
THIS EXAMPLE: ***1999***
This first reissue of the Jet Fire Bird (now "Firebird") was available from 1989 to 2003 and matched the control layout of the original model: a volume knob per pickup and a master tone knob (by the bridge), a master volume (on the cutaway), and a pickup selector switch.

The Gretsch Building in New York City, 1955.

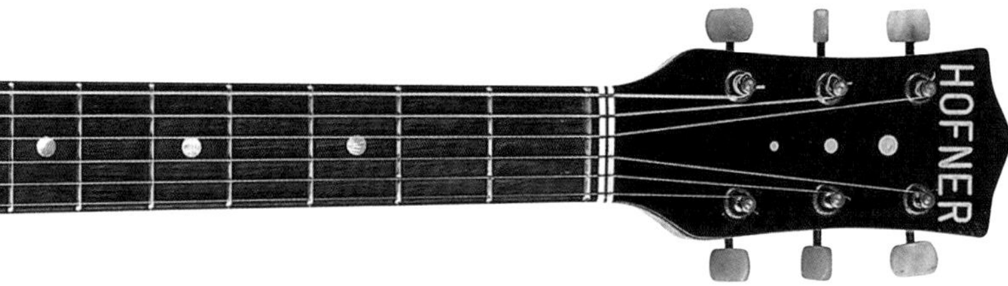

ORIGINAL **HOFNER CLUB 50**
THIS EXAMPLE: ***1956***
The Club 50 was the two-pickup version of the 40, and the guitars pictured here have Hofner's early-style round control panel, later changed to a rectangular shape.

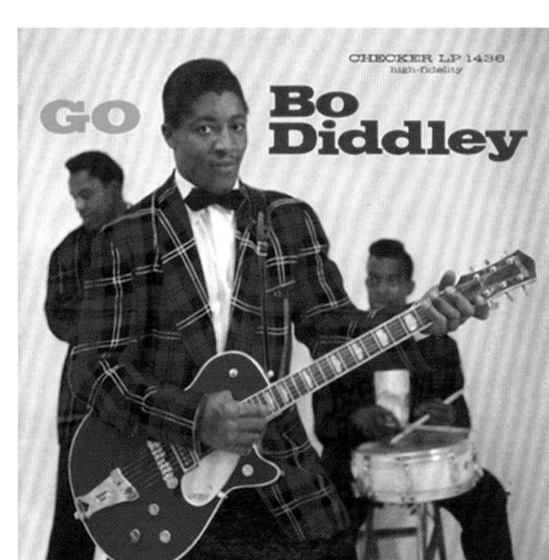

Bo Diddley goes with a Gretsch Jet Fire Bird, 1959.

ORIGINAL **GRETSCH JET FIRE BIRD 6131**
THIS EXAMPLE: ***1956***
The Jet Fire Bird, the latest addition to Gretsch's semi-solid Jet series, had a bright red front contrasted with a black back and sides. This one has single-coil DynaSonic pickups, which were changed to humbuckers around 1958, and early-style block markers.

The first commercial double-neck electric guitar incorporated the first electric twelve-string guitar. Introduced in 1955 as the Stratosphere Twin, it was designed by Russ and Claude Deaver in Springfield, Missouri. The lower neck was a regular six-string and the upper a twelve-string, tuned in a very unusual way and intended to provide the player with a harmony twin-guitar lead sound, without the need for a second guitarist. The Stratosphere Guitar Mfg Co's catalogue also featured single-neck six-string and single-neck twelve-string models, although the twelve probably didn't go into production.

The musician who made the Stratosphere Twin his own, even if briefly, was Jimmy Bryant. He's best known today for his instrumental duets he recorded in the 50s with pedal-steel virtuoso Speedy West and his early use of Fender electrics (as featured earlier in this book). Bryant used the Twin double-neck to play what Stratosphere described as "double-string lead as fast as you would ordinarily play single-string lead," using it on a few Bryant–West cuts, including the mind-boggling 'Stratosphere Boogie.' But the Stratosphere company was ahead of its time, and by 1959 it had ceased trading.

Supro in its earliest incarnation had been a brandname that the National-Dobro company used in the 30s for a number of early electric guitar models, mainly of the lap-steel variety. National-Dobro was sold in the early 40s, and the new owners changed the company's name to Valco, although they continued to use National, Dobro, and Supro as the principal brandnames on their guitars. The first modern Supro electrics made their debut in the early 50s, such as the Ozark, an early solidbody that was introduced in 1952. Further electrics included the Belmont, the solid wooden body of which was covered in pearloid plastic, and the Dual Tone, with an elegant monochrome finish.

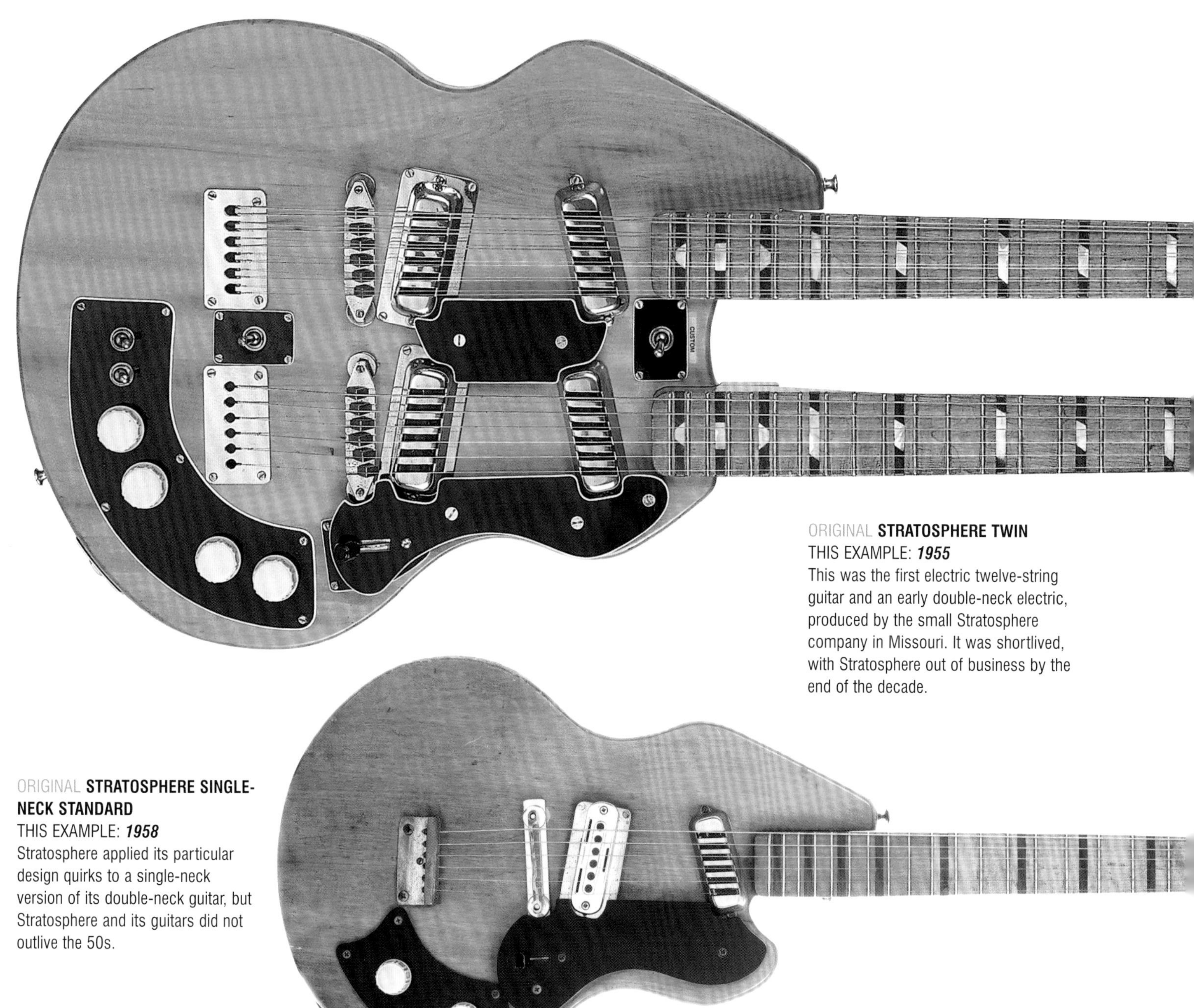

ORIGINAL **STRATOSPHERE TWIN**
THIS EXAMPLE: ***1955***
This was the first electric twelve-string guitar and an early double-neck electric, produced by the small Stratosphere company in Missouri. It was shortlived, with Stratosphere out of business by the end of the decade.

ORIGINAL **STRATOSPHERE SINGLE-NECK STANDARD**
THIS EXAMPLE: ***1958***
Stratosphere applied its particular design quirks to a single-neck version of its double-neck guitar, but Stratosphere and its guitars did not outlive the 50s.

Valco '54 ad highlighting its two electric brands, National and Supro.

ORIGINAL **SUPRO BELMONT**
THIS EXAMPLE: ***1955***
For this one, Supro pulled out the plastic, echoing Gretsch's use of body wraps to give a solidbody guitar a unique look. Never shy of a snappy name, Supro called the Belmont's "glowing red sherry maroon plastic" the No-Mar finish.

ORIGINAL **SUPRO DUAL TONE**
THIS EXAMPLE: ***1955***
Supro was a brand of the Valco company of Chicago, and the company proudly described the dual-pickup Dual Tone, new for 1955, as "brilliantly two-toned in glossy ebony black and sparkling arctic white."

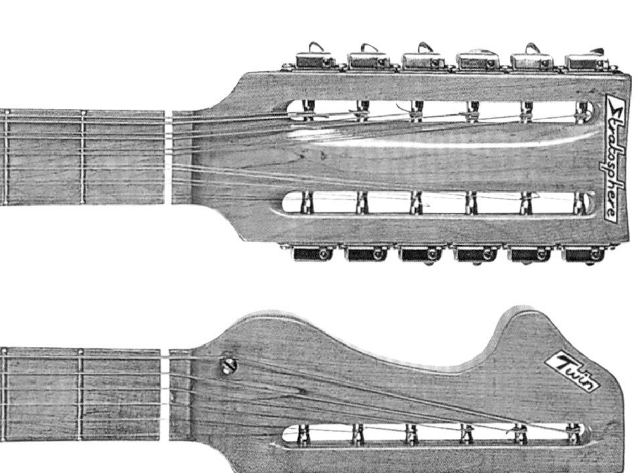

Jimmy Bryant with double-neck in Stratosphere's 1955 catalogue.

Played and recommended by **JIMMY BRYANT,** West Coast Radio, Television and Capital Recording Artist.
The "Stratosphere Boogie" and "Deep Water" are his latest hits.

The Supro brand expired with its owner, Valco, in 1968, following Valco's unwise purchase of the Kay guitar company and the bankruptcy that followed. The Supro name made a few appearances but largely disappeared for some time, briefly reappearing again in the early 80s. It was revived once more in 2013, when Absara Audio of New York bought the rights to the Supro name from the amplifier designer Bruce Zinky, who had made high-end custom amps for Fender.

Absara Audio has since concentrated on re-creating the renowned Supro amplifiers, but the company also has reissued some classic Supro electric guitars, including the Belmont, Coronado, Dual Tone, Martinique, and Sahara, as well as new retro-styled models such as the Hampton, Westbury, and Jamesport.

In 2018, Absara announced a special reissue of the original 50s Supro Dual Tone as played by a very famous musician. It developed the David Bowie Limited Edition model in collaboration with the David Bowie Archive. Bowie had bought and used a couple of Dual Tones while recording his 2003 album *Reality* and played them on the subsequent world tour. He can be seen holding aloft his favorite of the two Dual Tones on the cover of the 2010 live album, *A Reality Tour*.

Part of the appeal of the Dual Tone for Bowie was that it was one of the guitars played by his hero Link Wray. Wray is best known for the sinister instrumental hit 'Rumble' that he cut with his group The Ray Men in 1958, using distortion and tremolo to create an effectively disturbing atmosphere. The Eastwood company of Canada later produced a Dual Tone reissue in tribute to Wray. The instrument was adorned with a 50s-style illustration by the London-based artist Vince Ray, a specialist in pop surrealism and retro graphics.

EASTWOOD LINK WRAY TRIBUTE
THIS EXAMPLE: ***2014***
Eastwood's salute to the 50s electric-guitar pioneer Link Wray features an illustrated Dual Tone body by the artist Vince Ray, who called Wray's music the soundtrack of juvenile-delinquent rock'n'roll.

Mike Keneally digs in with a Supro Hampton, 2017.

SUPRO DUAL TONE BOWIE
THIS EXAMPLE: ***2018***
This special-edition reissue of Supro's 50s Dual Tone model was issued in 2018 to celebrate David Bowie's use of a couple of original Dual Tones for his 2003 *Reality* album and world tour.

SUPRO JAMESPORT
THIS EXAMPLE: ***2016***
Another updated Supro from the brand's new owner, Absara, draws on an original Ozark-shape body in the hope of attracting modern players to old-school style and tone.

Supro's revived 50s-style guitars in a 2018 ad.

SUPRO WESTBURY
THIS EXAMPLE: ***2016***
The revived Supro brand, owned by Absara Audio, called this a 21st-century update of the original 50s guitars, adding a tune-o-matic bridge to the original-style field-coil pickups.

SOUTHDALE
REGIONAL SHOPPING CENTER

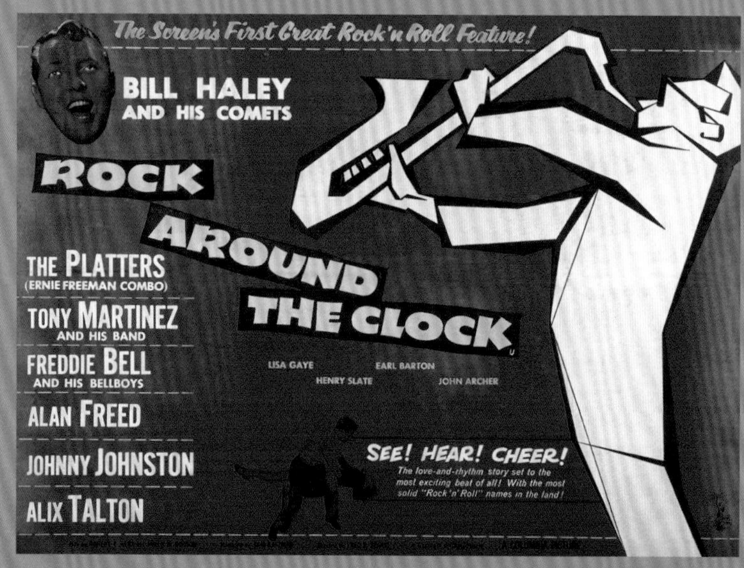
The Screen's First Great Rock 'n Roll Feature!
BILL HALEY
AND HIS COMETS
ROCK
AROUND
THE CLOCK
THE PLATTERS
(ERNIE FREEMAN COMBO)
TONY MARTINEZ
AND HIS BAND
FREDDIE BELL
AND HIS BELLBOYS
ALAN FREED
JOHNNY JOHNSTON
ALIX TALTON
LISA GAYE
EARL BARTON
HENRY SLATE
JOHN ARCHER
SEE! HEAR! CHEER!
The love-and-rhythm story set to the most exciting beat of all! With the most solid "Rock 'n' Roll" names in the land!

FRANK SINATRA · ELEANOR PARKER · KIM NOVAK
THE MAN WITH THE GOLDEN ARM
A film by
Otto Preminger

- **THE FIRST** underwater transatlantic telephone cable linking the US and the UK opens for service.
- **SOUTHDALE CENTER** "the world's biggest shopping town" opens in Minneapolis, with 72 stores on a ten-acre site. It becomes the model from which most other malls are cloned.
- **ROCK AROUND THE CLOCK** becomes a movie and defines the standard rock film plot about a manager who discovers an unknown group (Haley & His Comets) and hits it big. Meanwhile, Hollywood takes an early shot at drug addiction in Otto Preminger's *The Man With The Golden Arm*.

1956

- **THE HUNGARIAN** uprising is quelled by invading Soviet tanks as martial law is imposed.
- **BOXER** Rocky Marciano retires undefeated having won every one of his 49 professional fights, all but six by a knockout.
- **THE SUEZ CRISIS** develops when Israel, the UK, and France retaliate against Egypt for nationalizing the Suez Canal. Air attacks on Egypt ensue, and the USSR threatens a nuclear response. A ceasefire in November at last calms a tense, fearful world.

1956

Nathan Daniel began his career in the 30s making amplifiers, including some models for Epiphone's early Electar brand. He set up on his own as Danelectro in New Jersey in 1946, at first supplying amps to mail-order firms. In 1954, he began making guitars, with cloth or vinyl covered bodies and a few years later introduced the U series.

The bodies of the single-pickup U-1 and two-pickup U-2 models were constructed in an unconventional way, following Daniel's emphasis on cheap materials and simple production methods. He used a pine frame topped and backed with a shaped sheet of Masonite (a US brand of fiberboard) and edged with vinyl. The U guitars had clear plastic pickguards, distinctive headstocks, and the pickup cases were made from lipstick tubes. Novel "television-type" stacked controls on the U-2 offered a volume and tone per pickup, and a selector on the U-1 gave three tone changes (or regular pickup switching on the U-2).

The U guitars came in various colors, they were relatively cheaply priced, listing at $75 for the U-1 and $100 for the U-2, and for many beginners they provided a first taste of the possibilities of an electric six-string. Later, as we shall see, Danelectro would supply a number of instruments to the mail-order firm Sears, Roebuck. These, too, would encourage the initial fumblings of would-be guitar players across the United States.

In recent times, following Nathan Daniel's death in 1994, Evets acquired the rights to the Danelectro brand. Evets introduced Danelectro effects in 1997 and then a line of guitars the following year. The reissued Dan'os are mostly similar in look and construction to the old ones, including some classic U models with reproduction lipstick pickups. By 1999, Danelectro was also offering sparkle finishes and revised switching that added modern touches to the old-style appeal.

ORIGINAL **DANELECTRO U-1**
THIS EXAMPLE: ***1957***
Danelectro's U series, introduced around 1956, at first consisted of the single-pickup U-1 model (this one finished in "ivory leatherette") and the two-pickup U-2, both boldly styled and made with basic, inexpensive materials.

ORIGINAL **DANELECTRO U-2**
THIS EXAMPLE: ***1958***
The U-2 was one of the two early U-series Dan'o guitars, featuring a pine-frame body with fiberboard top and back (this one finished in "coral lacquer") and two pickups with lipstick-tube cases.

Danelectro 1956 catalogue shows U-1 and U-2 with "coke bottle" head.

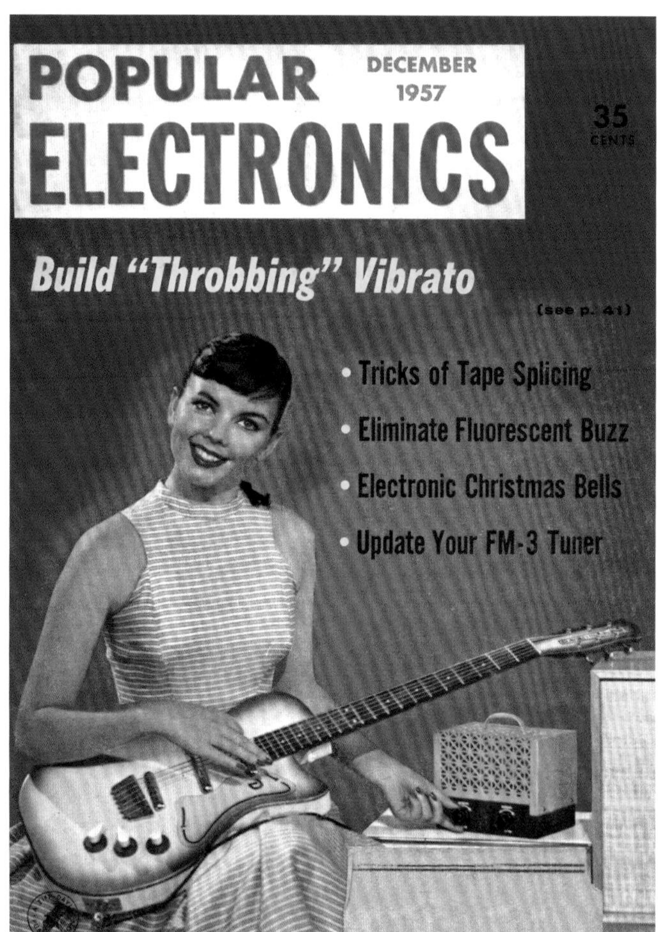

Magazine cover star, 1957, with the later three-pickup U-3.

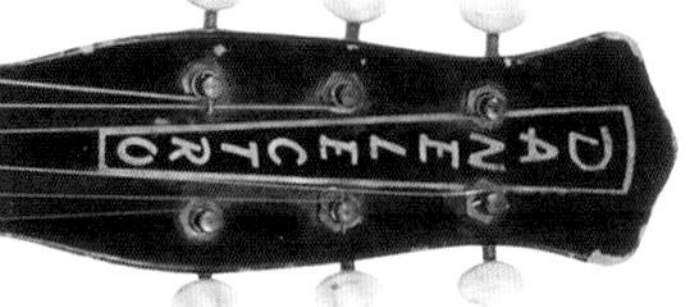

2005 Dan'o ad recalling the spirit of 1956.

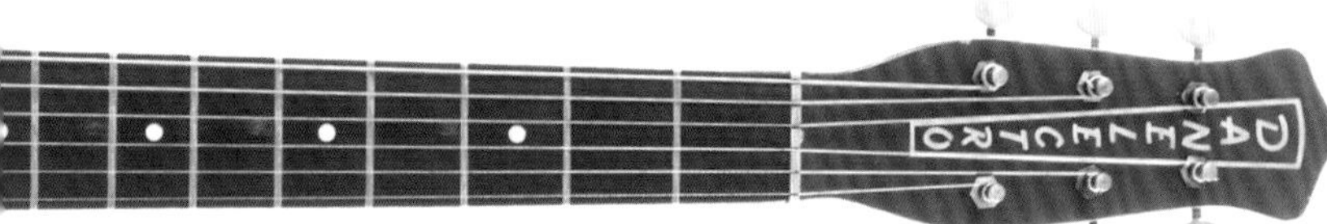

DANELECTRO BARITONE
THIS EXAMPLE: ***2017***
One of several reissues of the original U-style Danelectro guitars, this modern baritone variant provides a vintage-style low-tuned guitar.

1956

DUO-SONIC AND MUSICMASTER THREE-QUARTER SIZE GUITARS

The Duo-Sonic dual pickup and Musicmaster single pickup ¾ size guitars are the latest in design and styling of instruments of their kind. Each one is especially designed for the adult and young musician with small hands. The playing characteristics of these instruments are such that they represent the finest guitars of their type on the musical market today. The specially designed neck facilitates easier fretting and faster action. In addition, this one-piece neck not only is reinforced with an adjustable tension rod which maintains perfect neck alignment, but it is also easily adjustable. The neck is easily replaceable by the owner and this feature in itself will eliminate costly and time-consuming repairs. The high fidelity pickups on these instruments are fully adjustable and will provide any desired tone desponse. Both guitars have a full range tone control and, in addition, the Duo-Sonic Guitar is provided with a three-position pickup, selector switch which affords instant changes from lead tone to soft rhythm tone. String action can be varied to suit the individual player with the string height adjustments located under the chrome bridge cover. Also, string length can be adjusted to insure perfect intonation. The guitar body features the modern cutaway design for ease of playing all 21 frets. The modern head design aligns the tuning keys so that there is direct string pull permitting easier and more accurate tuning. The instruments are trimmed with gold-finished pickguards and chrome controls and bridge cover. The Duo-Sonic and Musicmaster ¾ size guitars are truly outstanding instruments in their price range and will provide top performance for all those musicians desiring the finest in ¾ size instruments.

Fender's 1956/57 catalogue page for Duo-Sonic and Musicmaster.

A student with a Musicmaster on Fender's '58 brochure cover.

ORIGINAL **GRETSCH WHITE PENGUIN 6134**
THIS EXAMPLE: ***1956***
Launched in 1956, the White Penguin was a semi-solid companion to the White Falcon. But it failed to take off, very few were made, and the Penguin is now a rare collectable.

ORIGINAL **FENDER DUO-SONIC**
THIS EXAMPLE: ***1959***
Like the Musicmaster, the Duo-Sonic had a metal "gold-finished" anodized pickguard. Unfortunately, the anodized skin often wore through to the aluminum below, and the idea did not last long.

ORIGINAL **FENDER MUSICMASTER**
THIS EXAMPLE: ***1957***
The single-pickup Musicmaster and two-pickup Duo-Sonic, introduced in 1956, were Fender's first budget "student" solidbody guitars, with shorter string-length and basic appointments.

Some instrument stores of the 50s found a clever way to increase sales of guitars and other instruments by running a school or "studio," usually on the same premises, after-hours, offering lessons to would-be players. The schools were perfectly placed to sell startup instruments to beginners, and equally attentive when the new musicians felt their skills demanded better (more expensive) instruments to show off this new-found talent.

Fender, like its competitors, was aware of these marketing tactics, and in 1956 the company introduced a pair of suitable budget electrics. The guitars had a shorter, more manageable string-length than Fender's regular models: the company described the one-pickup Musicmaster and two-pickup Duo-Sonic as "three-quarter size" and "ideal for students and adults with small hands." The two guitars certainly looked cheaper than Fender's Stratocaster, Telecaster, and Esquire, and indeed they sat at the bottom of the contemporary pricelist. By early 1957, a Strat with vibrato listed at $274.50, a Tele at $199.50, an Esquire $164.50, Duo-Sonic $149.50, Musicmaster $119.50.

Meanwhile, Gretsch was still concerned with the prestige end of its catalogue. Just as it had issued a companion model to the Chet Atkins 6120, in 1956 Gretsch added a partner to the high-end White Falcon in semi-solid style, the White Penguin. It had many of the Falcon's features, but it had a little penguin waddling across the pickguard. Very few people bought one. The model didn't appear in any of the company's catalogues, it made only fleeting appearances on a couple of pricelists, and it was briefly name-checked in just one brochure. From the small number that surface today, it's obvious that very few Penguins were made, and the model has since become regarded as one of the most collectable (and valuable) of all Gretsch guitars.

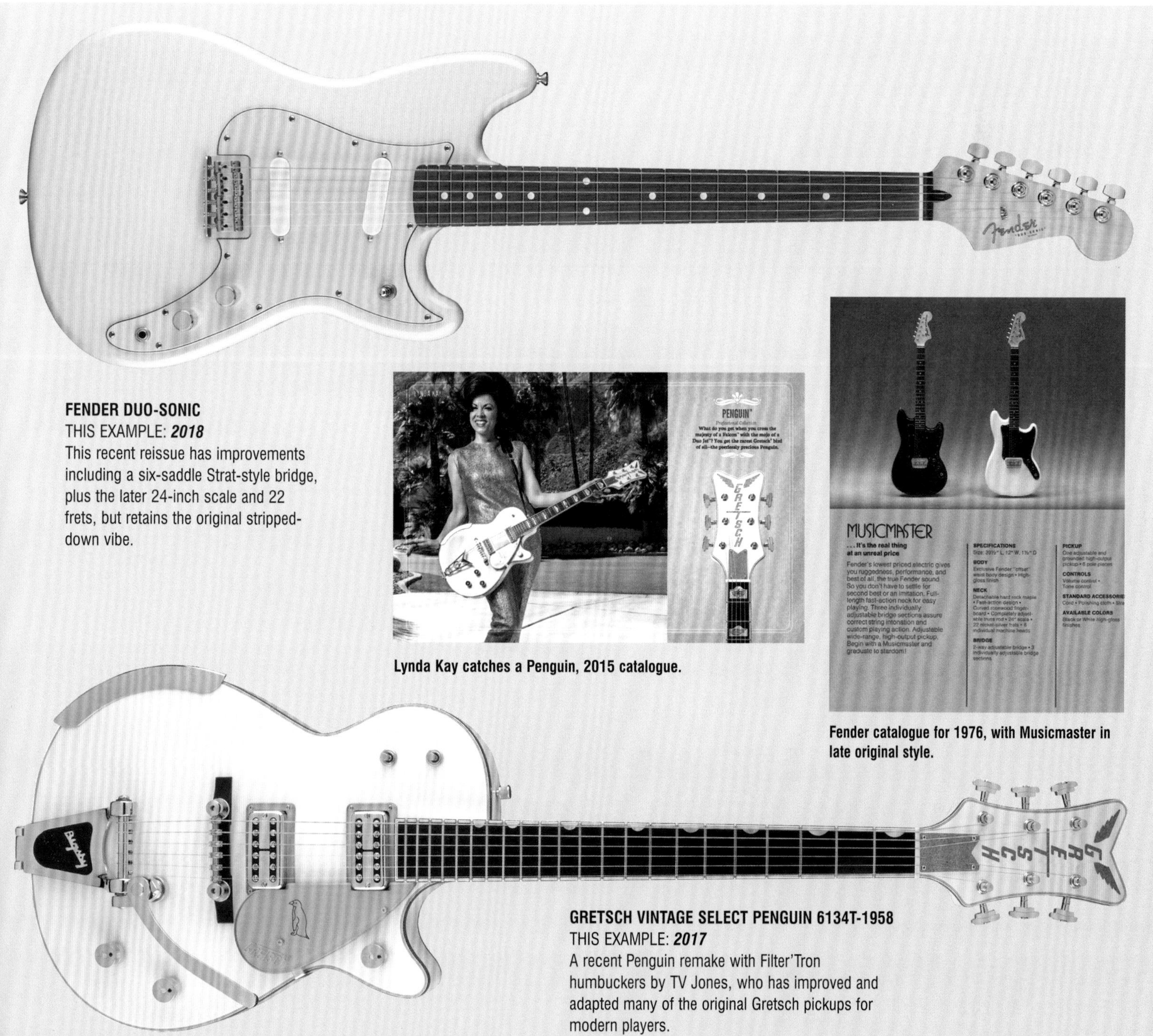

FENDER DUO-SONIC
THIS EXAMPLE: ***2018***
This recent reissue has improvements including a six-saddle Strat-style bridge, plus the later 24-inch scale and 22 frets, but retains the original stripped-down vibe.

Lynda Kay catches a Penguin, 2015 catalogue.

Fender catalogue for 1976, with Musicmaster in late original style.

GRETSCH VINTAGE SELECT PENGUIN 6134T-1958
THIS EXAMPLE: ***2017***
A recent Penguin remake with Filter'Tron humbuckers by TV Jones, who has improved and adapted many of the original Gretsch pickups for modern players.

ПОЧТА СССР
3·11·1957
ВТОРОЙ СОВЕТСКИЙ СПУТНИК ЗЕМЛИ
20к к20

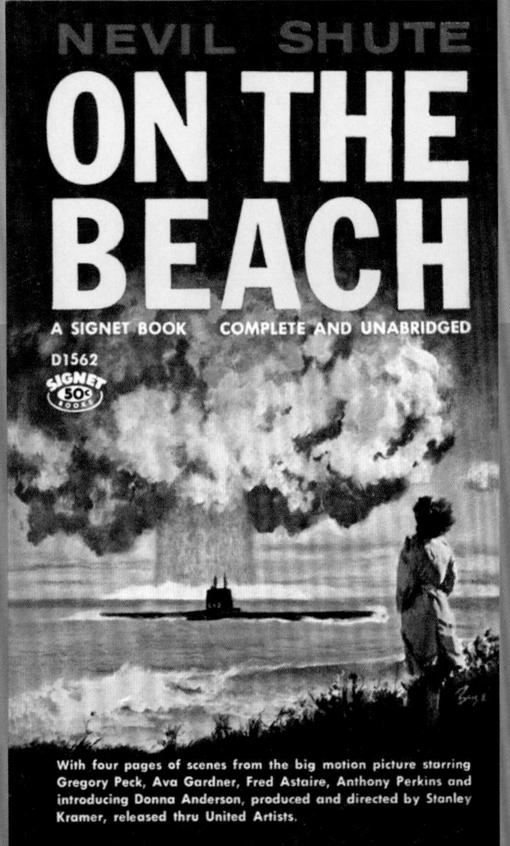
NEVIL SHUTE
ON THE BEACH
A SIGNET BOOK COMPLETE AND UNABRIDGED
D1562
SIGNET 50¢ BOOKS
With four pages of scenes from the big motion picture starring Gregory Peck, Ava Gardner, Fred Astaire, Anthony Perkins and introducing Donna Anderson, produced and directed by Stanley Kramer, released thru United Artists.

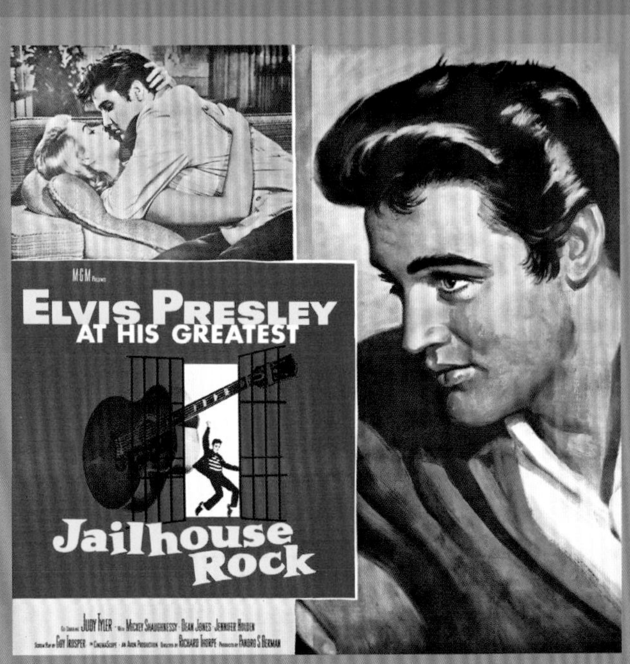
ELVIS PRESLEY
AT HIS GREATEST
Jailhouse Rock

- **THE SOVIET UNION** launches within a month Sputnik 1 and Sputnik 2, the first artificial satellites to orbit the earth. Sputnik 2 has a dog, Laika, on board, proving that life can survive (at least for a while) in space. A subsequent attempt to launch a satellite by the US in December fails. The space race begins.

- **IN THE UK**, the Wolfenden Report calls for homosexual acts between consenting adults to be decriminalized.

- **ELVIS PRESLEY** stars as Vince Everett in his third film, *Jailhouse Rock*, with a set of songs mostly composed by Jerry Leiber and Mike Stoller.

1957

- **NUCLEAR TESTS** in the Pacific are condemned by a mass protest in Tokyo, but the demos fail to stop Britain exploding its first H-bomb near Christmas Island. Nevil Shute's *On The Beach*, a horrific vision of worldwide nuclear devastation, is published.

- **RADIO** beams out guitar-soaked hits, not least 'Come Go With Me' (Del-Vikings), 'Peggy Sue' (Buddy Holly), and 'Bye Bye Love' (Everly Brothers).

- **TV DEBUTS** include *Wagon Train*, *Perry Mason*, and *Zorro* in the US, and *Emergency Ward 10*, *Pinky & Perky*, and *Six-Five Special* in the UK.

- **JACK KEROUAC** launches the Beat Generation with his novel *On The Road*, as Sal Paradise and Dean Moriarty roam America to a jazz soundtrack.

In 1957, the poll-winning jazz guitarist Barney Kessel endorsed a line of three models by the Kay company of Chicago that strikingly exemplified 50s design and style. Among the features of Kay's three Kessel signature models—the semi-solid Pro and hollowbody Artist and Jazz Special—was an impressive headstock of injection-molded plastic, nicknamed the Kelvinator by collectors because of its similarity to the refrigerator company's logo. The Kessel models enhanced Kay's image, but the guitarist's signature was later removed from the pickguard when he moved on to endorse a Gibson model.

Over at Gibson, Seth Lover developed a new humbucking pickup, which first appeared on the brand's guitars in 1957. It was intended to cut or "buck" the hum and electrical interference associated with regular single-coil pickups by using two coils with opposite magnetic polarity. Among the models that benefitted from the new humbuckers were the Les Paul Model (Goldtop) and the Les Paul Custom, and at the same time the Custom was promoted to a three-pickup guitar.

During 1953, Adolph Rickenbacker sold his musical-instrument business to Francis Cary Hall, including the Rickenbacker brandname. Hall's Radio & Television Equipment Co (Radio-Tel) in Santa Ana was an early distributor for Fender steels and amps, and in '53 Hall became a partner in the Fender Sales company, at the same time as he began to develop his new Rickenbacker operation. Roger Rossmeisl, a German guitar maker, joined Rickenbacker in 1954, and the firm launched its first Spanish electrics, the Combo 600 and 800. Hall's relationship with Fender ended in '55, when he shifted his attention full-time to Rickenbacker. In 1957, the Combo 650 and 850 were introduced, with a body shape among those Rickenbacker still uses today. But as we shall see, there were better things in store for the brand.

Kay's Barney Kessel Jazz Special in the 1959 catalogue.

ORIGINAL **KAY BARNEY KESSEL ARTIST**
THIS EXAMPLE: ***1957***
One of three impressive signature models named for the jazz and studio guitarist, with Kay's Gold K "Kleenex-box" pickups, plus a Melita bridge of the type used on some Gretsch models.

ORIGINAL **RICKENBACKER COMBO 850**
THIS EXAMPLE: ***1957***
An early Rickenbacker guitar still with the company's original "horseshoe" pickup at the bridge. This new body style would be used soon for the classic 325 model.

ORIGINAL **GIBSON LES PAUL MODEL**
THIS EXAMPLE: ***1958***
The earliest type of Gibson humbucking pickup, as on this Les Paul, is known as a PAF because of a small label hidden underneath with "Patent Applied For" on it.

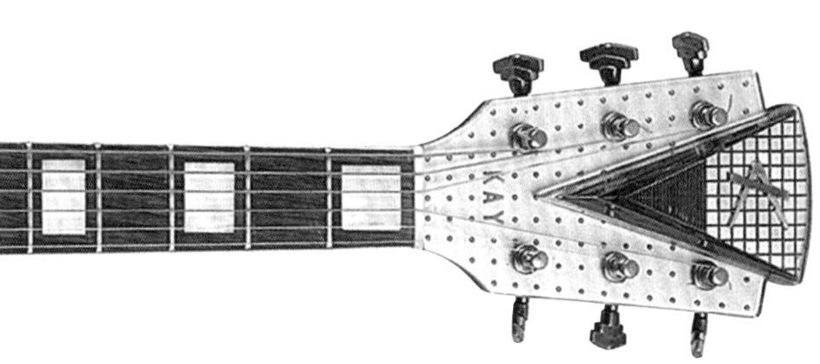

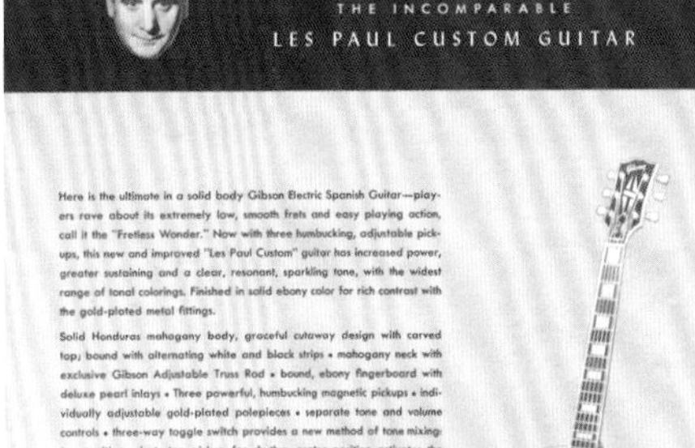

"The Fretless Wonder"
THE INCOMPARABLE
LES PAUL CUSTOM GUITAR

Here is the ultimate in a solid body Gibson Electric Spanish Guitar—players rave about its extremely low, smooth frets and easy playing action, call it the "Fretless Wonder." Now with three humbucking, adjustable pickups, this new and improved "Les Paul Custom" guitar has increased power, greater sustaining and a clear, resonant, sparkling tone, with the widest range of tonal colorings. Finished in solid ebony color for rich contrast with the gold-plated metal fittings.

Solid Honduras mahogany body, graceful cutaway design with carved top; bound with alternating white and black strips • mahogany neck with exclusive Gibson Adjustable Truss Rod • bound, ebony fingerboard with deluxe pearl inlays • Three powerful, humbucking magnetic pickups • individually adjustable gold-plated polepieces • separate tone and volume controls • three-way toggle switch provides a new method of tone mixing: top position selects top pickup for rhythm; center position activates the center and lower picks simultaneously for extreme highs and special effects; lower position operates lower pickup for playing lead. Tailpiece can be moved up or down to adjust string tension • Tune-O-Matic bridge permits adjusting string action and individual string lengths for perfect intonation • gold-plated Sealfast individual machine heads with deluxe buttons • gold-plated metal end pin and strap holder. Padded leather strap included.

SPECIFICATIONS
12¾" wide, 17½" long, 1¾" thick, 24¾" scale, 22 frets

Les Paul Custom—Ebony Finish $375.00
No. 537 Case—Faultless, gold plush lined 47.50
No. ZC-CLP Zipper Case Cover 21.50

Three-humbucker Les Paul Custom, 1958 catalogue.

ORIGINAL **GIBSON LES PAUL CUSTOM**
THIS EXAMPLE: ***1957***
Gibson's new humbucking pickups appeared in 1957, and the company took the opportunity to upgrade the Les Paul Custom to a three-pickup instrument.

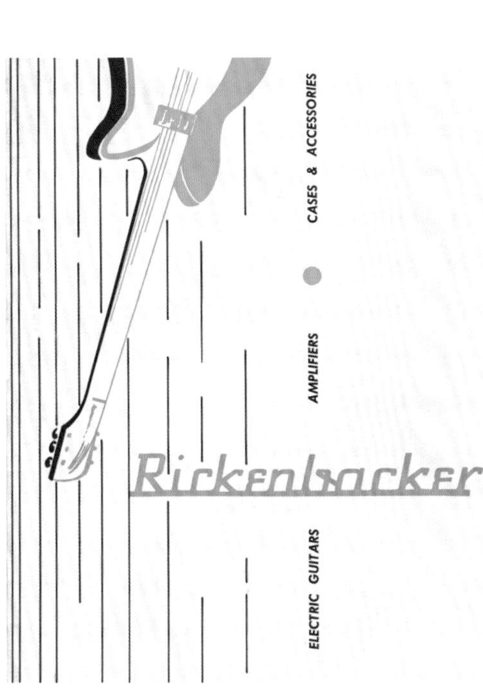

Rickenbacker's 1957 catalogue cover with earlier Combo body style.

Gibson first reissued the three-humbucker version of the Les Paul Custom in the early 90s, and the company's Custom Shop has given the model a few names through the years, including 1957 Les Paul Custom Black Beauty 3-Pickup (until the mid 2000s) and more simply 1957 Les Paul Custom 3-Pickup (from about 2006). "Black Beauty" is a nickname for the Custom derived from the black finish and the gold-plated metalwork that makes for a beautiful combination.

There haven't been many signature-model three-humbucker Customs. A significant exception was named for Peter Frampton, introduced by the Custom Shop in 2000 and based on Frampton's remodeled '54 Custom. Frampton's guitar was later stolen and considered lost forever, but it turned up and was returned to its owner in 2012. A painstaking Custom Shop re-creation of the restored guitar was issued in 2015.

The humbucker-equipped version of the Les Paul Model, or Goldtop as it's better known, was shortlived in its original incarnation, lasting about a year from mid 1957 before the finish was changed to sunburst in '58. Reissues have appeared since the early 80s, including models with aged finishes and with the Custom Shop's VOS finish, which means Vintage Original Spec—a process that Gibson said results in a lightly-aged look similar to that of "a well-cared-for 40-year-old guitar."

Vintage vibe and design has filtered down to many contemporary makers, such as the Rivolta brand, established by Dennis Fano as a more affordable companion to his Novo brand. The first Rivolta was the Combinata, a Rickenbacker-flavored mixture of Combo and 4001 bass ingredients. Eastwood's Airline brand drew on the Kay Barney Kessel Pro for the Tuxedo CB, though unlike the semi-solid original this remake was fully hollow.

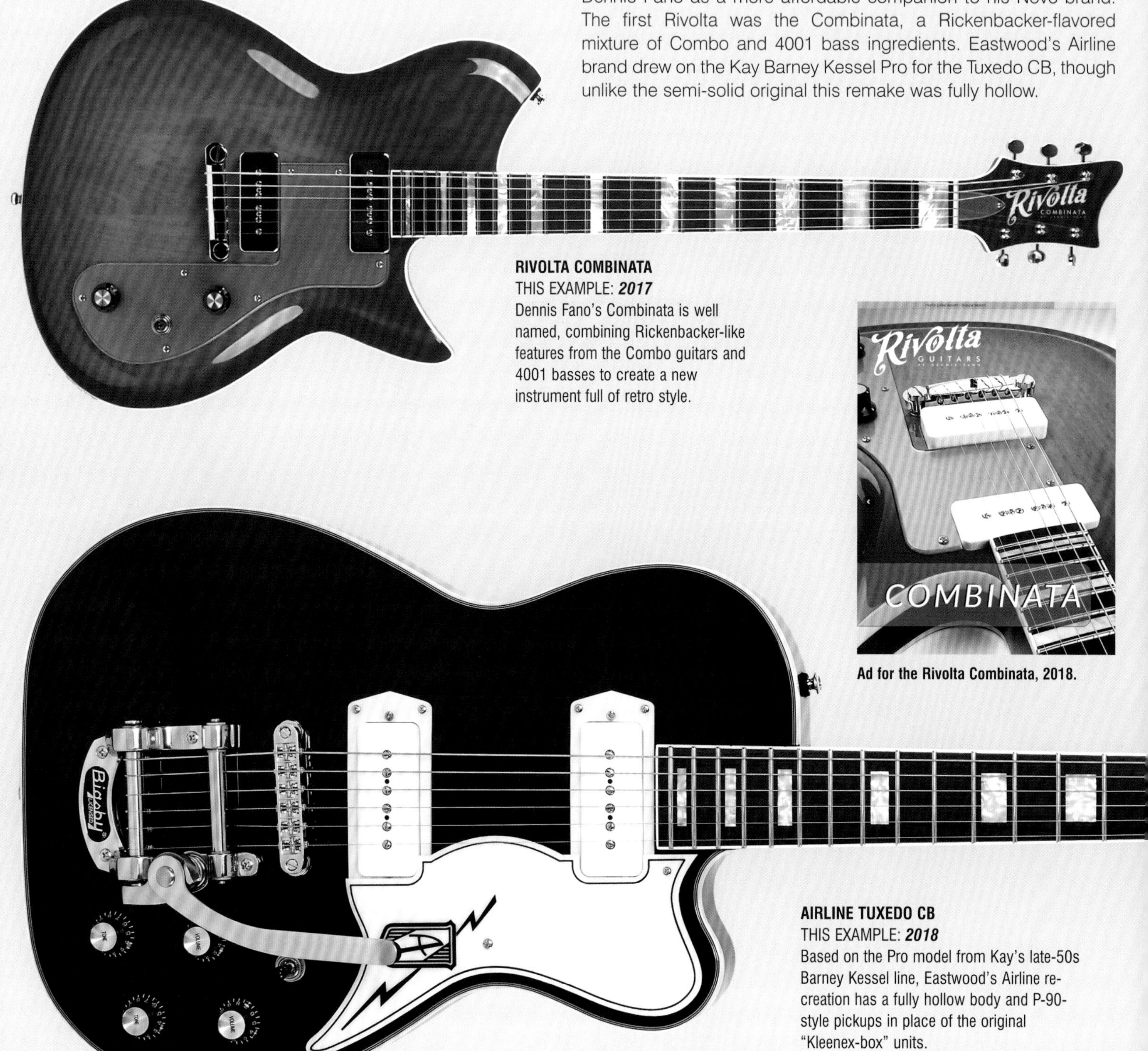

RIVOLTA COMBINATA
THIS EXAMPLE: ***2017***
Dennis Fano's Combinata is well named, combining Rickenbacker-like features from the Combo guitars and 4001 basses to create a new instrument full of retro style.

Ad for the Rivolta Combinata, 2018.

AIRLINE TUXEDO CB
THIS EXAMPLE: ***2018***
Based on the Pro model from Kay's late-50s Barney Kessel line, Eastwood's Airline re-creation has a fully hollow body and P-90-style pickups in place of the original "Kleenex-box" units.

An early reissue of the humbucker Goldtop, 1983.

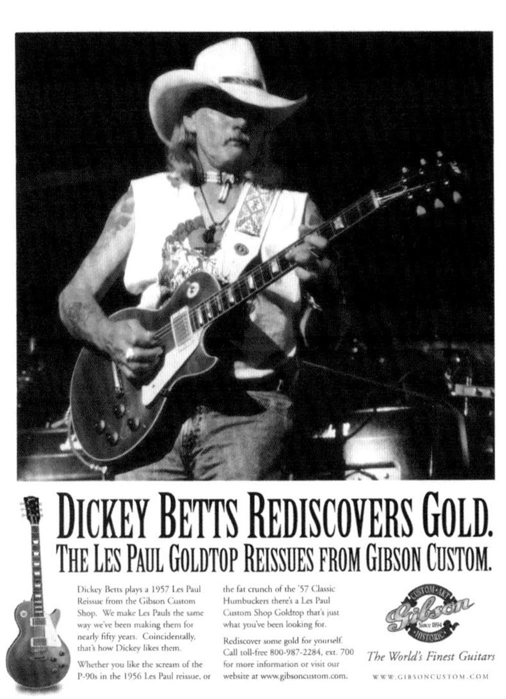

The Dickey Betts signature Goldtop, 2001.

GIBSON LES PAUL CUSTOM PETER FRAMPTON
THIS EXAMPLE: ***2000***
This signature model for Peter Frampton is based on the three-humbucker version of the Les Paul Custom that was made for a few years in the late 50s and early 60s.

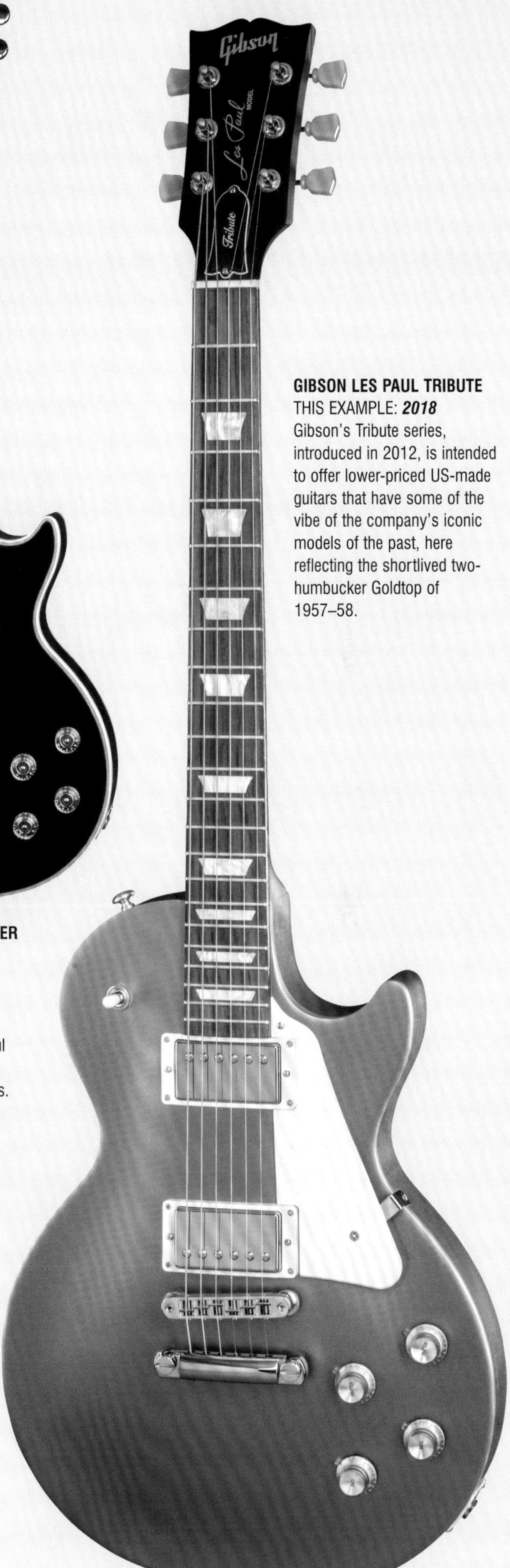

GIBSON LES PAUL TRIBUTE
THIS EXAMPLE: ***2018***
Gibson's Tribute series, introduced in 2012, is intended to offer lower-priced US-made guitars that have some of the vibe of the company's iconic models of the past, here reflecting the shortlived two-humbucker Goldtop of 1957–58.

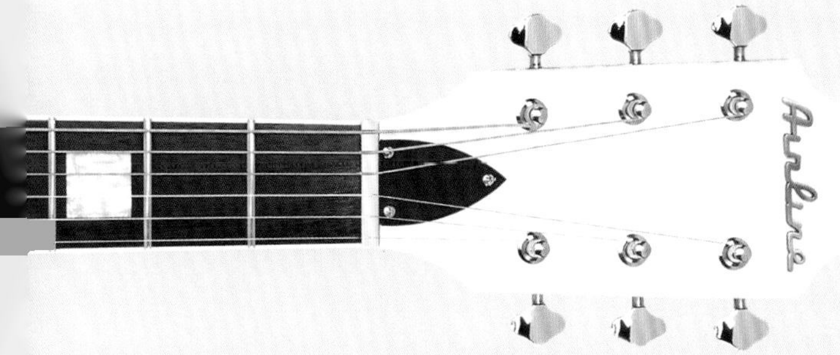

1957

Emile Grimshaw was a British banjo player who set up as a banjo and guitar maker in London in 1930 with his son Emile Jr., who took over the business when his father died in 1943. Grimshaw added electric guitars by the 50s, and as British-made electrics these were quite a rarity at the time, especially as import restrictions meant that new American guitars were virtually non-existent.

One model in particular, the SS De Luxe, proved popular with budding British rock'n'rollers such as Joe Brown, Bruce Welch, and Joe Moretti. It had a thinline semi-solid body, two pickups, cat's-eye soundholes, a short scale-length, and a curved control panel. Grimshaw continued into the 80s, and Emile Jr. died in 1987. But it was in the right place at the right time as British guitarists looked for a decent electric guitar in the early days of rock'n'roll.

The other brand widely available in the UK at the time was Hofner, made in Germany and imported to Britain by Selmer, which had Hofner make or modify models to its specifications. As well as the smaller sealed-top Club models, which we saw earlier, Selmer's bigger Hofner single-cutaway hollowbody electrics, introduced around 1957, were also popular.

The Committee was aptly named, apparently designed in collaboration with a group of six professional British guitarists: Frank Deniz, Ike Isaacs, Jack Llewellyn, Freddie Phillips, Roy Plummer, and Bert Weedon. It sat at the top of a trio of hollowbody electrics, with two pickups, fancy fingerboard markers, an ornate headstock, and an inlaid body back. The other two models, each with distinctive triple-dot fingerboard markers, were the two-pickup President and the single-pickup Senator. The Hofner company is still in business today and offers some modern instruments that use the classic model names.

ORIGINAL **HOFNER COMMITTEE**
THIS EXAMPLE: ***1959***
The other leading brand of electric guitar in Britain at the time was the German-made Hofner, and the Committee was the best regular model, with fancy inlays and two single-coil pickups.

6

ACOUSTIC/ELECTRIC MODELS

COMMITTEE ELECTRIC
Same specification as the famous Committee Model with the addition of two Hofner high sensitivity pick-ups, two tone controls, two volume controls, and on/off switches.
No. 395 Committee, blonde 75 gns. No. 396 Committee, brunette 75 gns.

PRESIDENT ELECTRIC
Same specification as the President model with the addition of two Hofner high sensitivity pick-ups, two tone controls, two volume controls and on/off switches.
No. 385 President, blonde 50 gns. No. 386 President, brunette 50 gns.

SENATOR ELECTRIC
Same specification as Senator model with the addition of one Hofner high sensitivity pick-up, tone and volume controls.
No. 387 Senator, blonde 30 gns.
No. 388 Senator, brunette 30 gns.

LEFT: **Hofner President, Committee, and Senator, 1957 catalogue.**

CENTER: **Selmer catalogue cover 1959–60 featuring Hofner.**

President
ELECTRIC

DOUBLE PLATE CONSOLE

PRESIDENT ELECTRIC
Same specification as the President Acoustic Model, with the addition of two Hofner high sensitivity pick-ups, and a "New Line" DOUBLE PLATE CONSOLE
No. 385 President, blonde .. .. .. 44 gns.
No. 386 President, brunette .. .. .. 44 gns.
No. 385T President, blonde thin model 44 gns.
No. 386T President, brunette thin model 44 gns.

Senator
ELECTRIC

SENATOR ELECTRIC
Same specification as the Senator Acoustic model, and fitted with a "New Line" SINGLE PLATE CONSOLE.
No. 387 Senator, blonde .. 27 gns.
No. 388 Senator, brunette .. 27 gns.
No. 387T Senator, blonde, thin 27 gns.
No. 388T Senator, brunette, thin 27 gns.

SINGLE PLATE CONSOLE

RIGHT: **President and Senator, 1959–60 catalogue.**

Committee with "New Line" control panel, 1959–60.

Grimshaw's retrofit vibrato on an SS Supreme, 1960.

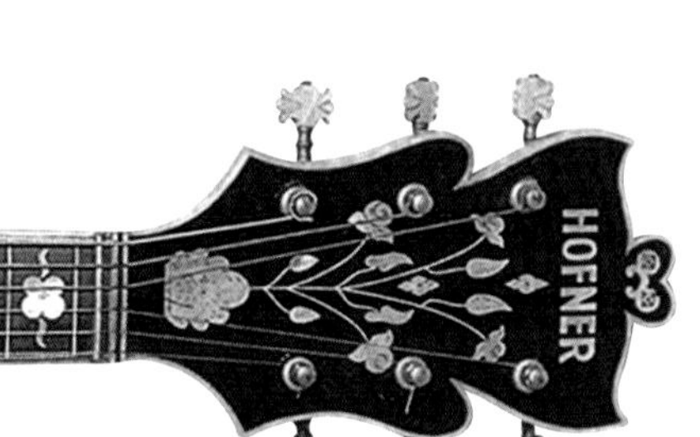

ORIGINAL **GRIMSHAW SS DE LUXE**
THIS EXAMPLE: ***1960***
Grimshaw made guitars in London, and with competition limited in 50s Britain, its electric guitars—notably the SS De Luxe—proved popular among many early rock'n'rollers in the UK.

Hofner's contemporary interpretation of the President, 2006.

HOFNER 457/12
THIS EXAMPLE: ***2017***
Hofner's 457 was the original German model from which Selmer's Hofner President was developed. This modern take on the 457 is a twelve-string version.

Harmony of Chicago had made cheap, basic electric Stratotone models since 1953, but by 1957 was in the process of moving on from the latest of those models, the H42, to make way for a new, wider range of Stratotones in '58, of which more later. For now, the H42, introduced in '55, had one stacked knob for volume and tone, a switch for bass or treble emphasis, and the colorful body had what Harmony called "chrome-like Harmometal wide edge bindings."

Danelectro, alongside Harmony and Kay, was meanwhile supplying guitars to the Sears, Roebuck mail-order company with Sears' own Silvertone brand. The New Jersey-based Danelectro had been making amplifiers for Sears for many years, and around 1954 it added electric guitars to the Silvertone-brand products, at first with a basic solidbody model, and then later some versions of the Dan'o U models. By '57, Sears was offering four Danelectro-sourced models in its catalogue: the 1317 (later 1302) single-pickup with black finish; the 1319 (1303) two-pickup black; the 1321 (1300) single-pickup with bronze finish; and the 1323 (1301) two-pickup bronze. Thousands of young would-be American guitarists, from Jerry Garcia to many more you've never heard of, started out with these cheap and effective Silvertones thanks to Nat Daniel and his team at Danelectro.

Magnatone started in the late 40s in Inglewood, California, and was best known for amplifiers: Buddy Holly and Lonnie Mack were early fans of the amps. There were guitars, too, including a stunning-looking steel, the shortlived Jeweltone of 1949, made of layered plastic. Solidbody Spanish models followed with design input by Paul Bigsby—the basic Mark III and Mark III Deluxe appeared around 1955, followed by the semi-solid set-neck Mark IV and (with vibrato) Mark V. Magnatone lasted in various forms to the early 70s, and the amplifiers have been recently revived.

ORIGINAL **HARMONY STRATOTONE NEWPORT H42/1**
THIS EXAMPLE: ***1957***
Introduced in 1955, the popular, cheap H42 was dropped in 1957 by the big Harmony company of Chicago to make way for an updated and improved line of Stratotone models.

ORIGINAL **SILVERTONE 1323**
THIS EXAMPLE: ***1957***
Silvertone was the guitar brand of the mighty Sears, Roebuck mail-order company, and 50s suppliers included Harmony and Kay, as well as Danelectro, which made this bronze-finish 1323, similar to a Dan'o U-2.

ORIGINAL **MAGNATONE MARK III DELUXE**
THIS EXAMPLE: ***1957***
A typical budget model of the period, the Mark III had a Formica pickguard covering the whole of the front, with Bakelite knobs and a bold M for Magnatone logo in the tailpiece.

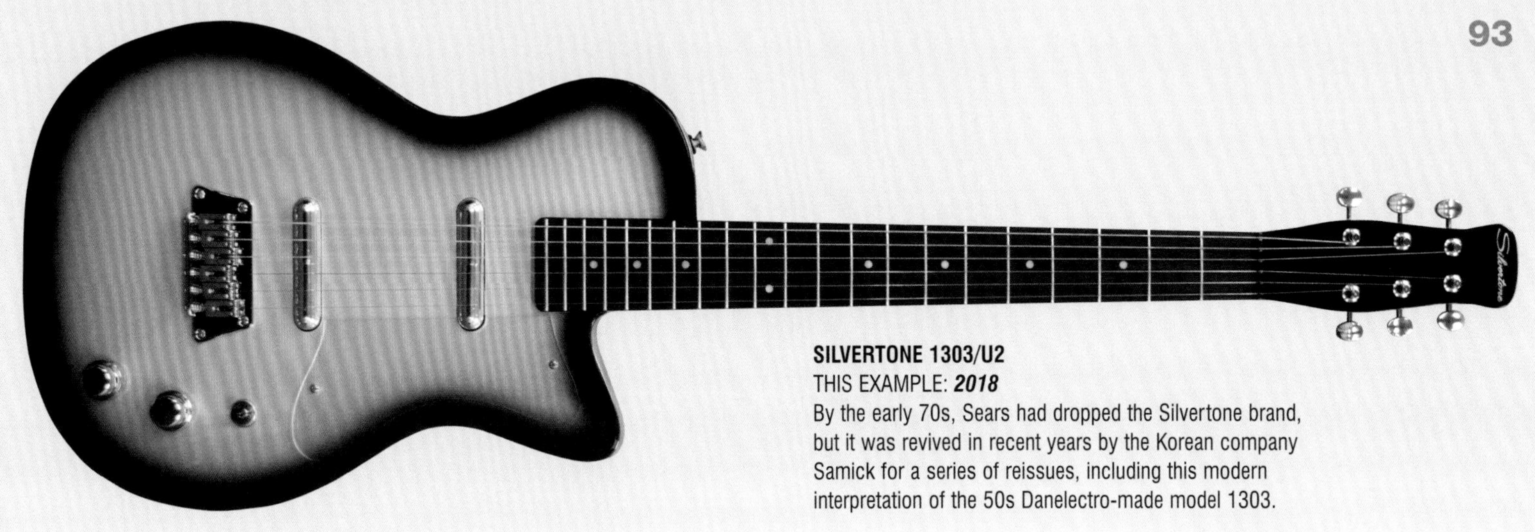

SILVERTONE 1303/U2
THIS EXAMPLE: ***2018***
By the early 70s, Sears had dropped the Silvertone brand, but it was revived in recent years by the Korean company Samick for a series of reissues, including this modern interpretation of the 50s Danelectro-made model 1303.

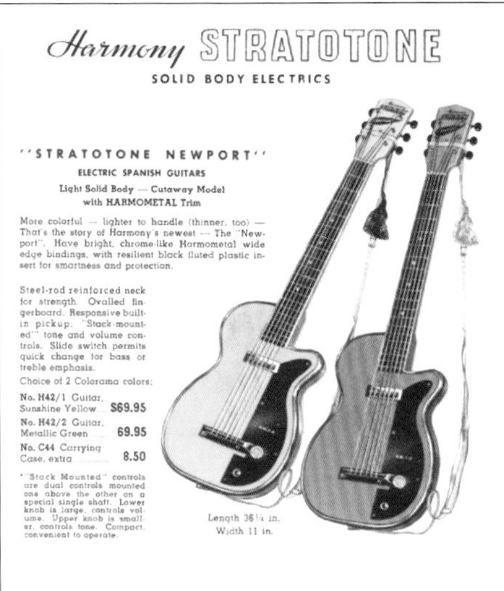

Harmony STRATOTONE
SOLID BODY ELECTRICS
''STRATOTONE NEWPORT''
ELECTRIC SPANISH GUITARS
Light Solid Body — Cutaway Model
with HARMOMETAL Trim
More colorful — lighter to handle (thinner, too) — That's the story of Harmony's newest — The "Newport". Have bright, chrome-like Harmometal wide edge bindings, with resilient black fluted plastic insert for smartness and protection.
Steel-rod reinforced neck for strength. Ovalled fingerboard. Responsive built-in pickup. "Stack-mounted"* tone and volume controls. Slide switch permits quick change for bass or treble emphasis.
Choice of 2 Colorama colors:
No. H42/1 Guitar, Sunshine Yellow ... $69.95
No. H42/2 Guitar, Metallic Green ... 69.95
No. C44 Carrying Case, extra ... 8.50
*"Stack Mounted" controls are dual controls mounted one above the other on a special single shaft. Lower knob is large, controls volume. Upper knob is smaller, controls tone. Compact, convenient to operate.
Length 36¼ in.
Width 11 in.

Yellow (/1) and green (/2) options for Harmony's H42, 1957.

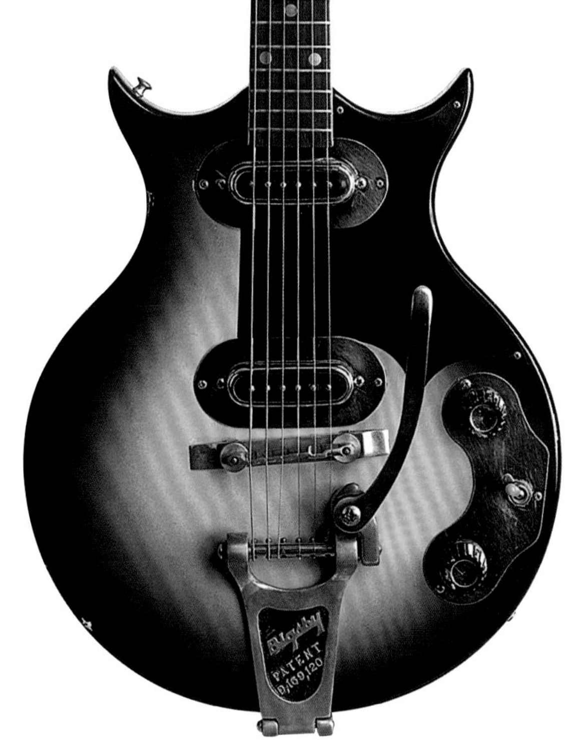

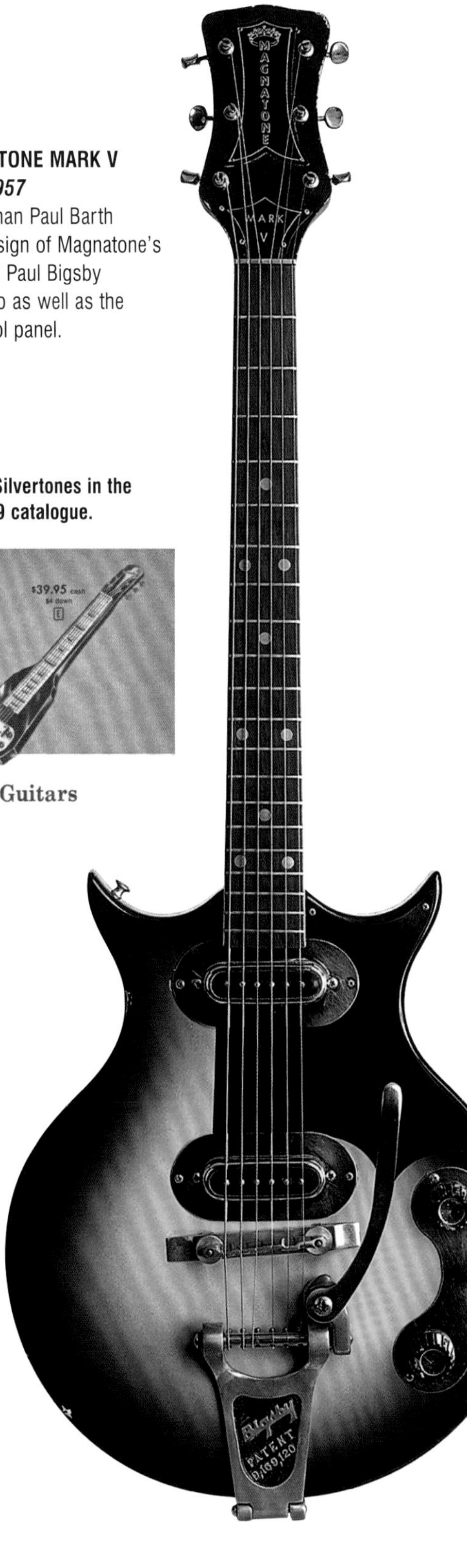

ORIGINAL **MAGNATONE MARK V**
THIS EXAMPLE: ***1957***
Ex-Rickenbacker man Paul Barth helped with the design of Magnatone's Mark IV and V, and Paul Bigsby supplied the vibrato as well as the pickups and control panel.

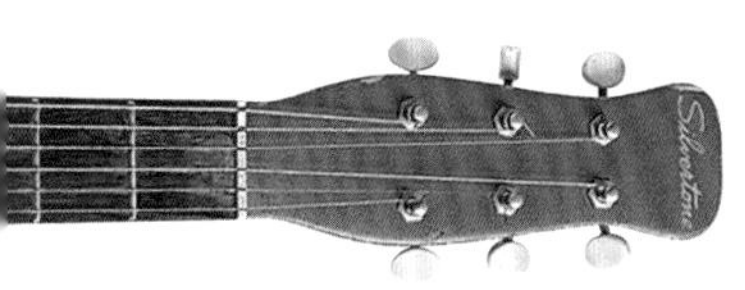

Danelectro-made Silvertones in the Sears, Roebuck '59 catalogue.

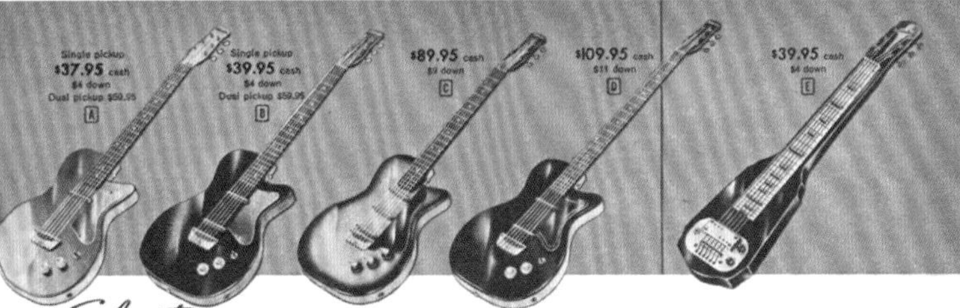

Single pickup
$37.95 cash
$4 down
A
Single pickup
$39.95 cash
$4 down
B
$89.95 cash
C
$109.95 cash
$11 down
D
$39.95 cash
$4 down
E
Silvertone Solid-body and Hawaiian Electric Guitars

MAGNATONE
ELECTRIC SPANISH GUITARS
MARK IV AND MARK V GUITARS
MAGNATONE takes great pride in presenting two exciting new models shown below. For the pattern and design of these models, Magnatone is indebted to America's Leading Guitar Authority, Paul Bigsby. The standards of these guitars will meet the most exacting requirements of the finest professional performer and their modest price will permit even the guitar "enthusiast" to enjoy ownership.
SPECIFICATIONS
HEAD
Artistically balanced. Individual chromed machine heads. Rich 24 karat gold medallion.
NECK
Consists of one solid piece of selected Honduras Mahogany from the top of the head to the end pin. In this rugged one-piece construction, the guitar is built around the neck—instead of neck being bolted on as on other guitars. New type cantilever action adjustment rods—which literally "float" the neck in perfect counter-balance to the string tension. Special guitar nut for greater response. Professional fret board with seven inlaid position markers. Precision-set frets. Fast action neck has "slim-line" contour
BODY
Size—14¼" wide, 2½" thick, 19" body length and 41" overall Hollowed-out body gives it the perfect balance, light weight and "feel" of a full sized auditorium guitar. Choice Mahogany and Basswood. Deep lustrous hand-rubbed finish. Double cut-a-way makes top positions easier
OTHER FEATURES
Dual pick-ups using power-packed Alnico VI magnets, the very latest in magnets. These together with Magnatone's own special windings enable the player to enjoy a tonal range and response of the highest calibre.
Each pick-up unit can be raised or lowered in its entirety—plus an individual adjustment for each string. Functional heavily chromed pick-up covers. Magnatone's exclusive Perfecto-Tuned Offset bridge made out of solid Beryllium copper for perfect intonation and harmonics—4-way adjustable scratch resistant handsomely fashioned pick guard. Simplified volume and tone control system. At the touch of a finger the single volume or tone control will instantly effect either or both of the pick-ups, thus permitting the performer the most intricate or extreme tonal or volume changes with a minimum of effort and confusion.
Equipped with Bobby Lee Straps.
MARK IV
Finished in a rich natural Mahogany.
Heavy duty chromed tail piece.
GENE DAVIS
MARK V
Sides and back finished in a deep rich Mahogany with Sunburst top.
Fitted with the World Famous Bigsby Vibrato Unit.
Bob Gibbons

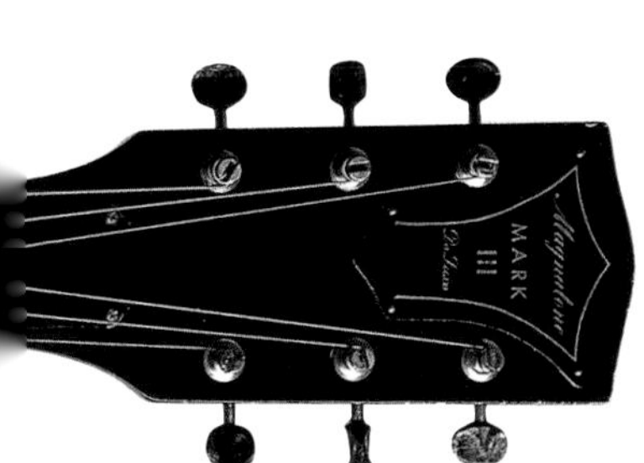

Magnatone 1958 catalogue with Mark IV and Mark V.

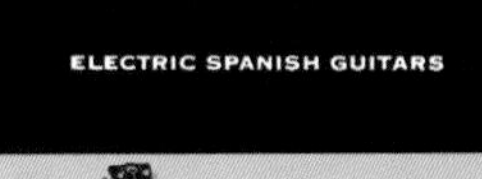

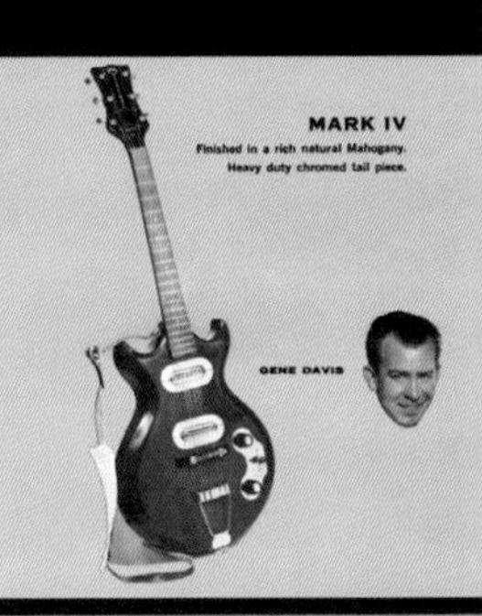

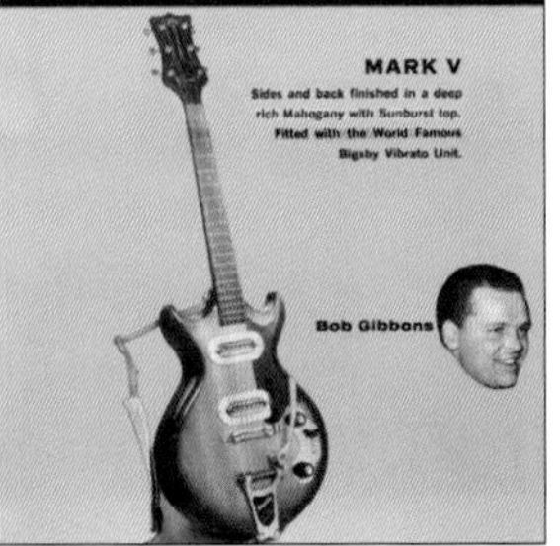

'58 MOTOROLA
Americana
PORTABLE TV
RIGHT-UP-FRONT TUNING
PUSHBUTTON ON-OFF
EXCLUSIVE MAGIC MAST ANTENNA

HAVE 'Twangy' GUITAR
STEREO
Will Travel
STEREO
Jamie

- **A GREAT** year for guitar-fueled records, including 'Summertime Blues' by Eddie Cochran and 'The Rumble' by Link Wray ... and meanwhile Chuck Berry's 'Johnny B. Goode' plays his guitar like ringing a bell.
- **AMERICA** launches a moon rocket that misses; blues popularizer W.C. Handy dies; the artist to be known as Prince is born.
- **INGVAR KAMPRAD** opens the first IKEA furniture store in Älmhult, Sweden.

1958

- **THE CAMPAIGN** for Nuclear Disarmament (CND) is launched in the UK, with its first protest march from London to the Atomic Weapons Research Establishment at Aldermaston. Over 9,000 scientists from 44 countries petition the UN to end nuclear weapons tests.
- **STEREO** comes to commercial records as the first stereo LPs are released, including Duane Eddy's debut, *Have Twangy Guitar Will Travel*.
- **TV OWNERSHIP** in the US is rocketing, with sets in over 75 percent of homes. And TV maker Philco encourages viewers to move the TV around the house with its new portable model the Slender Seventeen.

1958

There was an unwritten law that the design for the body of a guitar should follow a traditional shape. Until the Flying V and the Explorer, Gibson's new pair of so-called Modernistic guitars of 1958, guitars in general had familiar rounded outlines to the body, with an upper and lower bout straddling a waisted mid-section. This symmetrical figure-of-eight design led to the suggestion that a guitar was like a woman's body. The shape had endured for a long time, since the instrument's roots in earlier centuries, and every guitar more or less copied the template. After the two new Gibsons appeared, however, anything seemed possible.

The decision to ignore conventional guitar shapes and curves was a bold one. To some extent it reflected contemporary car design, especially the rise of the tail fin. Harley Earl at General Motors had borrowed a design detail from a Lockheed aircraft for a Cadillac or two, and the tail fin became a feature of many stylish American cars of the 50s, especially as developed by Chrysler's Virgil Exner and his "forward look."

The new guitars were not a success—for now, at least. Gibson's records indicate that it shipped 81 Flying Vs and 19 Explorers in 1958. For 1959, the final entries are lower still: 17 Vs and just three Explorers. This collapse of interest in the Modernistic guitars was a big disappointment.

For the short time the V and Explorer were in production, Gibson had made every effort to sell the new instruments. "Try one of these 'new look' instruments," the original publicity had insisted. "Either is a sure-fire hit with guitarists of today!" That was not the case, however. It would be the guitar players and the guitar designers of tomorrow who made them a hit.

ORIGINAL **GIBSON PROTOTYPE**
THIS EXAMPLE: ***1957***
Gibson sent this pre-production Flying V to its case supplier, Geib of Chicago, in order to design a case for the unusual new instrument. Non-standard features include the black pickguard and gold-color headstock logo.

Explorer and V promo in the Gibson Gazette, 1958.

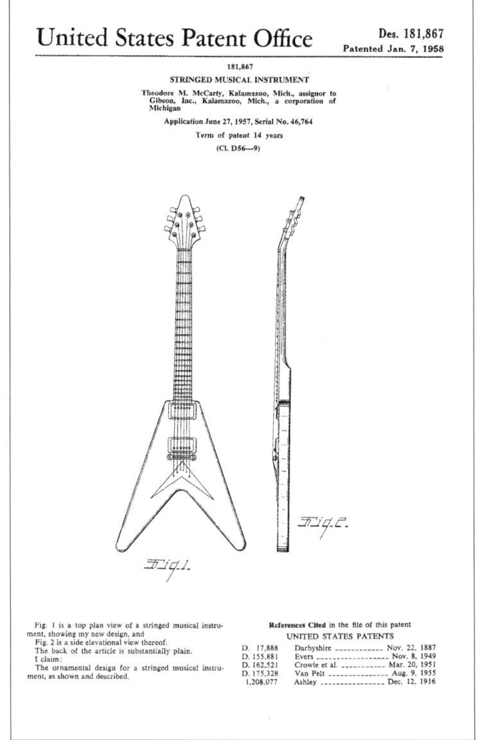

United States Patent Office — Des. 181,867 — Patented Jan. 7, 1958

181,867

STRINGED MUSICAL INSTRUMENT

Theodore M. McCarty, Kalamazoo, Mich., assignor to Gibson, Inc., Kalamazoo, Mich., a corporation of Michigan

Application June 27, 1957, Serial No. 46,764

Term of patent 14 years

(Cl. D56—9)

Fig. 1 is a top plan view of a stringed musical instrument, showing my new design, and

Fig. 2 is a side elevational view thereof.

The back of the article is substantially plain.

I claim:

The ornamental design for a stringed musical instrument, as shown and described.

References Cited in the file of this patent

UNITED STATES PATENTS

D. 17,888	Darbyshire	Nov. 22, 1887
D. 155,881	Evers	Nov. 8, 1949
D. 162,521	Crowle et al.	Mar. 20, 1951
D. 175,328	Van Pelt	Aug. 9, 1955
1,208,077	Ashley	Dec. 12, 1916

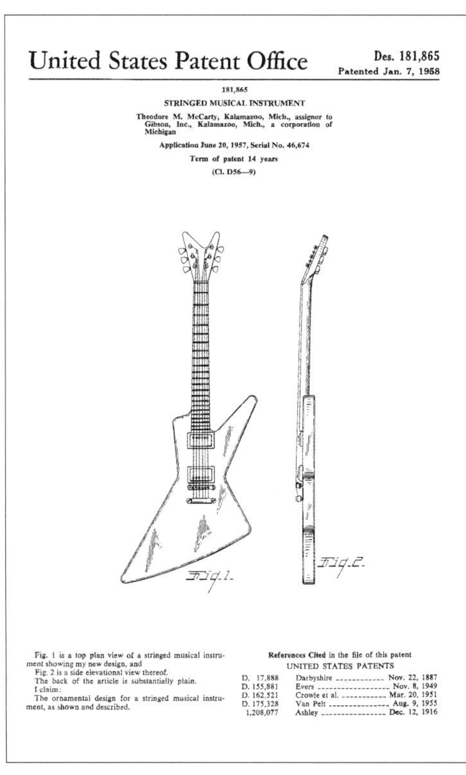

United States Patent Office — Des. 181,865 — Patented Jan. 7, 1958

181,865

STRINGED MUSICAL INSTRUMENT

Theodore M. McCarty, Kalamazoo, Mich., assignor to Gibson, Inc., Kalamazoo, Mich., a corporation of Michigan

Application June 20, 1957, Serial No. 46,674

Term of patent 14 years

(Cl. D56—9)

Fig. 1 is a top plan view of a stringed musical instrument showing my new design, and

Fig. 2 is a side elevational view thereof.

The back of the article is substantially plain.

I claim:

The ornamental design for a stringed musical instrument, as shown and described.

References Cited in the file of this patent

UNITED STATES PATENTS

D. 17,888	Darbyshire	Nov. 22, 1887
D. 155,881	Evers	Nov. 8, 1949
D. 162,521	Crowle et al.	Mar. 20, 1951
D. 175,328	Van Pelt	Aug. 9, 1955
1,208,077	Ashley	Dec. 12, 1916

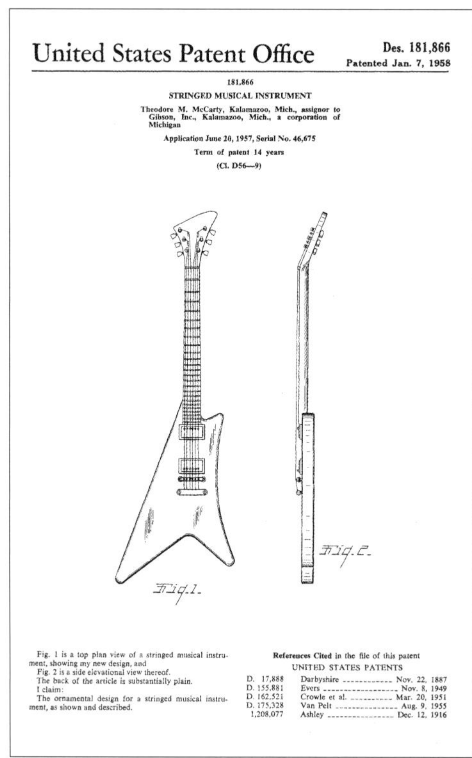

United States Patent Office — Des. 181,866 — Patented Jan. 7, 1958

181,866

STRINGED MUSICAL INSTRUMENT

Theodore M. McCarty, Kalamazoo, Mich., assignor to Gibson, Inc., Kalamazoo, Mich., a corporation of Michigan

Application June 20, 1957, Serial No. 46,675

Term of patent 14 years

(Cl. D56—9)

Fig. 1 is a top plan view of a stringed musical instrument, showing my new design, and

Fig. 2 is a side elevational view thereof.

The back of the article is substantially plain.

I claim:

The ornamental design for a stringed musical instrument, as shown and described.

References Cited in the file of this patent

UNITED STATES PATENTS

D. 17,888	Darbyshire	Nov. 22, 1887
D. 155,881	Evers	Nov. 8, 1949
D. 162,521	Crowle et al.	Mar. 20, 1951
D. 175,328	Van Pelt	Aug. 9, 1955
1,208,077	Ashley	Dec. 12, 1916

Patents for the Flying V and Explorer, 1958, and the unissued "Moderne."

The Gibson factory, Kalamazoo, from a 1958 catalogue.

ORIGINAL **GIBSON EXPLORER**

THIS EXAMPLE: ***1958***

The Explorer, named for America's first Earth satellite, found even less favor at the time than its companion Modernistic guitar, the Flying V. Both had unusual controls for a Gibson two-pickup guitar: a volume per pickup and just a single master tone.

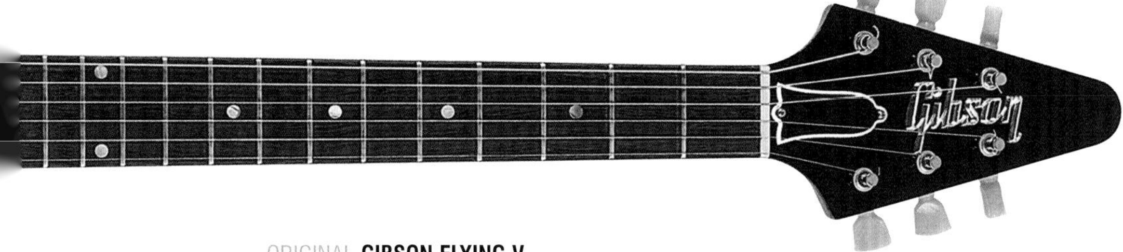

ORIGINAL **GIBSON FLYING V**

THIS EXAMPLE: ***1958***

The Flying V had a radical winged-shape body, made from korina, a West African hardwood that Gibson probably chose for its attractive light color.

Gibson's '58 catalogue cover emphasizes traditional products.

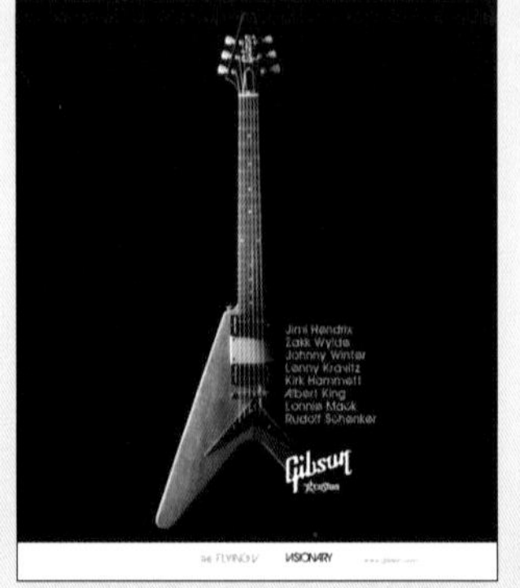

Roll-call of famous V players, Custom Shop ad, 2012.

Gibson would issue a redesigned Flying V in 1967, as we'll see later. Nonetheless, the 50s-style V design—the type with three controls in a straight line, where the revised '67 type has them in a triangular formation—has since inspired a number of reissues and reinterpretations following that original model's early death in 1959.

The first attempt at a period-style reissue of the 50s-style V came with the Flying V Heritage model of 1982. However, in the absence of a real original V to copy, Gibson's R&D team had to resort to an enlarged photograph, as supplied by a German vintage dealer, which was a less than ideal reference. Next came the 1958 Korina Flying V, introduced in 1991, which was a thoroughly more refined reissue with plenty of authentic detail, thanks to the Custom Shop having access to a real 50s Flying V (and an Explorer). A few years later, the 1958 Korina Flying V was grouped together with a reissued Explorer under the umbrella of Gibson's Historic Collection. This brought together the various elements of the Custom Shop's reissue programme, together with all the flagship Les Paul models and an impressive line of acoustics and electrics.

Gibson has at various times created other Vs that drew more loosely on the 50s-style instrument, and a few examples are pictured here. Despite the poor performance of the original model back in the late 50s, guitarists lucky to have played an original now realize that this experimental model, one of the pair that Gibson at the time called its Modernistic instruments, was a remarkable guitar. And as such it's an instrument that has proved influential on the large number of pointy creations that over the following decades would pour forth from guitar factories around the world.

An ad from 1982 for Gibson's first 50s-style V reissue.

GIBSON FLYING V CUSTOM
THIS EXAMPLE: ***2015***
A recent Gibson take on the mashup trend, this guitar imagines a meeting of a 50s-style Flying V and a Les Paul Custom, resulting in an instrument that looks somewhat overdressed.

Futura

BODY Maple construction, neck through body design ☐ A uniquely sculptured instrument featuring an innovative body taper for remarkable comfort and playability ☐ Gold-plated hardware including a Stop Bar™ tailpiece and Tune-O-Matic™ bridge ☐ One specially designed high output humbucking pickup at the bridge and one humbucking pickup at the neck ☐ Three-position toggle switch for pickup selection (individual or both simultaneously) ☐ Individual volume controls for each pickup and one master tone control mounted onto a revealed edge pickguard ☐ Black speed knobs ☐ Gold-plated "Posi-Lok"™ strap buttons.
Body Size: Length 16 1/16", Width 12 3/16", Depth 2".

NECK Width at first fret 1 11/16" ☐ Rosewood fingerboard with dot inlays ☐ Gold-plated, individually enclosed machine heads ☐ Gibson truss rod system and bell shaped truss rod cover.
22 frets ☐ 24¾" scale length.

New, solid brass Gibson Super Tune Vibrola incorporating the Gibson TP-6™ Fine Tuning tailpiece optional at extra cost.

Flying V

BODY Korina body construction ☐ Gold-plated Tune-O-Matic™ bridge and V-style tailpiece ☐ Two gold-plated Gibson Pat. Appl. For™ humbucking pickups ☐ Three "Top Hat" knobs ☐ Two volume and one master tone controls, each with dial pointer ☐ Pick-up selector switch (individual or both pick-ups simultaneously) ☐ Through-the-body string anchoring ☐ Black pickguard with white revealed edge ☐ Skid pad located on treble rim.

NECK Korina neck ☐ Rosewood fingerboard with dot inlays and corresponding side dots ☐ Original 1958 peghead shape and size, 17 degree peghead pitch ☐ Keystone emeraldescent machine head buttons with individually enclosed gears ☐ Raised Gibson peghead logo from original 1958 mold.
22 frets ☐ 24¾" scale length.

24

Gibson's oddball Futura and reissue Flying V, 1983 catalogue.

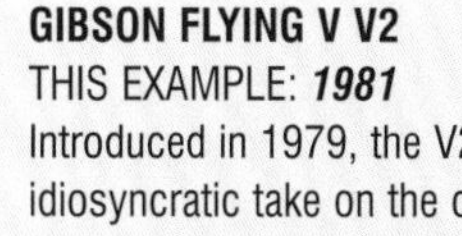

GIBSON FLYING V V2
THIS EXAMPLE: ***1981***
Introduced in 1979, the V2 was an idiosyncratic take on the original, partnered by the equally unusual Explorer E/2. Both had highly sculpted bodies, and the V2 had Boomerang V-shape pickups. Both were gone by '82.

GIBSON FLYING V '98 GOTHIC
THIS EXAMPLE: ***1998***
Despite the overwhelmingly black finish, this was otherwise a relatively straightforward 50s-influenced V, with a regular tailpiece, coverless humbuckers, and an unmarked fingerboard, apart from a goth-friendly moon-and-star inlay.

Like its companion Flying V, Gibson's original Explorer design has had a profound influence over the years since its early demise in 1959, inspiring quite a few reissues and reinterpretations. As with the V, Gibson's first attempt at a period-style reissue of the original Explorer came with the Explorer Heritage model, a little ahead of the companion Flying V, in 1981.

More significant in terms of period-correctness was the 1958 Korina Explorer, introduced in 1993, a more refined reissue that had plenty of authentic detail, not least because Gibson's Custom Shop enjoyed full access to a real 50s Explorer.

In a sumptuous Historic Collection catalogue issued in 1994, the company summed up the situation reasonably accurately. "The space age influenced consumer design in the late 50s," ran the blurb, "and Gibson answered with the 'modernistic' Korina Flying V and Explorer. These guitars are the most highly sought of any Gibson solidbody. Precisely measured from samples of original 1958 instruments, the Historic Collection's Flying V and Explorer offer the modern collector a chance to own these rare pieces."

Gibson also included in that page of the Historic Collection brochure a picture of the aging Ted McCarty, who was the boss at Gibson during the period when the originals were first introduced. McCarty must have drawn some satisfaction from this 90s reissue of the two instruments that were among the least successful during his tenure at the head of the company.

Explorer and Flying V variations of the Designer series, 1984 ad.

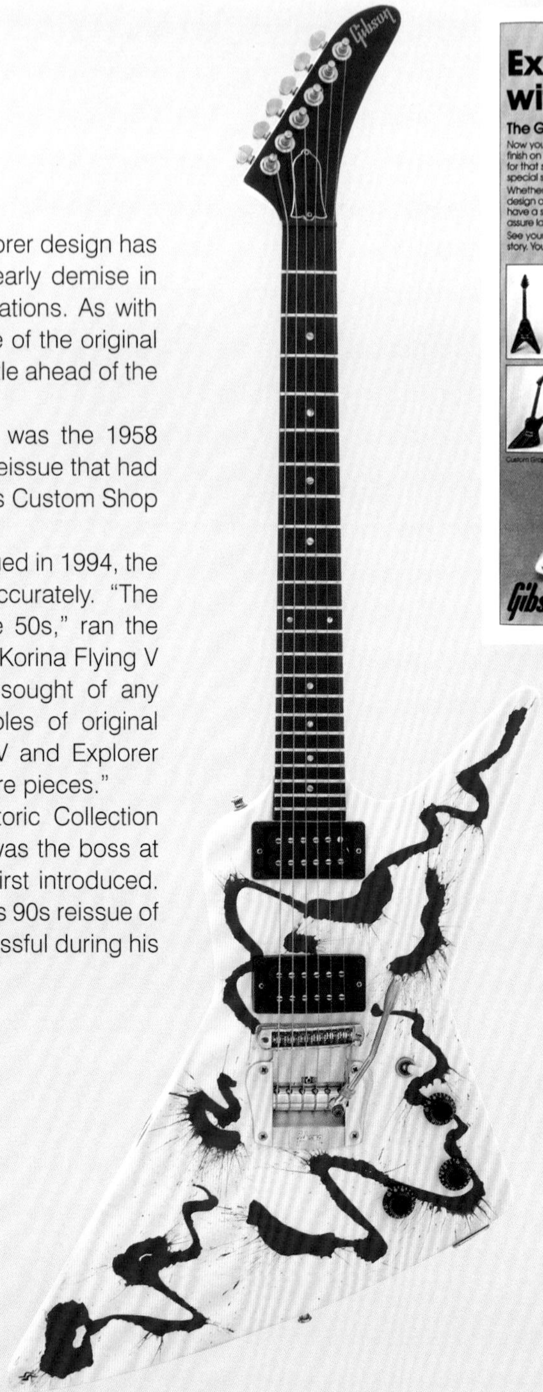

GIBSON EXPLORER DESIGNER
THIS EXAMPLE: ***1984***
Gibson's attempt to ride the 80s trend for wild color schemes resulted in the painted doodles seen across the bodies of the shortlived Designer Series.

GIBSON X-PLORER NEW CENTURY
THIS EXAMPLE: ***2006***
Introduced in 2003, the X-Plorer was the regular mahogany-body Explorer model of its time, and the New Century variant added a full-body mirror finish.

1958

Ted McCarty and the design patents for the Flying V and the Explorer

The space age influenced consumer design in the late 1950s and Gibson answered with the "modernistic" Korina Flying V and Explorer. Constructed of Korina, a rare African mahogany, these guitars changed the look of rock and roll forever. Shipping records show that under 100 Flying Vs and under 50 Explorers were shipped during 1958-1959. As a result, these guitars are the most highly sought of any Gibson solid body. Precisely measured from samples of original 1958 instruments, the Historic Collection's Flying V and Explorer offer the modern collector a chance to own these rare pieces. Limited in quantity and stamped with special serial numbers, these guitars include hardware cast from the original 1958 molds and dyes. Collectors have sought these masterpieces for years. Now they can include them in their collection.

'58 Korina Flying V *Natural*

Pickups	Two '57 Classic HBs
Controls	Volume, tone, 3-way switch
Hardware	Gold
Scale/Nut width	[illegible]
Fingerboard/Inlay	Rosewood, 22 fret / Dot
Binding	None
Bridge/Tailpiece	ABR-1 Tune-o-matic / Original "V"
Materials	Korina neck & body
Finish	Antique Natural

'58 Korina Explorer *Natural*

Pickups	Two '57 Classic HBs
Controls	Volume, tone, 3-way switch
Hardware	Gold
Scale/Nut width	[illegible]
Fingerboard/Inlay	Rosewood, 22 fret / Dot
Binding	None
Bridge/Tailpiece	ABR-1 Tune-o-matic / Stop Bar
Materials	Korina neck & body
Finish	Antique Natural

50s-style reissues highlighted in a 1994 catalogue.

GIBSON MODERNE
THIS EXAMPLE: ***1982***
One of the three original 50s Modernistic designs was never produced, but in 1982 Gibson conjured the design that collectors named the Moderne, resulting in a "reissue" ... of a guitar that never existed.

GIBSON EXPLORER 2018
THIS EXAMPLE: ***2018***
This relatively budget-price 50s-style Explorer reissue differs from the original thanks to its mahogany body and neck (not korina) and granadillo fingerboard (not rosewood).

The Explorer and Flying V may have died a very early death after Gibson first made them available in the late 50s, but the shape and look of these two guitars have since inspired many guitar-makers and musicians, who have drawn on and paid homage to what we now recognize as a pair of startling innovations from Kalamazoo, Michigan.

Some makers decided to copy the designs almost exactly, and one of the first of these was Ibanez, a brand used for guitars by the Hoshino company of Japan. The earliest Ibanez guitars borrowed rather loosely from Western guitar design, notably elements of Fender and Burns instruments, with added twists of Eastern taste. But in the 70s, Ibanez turned to more blatant copying. Among other copies of American designs, Ibanez introduced a Flying V copy in 1972 and an Explorer in '75. Ibanez was not alone—many of the sizable Japanese manufacturers followed the same path—but the brand serves as a good example to illustrate the history.

Ibanez moved on to original designs, such as the 1975 Iceman, and Gibson tried legal action later in the 70s that deterred some copyists. But the influence of Gibson's Explorer and Flying V designs would spread into the general language of the modern electric guitar and to many different brands. This became particularly evident in the late 70s and into the 80s when metal guitarists took a shine to guitars that had a pointy look, guitars designed for the particular techniques that metal had begun to demand. Makers such as B.C. Rich, Dean, Hamer, and indeed Ibanez, saw not only that a solidbody guitar could be made in any shape the designer cared to create, but that some players welcomed the kind of extreme visuals that would suit their extreme music.

B.C. RICH MOCKINGBIRD
THIS EXAMPLE: ***1981***
Another pioneer of pointy guitars who drew on Gibson's 50s Modernistic guitars—especially in this instance the Explorer—was Bernardo Rico. His B.C. Rich company introduced the Mockingbird in 1976.

DEAN ML
THIS EXAMPLE: ***1977***
Dean Zelinsky's ML design from the late 70s effectively matched the top half of an Explorer with the lower half of a Flying V for an arrestingly unusual multi-point solidbody.

Hamer's Explorer clone with Tom Dumont, 1997.

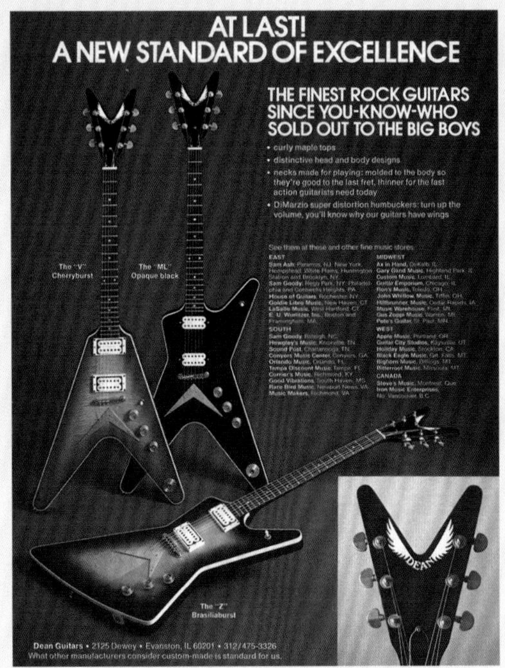

Dean's three original pointy models star in a 1977 ad.

A 1975 Ibanez ad for knock-offs of the Explorer, Moderne, and Flying V.

IBANEZ XV-500
THIS EXAMPLE: ***1985***
Ibanez was one of the first Japanese firms to copy the Flying V and Explorer in the 70s, but by the time of this XV-500 it had found its own way, offering ultra-pointy creations alongside many other styles of guitar.

Antonio Wandrè Pioli deserved a prize for outlandish guitar design. The Italian guitar maker worked from the late 50s into the 60s, based in Cavriago, near Reggio Emilia in northern Italy. He designed and produced a series of remarkable looking guitars with some notable design features, among them the Rock Oval (introduced around 1958), the Selene (1960), and the Bikini (1961). His guitars appeared with a variety of brandnames, including Wandrè, Framez, Davoli, Noble, and Orpheum.

Most striking at first glance were the unconventional shapes of some of Pioli's designs. The Rock Oval was apparently inspired by a fish hook. The bass side of the plywood body had an exaggerated waisted shape with strong curves, while the treble side had a quarter of the body missing, scooped out for the hook shape. The Bikini, one of the first guitars with a small onboard amplifier, was designed in two sections—hence the name—with amp-and-speaker in a curved pod attached to the body. Pioli used an unusual aluminum neck section, sometimes adding molded plastic pickguards and headstock plates. He produced guitars with bright and sometimes shockingly colorful finishes, ranging from figurative illustrations to strands of color that merged into one another. However, he faced mounting business problems, and Pioli closed his factory in 1968. He stopped building instruments a few years later, and he died in 2004 at the age of 78.

Meanwhile, Kay in Chicago followed the trend for unusual body designs and made its own plain take on the idea, introduced in 1958 in the shape of the Solo King model. It did not last long. Elsewhere in the extensive Kay lines, more conventional hollowbody and solidbody electrics held sway, and the firm was still providing a number of Silvertone-brand guitars to the Sears, Roebuck mail-order company.

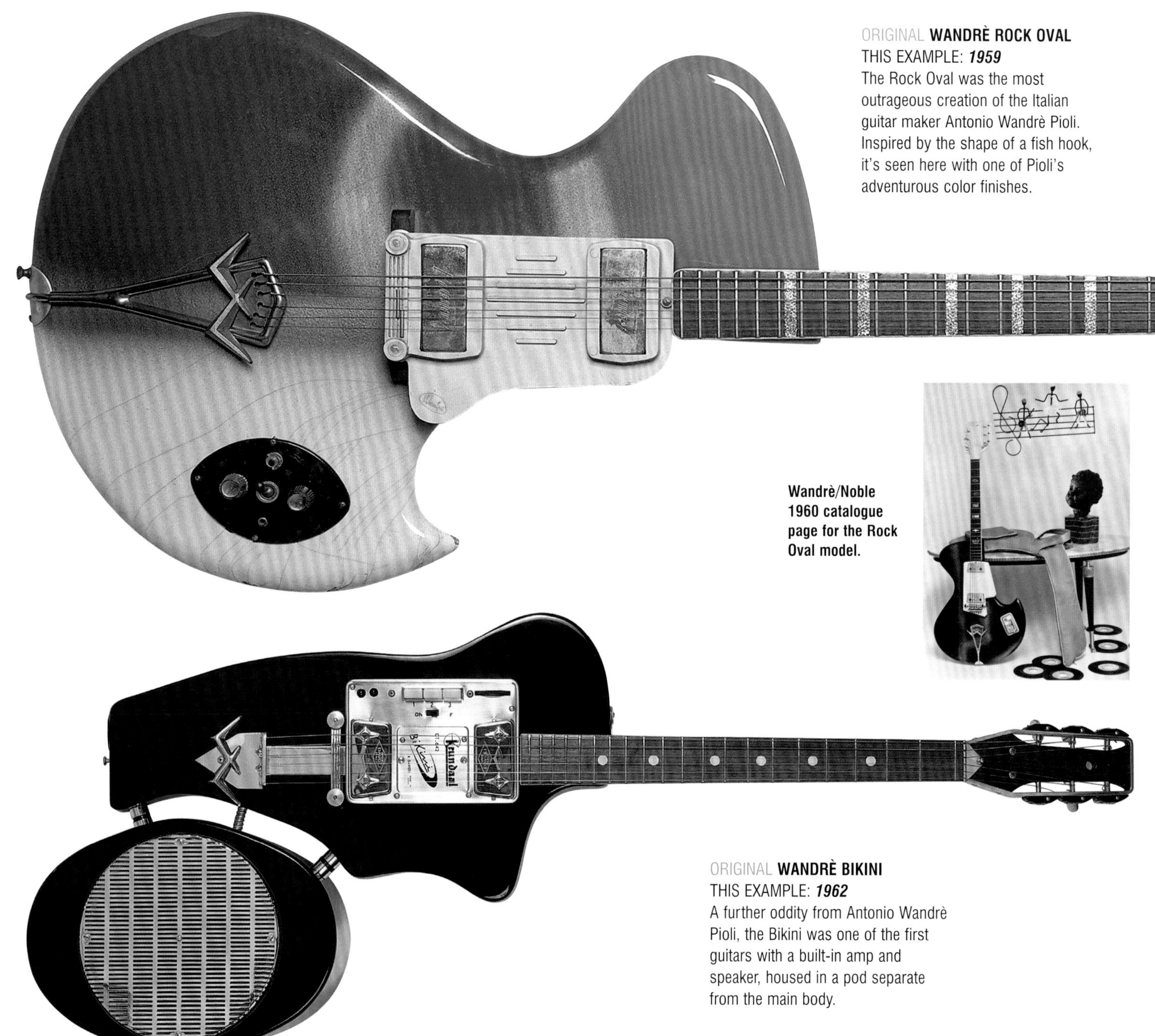

ORIGINAL **WANDRÈ ROCK OVAL**
THIS EXAMPLE: ***1959***
The Rock Oval was the most outrageous creation of the Italian guitar maker Antonio Wandrè Pioli. Inspired by the shape of a fish hook, it's seen here with one of Pioli's adventurous color finishes.

Wandrè/Noble 1960 catalogue page for the Rock Oval model.

ORIGINAL **WANDRÈ BIKINI**
THIS EXAMPLE: ***1962***
A further oddity from Antonio Wandrè Pioli, the Bikini was one of the first guitars with a built-in amp and speaker, housed in a pod separate from the main body.

Orpheum "COLOR-RAMA" GUITARS

A completely radical change that is so new and different it puts this Orpheum line years ahead. Modernistic, ultra thin cutaway bodies of a high quality veneer covered with high gloss laminated polyester. These intriguing body contours add greatly to the beauty of the sparkling colors. All aluminum head-piece, neck and adjusting thumb screw for easy neck tilt. Rosewood finger-boards, Fret-O-Matic adjustable bridge and specially designed individual magnetic pickups for each string combine to give you flawless electronic reproduction.

From every angle — in basic DESIGN, SIZE, COLOR and PERFORMANCE this blossoming array of instruments are geared to meet the demands of todays' progressive Guitarists.

"TEEN AGER"
MODEL 900 — Hollow body guitar with F holes. Single electric pickup with volume and tone controls. Available in Fire Engine Red or Nassau Blue finish.
$109.00

"SPATIAL"
MODEL 905 — Dual pickups with volume and tone controls and treble-bass switch. Individual string fine tuners and concave shape gives truly exciting tone. Available in sparklized Royal Blue and Red Maroon finish.
$135.50

Lipsky

"ROCK OVAL"
MODEL 910—Same as above in an entirely new concept in Guitar design — oval elongated body with a deep low cutaway. Finished in a multicolor blend of Fiery Red, Sun Orange, Sky Blue and Garden Green.
$144.50

"VIBRATO"
MODEL 915 — Hollow body with double pickup, volume and tone controls and treble-bass switch. Vibrato arm mounted and pre-adjusted enabling the player to change the tone above and below pitch, for true vibrato and other tonal effects. Swivel handle swings out of the way for rhythm playing. Available in Fire Engine Red or Nassau Blue finish.
$175.50

All of the above models are equipped with ORPHEUMATIC HI-POWER STRINGS and are complete with cables and Guitar straps.

CASES TO FIT
Specially designed, laminated presto guitar cases made to fit these models. Blue alligator waterproof covering.

No. 144T	— For No. 900	$10.50
No. 144	— For No. 915	$10.50
No. 20	— For No. 905	$13.50
No. 15	— For No. 910	$13.50

Four Wandrè models branded Orpheum for an American distributor, 1961.

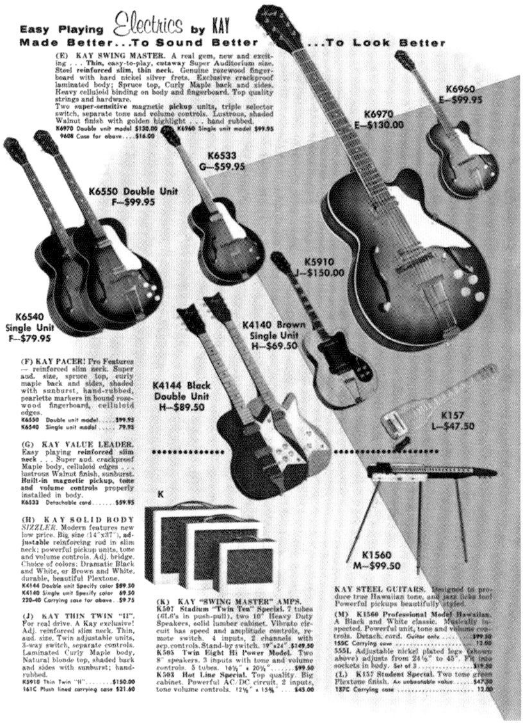

Easy Playing Electrics by KAY
Made Better...To Sound Better ...To Look Better

(E) KAY SWING MASTER. A real gem, new and exciting . . . Thin, easy-to-play, cutaway Super Auditorium size. Steel reinforced slim, thin neck. Genuine rosewood fingerboard with hard nickel silver frets. Exclusive crackproof laminated body; Spruce top, Curly Maple back and sides. Heavy celluloid binding on body and fingerboard. Top quality strings and hardware.
Two super-sensitive magnetic pickup units, triple selector switch, separate tone and volume controls. Lustrous, shaded Walnut finish with golden highlight . . . hand rubbed.
K6970 Double unit model $130.00 K6960 Single unit model $99.95
9608 Case for above....$16.00

K6960 E—$99.95
K6970 E—$130.00
K6533 G—$59.95
K6550 Double Unit F—$99.95
K6540 Single Unit F—$79.95
K5910 J—$150.00
K4140 Brown Single Unit H—$69.50
K4144 Black Double Unit H—$89.50
K157 L—$47.50
K
K1560 M—$99.50

(F) KAY PACER! Pro Features — reinforced slim neck. Super aud. size, spruce top, curly maple back and sides, shaded with sunburst, hand-rubbed, pearlette markers in bound rosewood fingerboard, celluloid edges.
K6550 Double unit model......$99.95
K6540 Single unit model...... 79.95

(G) KAY VALUE LEADER. Easy playing reinforced slim neck . . . Super aud. crackproof Maple body, celluloid edges . . . lustrous Walnut finish, sunburst. Built-in magnetic pickup, tone and volume controls properly installed in body.
K6533 Detachable cord.......$59.95

(H) KAY SOLID BODY SIZZLER. Modern features new low price. Big size (14"x37"), adjustable reinforcing rod in slim neck; powerful pickup units, tone and volume controls. Adj. bridge. Choice of colors: Dramatic Black and White, or Brown and White, durable, beautiful Plextone.
K4144 Double unit Specify color $89.50
K4140 Single unit Specify color 69.50
220-40 Carrying case for above..$9.75

(J) KAY THIN TWIN "II". For real drive. A Kay exclusive! Adj. reinforced slim neck. Thin, aud. size. Twin adjustable units, 3-way switch, separate controls. Laminated Curly Maple body, Natural blonde top, shaded back and sides with sunburst; hand-rubbed.
K5910 Thin Twin "II"........$150.00
161C Plush lined carrying case $21.60

(K) KAY "SWING MASTER" AMPS.
K507 Stadium "Twin Ten" Special. 7 tubes (6L6's in push-pull), two 10" Heavy Duty Speakers, solid lumber cabinet. Vibrato circuit has speed and amplitude controls, remote switch. 4 inputs, 2 channels with sep. controls. Stand-by switch. 19"x24" $149.50
K505 Twin Eight Hi Power Model. Two 8" speakers. 3 inputs with tone and volume controls. 5 tubes. 16½" x 20½"........$99.50
K503 Hot Line Special. Top quality. Big cabinet. Powerful AC/DC circuit. 2 inputs, tone volume controls. 12½" x 15¾" ... $45.00

KAY STEEL GUITARS. Designed to produce true Hawaiian tone, and jazz licks too! Powerful pickups beautifully styled.
(M) K1560 Professional Model Hawaiian. A Black and White classic. Musically inspected. Powerful unit, tone and volume controls. Detach. cord. Guitar only $99.50
155C Carrying case 12.00
555L Adjustable nickel plated legs (shown above) adjusts from 24½" to 45". Fit into sockets in body. Set of 3 .... $19.50
(L) K157 Student Special. Two tone green Plextone finish. An unbeatable value......$47.50
157C Carrying case 12.00

Part of Kay's large range of guitars in the 1959 catalogue.

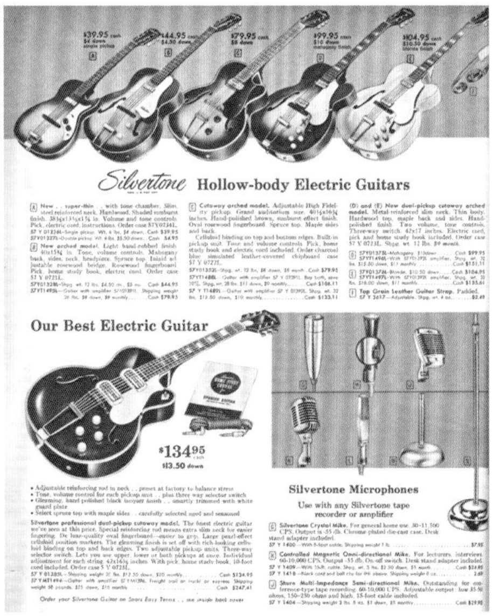

Silvertone Hollow-body Electric Guitars

Our Best Electric Guitar

$134.95

Silvertone Microphones
Use with any Silvertone tape recorder or amplifier

Sears, Roebuck 1959 catalogue with some Kay-made Silvertones.

ORIGINAL KAY SOLO KING K4102
THIS EXAMPLE: ***1958***
As if to prove that anything Gibson could do with its Flying V and Explorer, Kay could do worse, the Solo King was a misshapen addition in 1958 to Kay's broad catalogue of electric guitars.

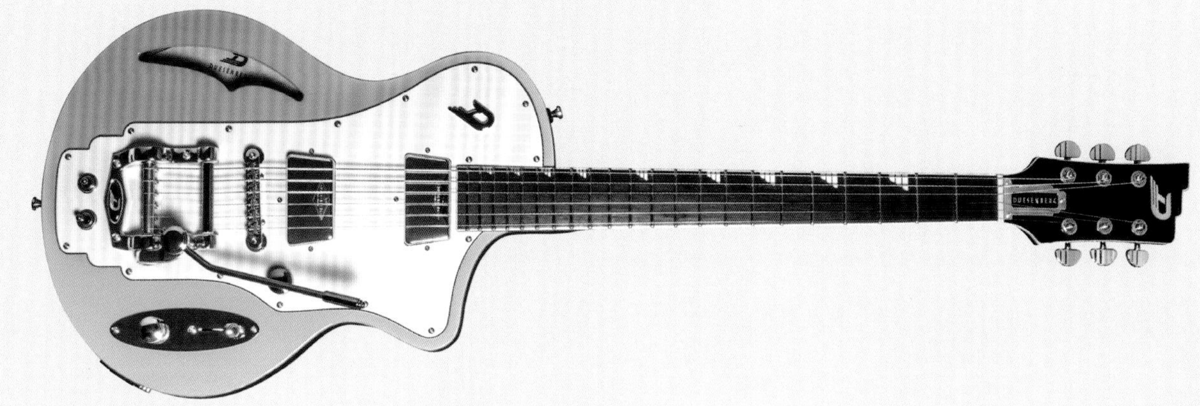

DUESENBERG JULIA
THIS EXAMPLE: ***2018***
Dieter Gölsdorf started Duesenberg in Hannover, Germany, in 1995 with an interest in retro design and modern technology. The new-for-2018 Julia draws on Wandrè's Soloist, a 60s model favored more recently by Buddy Miller and Bill Nelson.

Double Mandolin alongside the Double 12, 1960 catalogue.

Custom-built Doubles

DOUBLE 12

DOUBLE MANDOLIN

Gibson's first electric double-neck guitars appeared in 1958, a pair of thinline hollowbody models with double pointed cutaways and no f-holes. We've seen that Paul Bigsby made the first electric double-neck, in California in 1952, as a custom instrument, and that Stratosphere in Missouri produced a Twin model in 1954 that combined six-string and twelve-string necks. Gibson's new EDS-1275 Double 12 had the six-string and twelve-string combination, too, while its EMS-1235 Double Mandolin mixed a regular six-string neck plus a short-scale neck with six strings tuned an octave higher than a guitar and supposedly mimicking a mandolin sound.

In 1958, Gibson made a radical design change to three of the Les Paul models and, as we shall see, a cosmetic alteration to another. The company heralded the moves in its *Gibson Gazette* promotional magazine. "Guitarists the world over are familiar with Gibson's famous series of Les Paul Guitars," the *Gazette* report proclaimed. "They include some of the finest solidbody instruments manufactured today—and lead the field in popularity. It is with great pride that Gibson announces exciting improvements."

Those improvements meant that the Les Paul Junior, Les Paul Junior Three-Quarter, and Les Paul TV models were redesigned with a new double-cutaway body shape. The fresh look of the Junior and Junior Three-Quarter was enhanced with a new cherry red finish, and the TV, which adopted the new double-cutaway design as well, came with a yellower version of the TV finish (Gibson called it "cream").

The Junior Three-Quarter had been available since 1956. It was a Junior with a shorter neck, resulting in a string-length some two inches shorter than the regular version. Gibson explained in its brochure at the time that the Junior Three-Quarter was designed to appeal to "youngsters, or adults with small hands and fingers."

ORIGINAL **GIBSON EDS-1275 DOUBLE 12**
THIS EXAMPLE: ***1959***
Gibson's first electric twelve-string guitar appeared in this new double-neck model, with a thinline hollow body. Promotional material emphasized that the new double-necks were custom-built to order only, and very few were made.

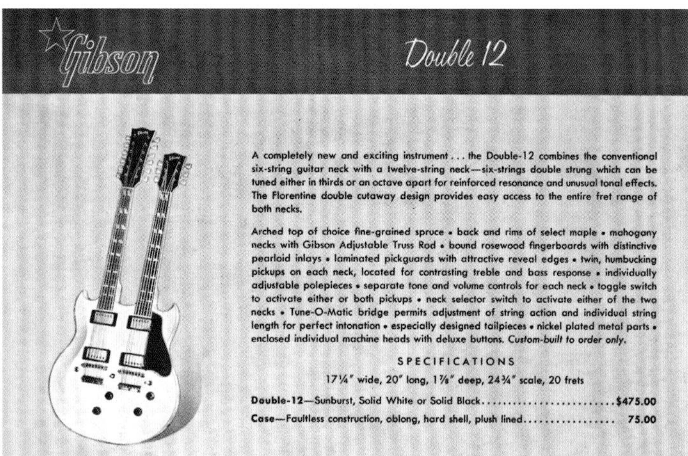

Gibson

Double 12

A completely new and exciting instrument . . . the Double-12 combines the conventional six-string guitar neck with a twelve-string neck—six-strings double strung which can be tuned either in thirds or an octave apart for reinforced resonance and unusual tonal effects. The Florentine double cutaway design provides easy access to the entire fret range of both necks.

Arched top of choice fine-grained spruce • back and rims of select maple • mahogany necks with Gibson Adjustable Truss Rod • bound rosewood fingerboards with distinctive pearloid inlays • laminated pickguards with attractive reveal edges • twin, humbucking pickups on each neck, located for contrasting treble and bass response • individually adjustable polepieces • separate tone and volume controls for each neck • toggle switch to activate either or both pickups • neck selector switch to activate either of the two necks • Tune-O-Matic bridge permits adjustment of string action and individual string length for perfect intonation • especially designed tailpieces • nickel plated metal parts • enclosed individual machine heads with deluxe buttons. *Custom-built to order only.*

SPECIFICATIONS

17¼" wide, 20" long, 1⅞" deep, 24¾" scale, 20 frets

Double-12—Sunburst, Solid White or Solid Black........................**$475.00**
Case—Faultless construction, oblong, hard shell, plush lined................. **75.00**

Gibson's 1958 catalogue introduces the "new and exciting" Double 12.

Electric Spanish Guitars

SOLID BODY MODELS

LES PAUL JUNIOR
LES PAUL JR. 3/4

A best seller that's now even better—with its handsome new cherry-red finish and its highly desirable new double cutaway design, and its very low popular price. You get Gibson quality and top performance. A small, thin, sturdy, solid body guitar, its beautiful cherry-red finish on the finest mahogany. Nickel-plated metal parts and quality machine heads. Leather strap included.
Available also with three-quarter size neck and fingerboard that joins the double cutaway body at the 15th fret.

- Slim, fast, low-action neck—with exclusive extra low frets, joins body at the 22nd fret
- One-piece mahogany neck, adjustable truss rod
- Rosewood fingerboard, pearl dot inlays
- Combination bridge and tailpiece, adjustable horizontally and vertically
- Powerful pickup with individually adjustable polepieces
- Separate tone and volume controls which can be pre-set

12¾" wide, 17¼" long, 1¾" thin . . . 24¾" scale, 22 frets

Les Paul Jr. Cherry-red finish

Les Paul Jr. ¾ Cherry-red finish

115 Durabilt case

1960 catalogue with double-cutaway Les Paul Junior.

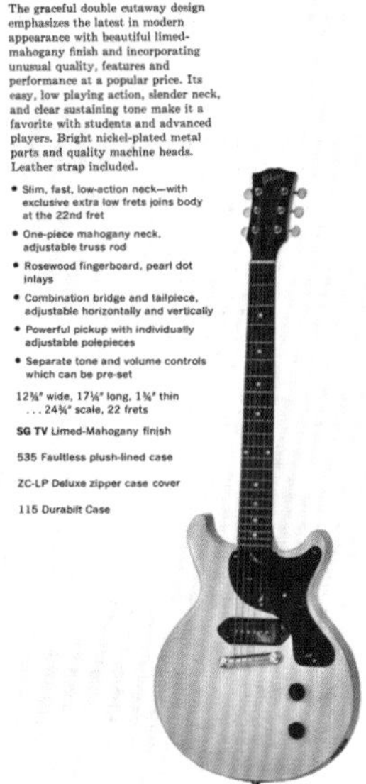

TV

The graceful double cutaway design emphasizes the latest in modern appearance with beautiful limed-mahogany finish and incorporating unusual quality, features and performance at a popular price. Its easy, low playing action, slender neck, and clear sustaining tone make it a favorite with students and advanced players. Bright nickel-plated metal parts and quality machine heads. Leather strap included.

- Slim, fast, low-action neck—with exclusive extra low frets joins body at the 22nd fret
- One-piece mahogany neck, adjustable truss rod
- Rosewood fingerboard, pearl dot inlays
- Combination bridge and tailpiece, adjustable horizontally and vertically
- Powerful pickup with individually adjustable polepieces
- Separate tone and volume controls which can be pre-set

12¾" wide, 17¼" long, 1¾" thin . . . 24¾" scale, 22 frets

SG TV Limed-Mahogany finish

535 Faultless plush-lined case

ZC-LP Deluxe zipper case cover

115 Durabilt Case

Double-cutaway Les Paul TV in Gibson's 1960 catalogue.

Evidence of the Junior's widespread influence, Collings ad, 2016.

GIBSON BILLIE JOE ARMSTRONG LES PAUL JUNIOR DOUBLE CUT
THIS EXAMPLE: ***2012***
Signature models of the double-cutaway Junior have not been plentiful, but in 2012 Gibson announced this teaming with Green Day frontman Billie Joe Armstrong.

ORIGINAL **GIBSON LES PAUL TV**
THIS EXAMPLE: ***1959***
The TV also received the new double-cutaway body shape in 1958, and around the same time the Kalamazoo paint shop adapted the TV color to a rather more yellow-ish hue.

ORIGINAL **GIBSON LES PAUL JUNIOR**
THIS EXAMPLE: ***1960***
Gibson redesigned the Junior in 1958 with a cherry red finish on a new double-cutaway body, intended to provide players with better access to the guitar's upper frets.

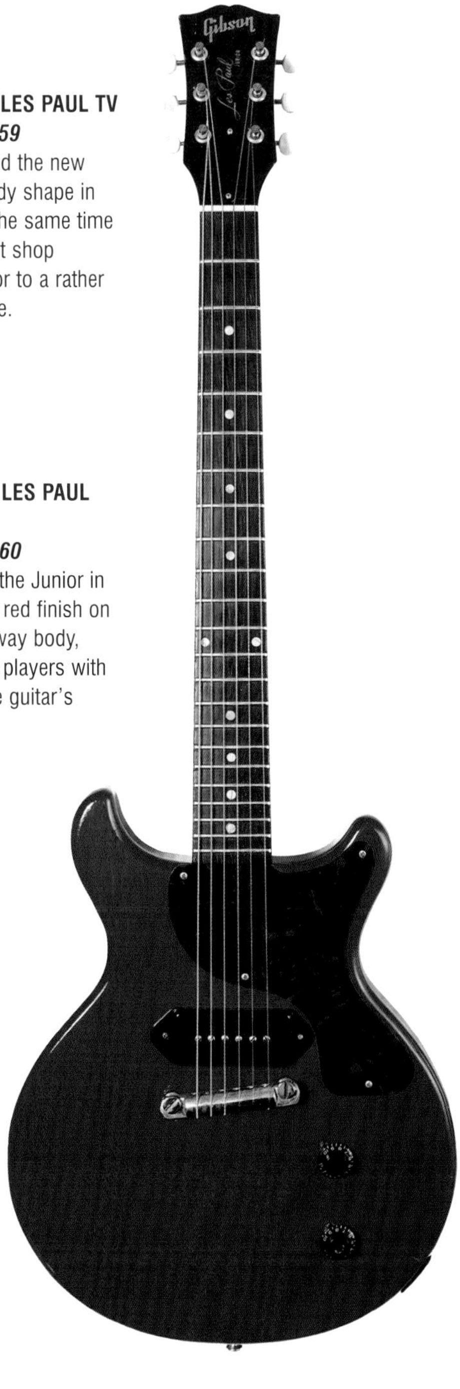

Gibson devised a revolutionary body design and construction for its ES-335, introduced in 1958. It was a true first for Gibson: a double-cutaway semi-solid electric guitar. Sales of its solidbody models were slipping, so perhaps a guitar with the benefits of a solidbody in a hollowbody-like package might prove more appealing?

The company devoted a half-page splash in its 1958 catalogue to the 335, hinting at "semi-solid thin styling" and "new body construction, with solid fitting neck, pickups and adjustable bridge, providing the solidity essential for clear, sparkling, sustaining tone – while retaining a body size and shape that is easy and comfortable to hold." None of this revealed the precise truth: the 335 had a solid block of wood running through the inside of its hollow body.

The 335's body consisted of a pressed laminated top and back, a pair of laminated rims, or sides, and the solid internal block. It had two generous, rounded, symmetrical cutaways that met the neck either side of the nineteenth fret. The laminated wood was three-ply: two outer plies of maple, with the same grain direction, and between them a ply of softer wood, usually poplar, with the grain running at ninety degrees to the maple. The internal maple block ran almost the entire length of the body.

Players soon found that the new ES-335 really did combine the qualities of a hollowbody and solidbody guitar, and guitarists have lined up ever since to taste its attractively different flavors. In its early days, the new guitar came only in natural or sunburst finish: at first, in natural it was the ES-335TN or ES-335TDN, and in sunburst the ES-335T or ES-335TD. Gibson added more colors, including cherry red in 1961 (ES-335TDC), walnut in 1968, and occasional custom colors such as black or Pelham blue.

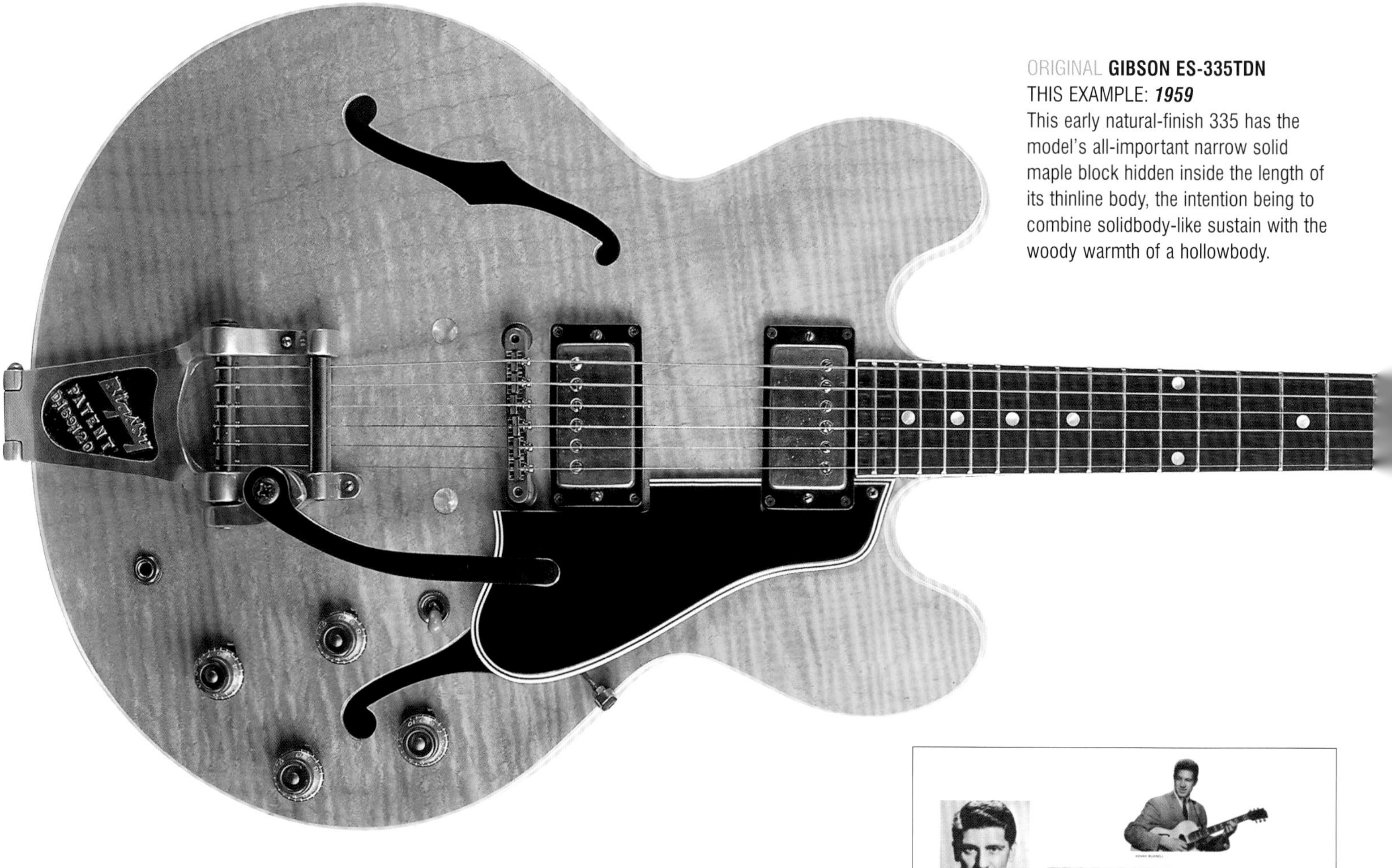

ORIGINAL **GIBSON ES-335TDN**
THIS EXAMPLE: ***1959***
This early natural-finish 335 has the model's all-important narrow solid maple block hidden inside the length of its thinline body, the intention being to combine solidbody-like sustain with the woody warmth of a hollowbody.

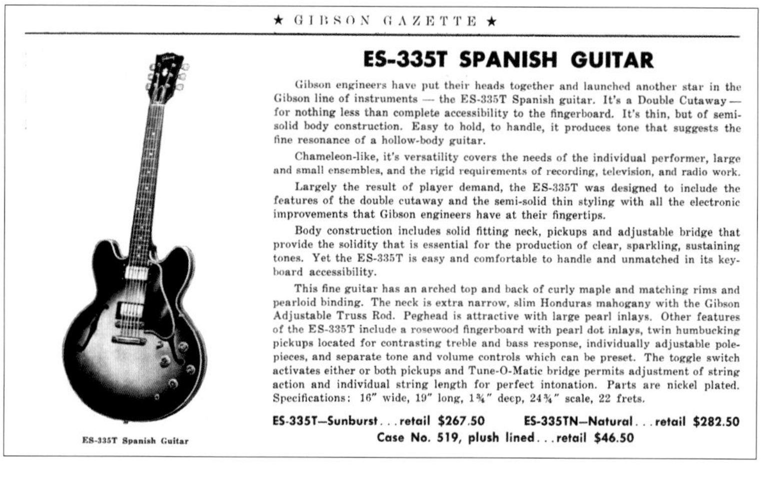

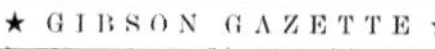

★ GIBSON GAZETTE ★

ES-335T SPANISH GUITAR

Gibson engineers have put their heads together and launched another star in the Gibson line of instruments — the ES-335T Spanish guitar. It's a Double Cutaway — for nothing less than complete accessibility to the fingerboard. It's thin, but of semi-solid body construction. Easy to hold, to handle, it produces tone that suggests the fine resonance of a hollow-body guitar.

Chameleon-like, it's versatility covers the needs of the individual performer, large and small ensembles, and the rigid requirements of recording, television, and radio work.

Largely the result of player demand, the ES-335T was designed to include the features of the double cutaway and the semi-solid thin styling with all the electronic improvements that Gibson engineers have at their fingertips.

Body construction includes solid fitting neck, pickups and adjustable bridge that provide the solidity that is essential for the production of clear, sparkling, sustaining tones. Yet the ES-335T is easy and comfortable to handle and unmatched in its keyboard accessibility.

This fine guitar has an arched top and back of curly maple and matching rims and pearloid binding. The neck is extra narrow, slim Honduras mahogany with the Gibson Adjustable Truss Rod. Peghead is attractive with large pearl inlays. Other features of the ES-335T include a rosewood fingerboard with pearl dot inlays, twin humbucking pickups located for contrasting treble and bass response, individually adjustable pole-pieces, and separate tone and volume controls which can be preset. The toggle switch activates either or both pickups and Tune-O-Matic bridge permits adjustment of string action and individual string length for perfect intonation. Parts are nickel plated. Specifications: 16" wide, 19" long, 1¾" deep, 24¾" scale, 22 frets.

ES-335T—Sunburst . . . retail $267.50 **ES-335TN—Natural . . . retail $282.50**
Case No. 519, plush lined . . . retail $46.50

ES-335T Spanish Guitar

Gibson announces the ES-335 in its Gazette magazine, 1958.

in the Gibson Galaxy of Stars

Fine guitarists demand fine instruments . . . that's why there are so many stars in the Gibson galaxy, why so many fine musicians everywhere choose Gibson. They appreciate Gibson tonal perfection, superb response, and ease of playing—so fast and low and light. They appreciate, too, the beauty of their instruments. Top performers in the guitar world are shown throughout this book—they're Gibson artists all!

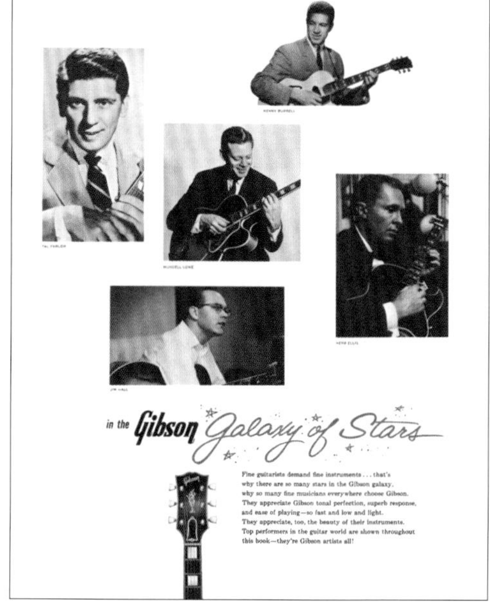

Gibson '60 catalogue emphasizes links with the jazz establishment.

• **Gibson Tune-O-Matic bridge** makes it possible to tune your guitar to perfect accuracy on each individual string, at the bridge. It permits precise adjustment for intonation and each saddle can be reversed individually, for full range tuning. Easily adjusted for fast, low action.

• **Gibson wonder-straight neck—with adjustable truss rod** . . . first developed by Gibson. Positively keeps the neck from twisting or warping because of climatical change or string tension . . . keeps tuning exact in the upper register. Neck can be adjusted perfectly in minutes. This is the famous slim, fast, low-action neck.

• **Gibson humbucking pickup** is a new approach to tone generation from string vibration. This high impedance pickup is sensitive to the smallest string vibration but rejects interference in the form of hum, static, or radiated noise. Two methods are provided to set the pickup: 1.) adjusting screws set pickup; 2.) adjusting individual polepieces set each string.

Electric Spanish Guitars • THIN BODY MODELS

An all-star guitar series for the most discriminating players . . . providing brilliant sustaining tone, fast action, and easy handling. Wonder-thin and light, these Gibson electric guitars fit close and comfortably against the body, giving easy access to the entire fret range. The slender neck with low-action frets is extremely fast and easy to finger . . . strings seem feather light. The feel is just right! Famous Gibson firsts—the electric guitar and the wonder-thin silhouette —are combined in these fine instruments.

• **Gibson wonder-thin silhouette** . . . only 1¾" to 2¼" thin.

The benefits of a thin body, 1960 catalogue.

ORIGINAL **GIBSON ES-335TD**
THIS EXAMPLE: ***1958***
Gibson's 335, introduced in 1958, was a new type of electric guitar that combined the benefits of hollowbody and solidbody in one double-cutaway design. It has proved to be one of the company's greatest instruments.

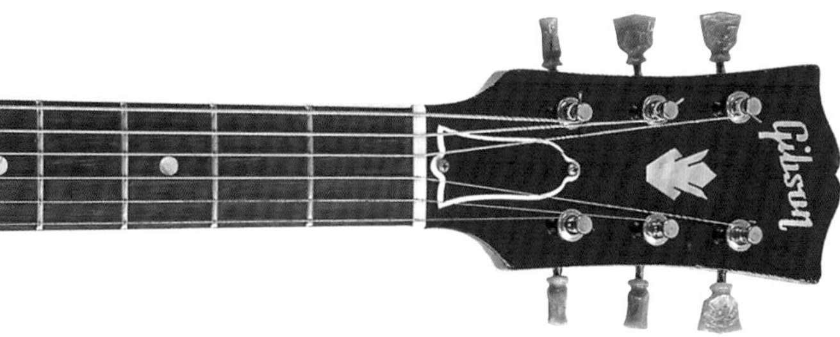

ELECTRIC
Spanish Guitars
THIN MODELS

The electric Spanish guitar, developed in the mid 1930's enabled the guitarist to emerge from a background of rhythm performance into the spotlight of the soloist. This new electronic voice was equal in dynamics to that of the brasses and the saxophones . . . the man with the guitar was able to express himself musically, to create his own solo version of each musical composition.

In the late 1940's as the larger dance bands dwindled in numbers, smaller musical groups were formed around the artistry of the electric guitar and new exciting musical combinations were created and enjoyed. Today we admire and respect hundreds of guitar artists, performing with unusual ability in all types of musical ensembles, their performance enhanced by the acoustical properties of their amplified electric guitar.

Gibson electrics span the requirements of all discerning musicians and are more than equal to the demands of each type of musical expression. As a typical example,—the new thin-body Gibson electric guitars provide new body-hugging comfort, plus unusally responsive action and free-playing performance.

Gibson provides an unusual variety of electric guitars . . . more satisfaction for your playing needs than any guitar . . . anywhere! Try a Gibson . . . You'll be amazed!

ES-335TDC
Thin, double cutaway—a newsmaker from its first appearance, this model offers outstanding performance for ensembles, recording, radio and TV at an amazingly modest price.
FEATURES: Curly maple arched top and back, nickel-plated metal parts. Slim, fast, low-action neck joins body at 20th fret. One-piece mahogany neck, adjustable truss rod. Rosewood fingerboard, pearl block inlays. Adjustable Tune-O-Matic bridge. Twin humbucking pickups with separate tone and volume controls which can be pre-set. Three-position toggle switch to activate either or both pickups. 16" wide, 19" long, 1¾" thin, 24¾" scale, 22 frets.
ES-335TDC Cherry finish
ES-335TD Sunburst finish
519 Faultless plush-lined case
304 Archcraft plush-lined case
ZC-19 Deluxe zipper case cover

ES-330TD
A wonderful instrument with truly magical tone available in single and double pickup models. The double cutaway body and thin silhouette make it wonderfully easy to hold and play.
FEATURES: Constructed from the finest curly maple and rosewood, nickel-plated metal parts. Slim, fast, low-action neck joins the body at 16th fret. One-piece mahogany neck, adjustable truss rod. Rosewood fingerboard, pearl dot inlays. Adjustable Tune-O-Matic bridge. Powerful pickups with individually adjustable pole-pieces. Separate tone and volume controls. Three-position toggle switch to activate either or both pickups. 16" wide, 19" long, 1¾" thin, 24¾" scale, 22 frets.
ES-330TDC Cherry finish
ES-330TD Sunburst finish
519 Faultless plush-lined case
304 Archcraft plush-lined case
104 Durabilt case
ZC-19 Deluxe zipper case cover

1963 catalogue: block-marker 335; hollowbody 330.

2014 ad with signature 335 for Warren Haynes (Gov't Mule, Allman Brothers).

The 335 has proved to be an important member of Gibson's electric guitar line since its introduction in 1958, and the company has since issued an array of reissues, variations, and models influenced by the originals, a sample of which is illustrated here.

Gibson's first period-correct reissue came in 1981 with the arrival of the ES-335 Dot. The clue to the main visual feature of this reissue was in the name. The 335 that Gibson made at the time still had block inlays in the fingerboard, a feature that had remained more or less unchanged since the early 60s. The reissue went back to the dot inlays of the original 1958-style guitar. This may seem a trivial detail, but some players, especially those who liked to use vibrato and bends, didn't care for the disturbance to their fingers that the block inlays could cause, preferring the feel of as much wooden board as possible. A return to the dots was ensured.

The 335 Studio, new for 1986, had a sealed body, in other words one without the regular f-holes. Meanwhile, there have been many famous 335 players—everyone from Alvin Lee to Lee Ritenour has put the model to good musical use—but Larry Carlton has long had the nickname Mister 335, following his classic work with Steely Dan, The Crusaders, and Joni Mitchell among many others. Gibson introduced Carlton signature models in 2002 and 2004.

Some players find the size of the 335 too much, and in the mid 90s Gibson's Custom Shop launched the 336 (first as the ES-336 and later the CS-336), a scaled-down 335 with a smaller body made of routed mahogany with a routed maple top. But the first proper 335-style model with a scaled-down body was the ES-339, introduced in 2007 with a center-block body.

Thinline Series

Gibson's innovative synthesis of acoustic and electric guitar designs, pioneered during the 50's, marked another evolutionary milestone in the history of the modern guitar.

In response to the musical desires of the world's foremost players, Gibson defined an entirely new concept and brought forth an instrument which combined the luxurious, full-bodied sound of hand-carved, arch-top models with the thick, penetrating sustain of the Les Paul solid body. The result was a thin-bodied, arch topped ES (Electric Spanish) style guitar with a distinctive double cutaway.

A solid maple center block running the length of the body provides the sustain. And the character is defined by layers of close-grained spruce used to support the arch and warm the tone of the maple.

The ES-335 Dot. The very essence of classic elegance, one of the most admired and requested models in Gibson history. The balanced feel and extraordinary playability permit the instrument to come alive in the player's hands.

The B. B. King Custom "Lucille." An instrument of unparalleled beauty fashioned after B. B.'s original Gibson model – the one he rescued from a raging fire without a thought for his own safety. Need we say more about Lucille?

The ES Artist. A furtherance of the design concepts that created the original ES style guitar, the Artist emphasizes sustain while retaining the responsiveness and feel to produce a stunning range of popular sounds.

The ES-347. A model offering a number of extras included in the classic thin body design: ebony fingerboard, solid brass nut, block-style inlays and two high output Dirty Fingers™ humbucking pickups with extended frequency response.

ES-335 DOT

BODY Arched maple top and back with matching maple rims ☐ Vintage double venetian cutaway ☐ Top and back bound with cream colored binding ☐ Nickel-plated hardware ☐ Full maple center block for additional sustain and high frequency response ☐ Adjustable Tune-O-Matic™ bridge with Stop Bar™ tailpiece ☐ Black fingerrest with white revealed edge ☐ Two "Pat. Appl. For"™ humbucking pickups with individual volume and tone controls ☐ Three position toggle switch for pickup selection (individual or both pickups simultaneously) ☐ Original Gibson "Top Hat" knobs ☐ Ultra safe Gibson "Posi-Lok"™ strap button.
Body Size: 18 15/16". Width 16". Depth 1 3/4".

NECK Mahogany neck construction ☐ Width at first fret 1 11/16" ☐ Vintage SP-1 peghead with seventeen degree pitch ☐ Bound rosewood fingerboard with dot inlays and corresponding side dots ☐ Pearl inlaid head veneer ☐ Individually enclosed machine heads ☐ Gibson truss rod with traditional Gibson bell shaped truss rod cover. 22 frets ☐ 24 3/4" scale length.

The inset photo above illustrates a highly figured maple top, available through the Gibson Custom Shop. For more information on the Custom Shop, see page 26.

The ES-335 Dot reissue profiled in a 1983 catalogue.

GIBSON ES-335 STUDIO
THIS EXAMPLE: ***1986***
The Studio variant of the 335 drew on an idea that Gibson had used for its B.B. King signature model: a 335-style center-block body, but without f-holes.

GIBSON ES-339 FIGURED
THIS EXAMPLE: ***2012***
The ES-339 was a scaled-down version of the 335, its body just under two inches narrower than a 335 at its widest point, aimed by Gibson at players who found the regular 335s a bit of a handful.

GIBSON LARRY CARLTON ES-335
THIS EXAMPLE: ***2010***
Studio star Larry Carlton has long played a 335 on his many famous sessions, including stellar work with Steely Dan, and this signature model has his nickname "Mr. 335" on the truss-rod cover.

GIBSON ES-335 DOT
THIS EXAMPLE: ***2018***
The Dot, introduced in 1981, was Gibson's first period-aware re-creation of an original-style 335, complete with the all-important dot markers seen on the early models.

The high-end ES-347 model in a 1980 ad.

Ibanez's 335-influenced John Scofield model, 2001 ad.

1958

Gibson made a change in 1958 that seemed relatively unimportant at the time but would take on great significance. The company decided to make a cosmetic alteration to the Les Paul Model (Goldtop). Sales had declined, and something had to be done to stimulate renewed interest in this relatively high-price model. Gibson figured that many players found the Goldtop's unusual finish too unconventional and that this had caused its dip in popularity. A new three-color cherry sunburst finish was applied in a bid to attract new customers. The first two sunburst Les Pauls—known today as Standard models—were shipped from the factory in May 1958, and the company had more of the guitars ready to show off during a summer trade show in July.

At first, Gibson's hunch about a different look was proved right. Gibson's boss Ted McCarty and his team knew Goldtop sales had declined from a high of 920 during 1956 to just 434 in 1958, the year of the new Standard. After the revised model appeared, sales climbed to 643 in 1959, but they would dip again in 1960. Gibson then decided the change of finish had not been enough, and that the only way to attract new customers was to completely redesign the entire Les Paul line—of which more later. This meant the original sunburst Les Paul Standard was only produced from 1958 to 1960.

Almost ignored at the time, these sunburst Standards have since become ultra-collectable icons. Players and collectors came to realize that their inherent musicality and short production run added up to a modern design classic. This re-evaluation was prompted originally in the middle and late 60s when star guitarists discovered these Les Pauls had enormous potential for high-volume blues-based rock, and their special appeal has only grown since.

ORIGINAL **GIBSON LES PAUL STANDARD**
THIS EXAMPLE: ***1958***
With sales of the Les Paul Goldtop fading, Gibson figured the way to attract new customers was to change the finish of the model to a new three-color sunburst look, introduced in 1958.

ORIGINAL **GIBSON LES PAUL STANDARD**
THIS EXAMPLE: ***1959***
Collectors now consider 59s the finest of the 58–60 bunch, although the original Bigsby vibrato fitted to this example, said to meddle with the tone, would shift the value down a notch or two.

Gibson's catalogue cover, 1960, with sedate bow-tied jazzman.

LES PAUL STANDARD

This beautiful solid body guitar incorporates many unusual Gibson features. Cherry sunburst carved maple top, mahogany body and neck. Combination bridge and tailpiece is a Gibson first. Tailpiece can be moved up or down to adjust tension. Tune-O-Matic bridge permits adjusting string action and individual string lengths. Finish in the striking cherry sunburst. Nickle-plated metal parts and individual machine heads with deluxe buttons. Deluxe padded leather strap included.

- Slim, fast, low-action neck—with exclusive extra low frets, joins body at 16th fret
- One-piece mahogany neck, adjustable truss rod
- Rosewood fingerboard, pearl inlays
- Graceful cutaway design
- Adjustable Tune-O-Matic bridge
- Twin powerful humbucking pickups with separate tone and volume controls which can be pre-set
- Three-position toggle switch to activate either or both pickups

12¾" wide, 17¼" long, 1¾" thin . . . 24¾" scale, 22 frets

Les Paul Standard Cherry sunburst finish

535 Faultless, plush-lined case

ZC-LP Deluxe zipper case cover

The shortlived sunburst Standard's sole catalogue appearance, 1960.

ORIGINAL **GIBSON LES PAUL STANDARD**
THIS EXAMPLE: ***1960***
This rare left-handed sunburst Standard, from its final production year and complete with upside-down Les Paul logo, is owned today by Paul McCartney.

ORIGINAL **GIBSON LES PAUL STANDARD**
THIS EXAMPLE: ***1960***
The beautiful figured maple top of this Standard is just the sort of thing to set the pulse racing of aficionados of the model that's nicknamed the Burst, short for sunburst.

Gibson has developed a programme where it re-creates famous guitars in limited editions, and in 2010 it was the turn of the Eric Clapton Les Paul. This would prove quite an achievement for the Custom Shop team, because there was no guitar to copy. The almost mythical instrument in question is known among collectors as the Beano Burst, because it was the Burst (sunburst Les Paul) that Clapton used on the session for the *Blues Breakers John Mayall With Eric Clapton* album, better known as the *Beano* album. On the front of the original jacket, Clapton reads a copy of the *Beano* comic.

Clapton had joined the Mayall band in April 1965. The following month he bought the Beano Burst from a shop in London's West End, and he began using it immediately. By the time the *Beano* album was released in 1966, Clapton was rehearsing his next band with Jack Bruce and Ginger Baker. Clapton was distraught when his beloved Les Paul was stolen during one of those Cream rehearsals, before he'd had a chance to play it with the new group in public or in the studio. The guitar has never been seen since and is considered lost. Should it ever turn up, it would be among the most valuable guitars in the world, such is the interest among collectors for the guitar that Clapton used for what many consider some of his finest recorded performances.

The 2010 Eric Clapton 1960 Les Paul limited edition came in several versions: a small number with aged finish, and signed by Clapton; a further small batch aged but not signed; and a larger edition of V.O.S. models (Vintage Original Spec, Gibson Custom's lightly-aged finishing process). Gibson's mission to re-create famous sunburst Les Pauls has also included models named for Paul Kossoff, Michael Bloomfield, and many others.

GIBSON LES PAUL STANDARD REISSUE
THIS EXAMPLE: ***1985***
Here's Gibson's original signature-model solidbody electric—with a second signature, thanks to Les Paul himself signing the pickguard of this 80s sunburst Standard reissue.

A roll-call of famous Burst players, 2012 ad.

GIBSON DUANE ALLMAN 1959 LES PAUL STANDARD
THIS EXAMPLE: ***2003***
Duane Allman used two Bursts during his short career, and Gibson has reproduced both in recent years. This one is the "darkburst " guitar, nicknamed Hot 'Lanta, that he acquired in 1971, shortly before his untimely death.

Clapton with Beano remake, 2010.

GIBSON ERIC CLAPTON 1960 LES PAUL AGED

THIS EXAMPLE: ***2010***

Clapton's "Beano" Burst, bought in '65 and stolen the following year, has become a legendary (and still missing) guitar. Gibson managed to re-create the non-existent original for this limited-edition run.

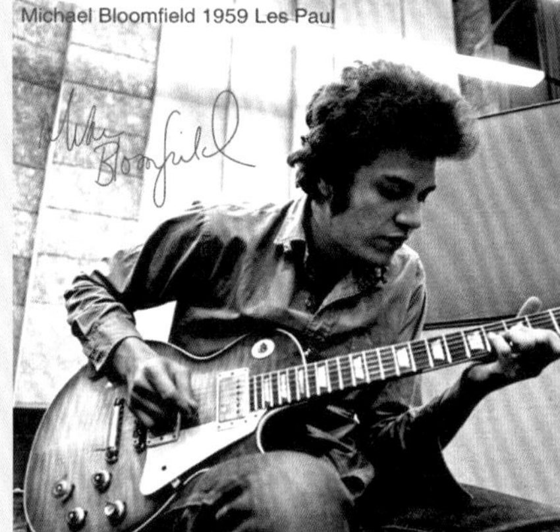

Michael Bloomfield Les Paul, sales material, 2010.

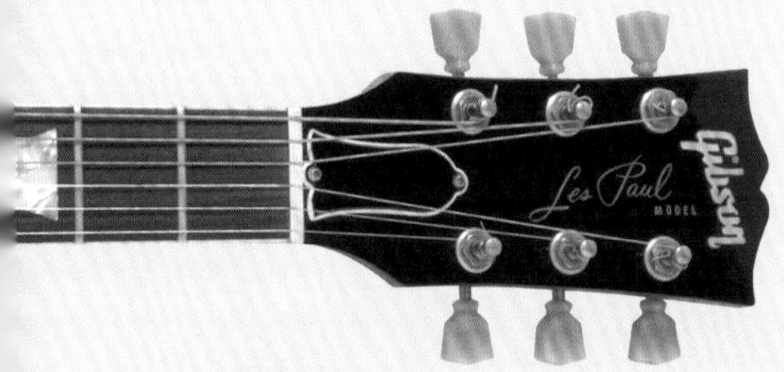

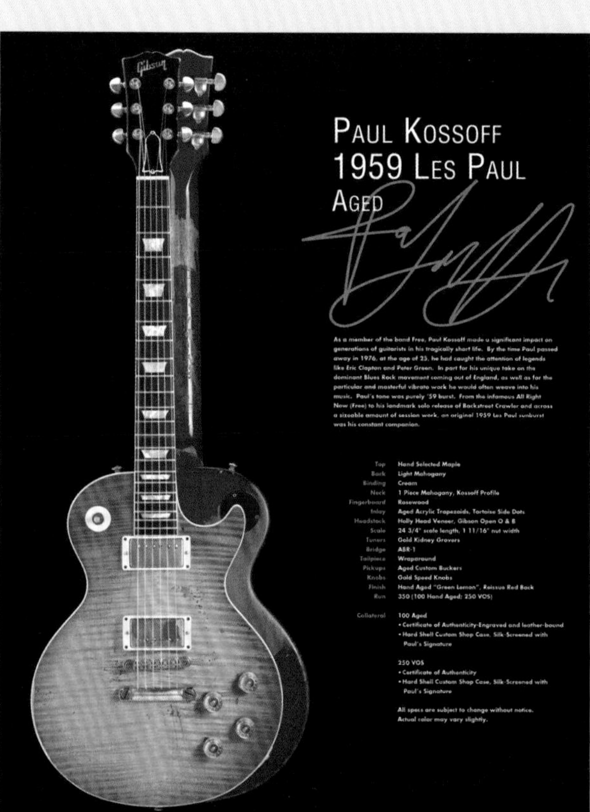

Promotional leaflet for a Paul Kossoff Burst, 2012.

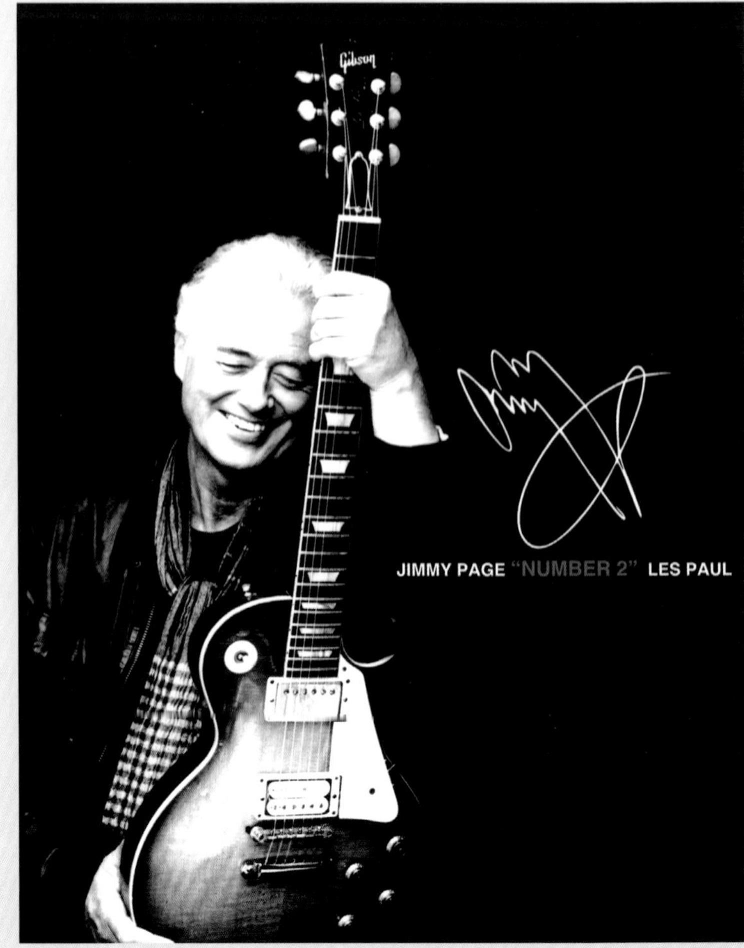

Jimmy Page “Number 2” sales material, 2009.

If Eric Clapton’s missing Beano Burst excites fans of the Gibson Les Paul Standard the most, then a close second (and third) would be the two Les Pauls that Jimmy Page used during his time with Led Zeppelin. And in this case, the two guitars certainly still exist, quite safe in Page’s keeping.

Page acquired his first Burst when Joe Walsh turned up at a Zep gig in San Francisco in 1969. Page was tiring of his road-weary Telecaster, and he quickly realized that Walsh’s Burst was gorgeous and easy to play. Later, Page recalled paying $500 for the guitar; Walsh remembered $1,200. Either amount would turn out to be a bargain, as the Les Paul served as Page’s main guitar through Led Zep’s glory years. He bought a second one, which inevitably became known as Number 2, in the 70s, a ’59 Burst that he used primarily as a backup to Number 1.

Not only did Page and Burst create a revered and unforgettable on-stage image, but in the studio he reminded a generation of guitarists and guitar fans just what a sunburst Les Paul could do in imaginative hands. For many, this would remain unsurpassed as the definitive combination of player and instrument, a 70s pairing to rival Clapton and Burst in the 60s.

In 2004, Gibson issued the Jimmy Page #1 1959 Les Paul, in three versions: a small number with aged finish, signed and hand-numbered by Page; some further limited-edition guitars aged but unsigned; and an unlimited edition with lightly-aged V.O.S. finish (known at the time as the Custom Authentic finish). A remake of Page’s Number 2 Burst followed five years later. Gibson has produced a number of other artist-model Bursts, including instruments named for Billy Gibbons, Mick Ralphs, and Slash, among many more.

GIBSON BILLY GIBBONS “PEARLY GATES” 1959 LES PAUL AGED

THIS EXAMPLE: ***2009***

ZZ Top guitarist Billy Gibbons acquired his beautiful ’59 Burst in 1968 and named it Pearly Gates. Gibson’s re-creation followed its Bursts named for Duane Allman, Jimmy Page, Gary Rossington, and Slash.

GIBSON JIMMY PAGE #1 1959 LES PAUL AGED
THIS EXAMPLE: ***2004***
Detailed re-creations of Jimmy Page's famous Les Pauls came in 2004 (this limited-edition lookalike of his Number 1 Burst) and 2009 (Number 2).

Slash "Appetite For Destruction" promo leaflet, 2010.

GIBSON MICK RALPHS '58 LES PAUL STANDARD REPLICA
THIS EXAMPLE: ***2017***
Gibson created this limited-edition remake in 2017 of a guitar once owned by Mick Ralphs, best known for his work with Bad Company.

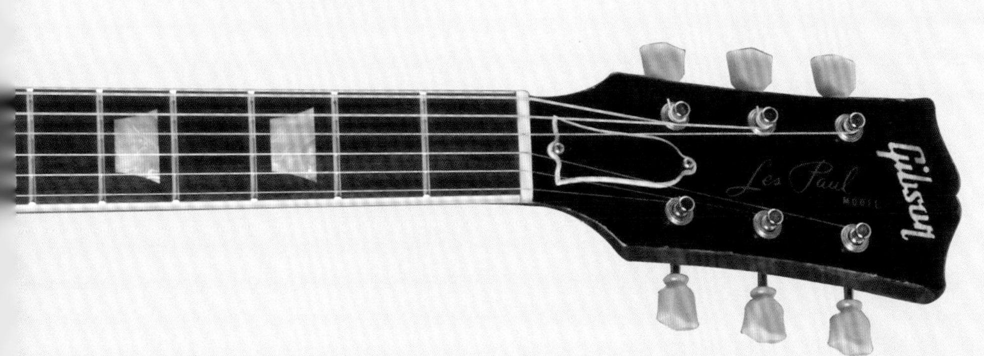

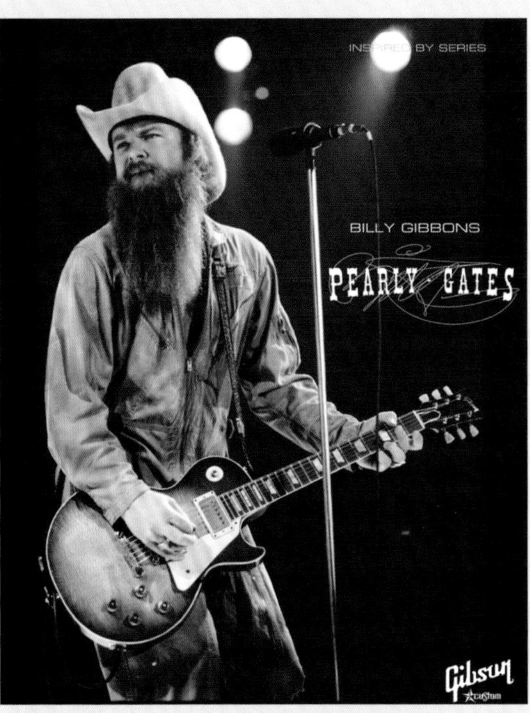

Promotional sheet for Billy Gibbons Pearly Gates model, 2009.

A number of US dealers in the 70s and 80s wanted new versions of the sunburst Les Paul Standard made originally from 1958 to '60, but Gibson seemed unaware of the demand that was growing for this kind of instrument among guitarists. Some of those dealers, including Strings & Things in Memphis and Jimmy Wallace at Arnold & Morgan in Dallas, persuaded Gibson to make specials for them.

Gibson's own first stab at making a production guitar intended to reflect the style of the original sunburst Les Paul came in 1980 with the shortlived Heritage Series Standard-80 models, which moved a little closer to older pickup specs and boasted pretty figured-maple tops. In 1982, Gibson's Kalamazoo factory made the limited-run Les Paul Standard 82, yet another try at a modern Burstalike, set apart from the Heritage primarily by its one-piece neck.

Gibson's Reissue Outfits, effectively an attempt to re-create more accurately the old-style Burst and Goldtop, were introduced in 1983, driven by continuing demand from customers who wanted the features of the hallowed 50s instruments. The Heritage models had been half-hearted reincarnations; these Outfits were the next steps, and they first appeared on the company's pricelists in '85. There was some way to go before detail-conscious customers were happier, but Gibson was at least starting to recognize some of the original features it needed to try to replicate more accurately.

Another step forward was the Les Paul Classic, introduced in 1990, which hinted at features of a '60 Burst, although the pickups were definitely modern. A year or so later, in '91, the regular Outfit-style reissue was revised and split into two models, effectively the Standard '59 Flametop Reissue and the Standard '60 Flametop Reissue—and this was where Gibson's proper, modern reissue started. The guitars had the "correct" details of the Classic plus some traditional-sounding humbuckers.

GIBSON LES PAUL REISSUE
THIS EXAMPLE: ***1987***
Gibson introduced a proper reissue programme in the early 80s, and this is an example that shows how the company was moving toward a more authentic re-creation of the originals.

GIBSON JIMMY WALLACE LES PAUL STANDARD
THIS EXAMPLE: ***1982***
Some US dealers, such as Jimmy Wallace in Texas, ordered Burst-like specials from Gibson, which at the time was not making production models of this type.

Les Paul Series

This is the guitar that transformed an era and became an industry standard. An instrument which transcends imprecise stylistic conventions. A guitar as much at home in the midst of mega-watt heavy metal as in the hands of a jazz musician.

This is the Gibson Les Paul model, namesake of a master innovator and peerless musician — thirty years after its introduction, still ahead of its time.

The composition of the Les Paul model is legend: the mahogany body for richness, warmth and broad harmonic spectrum; the arched maple top for brilliance, clarity and sustain.

Bonded to a one-piece mahogany neck and powered by Gibson's "Pat. Appl. For"™ humbucking pickups, the Les Paul model delivers a broad tonal range from crisp, biting treble to crystalline midrange to luxuriously smooth bass.

Today there is a family of Les Paul instruments, each bearing that unmistakable identity of tone recognized around the world as the Les Paul sound, yet each with important distinctions for the discerning player.

The Les Paul Standard represents the culmination of more than 30 years of design and technological evolution. We've combined the best ideas and most requested features from three decades of player input to provide you with the quintessential electric guitar.

Gibson provides the distinctive deep-dish arched top which originally set the Les Paul apart from assembly line instruments. We've revived the skinny SP-I headstock with its vintage 17-degree head pitch. It's part of what produced the country twang and blues shout so revered in classic models of the late 50's.

Gibson has also recreated its original "Pat. Appl. For"™ pickups — complete with robust bass response and glistening high end.

Today's Les Paul Standard is 30 years of electric guitar in the electric guitar that made history.

The Les Paul Custom is the time-tested classic of the line. The Custom is distinguished by a larger peghead, gold-plated hardware, multiple body bindings both top and back, and more elaborate pearl position markers and peghead inlay.

Many players express a preference for the Custom's ebony fingerboard, perceiving that it yields a brighter, more staccato response.

And for those who prefer the look of chrome, Gibson also offers the Les Paul Custom with chrome-plated parts.

The Les Paul Deluxe, cousin of the Les Paul Standard, features most of the same design innovations and aesthetic touches.

The real difference is in the electronics.

Smaller than Gibson's original humbucking pickup design, the Deluxe humbucking pickup is preferred by players who require a tighter, crisper sound. These pickups enable Deluxe Humbuckers™ to yield increased high frequency output, thus making the Les Paul Deluxe model ideal for players who require a sharp, distinctive attack.

For specifications on the Les Paul Standard, see the following page.

Sumptuous coverage of the reissue model, Gibson catalogue 1983

GIBSON LES PAUL CLASSIC
THIS EXAMPLE: ***1990***
Moving into higher gear as the 90s dawned, Gibson became yet more serious about remaking Burst-style instruments, hinted at here with the unsubtle "1960" on the pickguard of this first-year Classic model.

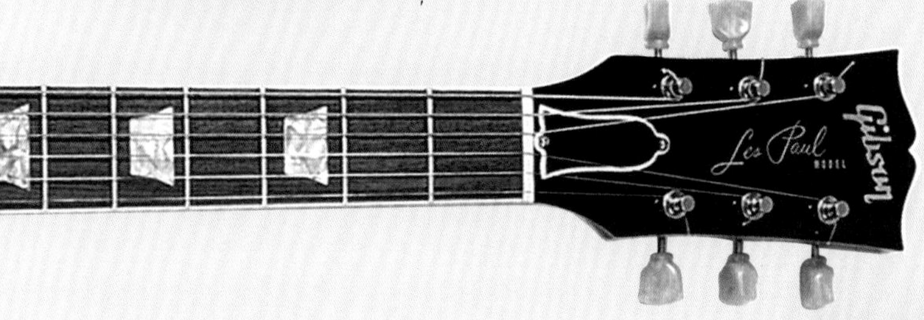

GIBSON HERITAGE STANDARD-80 ELITE
THIS EXAMPLE: ***1982***
The Heritage Standard Les Pauls, introduced in 1980, marked a turning point for Gibson, who seemed at last to become aware of the demand for Les Pauls with features similar to the 1958–60 sunburst classics.

Ibanez® ELECTRIC GUITAR
Model No. 2351M
FULL LENGTH: 40"   BODY: 17½" × 12⅜"
BODY DEPTH: 2"   NECK: 1⅝"
Solid body in contoured MAPLE top, back and sides are finished in mahogany. Detachable neck incorporating adjustable truss rod. Rosewood fingerboard with fancy pearloid position markers and white bound edges. Two chrome plated pickup units with separate polepieces. White laminated pickguard. Entire instrument is mirror polished by hand.
Complete with lead and plush-lined carrying case.

PRINTED IN JAPAN

Ibanez, an early Burst copyist, 1972 catalogue.

GIBSON '58 LES PAUL STANDARD 50th ANNIVERSARY AGED
THIS EXAMPLE: ***2008***
Fifty years after the first appearance of the sunburst Les Paul—the "Burst" to its fans—Gibson issued an anniversary model to mark the event, this one with a gently aged finish.

Nancy Wilson and Burstalike from Gibson's budget Epiphone brand, 2005.

In the early 90s, Gibson made a fresh start on the quality and detail of its Custom Shop reissues of classic 50s models, including the Les Paul Burst. In the process of sourcing original guitars to provide the kind of information they needed, the Custom Shop team examined several dozen Bursts from the '58–'60 period. They discovered that there was no super-correct guitar to reissue, and instead took the best attributes of each instrument—cosmetics, carving, and so on—and combined them.

Since that time, reissue Bursts have been in the Gibson line constantly, with various model names. Over the years, they've been gently and regularly tweaked to bring them ever closer to the original instruments of those hallowed three years. No detail has been too small for attention. Usually there's a '58, '59, and '60 model, sometimes with options on quality of top figure and, starting in 1999, an option of aged finish.

Tom Murphy developed the aged finish, at first at Gibson and from 1994 at his own Guitar Preservation company. Murphy's experience in refinishing and restoring old guitars made it natural to "age" the finished job, blending in new areas to sit more comfortably with the original worn guitar. He wasn't alone in developing this technique: some repairers had, like Murphy, been using a version of the idea in their own work, making good after visible repairs to merge them into the overall look and feel of an older instrument.

The first Gibson to benefit from the aged look was the Standard '59 Reissue Aged model, which officially started life as part of the Custom Shop line in 1999. The paint colors were made to look faded, the nickel parts on the instrument, such as the pickup covers, were realistically tarnished, and the lacquer "skin" was checked and effectively dulled. Remarkably, the guitar really did look old and broken-in.

1994 catalogue page for '59 and '60 Burst reissues.

1959 - 1960

In 1958, Gibson made one more change to the classic Les Paul Standard. By discontinuing the traditional Gold finish and introducing the new Cherry Sunburst effect, Gibson created what was to become the most collected guitar today - the "Sunburst" Les Paul Standard. The 1959 and 1960 Les Paul Reissues are direct descendants of this legendary instrument. As with the rest of the Historic Collection's Les Pauls, all of the necessary appointments are present. The AAA maple "dish" is carved with the same distinct character as the original Les Paul "Sunburst" and appointments such as a holly wood headstock veneer are topped off with a silk screened Les Paul logo. The '59 Reissue maintains the neck profile made famous by its historic counterpart while the '60 Reissue's neck provides the fast action made famous by the 1960 Les Paul. These guitars should be considered as the grand finale to any Les Paul collection.

'59 Les Paul Flametop
Heritage Cherry Sunburst

'59 / '60 Les Paul Flametops *Heritage Cherry Sunburst*

Pickups	Two '57 Classic HBs
Controls	Two volume, two tone, 3-way switch
Hardware	Nickel
Scale /Nut width2	24 ¾" / 1 11/16"
Fingerboard/Inlay	Rosewood 22 fret / Trapezoid
Neck Shape	1959 vintage / 1960 Slim taper LP
Binding	Body / Neck
Bridge/Tailpiece	Original ABR Tune-o-matic / Stop bar
Materials	Carved maple top, Mahogany back, One-piece mahogany neck
Finish	Heritage Cherry Sunburst, Heritage Darkburst

'60 Les Paul Flametop
Heritage Cherry Sunburst

A Custom Shop promo sheet, 2003.

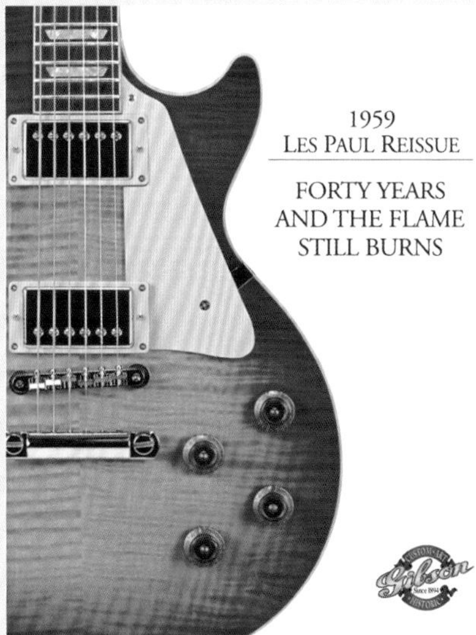

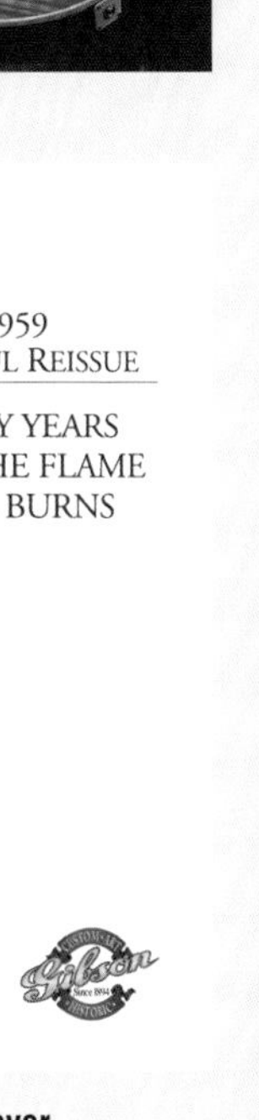

Fortieth birthday, 1999 catalogue cover.

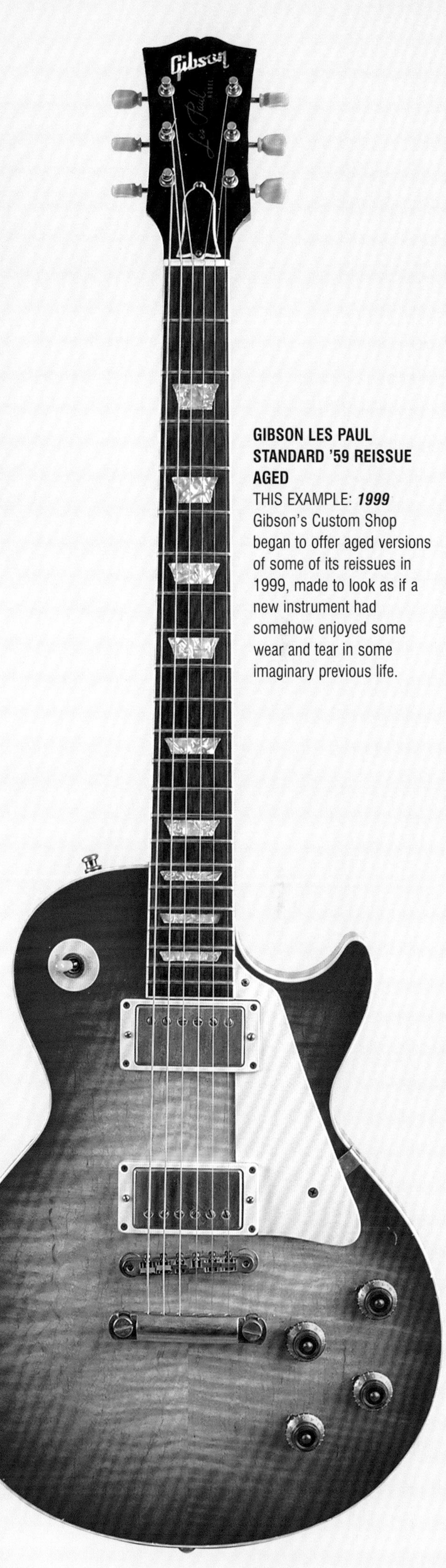

GIBSON LES PAUL STANDARD '59 REISSUE AGED
THIS EXAMPLE: ***1999***
Gibson's Custom Shop began to offer aged versions of some of its reissues in 1999, made to look as if a new instrument had somehow enjoyed some wear and tear in some imaginary previous life.

GIBSON LES PAUL HISTORIC 1959 REISSUE
THIS EXAMPLE: ***2001***
Into the 21st century, and Gibson's Custom Shop was gradually evolving and improving the detail and accuracy of its reissue models, a process that appeared to be continuing as this book went to press.

GIBSON LES PAUL STANDARD HP
THIS EXAMPLE: ***2018***
In 2015 Gibson introduced two levels of Standard: HP (High Power) or Traditional. The HP has a weight-relieved body with extra-flamey top and tapered heel, G-Force autotuners, zero fret, and various control options.

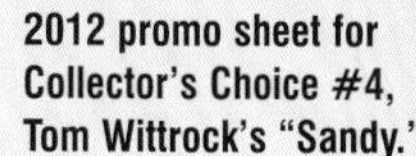

2012 promo sheet for Collector's Choice #4, Tom Wittrock's "Sandy."

2007 Gibson catalogue cover reveals the beauty of the Burst.

GIBSON COLLECTOR'S CHOICE #24 CHARLES DAUGHTRY 1959 LES PAUL "NICKY"
THIS EXAMPLE: ***2015***
Gibson Custom's Collector's Choice series continued with this gorgeous limited-edition re-creation of a classic '59 Burst owned by collector Charles Daughtry.

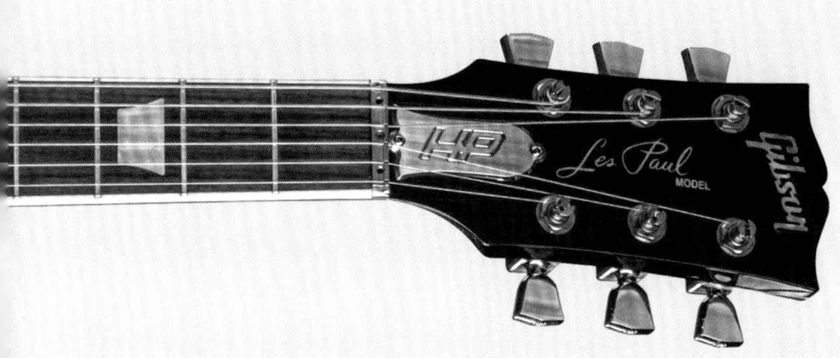

The first collectors were guitarists who simply began to accumulate more instruments as they needed or wanted them. If you own more than one guitar, you have a collection. Perhaps the small image of Eric Clapton with a Burst on the back of the 1966 *Beano* album started the old-electrics-are-good movement. The notion was well under way by the mid 70s that, somehow, only old guitars were worthy of attention by real players. Old guitars can be good or bad, of course, as can new guitars.

A development at Gibson that began in 2010 was what the Custom Shop called Collector's Choice. The idea here is to reproduce specific Bursts that have a reputation among collectors. The first was a reproduction of the ex-Peter Green, ex-Gary Moore Burst, but Collector's Choice Les Paul #2, which appeared in 2011, better defined the role of the series, being an exact-as-possible aged reproduction of a specific Burst owned by a leading collector. This one was Goldie—owners often give these Bursts names—an attractive faded '59 with wide, subtle flame, which has been owned by a number of collectors.

Gibson said in its promotional material for Collectors Choice: "Working with a specific '59 and its owner allowed Gibson Custom full access so that it could be analysed, digitally scanned, and measured from every conceivable perspective. … What is known is the guitar as it looks, feels, and plays today; the effects of time, light, dust, DNA, and every encounter that Goldie has had over the last 50 years has resulted in what Gibson Custom has worked so hard and for so long to bring to a very limited number of owners." More Collector's Choice limited-editions have followed, usually of 300 pieces, and each is issued with a certificate of authenticity.

GIBSON TRUE HISTORIC 1959 LES PAUL REISSUE
THIS EXAMPLE: ***2016***
The latest name at the time of writing for the Gibson Custom Shop's fastidiously accurate reissues was True Historic, which apparently offered "molecular level analysis" of some of its materials.

GIBSON LES PAUL TRADITIONAL
THIS EXAMPLE: ***2018***
Introduced in 2015 alongside the high-end HP, the Traditional model aimed to have 50s-style looks and features in a modern instrument, made at Gibson's Nashville factory.

The ES-355 was the first model Gibson added to the existing 335 to create a line of semi-solid thinline double-cut models. A handful of 355s were shipped at the end of '58, with production properly under way early the next year. The 355 was first seen in a late '58 ad in a trade magazine, where it was described as "Gibson's beautiful cherry-red ES-355T double cutaway model." It was obvious that the new model would be at the top of the new semi-solid line. Gibson called it "the ultimate in a double cutaway thin model Jazz guitar," hinting at the audience the company felt best suited to this new type of electric instrument.

Gibson declared the new model "a professional's guitar" with a "gleaming beauty" that made it "the focus of attention," and its features positioned the 355 well above the 335. It had an "ebony fingerboard [with] pearl block inlays," its Bigsby "manual vibrato" was gold-plated, as was the rest of the metalwork, and at first it was offered only as a regular mono guitar. The luscious new semi-solid had a faux-tortoiseshell pickguard and boasted multiple binding on the neck, on the body, and on the headstock, which also featured the luxurious split-diamond inlay that Gibson reserved for its high-end models.

The ES-355 had what Gibson called a "beautiful cherry-red finish." The company created the cherry finish on the 355 by staining the wood with a red dye and then adding a coat or two of clear lacquer on top, an appealing semi-transparent look that revealed any figuring present in the upper ply of maple on the body. With examples produced during the model's earliest years, the red proved likely to fade over time, and this sometimes developed into unusual and often pleasing shades of orange, watermelon, or brown.

Luxury in cherry red: ES-355, 1963 catalogue cover.

ORIGINAL **GIBSON ES-355TDSV**
THIS EXAMPLE: ***1960***
From 1959, the cherry-finish 355 was offered with regular mono wiring (355TD), or with stereo wiring and the addition of a six-way Varitone selector (355TDSV) like this example.

ORIGINAL **GIBSON ES-355TD**
THIS EXAMPLE: ***1959***
The 355 was a high-end Gibson, with fancy inlays and gold-plated metalwork. The optional Bigsby vibrato fitted to this 355 required two pearl dots to cover the holes already drilled for the regular (but now unnecessary) tailpiece.

GIBSON ES-355 REISSUE
THIS EXAMPLE: ***2016***
A recent version of the 355 as produced by Gibson's Memphis factory, which had specialized in the company's hollowbody and semi-solid models since it was opened in 2000, although it faced closure as this book went to press.

GIBSON B.B. KING LUCILLE
THIS EXAMPLE: ***2010***
B.B. King started using an ES-355 in the 60s and played one throughout his career. Gibson first produced a King signature model in 1981, named the Lucille after King's nickname for his favorite guitars.

The man and the woman.

The man: B. B. King.
The woman: Lucille, the King's Gibson guitar.
They've been places few ever dream of getting.
To street and alley sounds that sting like brass on brick.
To the quiet, sharp crack of heartbreak.
To the chain-heavy thunder of a troubled mind.
To the cold singing of flophouse bed springs.
To long cold ribbons of misery-crying.
To the muffled wetness of pillow-hidden weeping.
To the bluest. The lostest. The downest.
To the top of the heap. The mountain. The world.
If you're going places on the guitar, wouldn't it be great to travel with a woman like Lucille?

Gibson
Chicago Musical Instrument Co.
7373 North Cicero Avenue, Lincolnwood, Illinois 60646.

B.B. King and one of his Lucille 355s in a 1972 ad.

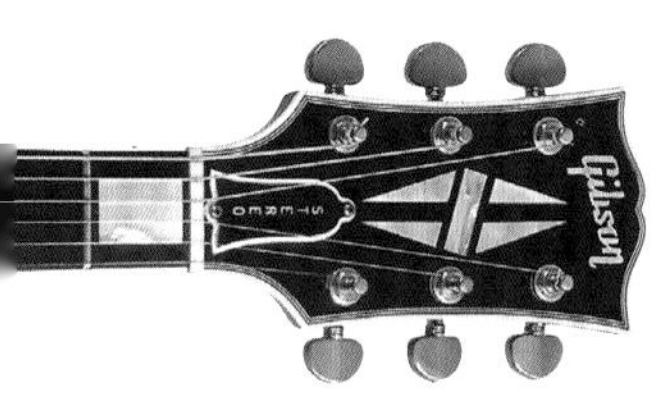

Gibson thin-body guitars feel just right

Whenever guitar players get to talking about their favorite instrument there's one thing they'll always say: *the feel is right!* And that's just what they've all been saying about Gibson's great new series of thin-body electrics. Yes, every one of these models—each with the Gibson *wonder-thin silhouette*—really does have that certain "feel" to it. And fitting so close and comfortably to your body, it'll let you reach many chords easily you've never played before.* You'll find the slender Gibson neck feels just right in your hand, and it's so easy to finger. That extremely fast, low action will make the strings seem feather-light to your touch. If you haven't done so already, be sure to find out all about this new all-star line of light-weight low-action thin-body Gibsons . . . each model so easy to handle, so easy to play. All have that quick response, balanced tone that always says instantly—Gibson.

Gibson INC.
KALAMAZOO, MICHIGAN

Gibson's "artist-enthusiast" Andy Nelson demos an early 355, 1958.

Tony Mottola goes stereo with a 355TDSV in this 1960 ad.

Catalogue cover, 1961, with olympic white Jazzmaster.

Fender decided to aim a new model at jazz players, naming it appropriately the Jazzmaster, introduced toward the end of 1958 at $329.50 as the firm's top-of-the-line solidbody. It had a striking body design, the waist with a more exaggerated offset than the Stratocaster. Fender applied for a utility patent for the offset design in 1958, granted a couple of years later. The patent was entirely concerned with what the company saw as the advantages the design would have for a seated guitarist—another clue that Fender believed the model would be taken up by jazz guitarists.

For the first time on a Fender, the Jazzmaster featured a rosewood fingerboard, aimed to provide a conventional appearance and feel for the targeted jazzmen. The guitar's floating vibrato system was new, too, with a tricky "lock-off" facility designed to prevent tuning problems if a string should break, but it did not succeed as well as the Strat vibrato.

The controls were elaborate for the time, designed so the guitarist, jazz-inclined or otherwise, could set up a rhythm sound and a lead sound, and then flick a small slide-switch to choose one or the other. But the system seemed complicated to players brought up on straightforward volume and tone controls.

The new model marked a change for Fender, an effort to extend the scope and appeal of its guitar line. Ironically, this was in part responsible for the Jazzmaster's lack of popularity relative to the Strat and Tele, mainly because many guitarists were not struck by the guitar's sounds and playability. But the idea of attracting flocks of jazz guitarists didn't work, because there was little to appeal to them in this new and rather awkward solidbody. They stuck with their hollowbody archtops, and mainstream Fender fans largely stuck with their Stratocasters and Telecasters.

User manual for the Jazzmaster, 1959.

Fender's ad-agency man Bob Perine came up with a series of striking ads that set guitars in unlikely situations.

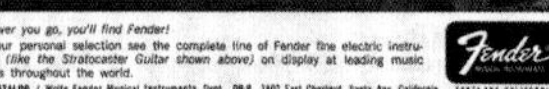

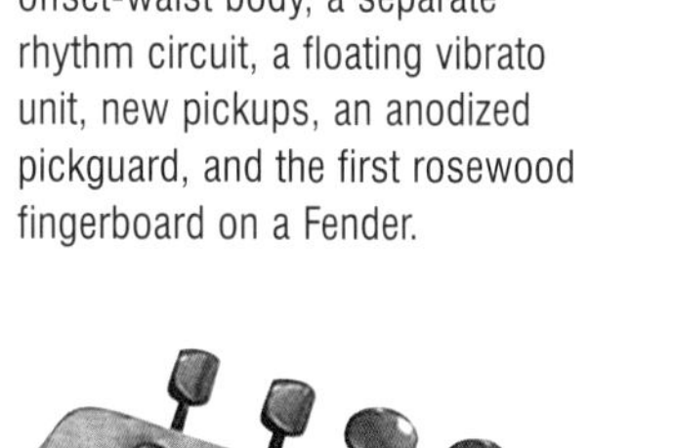

ORIGINAL **FENDER JAZZMASTER**
THIS EXAMPLE: ***1959***
The Jazzmaster had an enlarged headstock design and a distinctive offset-waist body, a separate rhythm circuit, a floating vibrato unit, new pickups, an anodized pickguard, and the first rosewood fingerboard on a Fender.

ORIGINAL **FENDER JAZZMASTER**
THIS EXAMPLE: ***1960***
The anodized guard of the original Jazzmaster was soon changed to a more practical plastic one in tortoiseshell or white, and Fender's custom colors—like this fiesta red—were becoming available.

Jazzmaster among the Fenders, 1959 ad.

Despite the failure of the original Jazzmaster to capture the imagination of jazz guitarists in the way that Fender seemed to have intended, in later years the model would have an impact on some other makers' designs and later still on a number of modern players. The design influence came from the Jazzmaster's offset-waist body, a relatively simple device that had an effect on a number of makers in Japan as well as in the United States and Europe.

During the 70s, Fender's CBS management cut back on the existing product lines and offered hardly any new models. The last Esquires and Duo-Sonics of the period were made in 1969, and by 1980 the Jazzmaster, and the Musicmaster, too, had been phased out of production. Most would be reissued later, but back in the day it made for a bare catalogue. However, this coincided broadly with a new popularity for some of those models among punk and new-wave guitarists. The punk ethic deemed it necessary to demonstrate that, at least in theory, you had little money. Jazzmasters and similar models were relatively unloved and therefore relatively cheap on the secondhand market compared to the burgeoning prices of what were now being touted as "vintage" Stratocasters and Telecasters.

One of the most notable of the new breed was Tom Verlaine in the New York group Television. Verlaine played a '58 Jazzmaster and showed its versatility on 1977's classic *Marquee Moon* album. In Britain, there was Robert Smith in The Cure and Elvis Costello fronting his Attractions, and both chose a Jazzmaster as their six-string of choice. A little later, back in the States, J. Mascis in Dinosaur Jr. relied on various Jazzmasters, notably a modified '63 that he'd picked up for $300. Fender would later introduce signature models for Mascis (2007) and Costello (2008).

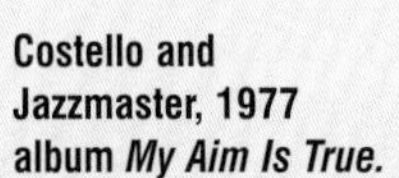

Costello and Jazzmaster, 1977 album *My Aim Is True.*

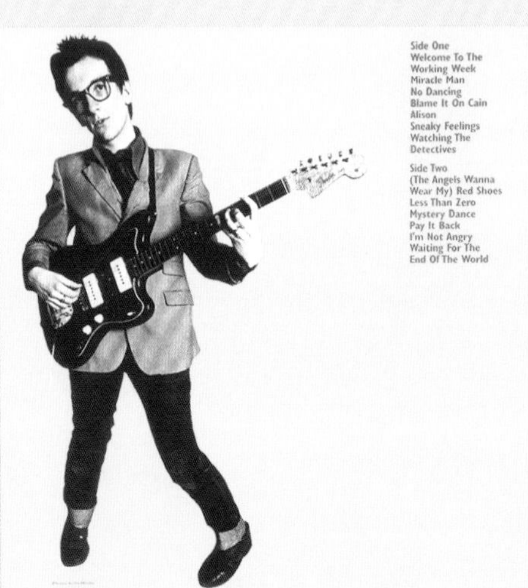

American Vintage '65 Jazzmaster in the 2013 catalogue.

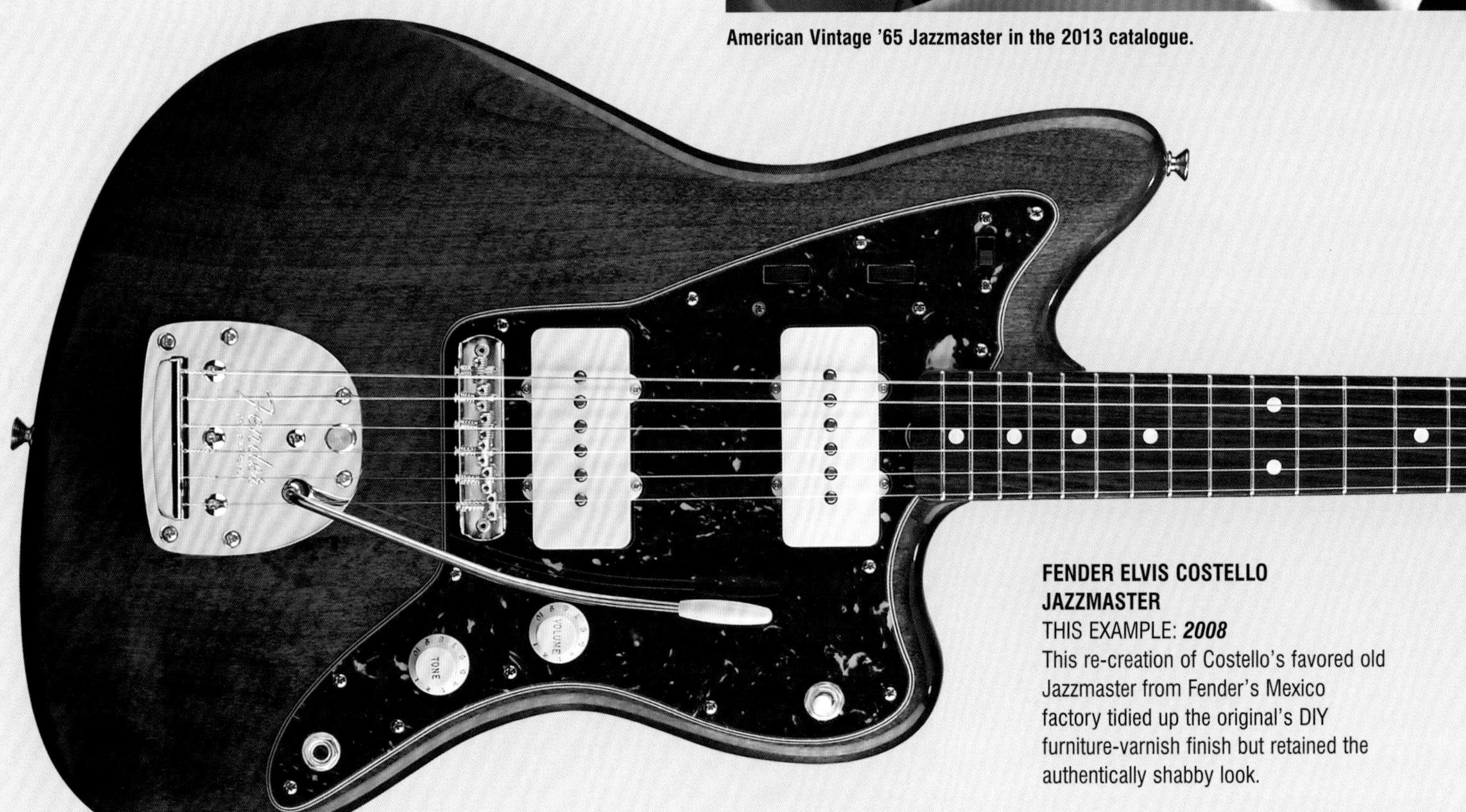

FENDER ELVIS COSTELLO JAZZMASTER
THIS EXAMPLE: ***2008***
This re-creation of Costello's favored old Jazzmaster from Fender's Mexico factory tidied up the original's DIY furniture-varnish finish but retained the authentically shabby look.

FENDER LIMITED EDITION 60th ANNIVERSARY '58 JAZZMASTER
THIS EXAMPLE: ***2018***
Fender's birthday celebrations for the 60-year-old Jazzmaster included this limited-edition re-creation of an early prototype, which had black pickup covers and Telecaster-style knobs.

2008 ad for a concert celebrating the Jazzmaster's 50th birthday.

FENDER J. MASCIS JAZZMASTER
THIS EXAMPLE: ***2007***
With its arresting purple sparkle finish and matching headstock, the Mascis signature Jazzmaster featured Fender's new Adjusto-Matic vibrato, which overcame the original's tendency to shift about or pop strings.

1958

Later mono and stereo Falcons on the '61 catalogue cover.

Gretsch released a new Chet Atkins model, the high-end Country Gentleman, in '58, and it became Atkins's favored guitar. It had a sealed body with "fake" f-holes and was the first Chet model with Gretsch's new Filter'Tron humbucking pickups, developed for the company by Ray Butts. It was also the first Gretsch hollowbody with a thinline body, about two inches deep, as opposed to other Gretsch models that were around an inch deeper.

Meanwhile, Jimmie Webster at Gretsch came up with Gretsch's Project-o-Sonic stereo guitars. In the first version of the idea, Webster and Butts simply split the windings of regular Filter'Tron humbuckers. When the player picked the lower three strings, sound was fed to one amp, while the top three strings fed sound to a second amp.

The system was launched during '58 as an option available on the Country Club and the White Falcon, but as we'll see there would be later variations. Through the rest of the 50s and into the early 60s, Gretsch called the system Project-o-Sonic (Country Club) and Super Project-o-Sonic (Falcon), only calling the models Stereo in pricelists and catalogues from about 1967.

These first stereo Gretsch guitars had the bridge pickup located much closer to the neck pickup than usual. The control layout and functions were similar to a regular guitar with two Filter'Trons, but the master volume knob on the cutaway bout was replaced with a three-way switch that selected various combinations of pickups and amps, while the two switches on the upper bout offered independent control of tonal emphasis for each pickup. A special Dual Guitar Cord connected the guitar to a Dual Jack Box, which provided two more jacks to connect to the two amplifiers necessary for stereo reproduction. Gretsch offered its own pair of amps to make a complete stereo outfit.

ORIGINAL **GRETSCH COUNTRY CLUB PROJECT-O-SONIC 6103**
THIS EXAMPLE: ***1959***
The stereo Country Club was called the Project-o-Sonic, while the stereo White Falcon was promoted to the Super Project-o-Sonic, and they had modified control layouts.

Jimmie Webster's stereo showcase album, Unabridged, 1958.

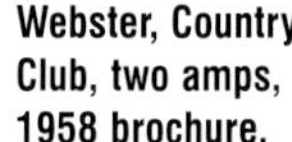

Webster, Country Club, two amps, 1958 brochure.

ORIGINAL **GRETSCH CHET ATKINS COUNTRY GENTLEMAN 6122**
THIS EXAMPLE: ***1959***
A high-end addition to the Chet Atkins line, the Country Gent had new Filter'Tron humbuckers and a sealed body with "fake" f-holes.

ORIGINAL **GRETSCH WHITE FALCON SUPER PROJECT-O-SONIC 6137**
THIS EXAMPLE: ***1958***
Gretsch's Project-o-Sonic models, launched in '58, were the first stereo guitars. They had split pickups that fed sound to two separate amps.

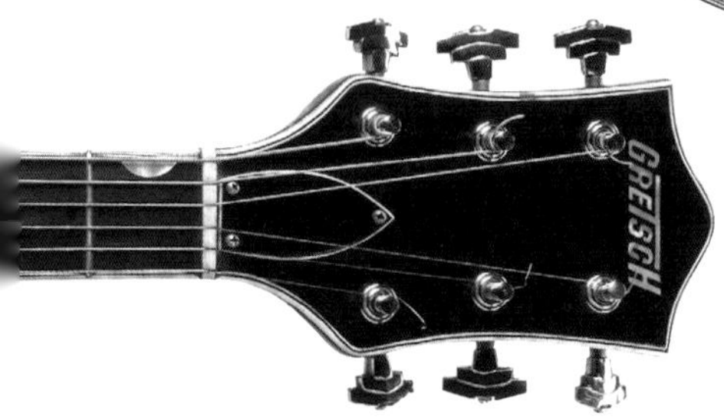

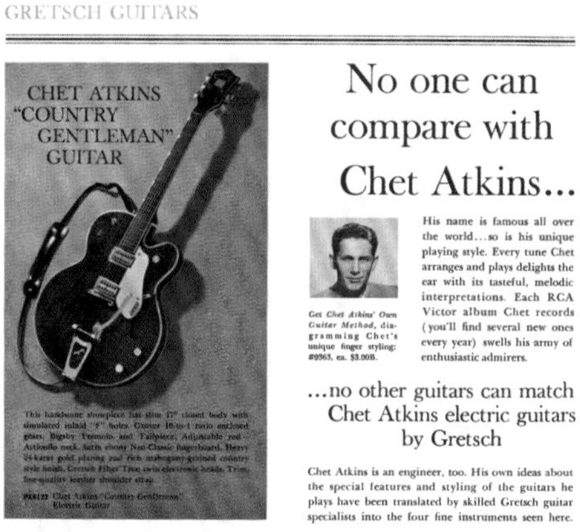

The "handsome showpiece" Country Gent in Gretsch's 1959 catalogue.

GRETSCH GUITARS

CHET ATKINS "COUNTRY GENTLEMAN" GUITAR

No one can compare with Chet Atkins...

Get *Chet Atkins' Own Guitar Method*, diagramming Chet's unique finger styling: #9363, ea. $3.00B.

His name is famous all over the world...so is his unique playing style. Every tune Chet arranges and plays delights the ear with its tasteful, melodic interpretations. Each RCA Victor album Chet records (you'll find several new ones every year) swells his army of enthusiastic admirers.

...no other guitars can match Chet Atkins electric guitars by Gretsch

Chet Atkins is an engineer, too. His own ideas about the special features and styling of the guitars he plays have been translated by skilled Gretsch guitar specialists into the four fine instruments seen here.

GRETSCH VINTAGE SELECT EDITION '59 CHET ATKINS COUNTRY GENTLEMAN HOLLOW BODY 6196T-59
THIS EXAMPLE: ***2017***
Gretsch's Vintage Select Edition series hosted this detailed reissue of the single-cut Gent, its '59 features updated with TV Jones Super'Tron pickups and a modified control layout.

1958

In 1958, Gretsch marked the 75th anniversary of its formation by issuing a pair of special Anniversary model guitars. The company had already tried the idea with 70th anniversary accordions in 1953. Anniversary models became relatively commonplace in later decades, usually an excuse to mark the birthday of the introduction of a classic model by offering a high-end re-creation. This was an early showing for the idea, and in this case it allowed the Gretsch company to demonstrate how much older it was than its competitors in the electric guitar world.

The two Anniversary models had all Gretsch's new appointments: one Filter'Tron pickup (Anniversary) or two (Double Anniversary), internal "trestle" bracing, arrow-through-G knobs, Space Control bridge, and Neo-Classic ("thumbnail") fingerboard markers. They came finished in an attractive two-tone green as well as sunburst. As instruments allegedly related to the importance of a solitary year in the company's history, they lasted remarkably well, continuing in the line until 1977 (and then revived in 1993). Nonetheless, the relatively low-end Anniversarys were stripped-down 6120s, something of a cheap celebration. "Priced for promotional selling" was the euphemism employed by Gretsch's admen.

Another new model launched by Gretsch in '58 was a further addition to the Chet Atkins line. Gretsch's scheme with the new relatively budget-price Chet Atkins Tennessean was to play on Atkins's growing fame to try to reach a wider audience. The red Tennessean was in effect a less fancy one-humbucker version of the 6120, with a list price upon its launch in 1958 of $295 (about $100 less than a 6120).

Gretsch now had three Chet Atkins models: relatively low (the $295 Tennessean); midrange (the $400 6120); and upper-mid (the $525 Country Gentleman). This followed the various systems used by many companies of offering clearly different models at a range of price-points.

ORIGINAL **GRETSCH ANNIVERSARY 6125**
THIS EXAMPLE: ***1959***
In 1958, Gretsch marked the 75th anniversary of the company's foundation with two models, this one-pickup Anniversary and the two-pickup Double Anniversary.

1958 Tennessean ad with Chet boosting the new mode.

Bow-ties and birthday cake, 1958 anniversary ad.

ORIGINAL **GRETSCH DOUBLE ANNIVERSARY 6118**
THIS EXAMPLE: ***1962***
The only hint of anniversary-style luxury on Gretsch's two birthday models, introduced in 1958, came with the optional two-tone green finish, officially known as smoke green.

ORIGINAL **GRETSCH CHET ATKINS TENNESSEAN 6119**
THIS EXAMPLE: ***1960***
The Tennessean, new for '58, was the lowest-priced Chet Atkins model, and at first it came with a single Filter'Tron humbucker, later swapped for two single-coils.

When Gretsch teamed up with Fender in 2004, a troubling omission from the new alliance's assets was the Chet Atkins name, along with some of the associated model names. This dated from Atkins's alliance with Gibson, which had begun in the 80s. A mutual acquaintance of Fender's Mike Lewis mentioned casually to him one day that he thought that someone closely linked to Chet Atkins's estate—Atkins had died in 2001—might be interested in Gretsch regaining the names. Lewis wasted no time in making contact, and luckily it happened to be the right time for all parties involved.

The news of the repaired links between the names of Gretsch and Chet Atkins was made public right at the start of 2007. "It is with great pleasure that Gretsch Guitars announces the return of the legendary Chet Atkins name to the iconic guitars he created and popularized throughout his storied multi-decade musical career," the press release declared. The newly allied Gretsch and Fender were already making these guitars, albeit some of them with necessarily altered names, so there was very little that needed to be done to change them, other than the name on the guitar. It seemed quite simply the right thing to do—and it was clear that Gretsch guitar fans felt the same way, too.

The renamed models would, in the coming years, be offered in various different styles and levels. Two names were completely reinstated: the Chet Atkins Hollow Body 6120 (since 1967 called the Nashville) and the Chet Atkins Country Gentleman 6122 (since 1989 called the Country Classic). Also, the Chet Atkins name was restored to the Solid Body 6121. The Chet Atkins Tennessee Rose 6119 was the only model that had to continue with its existing Gretsch name, because Gibson still had rights to the original name, the Tennessean.

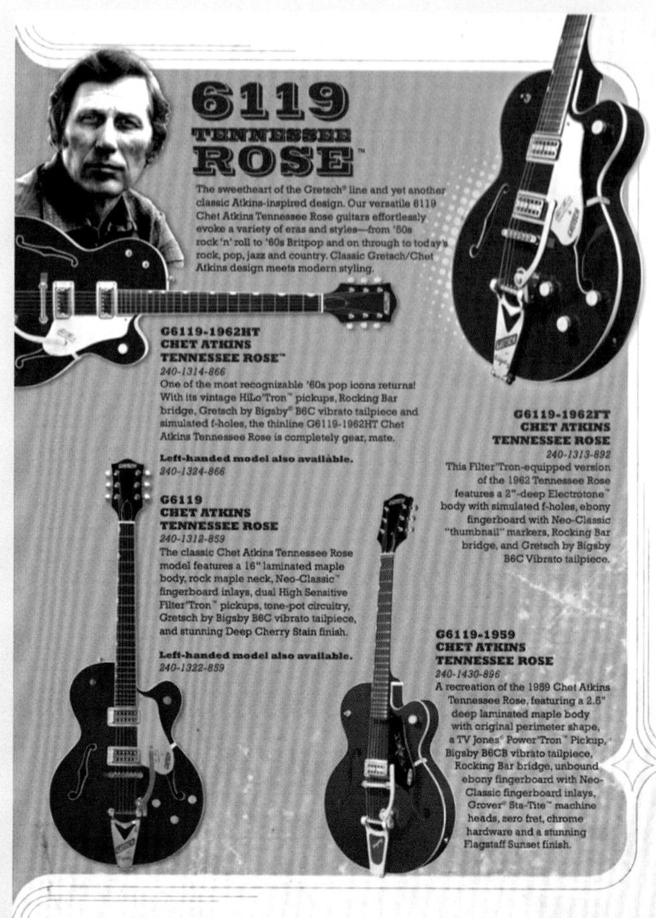

In this 2008 catalogue page, for Tennessean read Tennessee Rose.

GRETSCH VINTAGE SELECT EDITION '62 TENNESSEE ROSE HOLLOW BODY 6119T-62
THIS EXAMPLE: ***2017***
A remake of an early-60s Tennessean—although Gretsch cannot use that name because Gibson still has rights to the "Tennessean" name from the time when Chet Atkins was allied with that company.

No less than a 125th Anniversary model, 2008 catalogue.

A cool Anniversary model stars in this 2003 ad.

GRETSCH VINTAGE SELECT EDITION '60 ANNIVERSARY HOLLOW BODY 6118T-60

THIS EXAMPLE: ***2018***

The two-pickup Anniversary was first reissued in 1993, and this version in two-tone smoke green, a current model at the time of writing, is part of Gretsch's period-correct Vintage Select Edition series.

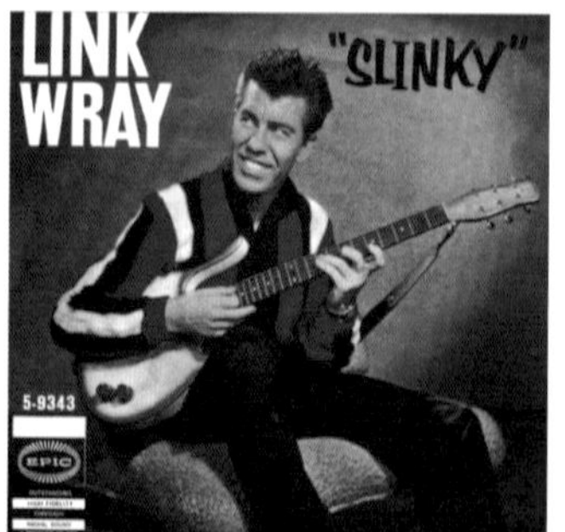

Link Wray and Guitarlin on a 45 from 1959.

Danelectro had introduced its U-series models earlier in the 50s, and the New Jersey company replaced them in 1958 with two new lines. The Guitarlin was a remarkable design, retaining the pine-frame and fiberboard construction style of the U models, but with a striking new body that had extremely deep double cutaways, allowing the bravest players to go for the highest of no fewer than 31 frets.

Danelectro's catalogue explained the model's name, claiming the extended fingerboard "combines the guitar and mandolin range … guitar tone in lower register shades to mandolin tone in upper register." The Guitarlin is also known as the Long Horn guitar, derived obviously from the shape of the body, but also this was the name given by Danelectro to the Guitarlin's bass brothers.

Also new for '58 was the Standard series, with a restrained double-cutaway body. The Standards are known also as Short Horn models, and again this relates obviously to the shape of the body, but also it derives from the name that Danelectro gave to a matching bass. The Standard came with one or two pickups and black or bronze finish: 3011 (one-pickup black), 3012 (one-pickup bronze), 3021 (two-pickup black), and 3022 (two-pickup bronze). The black Standard was also available with a simple vibrato bridge (and different headstock), which Danelectro called the Hand Vibrato models: 4011 (one-pickup) and 4021 (two-pickup), while a "white sunburst" Double Neck combined six-string guitar and four-string bass necks (3923).

The most visible player of a Danelectro Standard was Jimmy Page, who would acquire a 3021 during his pre-fame days as a studio guitarist in the mid 60s. When he went on to play his Dan'o on stage occasionally with The Yardbirds and then Led Zeppelin, he focussed attention on the model for a lot of players and collectors who otherwise would probably have continued to ignore it.

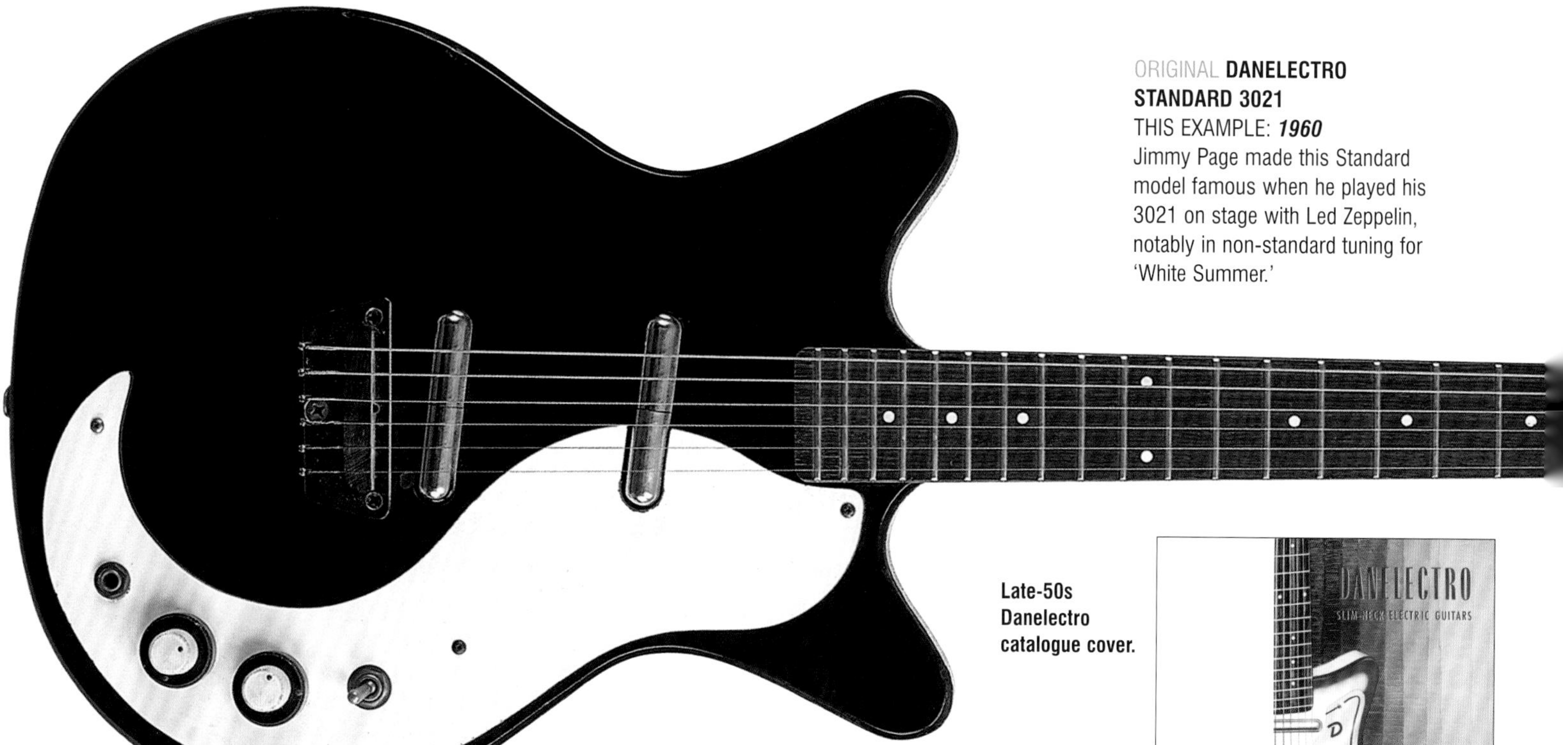

ORIGINAL **DANELECTRO STANDARD 3021**
THIS EXAMPLE: ***1960***
Jimmy Page made this Standard model famous when he played his 3021 on stage with Led Zeppelin, notably in non-standard tuning for 'White Summer.'

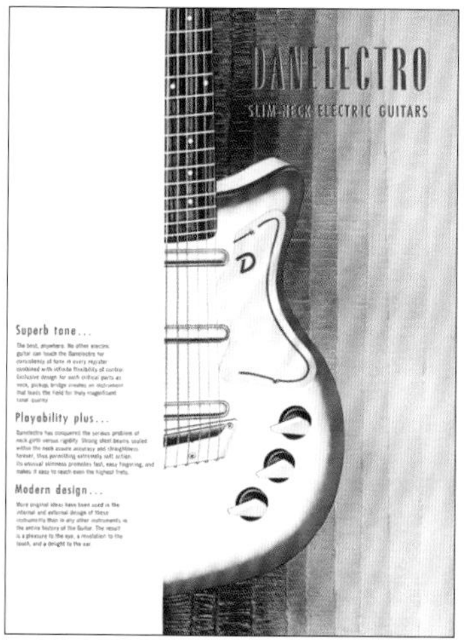

Late-50s Danelectro catalogue cover.

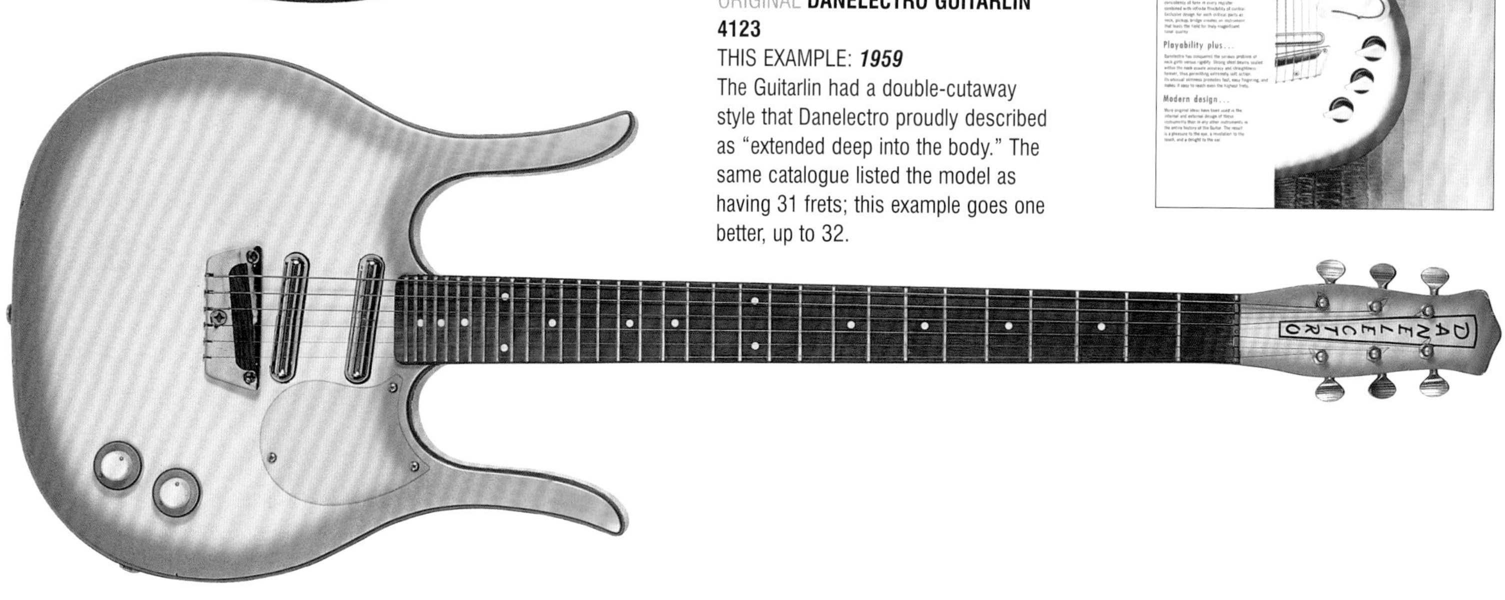

ORIGINAL **DANELECTRO GUITARLIN 4123**
THIS EXAMPLE: ***1959***
The Guitarlin had a double-cutaway style that Danelectro proudly described as "extended deep into the body." The same catalogue listed the model as having 31 frets; this example goes one better, up to 32.

ORIGINAL **DANELECTRO DOUBLE-NECK 3923**
THIS EXAMPLE: ***1964***

This double-neck, introduced in 1958, was relatively lightweight, thanks to the regular Dan'o construction using fiberboard front and back on a pine frame. The switch toggles between bass neck, guitar neck, or (for some reason) both necks.

The U-3 and two other U models were dropped in '58.

Dan'o Convertible, with or without pickup, 1959 catalogue.

Buy Both . . Save $10

Silvertone Single-pickup Electric Guitar plus Matching Amplifier

Separately total $67.90 $57.90

Beautifully matched for tone, performance and looks. Rich, gleaming lacquered brown finish.

Danelectro still supplied Sears with Silvertones, like this 1304, in 1958.

If there was one word that haunted the electric guitar industry in the 90s, it was retro. Toward the end of the decade, more guitar makers than ever were busily looking back to the past in a search for fresh inspiration, as the craze for retro flavors seemed to be everywhere. It's easy to understand why. Some makers felt there was almost no more to be done to the electric guitar, that it had reached its ultimate incarnations and that its general design, construction, and manufacturing systems were just about as perfect as they could get.

Instead of going forward, why not salvage the best factors that made past instruments so distinctive, and catch a bonus from the fashionable retro vibe? This was a grand theory, but in some ways it proved more difficult to put into practice. Getting too close to those atmospheric looks of the great guitars of the 50s and 60s could have nasty consequences if influence turned into theft. Some companies solved the problem by buying an old name and re-establishing the look.

Perhaps the most successful take on this idea was Danelectro, credited by many as popularizing the whole retro electric guitar movement. MCA had bought Danelectro, and then closed it in 1969. The founder, Nathan Daniel, died in 1994, and the following year the Evets Corporation obtained the rights to the Danelectro name. Evets introduced a line of Danelectro effects pedals in 1997, and then began to reissue Dan'o guitars during '98. The new Danelectros were similar in look and construction to the vintage instruments, including some classic-vibe models—such as the Longhorn, Standard, and Convertible—and some had reproduction lipstick-tube pickups. There were revised designs, too, such as the 59X, but the majority of these old-becomes-new models drew strongly from past glories.

DANELECTRO LONGHORN 58 GUITAR
THIS EXAMPLE: ***2015***
Based on the Guitarlin model first seen in 1958, this revised reissue settles on a more conventional 21-fret neck rather than the original's 31.

DANELECTRO CONVERTIBLE
THIS EXAMPLE: ***2014***
This one reproduces the original model, introduced in 1959, a double-cut acoustic guitar with a lipstick pickup fitted in the round soundhole, and adds a piezo pickup in the bridge.

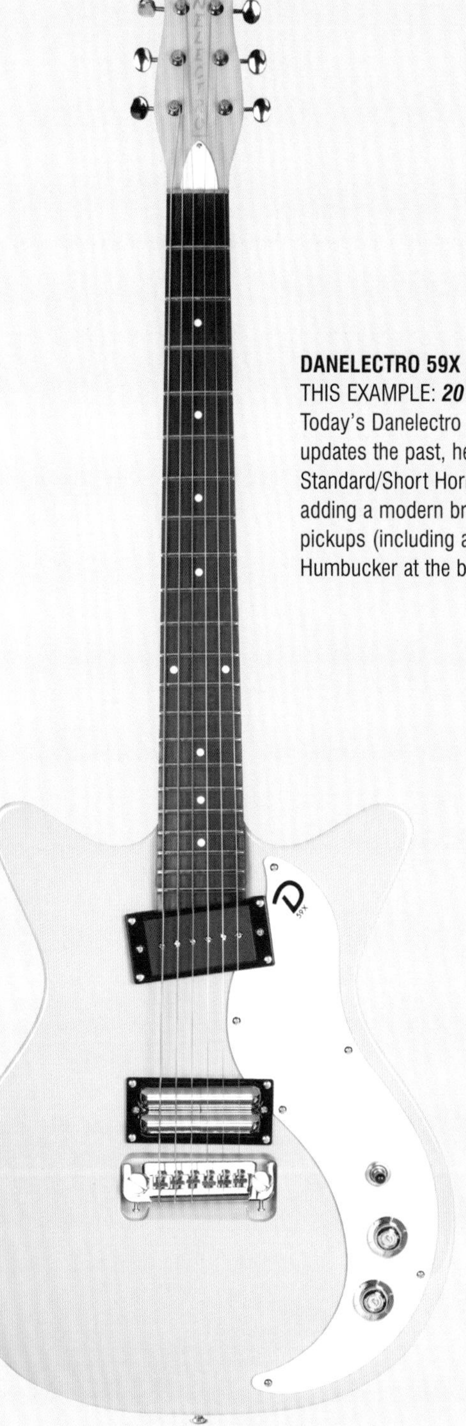

DANELECTRO 59X
THIS EXAMPLE: ***2018***
Today's Danelectro company updates the past, here taking the Standard/Short Horn style and adding a modern bridge and new pickups (including a Lipstick Humbucker at the bridge).

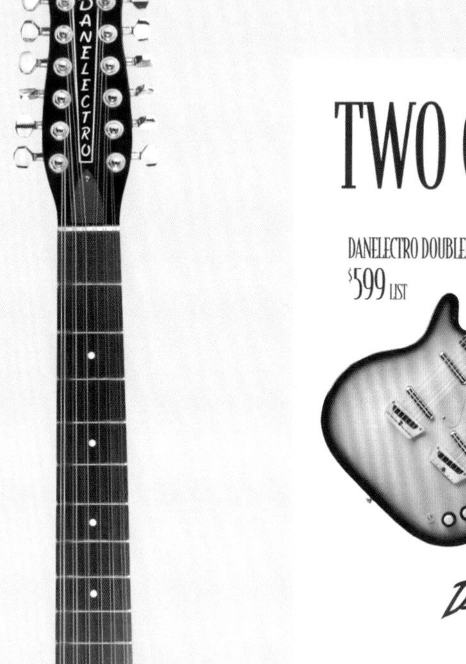

TWO COOL.

DANELECTRO DOUBLENECK
$599 LIST

For what you would pay for an "ordinary" guitar you can own a truly extraordinary one: The Danelectro Doubleneck. Choose 12 String or Baritone on top. 6 String on the bottom. Incredible tone. A blast to play.

Danelectro® SINCE 1947
TWO MUCH FUN.
www.danelectro.com

2000 ad confirms the return of the Double Neck.

DANELECTRO 12S
THIS EXAMPLE: ***2014***
A reissue of the Standard, late-50s style, also known as the Short Horn body, but here usefully offered as a twelve-string, a type that Danelectro never made back in the day.

Jimmy Page territory outlined in a 1998 reissue ad.

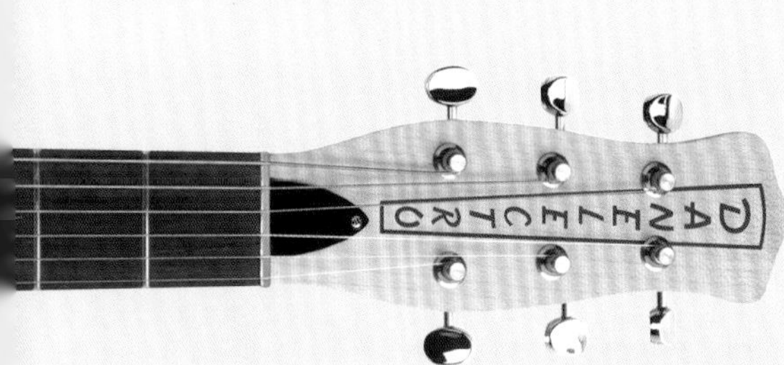

A new touch with Select-o-Matic in this Dan'o ad from 1999.

IT DOESN'T GET BETTER THAN THIS
www.danelectro.com

$299 LIST

Thousands of garage bands of the 60's cut their teeth on this one. The Danelectro 59-DC (Double Cutaway). Forty years later, top artists still record and perform with this great guitar.

Our re-issue features the genuine Lipstick® pickups. Dual concentric tone and volume controls. Same great Dano headstock. "Seal" pickguard. Large hollow inner cavity for a great open and "ringy" sound.

Don't miss out on the coolest new Dano!

Seven Great Colors!

DADDY O. YELLOW · COMMIE RED · LIMO BLACK · PEACHY KEEN · BEATNIK BURGUNDY · COOL COPPER · RETRO PURPLE

THE LEGEND CONTINUES

1958

Harmony of Chicago had a catalogue bursting with guitars by the late 50s, and there were some important additions to the line. The Meteor, introduced in 1958, was the company's first thinline hollowbody electric, with a shallow two-inch-deep body, fitted with a pair of DeArmond single-coil pickups and offered in sunburst (H70) or natural blonde (H71).

The Meteor proved popular among fledgling rockers, especially when Harmony was among the brands that became available in Britain after US import restrictions were lifted in 1959. Keith Richards bought a Meteor H70 in 1963 to fuel his early Stones efforts, no doubt influenced by Brian Jones's acquisition the previous year of a Stratotone H46, another model introduced by Harmony in 1958.

Left-handed guitarists in the 50s and 60s were often advised to learn to play right-handed, mainly because of the scarcity of left-handed instruments. Some left-handers turned a right-handed guitar around to face the "wrong" way, either without changing the strings (Albert King, for example) or taking the trouble to reverse the stringing (Jimi Hendrix, for very good example). The final option was to get a true left-handed guitar, with everything reversed. But the number of brands that offered them was limited, and it was always a matter of ordering one specially: a left-handed guitarist could not just walk in a store and try one. Gradually, this would ease, but back in the day, left-handers were poorly served.

Meanwhile in Japan, Guyatone was beginning to supply budget-price solidbody electrics to a number of overseas companies, including a few outlets in Europe. Guyatone had been in business since the 30s and introduced its first solidbody electric around 1955. The LG models that became available in the UK in '58 proved popular—some were branded Antoria or Star—and early customers included Hank Marvin and Jeff Beck.

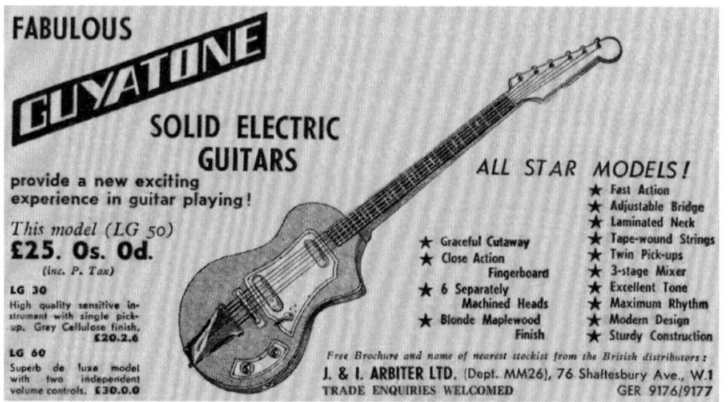

London shop ad for the Guyatone LG-50, 1960.

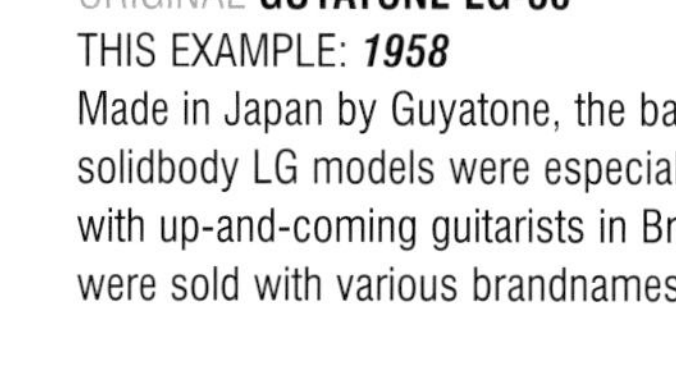

ORIGINAL **GUYATONE LG-30**
THIS EXAMPLE: ***1958***
Made in Japan by Guyatone, the basic solidbody LG models were especially popular with up-and-coming guitarists in Britain and were sold with various brandnames.

ORIGINAL **HARMONY STRATOTONE JUPITER H49**
THIS EXAMPLE: ***1960***
This semi-solid, introduced in 1958, has an array of controls that include a volume and tone knob per pickup, plus a "blend" control that adjusted the tonal balance between the two pickups when the selector was in the mid position.

The following four models are a new range of solid bodied instruments offering amazing value for money

The Guyatone L.G. 40 Model

Two pick-ups, tone, volume and selector controls all within easy reach when playing. Purfled edging to fingerboard and body. Single-sided machine heads. Beautiful shaded satinwood finish. Reinforced neck. Complete with lead.

Cash Price £21 . 0 . 0

Or by deposit of £2 and 12 monthly payments of £1 . 14 . 8 or 18 monthly payments of £1 . 4 . 2

The Guyatone L.G. 50 Model

An improved version of the above model

Attractive bird's-eye maple finish. Adjustable bridge. Pearloid fingerplate. Reinforced neck. Complete with lead.

Cash Price £25 . 0 . 0

Or by deposit of £2 . 10 . 0 and 12 monthly payments of £2 . 1 . 3 or 18 monthly payments of £1 . 8 . 8 or 24 monthly payments of £1 . 2 . 6

BELL

The Guyatone L.G. 60 Model

A superb instrument with improved pick-ups. Extra volume control. Reinforced neck. Micro adjustable bridge. Beautiful bird's-eye maple finish. Complete with lead.

Cash Price £30 . 0 . 0

Or by deposit of £3 and 12 monthly payments of £2 . 9 . 6 or 18 monthly payments of £1 . 14 . 6 or 24 monthly payments of £1 . 7 . 0

The Guyatone L.G. 120

A super double pick-up instrument with double cutaway. Large Pearloid fingerplate. Reinforced neck. Purfled edge fingerboard. Deep mahogany finish.

Cash Price £31 . 10 . 0

Or by deposit of £3 . 10 . 0 and 12 monthly payments of £2 . 11 . 4 or 18 monthly payments of £1 . 15 . 10 or 24 monthly payments of £1 . 8 . 0

Soft cover for all above models	£1 . 15 . 0
Fibre Case for all above models	£3 . 15 . 0
De luxe plush-lined plywood Case	£7 . 7 . 0

BELL

Britain's Bell mail-order catalogue features Guyatone models, 1961.

A bold claim in a 60s ad by Harmony.

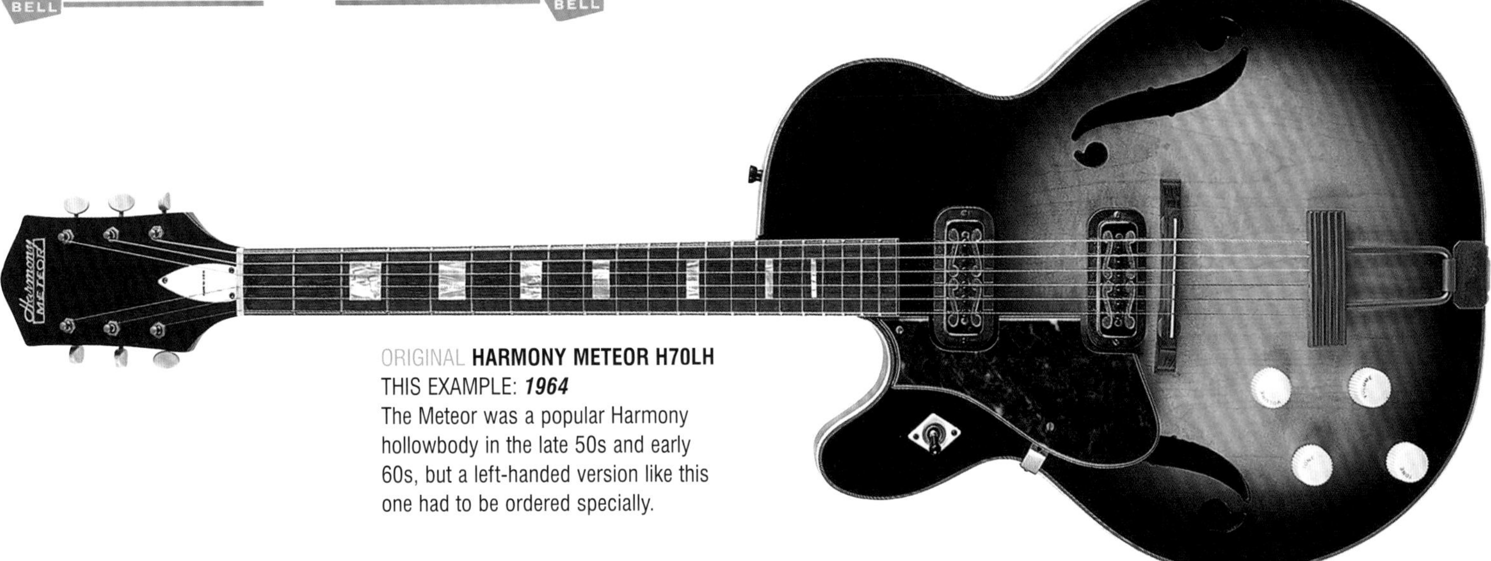

ORIGINAL **HARMONY METEOR H70LH**
THIS EXAMPLE: ***1964***
The Meteor was a popular Harmony hollowbody in the late 50s and early 60s, but a left-handed version like this one had to be ordered specially.

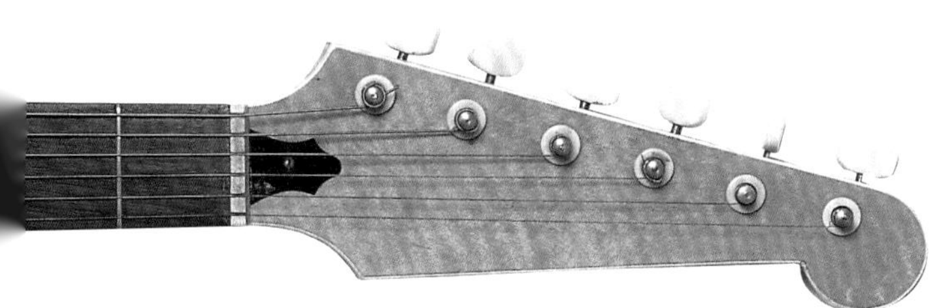

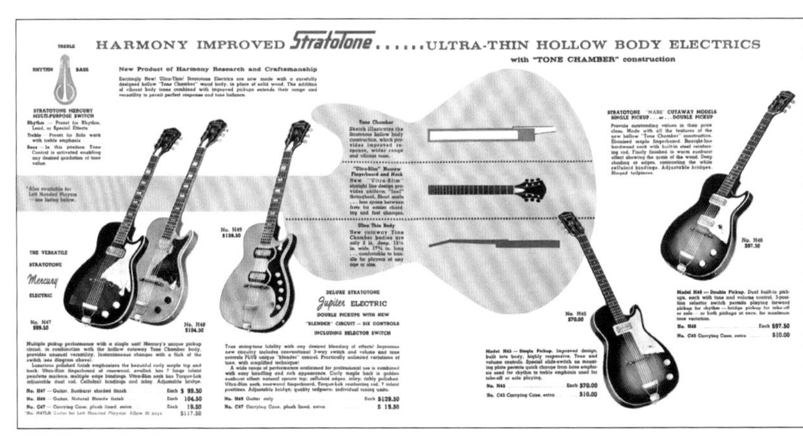

HARMONY IMPROVED Stratotone......ULTRA-THIN HOLLOW BODY ELECTRICS

with "TONE CHAMBER" construction

New Product of Harmony Research and Craftsmanship

STRATOTONE MERCURY MULTI-PURPOSE SWITCH

STRATOTONE "MARS" CUTAWAY MODELS SINGLE PICKUP . . . or . . . DOUBLE PICKUP

Harmony's Stratotone series, including Jupiter, 1959 catalogue.

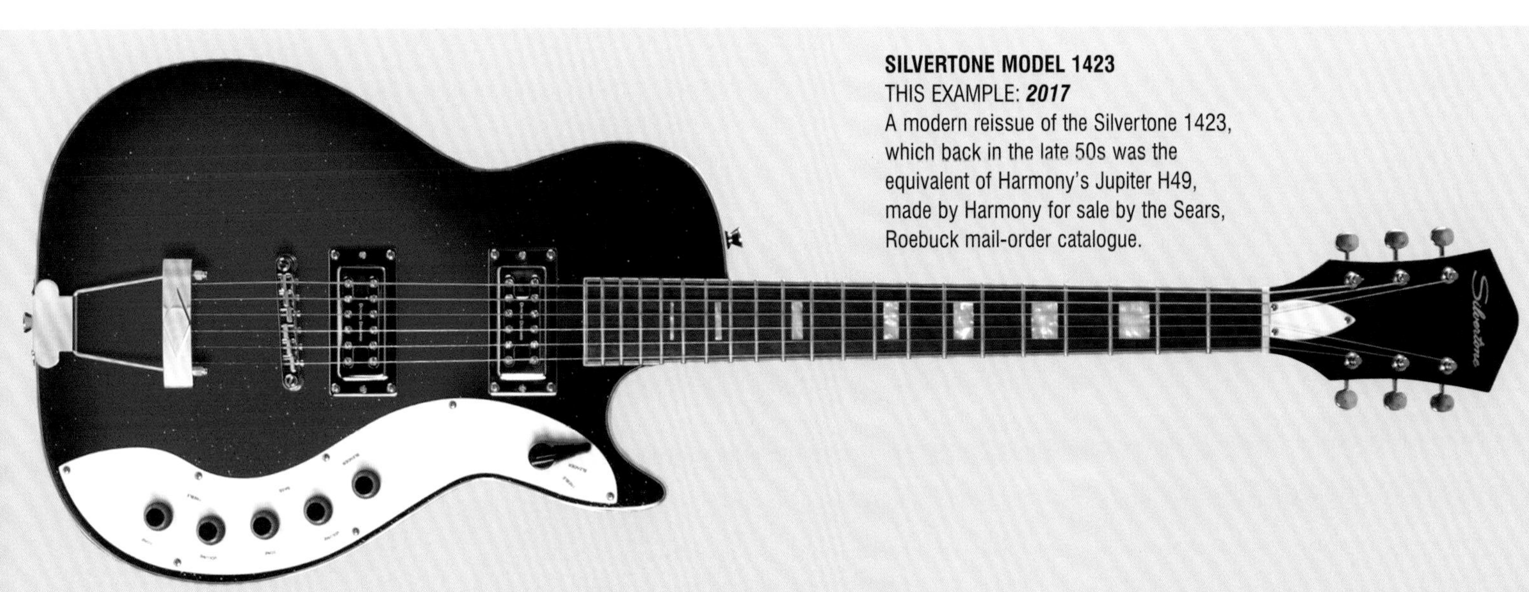

SILVERTONE MODEL 1423
THIS EXAMPLE: ***2017***
A modern reissue of the Silvertone 1423, which back in the late 50s was the equivalent of Harmony's Jupiter H49, made by Harmony for sale by the Sears, Roebuck mail-order catalogue.

North Iowa's Daily Newspaper Edited for the Home

MASON CITY GLOBE-GAZETTE

HOME EDITION

"The Newspaper That Makes All North Iowans Neighbors"

VOL. 97 | Associated Press and United Press International Full Lease Wires | MASON CITY, IOWA TUESDAY FEBRUARY 3, 1959 | No. 99

Four Killed in Clear Lake Plane Crash

- **BUDDY HOLLY** is killed in a plane crash in Iowa along with Ritchie Valens and The Big Bopper.

- **RUSSIA** launches Luna 1 into orbit around the sun, crashes Luna 2 into the moon, and uses Luna 3 to take the first photographs of the dark side of the moon.

- **CALIFORNIA** enacts the first car-exhaust emissions standards in the United States.

- **SOVIET LEADER** Nikita Khrushchev visits the United States. He is annoyed that for security reasons he is not allowed to tour Disneyland and is surprised at "how freely" women in America are dressed.

1959

- **BMC's** Mini, "the people's car," is launched on the UK market. Designed by Alec Issigonis, the £500 Mini is described by one newspaper as the vehicle "for which tens of thousands of economy motorists have been waiting." Meanwhile, the initial section of Britain's first motorway, the M1, is opened for traffic.

- **IN CUBA**, the government of dictator Fulgencio Batista is overthrown by a revolutionary movement led by Fidel Castro.

- **THE WORLD's** population is estimated at 2,900 million and is said to be increasing at just under two percent every year.

- **DIED**: Guitar Slim, Cecil B. De Mille, and Billie Holiday.

- **BORN**: Richie Sambora, Emma Thompson, and Bryan Adams.

1959

ORIGINAL **FENDER STRATOCASTER**
THIS EXAMPLE: ***1959***
During 1959, Fender changed the look of the Strat, most obviously by fitting it with a rosewood fingerboard, but also changing the pickguard to three-layer plastic and adding red into the sunburst finish.

'60 catalogue with Custom Esquire and Telecaster alongside regular models.

Bound bodies on Custom Esquire and Tele, 1960 ad.

ORIGINAL **FUTURAMA**
THIS EXAMPLE: ***1959***
The Czech-made Futurama was a loosely Strat-like solidbody distributed in the UK by Selmer of London, and it proved popular with early British rock'n'rollers, including George Harrison.

In the late 50s, Fender made a few adjustments to its electric guitars. We've seen how the Jazzmaster was the company's first electric with a rosewood fingerboard, and this was adopted for other Fenders around 1959, including the mighty duo of Stratocaster and Telecaster. The darker look of the rosewood board contrasted the pale color of the earlier maple, and as a general rule (despite various options at different times) it's a crude way to identify many 60s Strats and Teles from the earlier models.

Fender altered the look of the Strat's sunburst finish at the time, too, adding red to give a three-tone yellow-to-red-to-black effect. To cope with increased demand, four new factory buildings and a warehouse had been added in 1958 to the growing Fender site in Fullerton, and by '59 the number of employees at the various Fender locations had for the first time hit 100.

The last new Fender electrics of the 50s were the bound-body Custom versions of the Esquire and Telecaster, launched in 1959 and intended to add a little touch of luxury to the other otherwise somewhat spartan Tele. The Custom Esquire listed at $194.50 and the Custom Telecaster at $229.50, each $30 more than the regular unbound versions.

In Britain at the start of 1959, guitarists were still unable to buy new American guitars, thanks to longstanding US import restrictions. An alternative to the unobtainable Stratocaster came in the shape of the Futurama, produced in Czechoslovakia (now the Czech Republic) and first seen in Britain in 1958 thanks to Selmer, who also conceived the modern brandname. It at least looked something like a Strat, and as such proved popular, with early adopters including Tony Sheridan, who could be seen with his on the TV pop show *Oh Boy!*, as well as George Harrison and Jimmy Page.

ORIGINAL **FENDER CUSTOM TELECASTER**
THIS EXAMPLE: ***1963***
The Custom Esquire and Telecaster, introduced in 1959, had a different look, finished in the sunburst style of the Strat and with bound white edges to the body.

Instant modernity with Selmer's 1960 Futurama ad.

Of the thousands of guitarists who've found a rosewood-board Strat to their liking, one of the most highly regarded by his fellow musicians was Stevie Ray Vaughan. The Texan blues-rocker brought the Strat's capabilities spectacularly to notice in 1983 when he made a surprisingly effective pairing with David Bowie on Bowie's *Let's Dance* album. Vaughan's own *Texas Flood* of the same year went on to reveal more of his abilities, including some inspired Hendrix-flavored work.

Vaughan died prematurely in a helicopter crash in 1990, but not before he redefined contemporary blues-rock guitar playing, mostly performed on his distinctively careworn Strat known as Number One. Vaughan acquired it in 1973 in Austin, Texas, where he saw a beat-up '62–'63 Strat in the window and traded a black Strat for it. He had a few other Strats, but Number One was his primary choice.

Fender's "hot" Texas Special Strat-type single-coils first appeared on a new Stevie Ray Vaughan signature Strat introduced in 1992. The model had been agreed before Vaughan's tragic death, when the guitarist's career was at a peak. The signature model was based on Number One, and featured an SRV logo on the pickguard similar to the one on the original instrument. It had an unusual left-handed vibrato system, as favored by the right-handed Vaughan, a result of his strong stylistic link with left-hander Jimi Hendrix. The idea was that a left-handed vibrato ought to provide a right-handed player (for example Vaughan) with similar tonal peculiarities that a right-handed vibrato would give to a left-hander (for example Hendrix).

Fender has produced other signature Strats of the rosewood-board variety named for a number of players, including Jeff Beck, Ritchie Blackmore, Robert Cray, Dick Dale, Rory Gallagher, Mark Knopfler, John Mayer, Dave Murray, Bonnie Raitt, Chris Rea, and Kenny Wayne Shepherd.

John Mayer wishes Fender a happy 60th, 2006.

FENDER ROBERT CRAY STRATOCASTER
THIS EXAMPLE: ***2014***
Like the Stevie Ray Vaughan Strat featured here, this 60s-style "hardtail" (non-vibrato) signature model for Robert Cray first appeared in the early 90s and is still in the Fender line today.

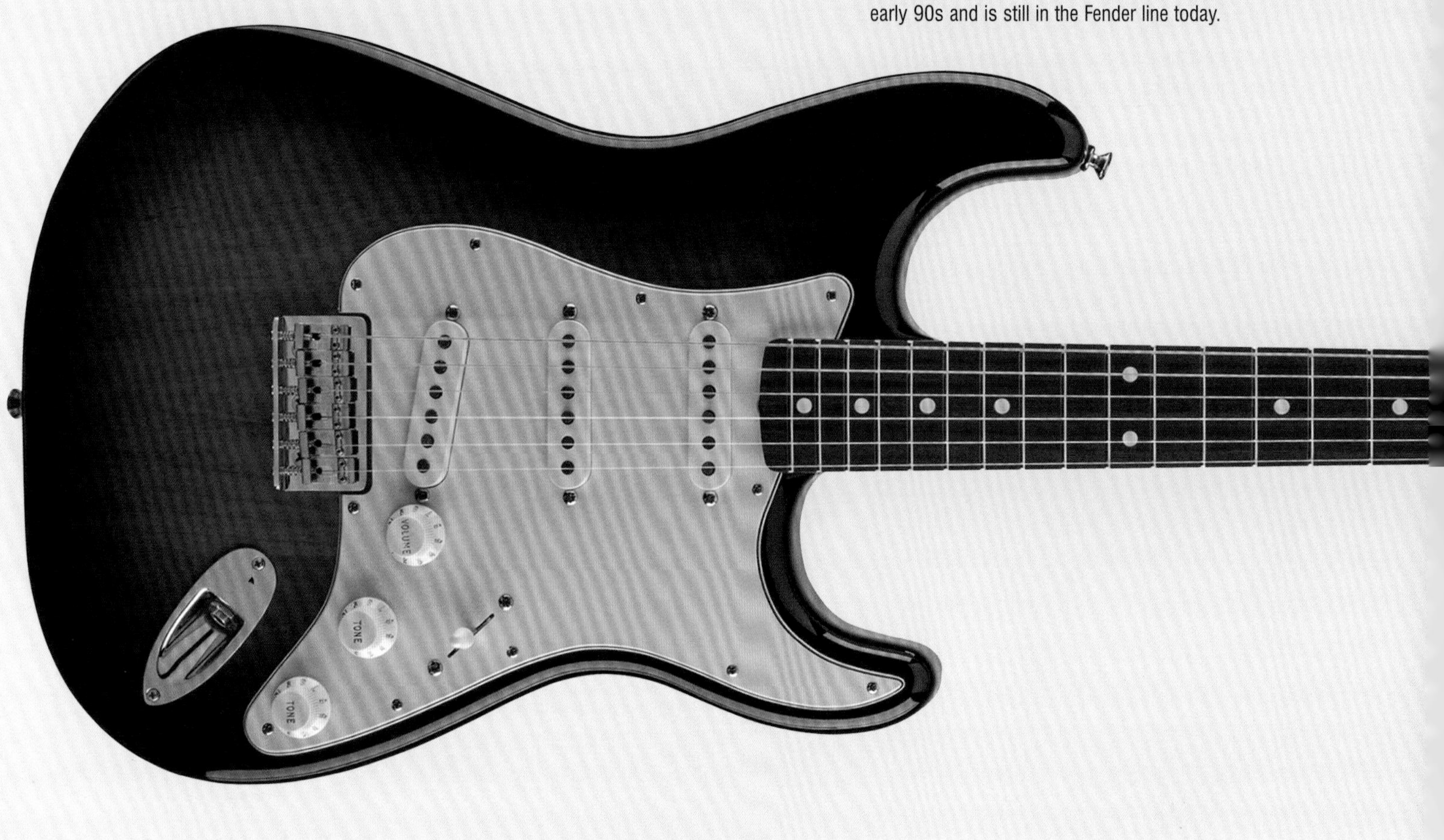

Robert Cray joins in the 2006 birthday wishes.

Swamp Ash Body
Texas Special Pickups
Vintage '62 Neck
Hot Rod Red Lacquered Finish
Medium Jumbo Frets

Mark Knopfler Signature Stratocaster

Two of the finest names in music have got together to produce one great guitar... A Stratocaster built to unique specifications and of enduring quality!

See your local dealer today & let the Sultans swing !!!

Fender

Mark Knopfler's signature Strat in early-60s style, 2004 ad.

FENDER STEVIE RAY VAUGHAN STRATOCASTER
THIS EXAMPLE: ***1992***
First issued in 1992, the Stevie Ray Vaughan Strat marked a tribute to the late bluesman, who had died two years earlier in a helicopter accident. There's no missing the SRV logo, but note also the left-handed vibrato.

1990 ad featuring Stevie Ray Vaughan and Jeff Beck.

Modifying and updating the original 50s and 60s-style Stratocaster has been a longterm occupation at Fender, where designers have to balance the two extremes among the guitarists they're aiming at. Sitting at one extreme is the purist who demands that every little detail matches the hallowed originals; at the other is the modern player who wants all the benefits of current developments in guitar technology. Somewhere in between is everyone else.

One such move came in 1980, when Fender finally applied the much-used abbreviation of the model name—Strat—to a new design. The new Strat was devised by Gregg Wilson, who combined the model's familiar looks with updated circuitry, a "hot" bridge pickup, and fashionable heavy-duty brass hardware. A reversion to the four-screw neck fixing and body-end truss-rod adjustment and the removal of the neck-tilt for the new Strat implied that Fender was already aware of the shortcomings of 70s Stratocasters. A few brighter colors were offered for the Strat, too, reviving Lake Placid blue, candy apple red, and olympic white. The model was significant as the first attempt at a modernized Stratocaster, and it retailed at $995, compared to $745 for the regular Stratocaster. The Strat was gone from the line by 1983.

Another shortlived guitar from the same period was the Elite Stratocaster (and an accompanying Telecaster), intended as a radical new high-end version of the old faithful. The Elite listed at $999 and had new pickups designed for humbucking noise cancellation and single-coil brilliance, linked to active circuitry. These generally good points were mostly overlooked, because the vibrato-equipped Elite Strat came saddled with a poor bridge. The Elite Strat also featured three pushbuttons for pickup selection, not to the taste of players brought up on the classic Fender switch. The model was dropped by the end of 1984.

FENDER STRATOCASTER STANDARD
THIS EXAMPLE: ***1982***
New Fender management in the early 80s instigated a move to a more traditional look for the regular Standard Stratocaster, including body-end truss-rod adjustment, narrow headstock shape, and four-screw neck fixing.

FENDER STRAT
THIS EXAMPLE: ***1980***
Fender intended this model—shown here in Lake Placid blue finish—as a revised Stratocaster with modern features, including brass hardware, "hot" bridge pickup, and updated circuitry. It lasted only about three years in the line.

FENDER STRATOCASTER ELITE
THIS EXAMPLE: ***1983***
Two features let down this otherwise promising Stratocaster update: the poor Freeflyte vibrato, and the replacement of the regular pickup switch with three pushbuttons. This Elite is finished in blue stratoburst.

Fifty years since Leo founded his original firm, 1996 ad.

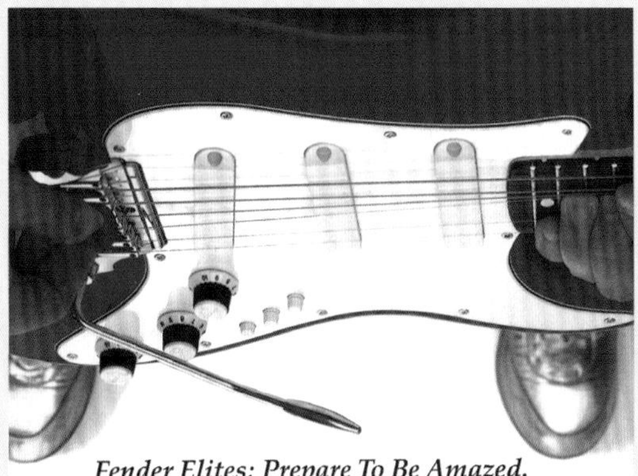

Fender's 1983 ad says the Stratocaster Elite is a "significant development."

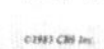

FENDER STRAT XII
THIS EXAMPLE: ***1990***
This 12-string Stratocaster was quite unlike Fender's earlier Electric XII from the mid 60s. The Strat XII stayed in the Fender catalogue until 1996, and it would be revived for a few more years in the 2000s.

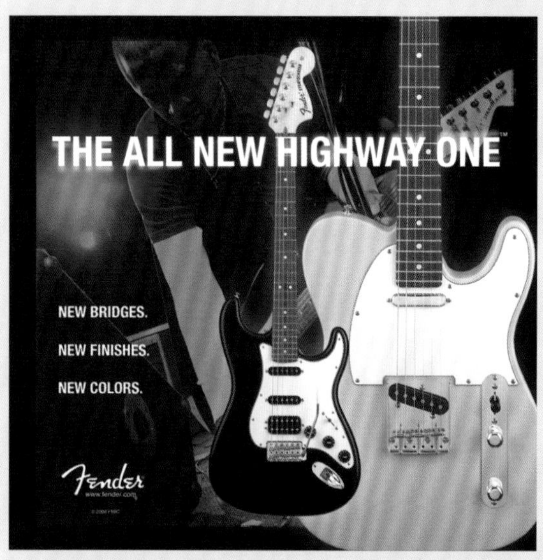

New and old with the Highway One Strat, 2006 ad.

FENDER AMERICAN ORIGINAL 60s STRATOCASTER

THIS EXAMPLE: ***2018***

A candy apple red finish brightens this most recent effort at a largely traditional 60s-style rosewood-board Strat. Fender said the model kept period features intact while adding modern feel and pickup switching.

FENDER AMERICAN PROFESSIONAL STRATOCASTER HH
THIS EXAMPLE: ***2017***
When updating the Strat for contemporary players, Fender often focusses on general feel and, more specifically, revised pickups. This model has Fender's modern "deep C" neck profile and a pair of Tim Shaw-designed ShawBuckers.

Modeling was a new technology applied to guitar-playing as the 21st century began, using digital re-creations of classic guitar and amp sounds. The California-based Line 6 was the innovator, with its Vetta amps and Pod boxes, and other amp makers followed. Line 6 also launched a modeling guitar, the Variax, in 2003. Fender entered this brave new world, at first in 2001 with the Cyber Twin amp, and then with the Fender American VG Stratocaster, launched in 2007 with a list price of $2,429 (about $1,100 more than a regular American Stratocaster).

Two Fender–Roland Strats had appeared earlier, in the late 90s, the shortlived American Standard Roland GR-Ready model and its replacement, the Mexico-made Standard Roland Ready Stratocaster. Both required an external synth to get new sounds, with Roland's VG-88 modeling module a popular choice. Now, Fender made everything happen inside the new VG Strat. The only connection the guitarist needed was through the regular jack to a regular amp: the modeling was done onboard. And the guitar could still play and sound exactly like a Strat, if necessary, using the regular magnetic pickups and controls.

The VG offered five sound settings: N for Normal (the regular Strat); S for modeled Stratocaster; T for modeled Telecaster; H for modeled Humbucking Pickups (which presumably Fender could not call the Les Paul mode); and A for modeled Acoustic. The VG's five-way selector gave logical variations within each of those settings, and the Tuning Control provided regular six-string tuning plus four alternative tunings and a simulated twelve-string. Despite all this innovation—or perhaps because of it—the VG lasted only a couple of years in Fender's line. Later, Roland offered the instrument as the G5 (from 2012), but this, too, was not a success with players and did not last long.

FENDER AMERICAN VG STRATOCASTER
THIS EXAMPLE: ***2007***
Four knobs on a Strat? This was Fender's attempt in collaboration with Roland to create a modeling guitar, as popularized by Line 6, with digitally created sounds. However, Fender fans seemed to want their Strats to remain in analogue territory.

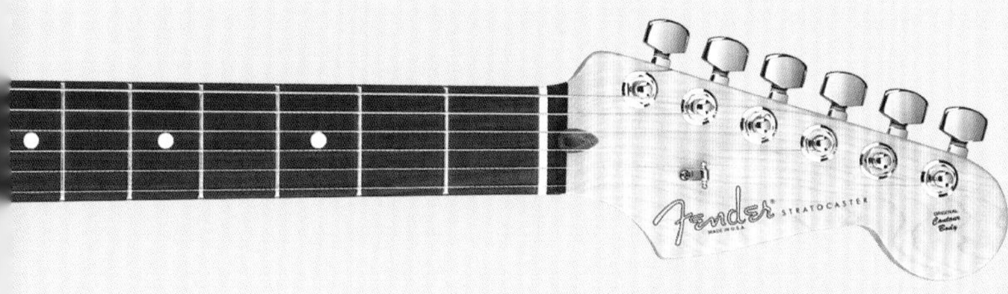

Aged-finish Strats in this Road Worn ad, 2011.

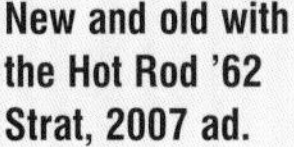

New and old with the Hot Rod '62 Strat, 2007 ad.

As far as the Fender Telecaster was concerned, the 70s was the decade of the humbucker. Part of Fender's distinction had come from using bright-sounding single-coil pickups, while fatter-sounding humbuckers were a Gibson mainstay. The bridge pickup on a Telecaster (or an Esquire) is praised as the heart of its sound, but some feel the neck pickup is the weak link. Some players ignore it; some find a useful jazz-like tone; others take matters into their own hands.

A popular choice was to replace a Tele's mellow neck pickup with a ballsier humbucker, often lifted from a Gibson, and the leader in this 70s trend was Keith Richards. He'd been playing Telecasters regularly with the Stones from around 1972, and his most famous is his black-guard early-50s model, nicknamed Micawber, which has a Gibson humbucker stuck on at the neck.

Fender recognized the trend, first modifying the Thinline Telecaster in '71 with two new Fender humbuckers. They were designed by Seth Lover, who in 1967 had come to Fender from Gibson, where he had devised its humbucking pickup in the 50s. The Telecaster Custom of '72 retained the classic Tele lead pickup but had a humbucker at the neck, and the control layout was opened out to a Gibson-like two volumes and two tones. The Telecaster Deluxe, new for '73, was like a cross between the big-headstock neck of the contemporary Stratocaster, the body of a Telecaster (but with a Strat-like rear contour), plus two humbuckers and, like the Custom, the controls of a Gibson.

These models were all gone by 1981, but in later years the idea of a humbucker'd Tele resurfaced to wide popularity. Meanwhile, there was the regular Telecaster, the start of vintage reissues, several more modified Teles, and a number of signature models to add to the mix.

FENDER TELECASTER DELUXE
THIS EXAMPLE: ***1973***
The Deluxe was one of Fender's revised humbucker'd Teles, quite a trend in the 70s, but one that would only achieve wider popularity in later decades. This one had two humbuckers, Gibson-like controls, and a Strat-style headstock.

FENDER '52 TELECASTER
THIS EXAMPLE: ***1984***
Fender's first modern reissue was the '52 Telecaster, introduced in 1982 and an attempt to recapture some of the feel and features of an original early-50s model.

A regular Tele steps out in a fanciful 1973 ad.

Tele Plus with Strat-like three-pickup layout, 1995 ad.

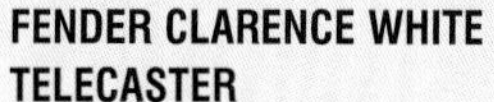

FENDER CLARENCE WHITE TELECASTER
THIS EXAMPLE: ***1993***
This tribute to the Byrds guitarist duplicated the late Clarence White's favored neck pickup, Scruggs tuners, and his B-bender string-pull, which made it possible to play string-bends within chords to emulate pedal-steel type sounds.

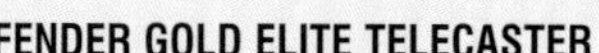

FENDER GOLD ELITE TELECASTER
THIS EXAMPLE: ***1983***
The Elite (emerald green finish here) marked a departure from the traditional Tele, with new pickups, active circuitry, and a six-saddle bridge, but it failed to make the right impact and lasted only a year or two.

The Telecaster is quite a guitar. It's the oldest solidbody electric guitar still going strong—not surprising when you know that it was the very first. As we've seen, way back in 1950, before anyone had even thought of rock'n'roll, Fender came up with this first commercial solidbody electric. Uncluttered and straightforward it may have been, but those are the attributes that remain at the heart of the Telecaster's appeal.

It's a simple, honest, playable guitar. We know some of the history and we can think of some great players who have turned to the Tele for help. But it's a constant source of delight to see these guitars turning up in all manner of new music. And, of course, it's always good to revisit the great music that defined the Tele as a modern classic. As James Burton told this author: "In studios they'll say oh, you've got to have this guitar, you've got to have that guitar. And I say, 'Why do I need all those guitars? It's right here.' Know what I'm saying?" We most certainly do, James.

There are many who think of the Tele as something of a grown-up guitar. It's a magnet for anyone who's been through all the gimmickry and gadgetry of the latest wonder-guitar. And those guitarists who haven't already succumbed are sure to come around at some point to appreciate the elegant, unpretentious simplicity of this instrument, one that effortlessly reflects the character and the will of the player in charge. So here it is, this vintage guitar, this brand new guitar. Here's the body, here's the neck. Here are the pickups, in old or some new configuration, and here are the knobs. Nothing more, nothing less. And still it feels just right.

FENDER AMERICAN CLASSIC TELECASTER
THIS EXAMPLE: ***1995***
The Custom Shop's American Classic, introduced in 1995, was a three-pickup high-end take on the factory-made American Standard—and check out that reversed control layout that puts the selector at the back of the panel.

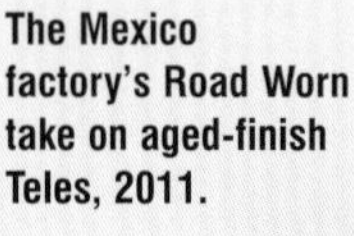

The Mexico factory's Road Worn take on aged-finish Teles, 2011.

FENDER AMERICAN ORIGINAL 60s TELECASTER
THIS EXAMPLE: ***2018***
Despite the model name, this is a reissue of the Custom Telecaster, the bound-body version introduced in 1959, and this stunner is finished in fiesta red, complete with period-correct rosewood fingerboard and three-ply pickguard.

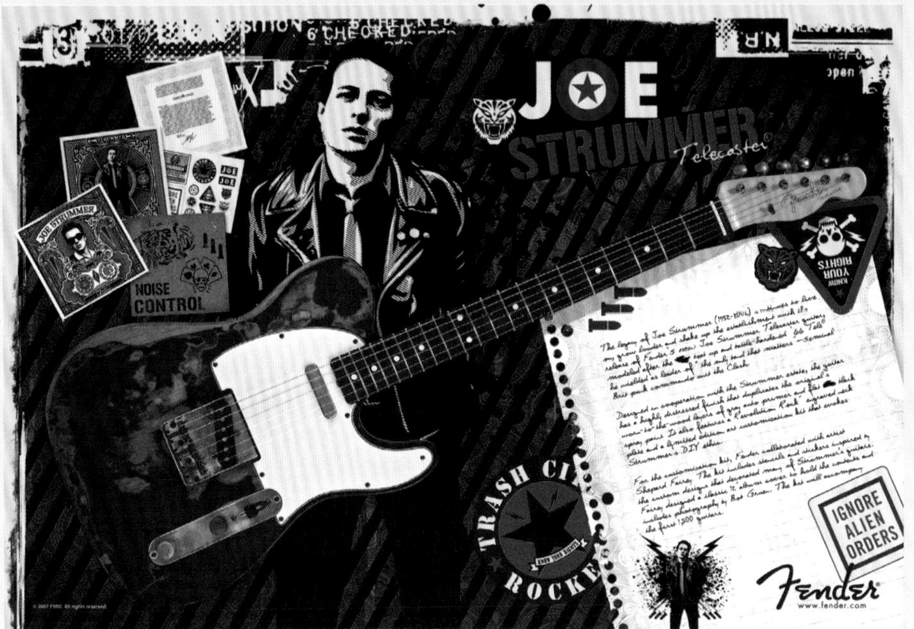

Fender's 2007 ad for a re-creation of Joe Strummer's careworn Telecaster.

Johnny Marr and Tele extend all good wishes, 2006.

FENDER '63 TELECASTER RELIC
THIS EXAMPLE: ***2001***
Fender decided in the mid 90s to market "aged" oldies, and soon the so-called Time Machine series had developed into three levels of finish, including the "knocked about" Relic look seen on this Lake Placid blue '63-style Tele.

1959

Gibson bought the old Epiphone brand of New York in 1957, primarily to gain control of Epiphone's upright bass business, but that lasted only a few years. More valuable was the acquisition of the Epiphone brand. Gibson set up a new Epi operation at Gibson's Kalamazoo base, and by 1959 it had released the first of its new Epiphones, in the process filling some of the gaps in the Gibson line they partnered. Some of these "new" guitars were continuations of existing Epiphone models, others were designed as Epiphone near-equivalents of Gibson models, although with different pickups and varied feature sets, and some were entirely new.

The high-end Emperor, for example, kept its three pickups, but along with the other hollow electrics—Century, Zephyr, and Deluxe—it was redesigned with a new thinline body. There was also a new full-depth hollow electric, the Broadway. There were solidbody models, too, the revised single-pickup Coronet and the new two-pickup Crestwood, which had double-cutaway bodies and, at first, Epi's New York-style pickups.

The Vega company began in Boston around 1900 as a maker of brass instruments and banjos, and by the 30s it had added guitars to the catalogue. The firm's electric models, such as the E-300 Duo-Tron introduced in 1949, were made using traditional techniques. Vega emphasized that "the electric parts in no way affect the body tone" thanks to a pickup fixed to the fingerboard and controls floating above the body on the guitar's tailpiece. In 1959, Vega decided to try a stereo guitar, with a spectacular result: the 12-pickup 1200 Stereo model, which listed at a steep $1,000. Vega to some extent followed the lead of Gretsch's recent Project-o-Sonic stereo models, splitting the output from the 1200's multiple pickups to two amplifiers. The model was shortlived.

A truly sensational solid body guitar with features that win it top rating from professionals who appreciate its tonal range, instant response, and easy action for professional performance. A thin solid body guitar with double cutaway, double pickup, and features that add up to outstanding value. Powerful pickups have adjustable polepiece screws to balance each string . . . separate tone and volume controls which can be preset . . . 3-way toggle switch to select either or both pickups. Tune-o-matic bridge permits precise tuning for perfect accuracy on each string. Handsome Honduras mahogany body in modern contoured design . . . all 22 frets above the cutaway. Mahogany neck with adjustable truss rod. Shell celluloid pickguard. Rosewood fingerboard with pearl dot inlays. Nickel-plated metal parts.

12¾" wide, 15¾" long, 1⅜" thin
24¾" scale, 22 frets

SB432	WILSHIRE, cherry finish	**$195.00**
1635	Case, hard shell, plush-lined	$ 50.00
1115	Case, chipboard	$ 14.75

New double-cut shape for Epi's Wilshire solidbody, 1960 catalogue.

ORIGINAL **EPIPHONE CRESTWOOD CUSTOM SB332**
THIS EXAMPLE: ***1959***
Under Gibson's new ownership, redesigned solidbody models were introduced in 1959, including the one-pickup Coronet, this two-pickup Crestwood Custom, and from 1963 the three-pickup Crestwood Deluxe.

Laurindo Almeida with Vega E-300, 1958 ad.

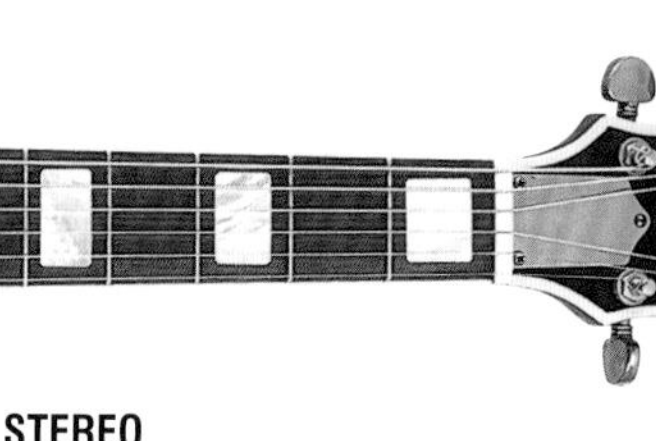

ORIGINAL **VEGA 1200 STEREO**
THIS EXAMPLE: ***1959***
Vega's 12 pickups on the 1200 Stereo are split into two groups of six, with two for each string. The rear six sense treble tones and the six nearest the neck are for bass response. This oddball model did not last long.

Gibson-era Epiphone catalogue cover, 1959.

Upright bass and guitar on 1958 Epiphone catalogue cover.

Reissue of later-style Wilshire solidbody in Epiphone's ad from 2011.

ORIGINAL **EPIPHONE EMPEROR E112TN**
THIS EXAMPLE: ***1959***
The mighty Emperor still sat at the top of Epiphone archtop electric line under the new Gibson ownership of the brand, and this natural-finish example still has the older New York style pickups, changed around 1961 to mini-humbuckers.

EPIPHONE JOE PASS EMPEROR II
THIS EXAMPLE: ***2011***
The Emperor name stayed in Epiphone's lines for many years, including this signature model named for the jazz guitarist Joe Pass, introduced in 1995 and still available at the time of writing.

Goya-badged Hagstroms for the USA, 1959 catalogue.

Gretsch in New York had drawn on expertise in drum making to use plastic covering for some of its early-50s solidbody models, including black plastic for early examples of the Duo Jet and an altogether more sparkly look for the Silver Jet. Several European makers used similar techniques, and in some cases they too drew on earlier expertise —but their inspiration came from accordions rather than drums.

One of the earliest was Hagstrom, a Swedish company set up by Albin Hagstrom in the 20s. Its Standard and De Luxe models introduced in 1959 had plastic fingerboards and brightly-colored sparkle or pearl plastic coverings on the front of the semi-hollow bodies. Combined with a control panel full of pushbuttons and roller wheels, and four pickups on the De Luxe model, these striking Hagstrom guitars (sold with the Goya brand in America) gave a burst of popularity to the use of plastic.

In 1946, Fred Wilfer founded Framus (Frankische Musikindustrie) in the Erlangen area of Bavaria in what was then West Germany. At first the firm made acoustic instruments, adding hollowbody electric guitars from the early 50s, and the first Framus semi-solid, the Hollywood, appeared at the end of the decade. Framus would become a prolific guitar maker as the 60s progressed, exporting its instruments far and wide and positioned alongside Hofner as the best-known of the German brands.

Hofner itself was developing more electric guitars during the late 50s and into the 60s, and Selmer, its UK agent, came up with a luxurious model in 1959, the Golden Hofner. It sat at the top of the pricelist and was by far the most ornate and attractive of Hofner's electrics. The Golden Hofner was, claimed Selmer in its catalogue, "a masterpiece of guitar perfection."

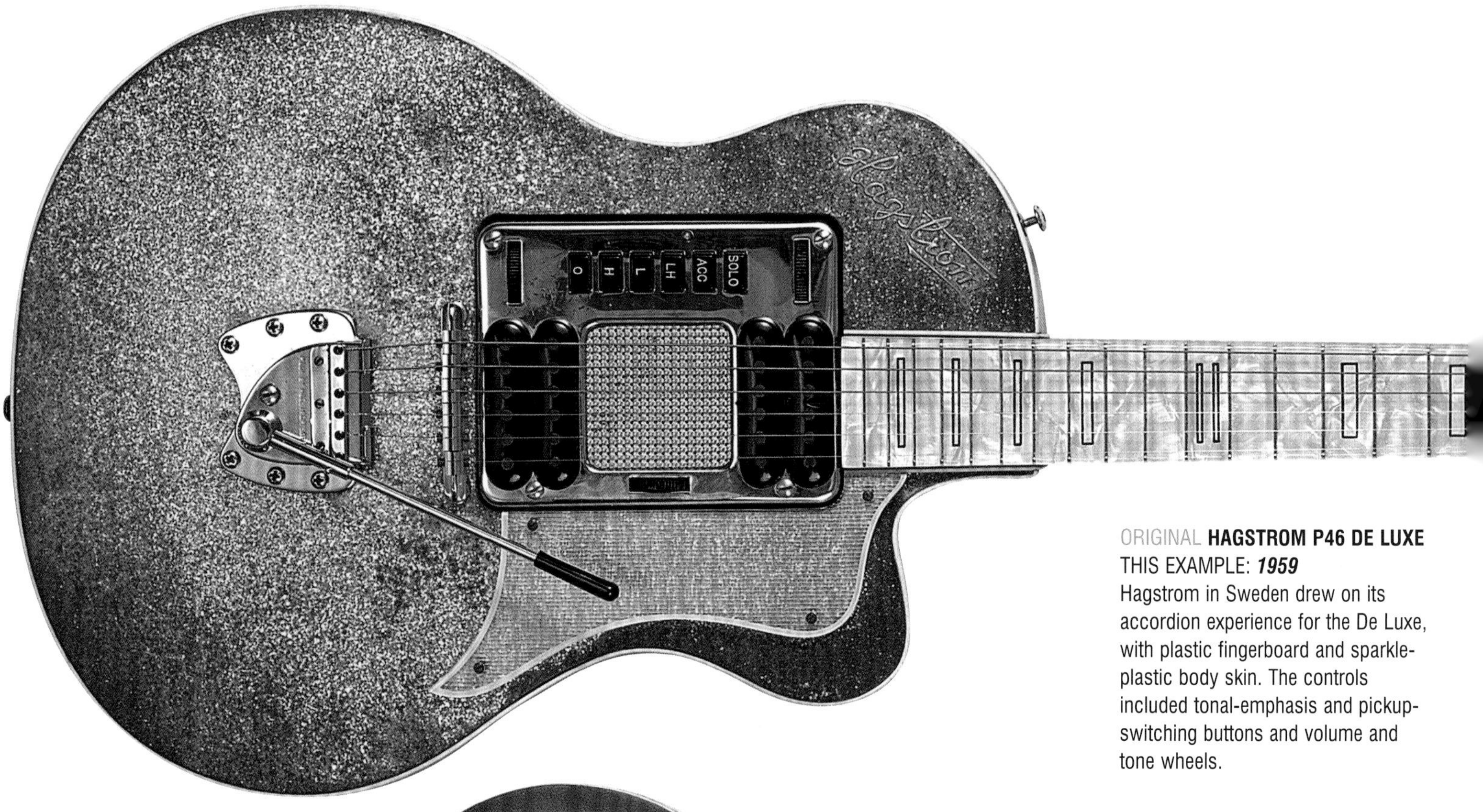

ORIGINAL **HAGSTROM P46 DE LUXE**
THIS EXAMPLE: ***1959***
Hagstrom in Sweden drew on its accordion experience for the De Luxe, with plastic fingerboard and sparkle-plastic body skin. The controls included tonal-emphasis and pickup-switching buttons and volume and tone wheels.

ORIGINAL **FRAMUS HOLLYWOOD 5/132**
THIS EXAMPLE: ***1959***
Framus introduced this semi-solid in the late 50s, echoing the shape of a Gibson Les Paul and offered with a choice of one, two, or three pickups and six finishes—this one is finished in what the German company called red-gold.

Selmer 1959 catalogue page for the Hofner Golden Hofner.

Golden Hofner

electric guitar

Built to the specification of guitar specialists, the Golden Hofner is unmatched in elegance and unequalled in tone.
Frets are of nickel silver, and machined heads are totally enclosed.

For complete specification see Golden Hofner Acoustic, page 2.

The Golden Hofner incorporates the "New Line" Flick Action console exclusive to all Hofner Electric Guitars. This enables quick changes from rhythm to solo playing and change of tone colours by the "flick" of a switch.

Cat. No. 523 .. .. 95 gns.
Thin model
Cat. No. T523 .. .. 95 gns.

A blue-sparkle P46 De Luxe on Hagstrom's 1959 catalogue cover.

ORIGINAL **HOFNER GOLDEN HOFNER THIN**
THIS EXAMPLE: ***1961***
The high-end Golden Hofner had fancy inlays on the fingerboard and the ornate headstock. This (thinline body) Thin version was owned by Bert Weedon, the British guitarist best known for his *Play In A Day* guitar tutor.

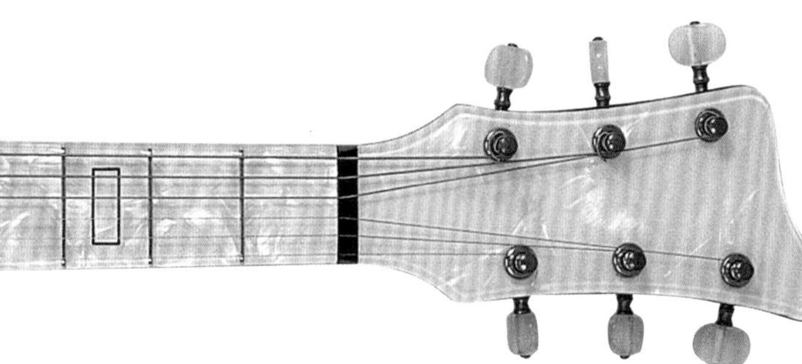

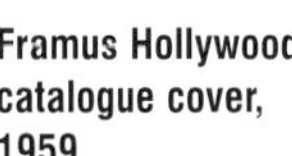

Framus Hollywood catalogue cover, 1959.

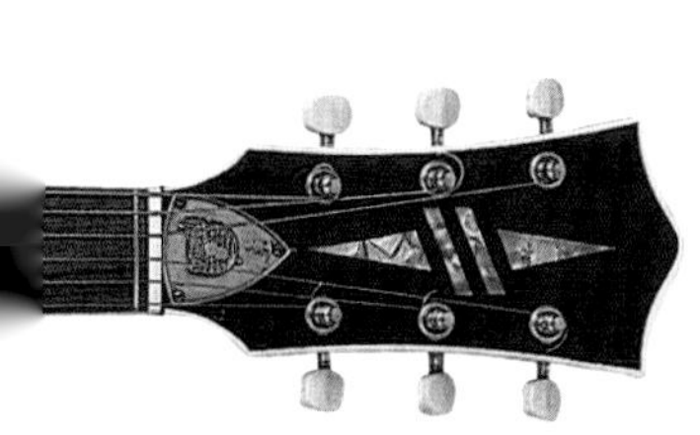

Grant Green with a sunburst 330, 1963 album cover.

Gibson's stereo ES-345 completed the company's semi-solid line when it was introduced in 1959 alongside the original 335 and the high-end 355. We've seen how Gretsch's Project-O-Sonic models of 1958 were the first stereo guitars, but also that year, Rickenbacker launched its Rick-O-Sound stereo system. This directed the output of each of two pickups to a separate amplifier or channel and featured two jacks: one for stereo output, the other for mono.

Gibson's two-pickup stereo circuitry was similar to the Rickenbacker system but had a single stereo-wired output jack. The new ES-345 came with a Y cable, which fed that output and split it to two mono jacks, and the guitarist would connect each of these to an amplifier (or a two-channel amp). Visual hallmarks of the 345 were its double-parallelogram fingerboard inlays (a pair of angled blocks), a triple-bound body top, and gold-plated metalwork.

There was a new Gibson gadget on the 345, the six-position Varitone switch, designed by Walt Fuller. It was a notch filter, which meant it took a "notch" out of the tonal frequency spectrum, reducing the frequency at each of five set points. In essence, the Varitone provided preset tonal sounds that could be adapted as necessary with the regular controls, but it did not prove popular.

Another new Gibson model added in 1959 was the ES-330, which had the look and style of the double-cut semi-solids but was fully hollow, without the body's internal block. As such, the 330 was Gibson's first fully hollow double-cut thinline. A further difference between the 330 and the semi-solid models was the way the neck was fitted further into the body and joined at the seventeenth fret. There was at first the option of one or two single-coil P-90s, with two or four controls as appropriate.

Freddy King with a cherry 345, 1965 album cover.

ORIGINAL **GIBSON ES-345TD**
THIS EXAMPLE: ***1959***
Gibson's new stereo guitar, introduced in 1959, was a further addition to its semi-solid thinline series. It had a stereo jack to feed two amps or one two-channel amp, and a six-way Varitone switch intended to provide tonal presets.

Magical stereo in Gibson's ES-345 catalogue, 1959.

Hank Garland and 345 in a roadster full of Gibsons, 1962.

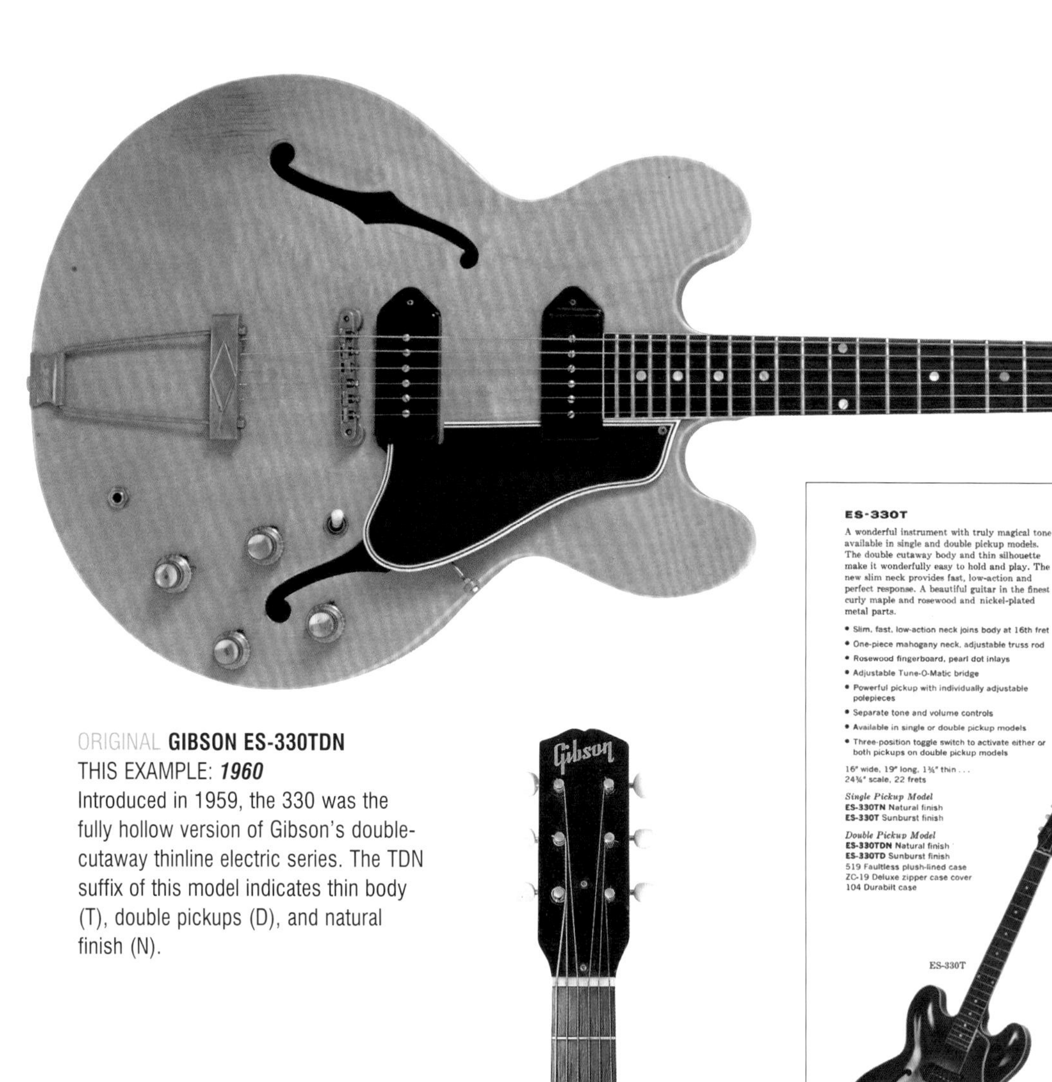

ORIGINAL **GIBSON ES-330TDN**
THIS EXAMPLE: ***1960***
Introduced in 1959, the 330 was the fully hollow version of Gibson's double-cutaway thinline electric series. The TDN suffix of this model indicates thin body (T), double pickups (D), and natural finish (N).

ES-330T

A wonderful instrument with truly magical tone available in single and double pickup models. The double cutaway body and thin silhouette make it wonderfully easy to hold and play. The new slim neck provides fast, low-action and perfect response. A beautiful guitar in the finest curly maple and rosewood and nickel-plated metal parts.

- Slim, fast, low-action neck joins body at 16th fret
- One-piece mahogany neck, adjustable truss rod
- Rosewood fingerboard, pearl dot inlays
- Adjustable Tune-O-Matic bridge
- Powerful pickup with individually adjustable polepieces
- Separate tone and volume controls
- Available in single or double pickup models
- Three-position toggle switch to activate either or both pickups on double pickup models

16" wide, 19" long, 1¾" thin . . .
24¾" scale, 22 frets

Single Pickup Model
ES-330TN Natural finish
ES-330T Sunburst finish

Double Pickup Model
ES-330TDN Natural finish
ES-330TD Sunburst finish
519 Faultless plush-lined case
ZC-19 Deluxe zipper case cover
104 Durabilt case

ES-330T

1960 catalogue page for the hollowbody ES-330.

ORIGINAL **GIBSON LES PAUL SPECIAL**
THIS EXAMPLE: ***1959***
Gibson redesigned its lower-price Les Paul models with a new double-cutaway body, launching the new Junior and TV in 1958 and the revised Special in '59, seen here with a cherry-red finish.

ORIGINAL **GIBSON MELODY MAKER**
THIS EXAMPLE: ***1960***
This new budget single-cutaway model was introduced in 1959 as the lowest-price Gibson solidbody, sitting below the company's $132.50 Les Paul Junior and listing at $99.50.

Gibson's double-cutaway thinline ES guitars have proved mainstays of the company's lines through the decades that followed the introduction of the originals during the 50s. Gibson like many makers is well aware of the usefulness of a double-cutaway and has sometimes applied the idea to its other series, including its most famous Les Paul models.

The first Les Pauls with a double cutaway were the redesigned versions of the budget flat-topped Junior, TV, and Special models, introduced in 1958 and 1959. Higher-end Les Pauls with the carved-top body style had to wait until 1984 and the Les Paul Double-Cutaway XPL to gain the extra cutaway. The XPL model was an attempt by Gibson to align a Les Paul-named model with the rising trend at that time for so-called superstrats, thanks mostly to the new Gibson's Kahler vibrato and the visual clue of an Explorer-style drooping headstock shape, of the type widely seen on superstrats by Jackson and other 80s US makers. Not surprisingly, the oddball XPL was shortlived.

By the 90s, PRS guitars were established instruments, melding a Les Paul-like carved, figured maple top and humbuckers with Stratocaster-style double cutaways and through-body stringing. PRS was attracting players who might otherwise have opted for a Les Paul or a Strat. When Gibson's new double-cutaway Les Paul DC models appeared in 1997, it seemed that the growing demand for a double-cutaway carved-top guitar had not gone unnoticed at Gibson's HQ in Nashville. The DC line started with a Custom Shop model, the Pro, effectively merging the late-50s Junior and Special double-cut shape with the Standard's carved top. The DCs survived into the 2000s, but at the time of writing, double-cut carved-top Les Pauls were limited to the Classic Double Cutaway, Standard Double Cutaway, and Tak Matsumoto Doublecut Custom Ebony.

GIBSON 1964 ES-345TDC FIGURED
THIS EXAMPLE: ***2015***
Gibson's period-correct reissue of the ES-345 was first sold in 2014, complete with stereo circuitry and Varitone selector. This one is in a transparent cherry finish, which enhances the optional figured top.

GIBSON LES PAUL DC PRO
THIS EXAMPLE: ***1997***
This DC Pro was one of three models, alongside the DC Studio and DC Standard, that reflected influences from PRS guitars, including a double-cutaway body with figured maple top, and a restyled headstock.

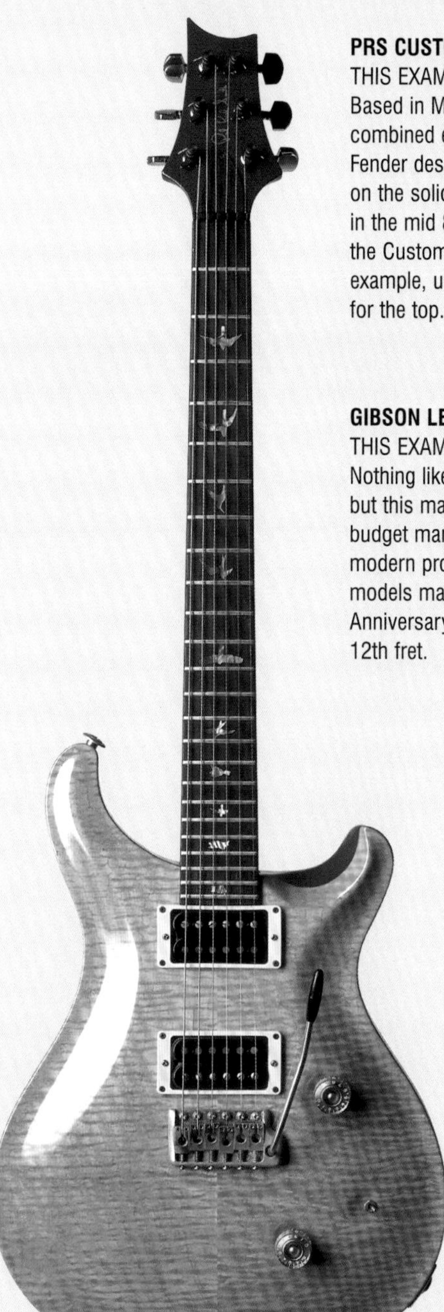

PRS CUSTOM
THIS EXAMPLE: ***1985***
Based in Maryland, Paul Reed Smith combined elements of Gibson and Fender design to create a new take on the solidbody electric, beginning in the mid 80s and exemplified by the Custom—often, as with this example, using fine figured maple for the top.

GIBSON LES PAUL MELODY MAKER
THIS EXAMPLE: ***2014***
Nothing like an original Melody Maker, but this mashup at least aims at a budget market, with the advantage of modern production. Several Gibson models made in 2014 had a 120th Anniversary inlay as seen here at the 12th fret.

GIBSON LES PAUL SPECIAL DOUBLE CUT
THIS EXAMPLE: ***2017***
The new double-cutaway body style was originally applied to the budget Les Paul Special model in 1959, and this Custom Shop reissue of that type is finished in TV white.

Thin Line Series

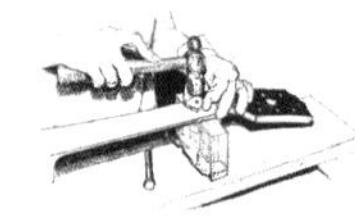

Positioning pin for fingerboard installation

ES-345TDSV/BODY SPECIFICATIONS
Arched maple top □ Arched maple back with matching maple rims □ Double Venetian cutaway offers easy access to higher playing positions □ Top and back bound in multiple black/white binding □ Adjustable, gold-plated Tune-o-matic bridge □ Gold-plated bail tailpiece □ Black fingerrest with white revealed edge □ Two gold-plated Gibson Humbucking pickups with individual volume and tone controls □ 3-position toggle switch for pickup selection (individual or both pickups simultaneously) □ Stereo electronics □ 6-position Vari-Tone control for additional tonal capabilities □ Body size: Length 19," width 16," depth 1¾"
NECK SPECIFICATIONS
Laminated maple construction □ Width at fingerboard nut 1 11/16" □ Rosewood fingerboard with divided block inlays and corresponding white side dots □ Pearl inlaid head veneer □ Deluxe, gold-plated machine heads □ Gibson truss rod with inscribed truss rod cover □ 22 frets □ 24¾" scale length
ES-345TDSV □ Sunburst, Wine Red, or Walnut finish
519 Faultless plush lined case

ES-335TD/BODY SPECIFICATIONS
Arched maple top □ Arched maple back with matching maple rims □ Double Venetian cutaway offers easy access to higher playing positions □ Top and back bound in multiple black/white binding □ Adjustable, chrome-plated Tune-o-matic bridge □ Chrome-plated bail tailpiece □ Black fingerrest with white revealed edge □ Two chrome-plated "Super Humbucking" pickups with individual volume controls □ 3-position toggle switch for pickup selection (individual or both pickups simultaneously) □ Coil tap switch to place either humbucking pickup into a single point non-humbucking mode □ Body size: Length 19," width 16" depth 1¾"

NECK SPECIFICATIONS
Laminated maple construction □ Width at fingerboard nut 1 11/16" □ Bound rosewood fingerboard with block inlays and corresponding side dots □ Pearl inlaid head veneer □ Chrome-plated, individual machine heads □ Gibson truss rod with inscribed truss rod cover □ 22 frets □ 24¾" scale length
ES-335TD □ Wine Red, Sunburst, Walnut, or Natural finish
519 Faultless plush lined case

17

Gibson's 1978 catalogue with wine-red 345 and natural 335.

"The 60s electric guitar was bent, reverb'd, and distorted to drive some of the most extraordinary music ever created."

PENGUIN BOOKS
LADY CHATTERLEY'S LOVER
D.H. LAWRENCE
COMPLETE AND 3/6 UNEXPURGATED

BANK of ENGLAND
A08 678204
I Promise to pay the Bearer on Demand the sum of
One Pound
Elizabeth R
1
1
LONDON
For the Gov. and Comp. of the BANK of ENGLAND
Chief Cashier
A08
1946
FARTHING

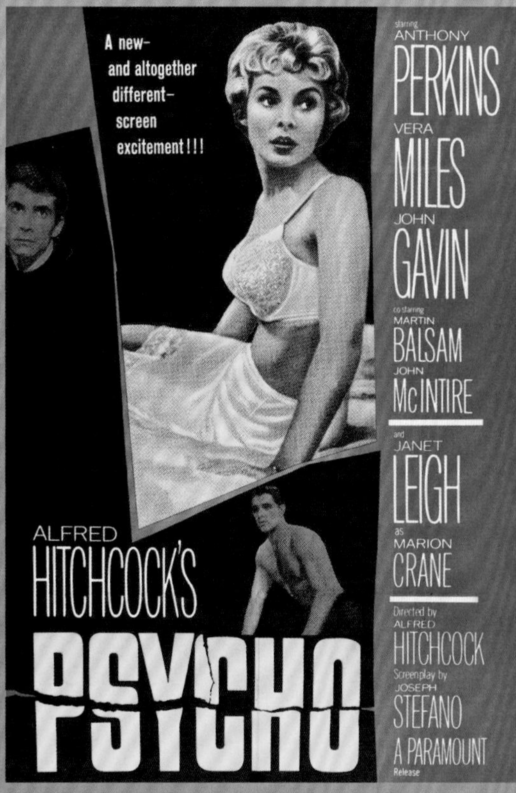

A new-
and altogether
different-
screen
excitement!!!
ANTHONY
PERKINS
VERA
MILES
JOHN
GAVIN
MARTIN
BALSAM
JOHN
McINTIRE
JANET
LEIGH
as
MARION
CRANE
Directed by
ALFRED
HITCHCOCK
Screenplay by
JOSEPH
STEFANO
A PARAMOUNT
Release
ALFRED
HITCHCOCK'S
PSYCHO

- **ELVIS PRESLEY** leaves the army, heading for a film career. Eddie Cochran is killed in a car crash on his way to London Airport.

- **A NEW £1** banknote design is issued in Britain, the first to show Queen Elizabeth. The farthing coin, worth just a quarter of a penny, is withdrawn from circulation.

- **AN AMERICAN U2** spy plane is shot down over Russia in May. The flight is optimistically described as a "weather research" mission, but the Russians sentence pilot Gary Powers to ten years' detention. He is released in 1962, exchanged for the Soviet spy Rudolf Abel.

1960

- **SIXTY-NINE PEOPLE** are killed by police after demonstrations in Sharpeville, Transvaal. Later, prime minister Verwoerd is shot in an assassination attempt.

- **ALFRED HITCHCOCK** deploys a TV crew and a tiny budget to set the movie *Psycho* in a lonely motel owned by psychopathic Norman Bates. The shower room is shared.

- ***LADY CHATTERLEY'S LOVER***, D.H. Lawrence's 1920s novel about the sexual exploits of Chatterley and her gamekeeper, is found not obscene by a London court. The prosecuting counsel famously asks the jury: "Is it a book you would even wish your wife or your servants to read?" After the trial 200,000 copies are sold immediately.

Gretsch double-cut mono Falcon and friends, 1963 catalogue.

In 1959, Gretsch had modified its stereo-guitar system to create a more complex version. Jimmie Webster and Ray Butts again split the 12 poles of each pickup into two but added two more three-way selector switches on the upper bout for a total of four there, making a grand (and perhaps overwhelming) total of two control knobs and five selectors. The new pair of switches provided nine combinations of the split pickup sections, and Gretsch calculated that this, in combination with the six tonal options provided by the other two selectors, offered what it called "54 colors and shadings in stereo sound."

In 1960, Gretsch shifted the revised version of the stereo Falcon Super Project-o-Sonic to a new double-cutaway body, the first of many Gretsch models to adopt the new shape. At the same time, the revised stereo Country Club Project-o-Sonic appeared, and Gretsch would also issue an Anniversary stereo model in 1961, using the original control layout but with split HiLo'Tron single-coil pickups. However, Gretsch had underestimated the conservative nature of many guitar players. Despite Webster's rich imagination and Butts's technical prowess, the stereo models did not sell well—although stereo Falcons, with further revisions to the way the controls were laid out, continued to appear until about 1980.

Gibson, too, made a change to the look of some of its guitar bodies, focussing at first, toward the end of 1960, on its two high-end full-body hollow electrics, the Super 400CES and the L-5CES. The earlier rounded cutaway (the type that, with a flourish, Gibson called Venetian) was replaced with a new sharp cutaway (this one termed by Gibson as the Florentine). It was intended to provide better access to the higher frets, and the design feature lasted to the end of the decade, later appearing on some period-specific reissues.

ORIGINAL **GRETSCH WHITE FALCON SUPER PROJECT-O-SONIC 6137**
THIS EXAMPLE: ***1962***
The Falcon moved from single-cut to a new double-cut body in 1960, the first of many Gretsch models to do so. The company's revised stereo system now had five selectors and two knobs, and there were two angled string-mute controls.

Wes Montgomery with Gibson L-5CES, 1965 ad.

ORIGINAL **GIBSON L-5CESN**
THIS EXAMPLE: ***1964***
The L-5CES had a new cutaway in 1960, moving from rounded ("Venetian") to sharp ("Florentine"). The Byrdland and ES-350T changed, too, but some models, such as the ES-175 and ES-140, had always had the sharp type.

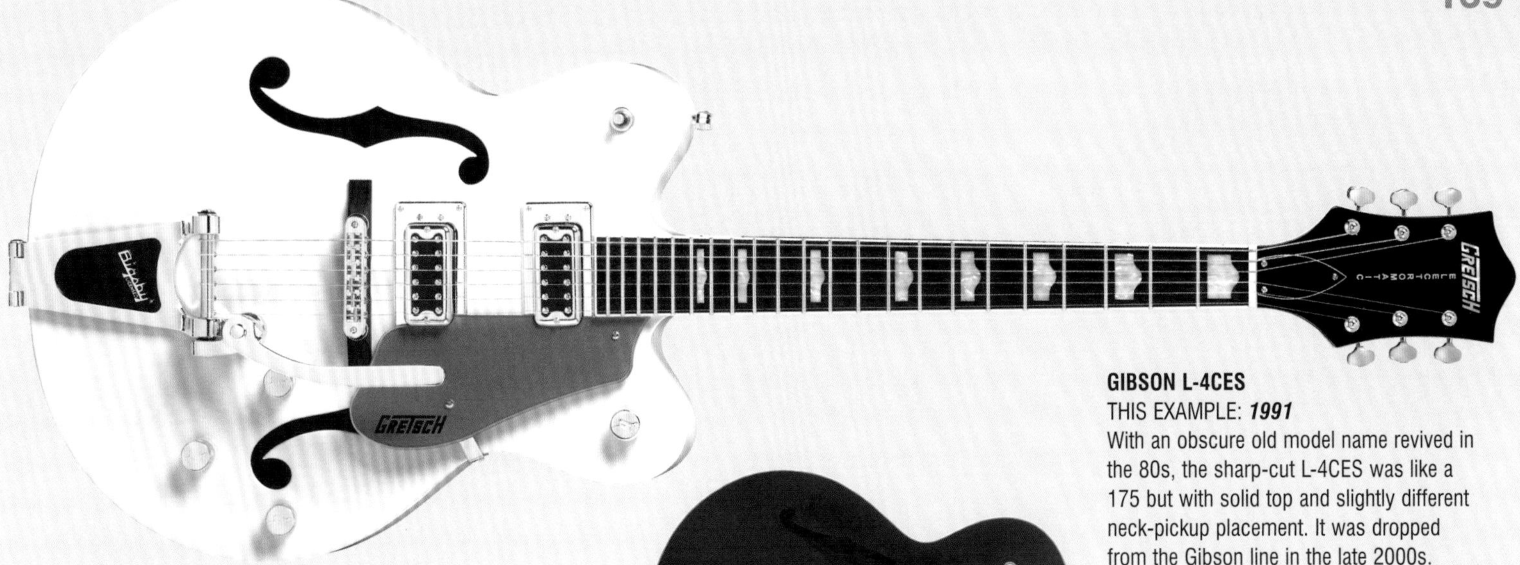

GIBSON L-4CES
THIS EXAMPLE: ***1991***
With an obscure old model name revived in the 80s, the sharp-cut L-4CES was like a 175 but with solid top and slightly different neck-pickup placement. It was dropped from the Gibson line in the late 2000s.

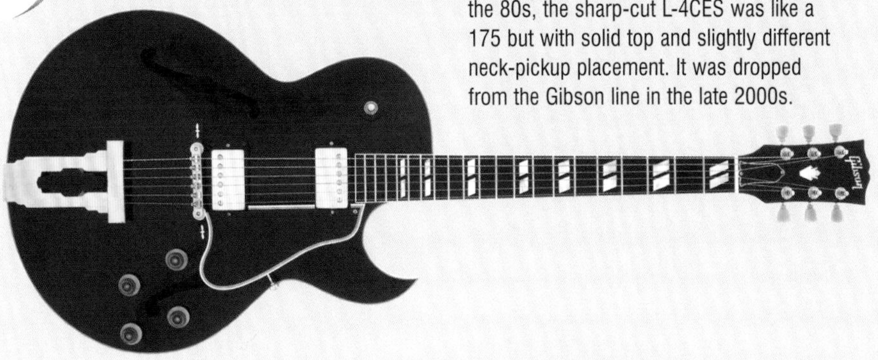

GRETSCH ELECTROMATIC HOLLOW BODY DOUBLE-CUT 5422-TDGC
THIS EXAMPLE: ***2014***
Gretsch first used the old Electromatic name as a brand in the late 90s, and in 2004 began using Gretsch Electromatic for a revised budget line. This double-cut Falcon is typical of the style and quality of recent Electromatic models.

Gretsch double-cut stereo Falcon, 1965 catalogue.

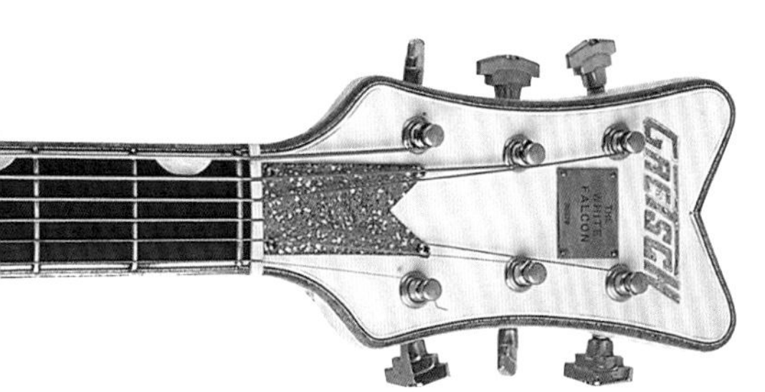

GRETSCH GUITARS

THE ULTIMATE SOUND OF THE TIMES

THE WHITE FALCON
- THE MOST BEAUTIFUL GUITAR MADE
- NEW GRETSCH "T" ZONE TEMPERED TREBLE
- DOUBLE CUTAWAY
- HOLLOW BODY

PX6137

No guitar can match its eye-stopping white and gold beauty or its rainbow of tonal colors. It is the ultimate guitar. No expense has been spared to make it what it is. The guitarist who must have the best will have no other.
The "White Falcon" features a slim 17" double cutaway gleaming white body of 2" thickness with 24-karat gold-plated metal parts, with multiple binding thru-out body and neck. Body finished in white lacquer, hand rubbed to a high luster. Exclusive Gretsch Vibrato*for that exciting tremolo effect. Satin ebony Neo-Classic fingerboard. Gretsch Deluxe High Ratio gears. Double Filter 'Tron pickups. Double muffler. Standby switch. Padded Back for extra comfort. 54 tone-color variations available at the flip of a switch! Made possible by four split Filter 'Tron heads ...two bass, two treble which you can custom-blend in nine different settings. Three-way bass and treble tone-color switches provide six tone settings for each head combination... the exclusive Gretsch "T" Zone Tempered-Treble (Patent #3,103,846) for perfect high note intonation...

PX6137 Gretsch White Falcon Guitar with Super Project-O-Sonic electrification. 24-karat gold-plated metal parts ....
PX6136 Gretsch White Falcon Guitar with standard Gretsch electrification. 24-karat gold-plated metal parts. (not illustrated) ....

* Patent Pending

Gibson Super 400CES, 1966 catalogue.

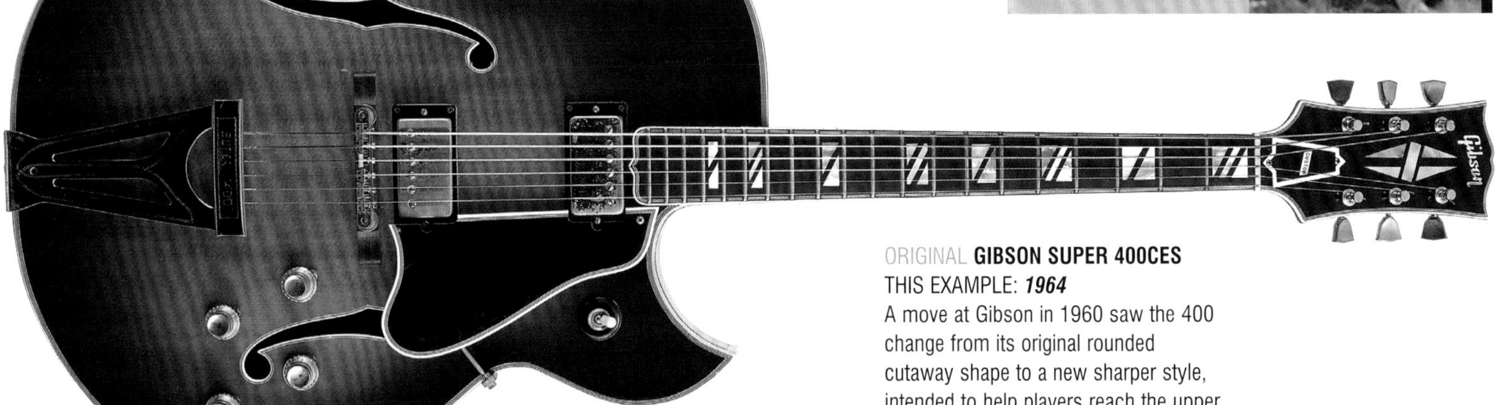

ORIGINAL **GIBSON SUPER 400CES**
THIS EXAMPLE: ***1964***
A move at Gibson in 1960 saw the 400 change from its original rounded cutaway shape to a new sharper style, intended to help players reach the upper frets more easily. The change also required a slightly shorter pickguard.

ORIGINAL **HOFNER VERITHIN**
THIS EXAMPLE: ***1960***
While the "flick-action console" and bar-shape fingerboard unlays mark this out as a typical product of the Hofner factory in Germany, the Verithin was in the American style of Gibson's thinline double-cut models such as the ES-330.

ORIGINAL **KAY UP-BEAT K8995J**
THIS EXAMPLE: ***1960***
A pair of Gold K Up-Beat models first appeared in Kay's 1960 catalogue, with two pickups (K8990) or, like this impressive example, three (K8995), and they were offered in shaded walnut (S), golden blond (B), or jet black (B).

Gold K Pro and Up-Beats, Kay catalogue 1960.

ORIGINAL **HARMONY ROCKET H59**
THIS EXAMPLE: ***1966***
This three-pickup version of Harmony's Rocket looked ready and willing to deliver a multitude of sounds thanks to its six controls (a volume and tone per pickup) and a four-way pickup selector (providing each pickup or all three).

British ad, 1960, for the new Hofner Verithin.

The Kay company of Chicago moved up a gear as the 60s began, and the already sizable operation would prove to be a powerhouse of guitar production as the demand for instruments at all levels grew dramatically during the decade. Kay expanded its guitar lines accordingly, adding new thinline models such as the Swingmaster and Speed Demon alongside the hollowbody Up-Beat, as well as new solidbody models like the imaginatively named Double Cutaway Solid, and also the Vanguard Contour.

In 1964, the company would make a move to a new factory at the Elk Grove Village industrial park, north-west of Chicago. Two years later, Kay was bought by Seeburg, a large company best known for its jukeboxes. As we shall see, this would be a relatively brief relationship for the Kay brand.

Meanwhile, Harmony was growing, too, in parallel with the increased interest in guitar playing across America and beyond. The models kept on coming, including the popular thinline hollowbody Rocket, and the H59 three-pickup version with its distinctive curving row of controls joined the existing single and double-pickup versions in 1960.

Harmony celebrated its 70th anniversary in 1962, the same year it moved to what it described as "the newest guitar plant in the world" at Archer Heights, near Chicago's Midway airport. The company added a second plant there a few years later to create a vast 125,000 square-foot space.

In Germany, Hofner was eyeing up new developments and creating its weapons for the rock'n'roll guitarist. A new model for 1960 was the Hofner Verithin, which reflected the influence of Gibson's ES-335 shape on other makers. There's no doubting by the name that the Verithin was a thinline, and it had the 335's double cutaway, too, but lacked the internal block.

One, two, and three-pickup Rockets, Harmony catalogue 1960.

HOFNER VERYTHIN CT
THIS EXAMPLE: ***2017***
Hofner's more recent take on its 60s Verithin style, updated and revised for modern players who seek a double-cut touch of German-style retro.

AIRLINE H59
THIS EXAMPLE: ***2018***
A modern take on the classic three-pickup Harmony Rocket, rebranded to join the line of Airline period re-creations by the Canadian company Eastwood.

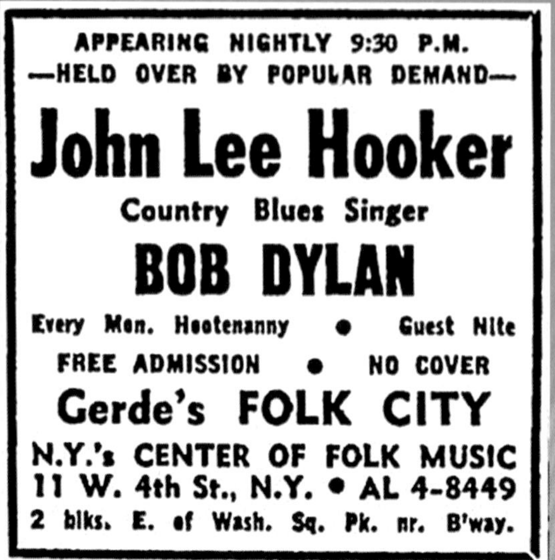

APPEARING NIGHTLY 9:30 P.M.
—HELD OVER BY POPULAR DEMAND—

John Lee Hooker

Country Blues Singer

BOB DYLAN

Every Mon. Hootenanny • Guest Nite

FREE ADMISSION • NO COVER

Gerde's FOLK CITY

N.Y.'s CENTER OF FOLK MUSIC
11 W. 4th St., N.Y. • AL 4-8449
2 blks. E. of Wash. Sq. Pk. nr. B'way.

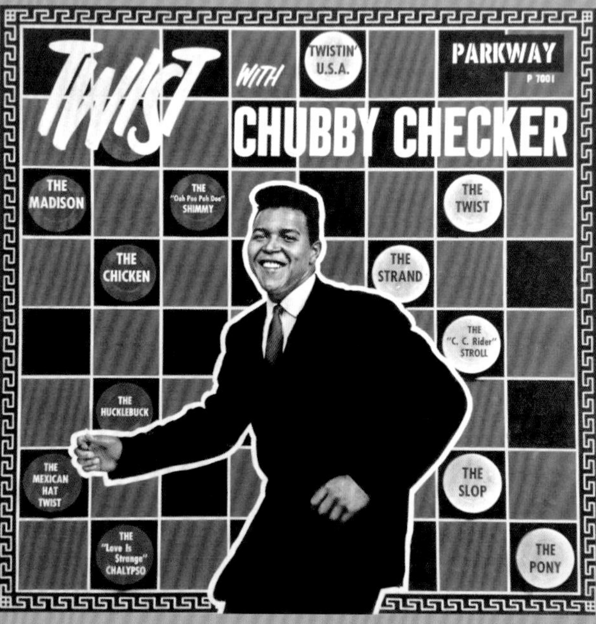

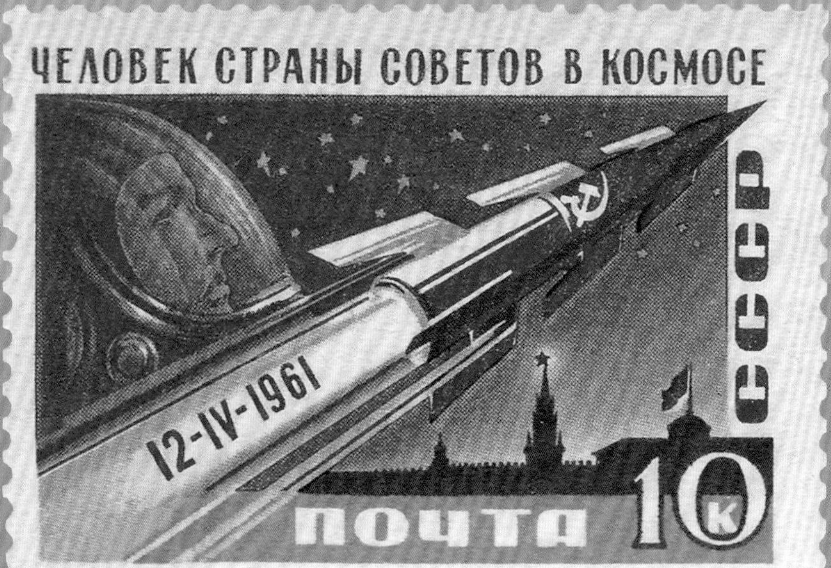

ЧЕЛОВЕК СТРАНЫ СОВЕТОВ В КОСМОСЕ

12-IV-1961

СССР

ПОЧТА 10 К

- **YURI GAGARIN** is the first man in space. The Russian orbits earth in Vostok 1 for a little under two hours. A month later, Alan Shepard is the first American in space, fired 116 miles up for a fifteen-minute leap. In August, Gherman Titov orbits in Vostok 2 for 25 hours.

- **GEORGE FORMBY**, British screen star and ukulele wizard, dies. David Evans is born in Essex, England. At the end of the next decade he will become guitarist Edge in U2.

- **THE BERLIN WALL** is built to prevent East Berliners reaching the West. Elsewhere, the contraceptive pill is on general sale, aimed to control more personal incursions.

1961

- ***CATCH-22***, Joseph Heller's comic-surreal novel about American airmen in the wartime Mediterranean, is published. The title will pass into the language to describe deadlock.

- **THE TWIST** is the latest dance craze to rock America. Less rhythmically bound, Bob Dylan debuts in New York City folk clubs and is signed to the Columbia record company in September.

- **AMERICA's** recently elected president John F. Kennedy faces trouble abroad as an invasion of Cuba at the Bay of Pigs fails, and as the number of "military advisers" sent by the US to Vietnam steadily increases.

In Britain, Vox was the brand used by Jennings Musical Industries (JMI), owned by Tom Jennings, who had established his Jennings Organ Company in the late 40s and then JMI early in the 50s. JMI manufactured and distributed Vox amplifiers, devised by Dick Denney, and the firm's headquarters and factory were at Dartford, to the south-east of London.

During 1959, Vox began also to produce guitars. At first these were budget models, but soon Tom Jennings wanted a better instrument, and he instructed his in-house designers to produce a new design. JMI's designers came up with the Phantom, which Vox introduced in 1961. Most obviously different was the five-sided body, and like Gibson's earlier Flying V and Explorer, it had none of the curves of conventional designs. The Phantom in a number of variations remained in the original Vox line until 1968.

Jim Burns set up his Ormston Burns company in Essex, east of London. It began producing electric guitars in 1959, the most spectacular of which was the solidbody Bison, introduced in 1961. This first version of the Bison had a beautifully sculpted body with a pair of forward-sloping cutaway horns, an impressive vibrato, gold-plated metalwork, a patented gear-box truss-rod system, Split Sound switching, and low-impedance pickups. The following year, Burns would replace this four-pickup Bison with a redesigned version, which had three pickups and was generally less advanced than the original, although it did have the enticing Wild Dog setting among its tonal presets.

Charlie Watkins was based in south-east London, and by 1960 he had a line of three Watkins amplifiers (which gained the WEM logo around 1963–64) and the Copicat tape-echo box, as well as some imported German-made acoustic guitars. It was around this time that the best known of the Watkins electrics was introduced, the solidbody Rapier series.

Watkins Rapier models in the Bell mail-order catalogue, 1964.

The "new shape" Vox Phantom VI, 1963 ad.

ORIGINAL **VOX PHANTOM XII STEREO**
THIS EXAMPLE: ***1965***
The striking five-sided body appeared on a number of Phantom models, including this later Stereo XII, which has a bewildering array of controls designed to appeal to the keen 60s soundscaper.

ORIGINAL **BURNS BISON**
THIS EXAMPLE: ***1961***
The Bison was a good example of British engineering, but one Burns insider estimated the company made only 49 of them before the design had to be simplified, and a revised three-pickup version was introduced during 1962.

Ormston Burns
NOW PROUDLY PRESENT
the fabulous
BLACK BISON
with the new "split sound" (Pat. pend.)

WHAT IS SPLIT SOUND?
After years of research, top British hi-fi engineers have developed this exciting new sound, exclusive to this guitar and patented by Burns. Split sound means that the guitarist can have true stereo—sparkling treble and full, rich bass—at the same time from one amplifier! Remember—the Black Bison is the only guitar in the world with this wonderful innovation.

JUST LOOK AT THESE FEATURES!
★ Revolutionary ultra-sonic pick-ups.
★ Absolutely distortion-free.
★ Purest electric guitar sound ever.
★ New "string-lock" bridge* (roller action—6 individual ball bearings).
★ Brilliant new vibrato unit with unique micro-adjustment.*
★ Neck guaranteed 20 years.
★ New geared truss rod.*
★ Ebony fingerboard.
★ 24-carat gold-plated fittings.
★ "Satin lustre" black finish.
★ "Sculptured" body (Reg. Des. No. 902999).
*PATENTS PENDING

£300 WORTH OF VALUABLE INSTRUMENTS TO BE WON BY USERS OF BURNS GUITARS! WATCH THIS SPACE NEXT WEEK!!

WRITE FOR LEAFLETS

Manufactured exclusively by:—Ormston Burns Ltd., Cherry Tree Rise, Roding Valley, Buckhurst Hill, Essex
Trade Suppliers:—ROSE, MORRIS & CO. LTD., 79-85 PAUL STREET, E.C.2
BARNES & MULLINS LTD., 3 RATHBONE PLACE, W.1

Burns proudly launches the Bison, 1961 ad.

ORIGINAL **WATKINS RAPIER 33**
THIS EXAMPLE: ***1964***
The affordable Rapier models were stalwarts of the burgeoning beat scene in early-60s Britain. Many groups began with Watkins amps, too, and the WEM logo (Watkins Electric Music) was seen on PAs at many live events at the time.

In their original forms, neither Vox nor Burns would last beyond the 60s, but both British brands reappeared in later years. A number of Vox guitars had been made in Italy in the 60s in addition to British production, but in the 70s and 80s there was a revival of the Vox name on some Japanese-made models, none of which bore any similarity to the classic 60s instruments. Those who remembered the striking Phantom and Mark models were surprised to see that these models were not reissued.

More recently, as interest in those originals has grown, there have been two attempts at a revival of the style and feel of the classics, including the five-sided Phantom model. Phantom Guitarworks in the United States made one such effort, offering a number of remakes of vintage-style Vox guitars. In 1998, the Japanese musical electronics firm Korg launched new lines of Vox reproductions, and these would last in production until 2014.

Burns, meanwhile was sold to the US keyboard company Baldwin in 1965, but this was a relationship that had fizzled out by 1970. Jim Burns himself made some comebacks in the 70s and into the 80s, but while interesting, most of those guitars were without much reference to the vintage-style Burns models of the 60s. It was only in 1992 that Burns saw a proper revival, with Barry Gibson in charge (and Jim Burns a consultant until his death six years later). This relatively new Burns London operation continues today.

The revived Burns London company has offered several period-correct reissues of the classic models and also has developed a number of new models and modern-style remakes mostly divided into the Club series and the Custom Elite series. Those reissues have included re-creations of the original 1961-style four-pickup Bison, the revised three-pickup '62 version, and the '64-style Bison that had a scroll headstock and three-piece pickguard.

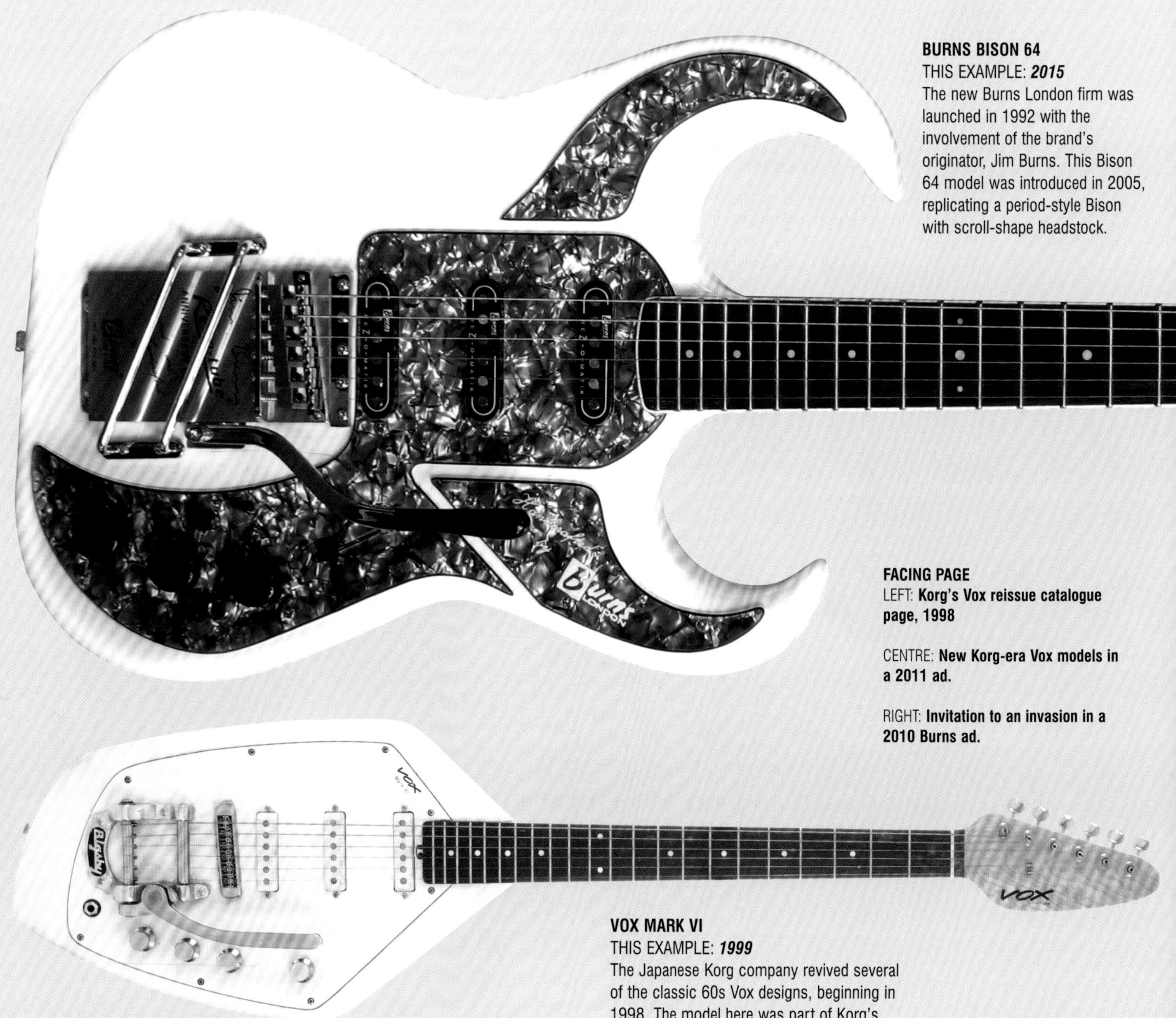

BURNS BISON 64
THIS EXAMPLE: ***2015***
The new Burns London firm was launched in 1992 with the involvement of the brand's originator, Jim Burns. This Bison 64 model was introduced in 2005, replicating a period-style Bison with scroll-shape headstock.

FACING PAGE
LEFT: **Korg's Vox reissue catalogue page, 1998**

CENTRE: **New Korg-era Vox models in a 2011 ad.**

RIGHT: **Invitation to an invasion in a 2010 Burns ad.**

VOX MARK VI
THIS EXAMPLE: ***1999***
The Japanese Korg company revived several of the classic 60s Vox designs, beginning in 1998. The model here was part of Korg's reissue series, which continued in production for about three years.

1962-style Bison reissue in Burns London's 2006 catalogue.

Vox Custom 25, Japanese solidbody, 1982 catalogue.

In the '60s, Vox crafted a line of distinctly designed, beautifully detailed electric guitars. Now we are proud to present replicas of these models recreated with original details using the same unique parts. At Vox our main goal is to offer products of the finest quality, so we have improved the playability and specifications over those of the originals to satisfy today's demanding musicians.

Shown: Mark III Custom, Mark III with tremolo, Mark VI

Mark III, Mark VI, Mark XII

Sculpted of poplar bodies with maple necks and rosewood fingerboards, the Vox Mark III, Mark VI and Mark XII are constructed in the U.S.A. With sleekly styled fittings, like Bigsby* tremolo systems and chrome knobs and original style pickup covers, they look as good as they sound. The droplet shaped Mark III comes with two single coil pickups and is available in two models – one with a fixed bridge and the other with a Bigsby tremolo system. The Mark III Custom comes in white and offers a painted headstock and chrome pickguard as used by one of the most famous guitarists of the '60s. The Mark VI's distinct body style is fitted with three single coil pickups and a Bigsby tremolo system. The Mark XII is a twelve string, droplet-shaped model that offers Vox styling and superior playability.

Colors available:

Mark III – black, red, ocean green
Mark III Custom – white
Mark VI – sparkle black, red, blue
Mark XII – black

Vox Mini 12 Guitar

This 19-fret little gem comes fully loaded with vintage alnico pickups. Commonly used on early 1960s British invasion recordings, the Mini 12's tuning and fingering are the same as a standard 12 string guitar, except that it is tuned to "A" instead of "E." With fully adjustable intonation for each of the 12 strings, a maple neck and a solid 2 piece hardwood body, the Mini 12 will add a unique flavor to your guitar performance. Available in suburst only.

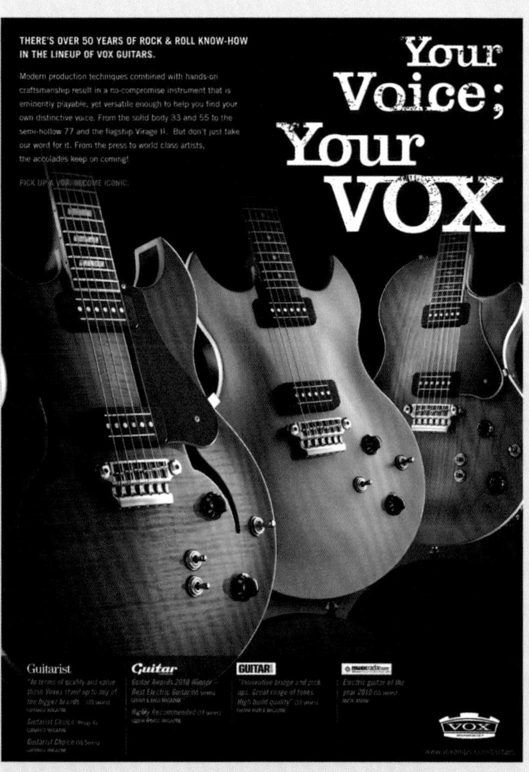

1961

Custom-color and sunburst Jazzmasters, 1962–63 catalogue.

Fender first issued a custom-finishes chart in 1961 to promote the available custom colors, although non-standard colors had been available earlier. Most Fenders at first came only in the standard finish: blond for Telecasters and Esquires; sunburst for Stratocasters and Jazzmasters. Since about 1954, the factory had turned out a few one-offs finished in solid colors, but not many players at the time seemed interested, and Fender's main production remained in regular-finish instruments.

The first official sign from Fender of its color options came in the 1956–57 catalogue, which noted that the Strat was available "in custom colors at 5% cost," and a '57 pricelist offered some models "in Custom DuPont Ducco finishes—5% extra cost." DuPont was the biggest supplier of paint to the car industry in America, and Fender used paints from its Duco nitro-cellulose lines, such as fiesta red or foam green, as well as the more color-retentive Lucite acrylics, like Lake Placid blue metallic or burgundy mist metallic.

Fender's first custom finishes chart offered options of black, burgundy mist metallic, Dakota red, daphne blue, fiesta red, foam green, inca silver metallic, Lake Placid blue metallic, olympic white, shell pink, sherwood green metallic, shoreline gold metallic, sonic blue, and surf green. Later 60s charts lost some of these and added others, including candy apple red metallic, firemist gold metallic, ocean turquoise metallic, and teal green metallic.

Decades later, Fenders with these original custom colors proved desirable among collectors, who rate them as prime catches. Back in the day, the colors didn't add much to the price. In 1961, a custom color added just $14.47 extra to a regular $289.50 sunburst Strat with vibrato. Be assured, however, that in today's market, the price differential between a sunburst '61 Strat and one in a genuine custom color would certainly be greater.

ORIGINAL **FENDER ESQUIRE**
THIS EXAMPLE: ***1959***
Esquires and Telecasters in custom colors are seen less often than Strats, and this Esquire from 1959 is finished in fiesta red, one of 14 colors that Fender first offered on its 1961 custom-finishes chart.

ORIGINAL **FENDER STRATOCASTER**
THIS EXAMPLE: ***1961***
An early-60s Strat finished in burgundy mist metallic, one of the DuPont paint colors that Fender offered as optional finishes on many of its solidbody electric models at the time.

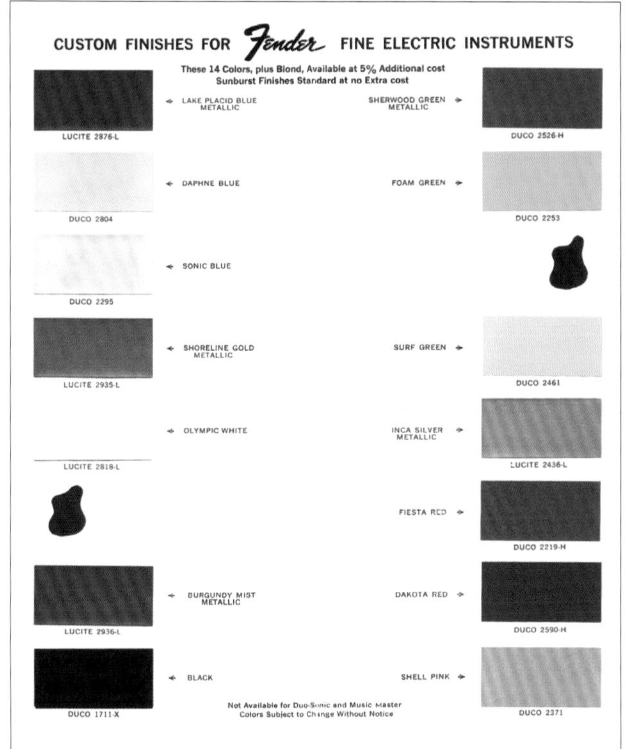

CUSTOM FINISHES FOR Fender FINE ELECTRIC INSTRUMENTS

These 14 Colors, plus Blond, Available at 5% Additional cost
Sunburst Finishes Standard at no Extra cost

Color	Code	Color	Code
LAKE PLACID BLUE METALLIC	LUCITE 2876-L	SHERWOOD GREEN METALLIC	DUCO 2526-H
DAPHNE BLUE	DUCO 2804	FOAM GREEN	DUCO 2253
SONIC BLUE	DUCO 2295		
SHORELINE GOLD METALLIC	LUCITE 2935-L	SURF GREEN	DUCO 2461
OLYMPIC WHITE	LUCITE 2818-L	INCA SILVER METALLIC	LUCITE 2436-L
		FIESTA RED	DUCO 2219-H
BURGUNDY MIST METALLIC	LUCITE 2936-L	DAKOTA RED	DUCO 2590-H
BLACK	DUCO 1711-X	SHELL PINK	DUCO 2371

Not Available for Duo-Sonic and Music Master
Colors Subject to Change Without Notice

Fender's first custom finishes chart, 1961.

Early fiesta red Strat on the 1958–59 catalogue cover.

ORIGINAL **FENDER TELECASTER**
THIS EXAMPLE: ***1963***
A Telecaster from the early 60s finished in shoreline gold metallic, one of the custom color options that Fender promoted through its catalogues, pricelists, and custom-finishes charts of the period.

ORIGINAL **FENDER JAZZMASTER**
THIS EXAMPLE: ***1962***
This Jazzmaster is finished in sonic blue. Many custom-color Jazzmasters of the period, like this one, had a matching headstock finish, and here the top lacquer at the head has yellowed somewhat with age.

Most of Fender's original custom color finishes were discontinued in the late 60s and early 70s. CBS management cut the Fender line back to the basics and did not seem much interested in offering too many colorful guitars.

A pricelist from late '74, for example, revealed that the Jazzmaster was back to the way it had started in the late 50s, with only a sunburst finish on offer. Meanwhile, the Stratocaster had been trimmed down to just six finishes: the regular sunburst look, plus options of natural, blond, black, white, or walnut finish, each for a small extra cost. The Telecaster, too, was now offered in only six finishes: the standard was blond, and there were options of just natural, sunburst, black, white, or walnut. All these could be bought new with the regular rosewood fingerboard of the period, but also a maple board was offered as an option. And there were optional left-handed versions, a Bigsby vibrato option for the Telecaster, and a vibrato-less option for the Stratocaster.

Fender brightened its available color schemes somewhat during the 80s, with a shortlived line of international colors in 1981 and some custom colors and "stratobursts" around '82. Some of the new hues were distinctly lurid, such as capri orange, aztec gold, or bronze stratoburst, and they were not much liked at the time. Also, in 1984, Fender made short runs of marble "bowling ball" finishes for some Strats and Teles, in streaky red, blue, or gold.

Into the 90s and on to more recent decades, and the idea of a decent selection of custom colors seemed to take firmer hold at Fender. Since those earlier uncertain days, the company today offers a full selection of colors to entice the guitarist who wants to have something beyond the regular sunbursts or blonds.

Custom Shop 2015 catalogue, blue ice metallic Tele.

FENDER TELECASTER STANDARD
THIS EXAMPLE: ***1984***
Fender decided to draw attention to the shortlived Standard model, which had no through-body stringing, with a short run of "bowling ball" or "marble" finishes in blue (pictured), gold, or red.

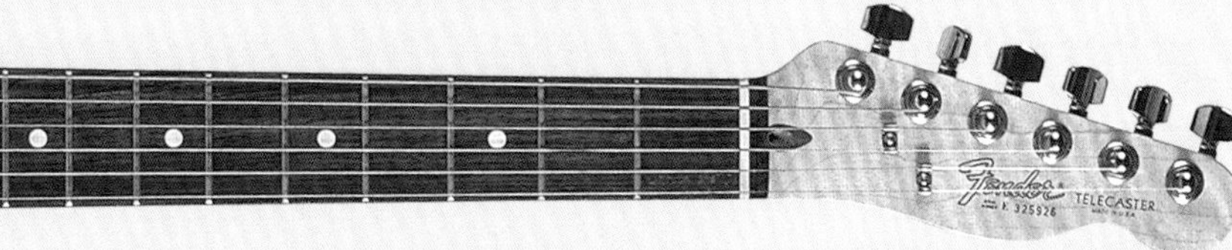

FENDER AMERICAN VINTAGE '62 STRATOCASTER
THIS EXAMPLE: ***2012***
The forerunner to Fender's more recent American Original series, the company's American Vintage models included a '62-style Stratocaster, this one finished in surf green.

American Vintage colors, 2002 ad.

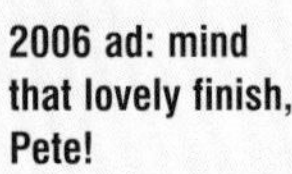

2006 ad: mind that lovely finish, Pete!

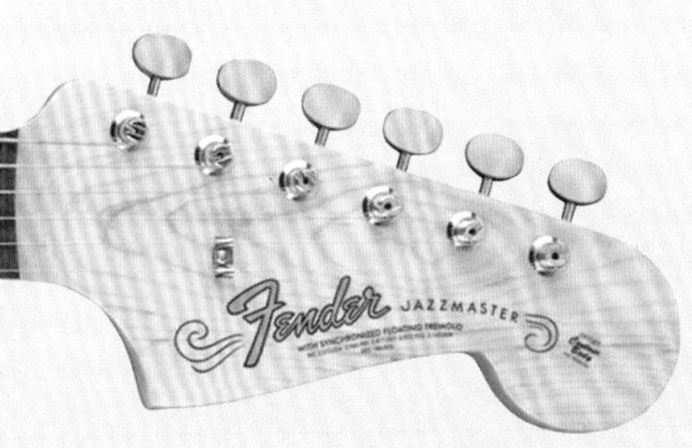

FENDER AMERICAN ORIGINAL 60s JAZZMASTER
THIS EXAMPLE: ***2018***
At the time of writing, this was the current 60s-style Jazzmaster made in Fender's US factory in California. This example is finished in ocean turquoise, which like the Strat pictured here uses one of Fender's original vintage-era color names.

Lee Roy Parnell with colorful Roadhouse Strats, 1997.

Epiphone, owned by Gibson since 1957, continued to add some new models to its lines that were near-equivalents of Gibson models, although with different pickups and varied feature sets. The Sheraton, a double-cutaway thinline model that Epiphone had introduced in 1959, was roughly equivalent to the Gibson ES-355, and at first it was the only semi-solid among the Gibson-made Epiphones. In 1961, the Sheraton gained Epiphone's mini-humbucking pickups, and also this year the vibrato, with its E-for-Epiphone logo, became a standard fitting. Epiphone introduced a new hollowbody double-cut thinline in 1961, too, the Casino, which was a close relation to the Gibson ES-330. The Casino's most famous players would be Paul McCartney, John Lennon and George Harrison, who each played one later in the 60s.

Rickenbacker introduced a higher-end model in 1961, the 460, which had triangle fingerboard markers—Rickenbacker's most obvious indicator of a deluxe model. It was the first with a modified control layout, which the California company would apply to nearly all its models over the coming years. A fifth "blend" control was added just behind the four regular controls, with a smaller knob, and it offered some increased versatility to the available tones.

The 460 also had Rickenbacker's new stereo output system, called Rick-O-Sound, following the earlier lead of Gretsch and Gibson's developments in this area.

Rickenbacker's system simply separated the output from the neck pickup and the bridge pickup, using a split cable to feed the individual signals to two amplifiers (or amp channels). It was made possible by a special double jack-plate fitted to Rick-O-Sound models, with one jack marked Standard, which alone offered regular mono output, and one marked Rick-O-Sound, which required a stereo plug connected to a Y cable. On stereo Rickenbackers, the new fifth knob functioned like a balance control between neck pickup and bridge pickup.

ORIGINAL **EPIPHONE CASINO E230TD**
THIS EXAMPLE: ***1965***
Another Gibson-like model in the Epiphone lines of the time was the Casino, introduced in 1961 and a near equivalent of Gibson's fully hollowbody ES-330 double-cutaway thinline model.

British catalogue, 1963, for Epiphone's Casino.

ORIGINAL **EPIPHONE SHERATON E212T**
THIS EXAMPLE: ***1961***
One of the schemes adopted by the newly Gibson-owned Epiphone brand was to create close relatives of near-equivalent Gibson models, and in the case of this Sheraton the Gibson relative was the high-end semi-solid ES-355.

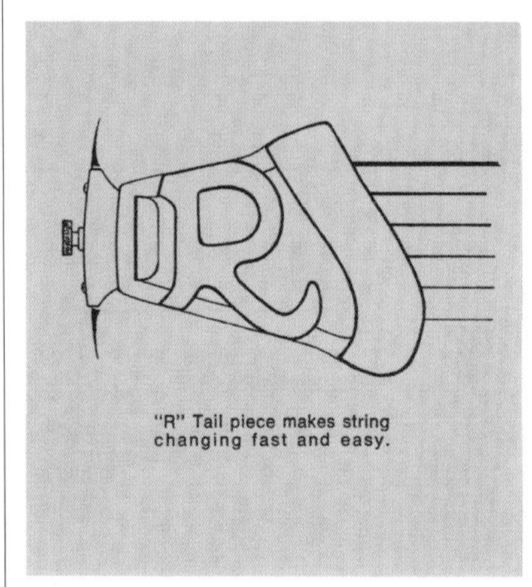

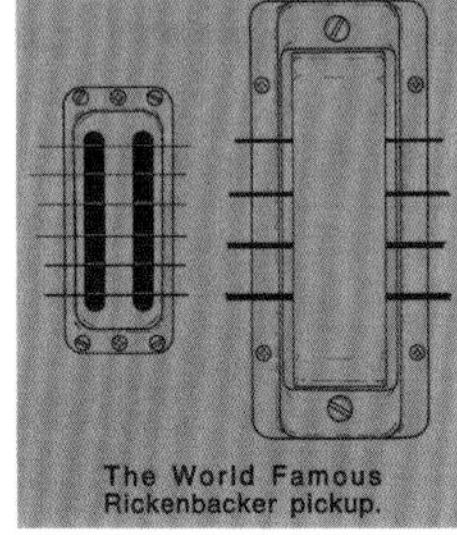

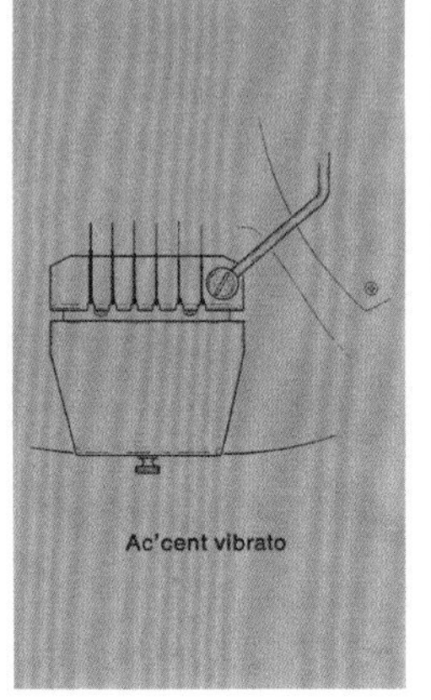

Rickenbacker features, including stereo, 1968 catalogue.

EPIPHONE NOEL GALLAGHER UNION JACK SUPERNOVA
THIS EXAMPLE: ***2005***
Noel Gallagher was an enthusiastic Epiphone player, and the patriotic finish of this production model of the early 2000s has the bold look of a custom model made for the Oasis guitarist.

1961 Epiphone ad for its Tremotone vibrato.

ORIGINAL **RICKENBACKER 460**
THIS EXAMPLE: ***1961***
Rickenbacker introduced its new 460 model in 1961, its first with the company's Rick-O-Sound stereo output system, and the first with a new fifth control knob that blended tones or (in stereo mode) balanced left and right output.

Paul Weller with Epiphone Elitist Casino, 2008 ad.

1961

Gibson began removing Les Paul's name from guitars in 1959, and by the end of that year the Les Paul TV and Special models became the SG TV and SG Special, with exactly the same features. For now, the Les Paul Junior kept its name. But a bigger change was coming, as Gibson managers saw sales tumbling of Les Paul-style guitars after most had peaked in '59. They decided it was time for a complete redesign.

Gibson considered the benefits of its recent developments, including thinner and double-cutaway bodies, new finishes, slimmer-profile necks with full access to the highest frets, and new pickups, as well as the tried-and-tested features of established instruments. The result was the design we know today as the SG.

The SG design was radical, almost as if a sculptor rather than a guitar-maker was at work. The double-cutaway body was a modernistic amalgam of bevels and points and angles, and the design invited players to reach the topmost frets with ease and speed. It was unlike anything any guitar maker had produced before. The official announcement of the first two new-design guitars—still for now called the Les Paul Standard and the Les Paul Custom—came in the early months of 1961 (although the new Standard had started to come off Gibson's production line at the very end of 1960).

Three further models with the new SG design, the Les Paul Junior, SG TV, and SG Special, were announced in 1961. Gibson had dropped the original-design single-cutaway Les Paul sunburst Standard and black Custom, and also the rounded-double-cutaway Les Paul Junior, Junior 3⁄4, SG TV, SG Special, and SG Special 3⁄4. In 1963, Gibson would finally drop the remaining Les Paul names, establishing the new-shape line as the SG TV, SG Junior, SG Special, SG Standard, and SG Custom.

ORIGINAL **GIBSON (SG) LES PAUL CUSTOM**
THIS EXAMPLE: ***1963***
The gorgeous new SG-shape Les Paul Custom, introduced in 1961, was the high-end guitar among the models with this new design. It lost its Les Paul markings and became known simply as the SG Custom during 1963.

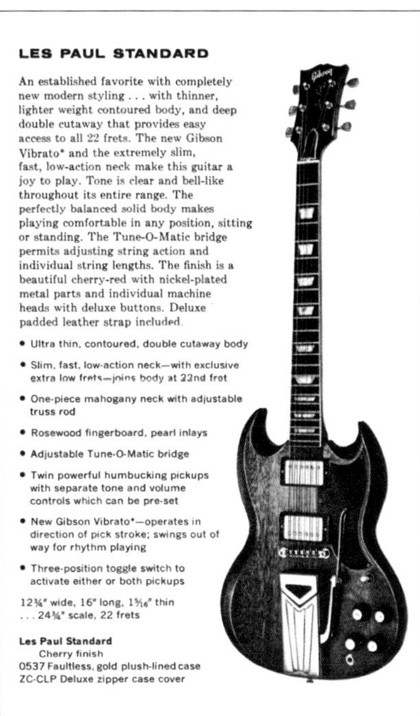

LES PAUL STANDARD

An established favorite with completely new modern styling . . . with thinner, lighter weight contoured body, and deep double cutaway that provides easy access to all 22 frets. The new Gibson Vibrato* and the extremely slim, fast, low-action neck make this guitar a joy to play. Tone is clear and bell-like throughout its entire range. The perfectly balanced solid body makes playing comfortable in any position, sitting or standing. The Tune-O-Matic bridge permits adjusting string action and individual string lengths. The finish is a beautiful cherry-red with nickel-plated metal parts and individual machine heads with deluxe buttons. Deluxe padded leather strap included.

- Ultra thin, contoured, double cutaway body
- Slim, fast, low-action neck—with exclusive extra low frets—joins body at 22nd fret
- One-piece mahogany neck with adjustable truss rod
- Rosewood fingerboard, pearl inlays
- Adjustable Tune-O-Matic bridge
- Twin powerful humbucking pickups with separate tone and volume controls which can be pre-set
- New Gibson Vibrato*—operates in direction of pick stroke; swings out of way for rhythm playing
- Three-position toggle switch to activate either or both pickups

12¾" wide, 16" long, 1 5/16" thin . . . 24¾" scale, 22 frets

Les Paul Standard
Cherry finish
0537 Faultless, gold plush-lined case
ZC-CLP Deluxe zipper case cover

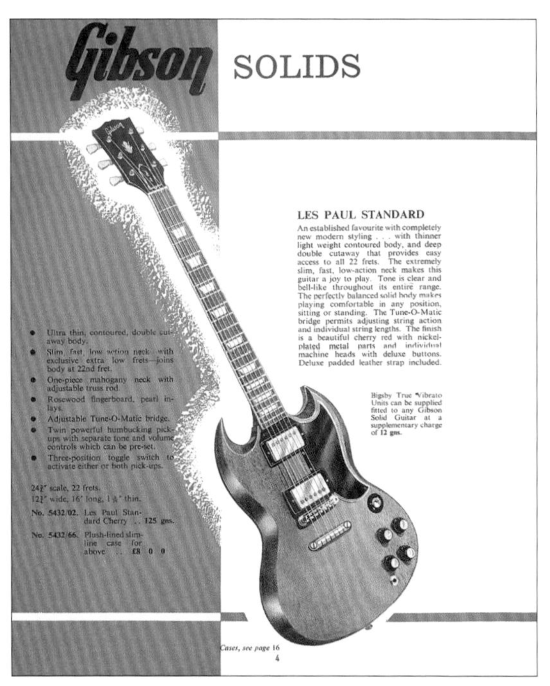

Gibson SOLIDS

LES PAUL STANDARD

An established favourite with completely new modern styling . . . with thinner light weight contoured body, and deep double cutaway that provides easy access to all 22 frets. The extremely slim, fast, low-action neck makes this guitar a joy to play. Tone is clear and bell-like throughout its entire range. The perfectly balanced solid body makes playing comfortable in any position, sitting or standing. The Tune-O-Matic bridge permits adjusting string action and individual string lengths. The finish is a beautiful cherry red with nickel-plated metal parts and individual machine heads with deluxe buttons. Deluxe padded leather strap included.

- Ultra thin, contoured, double cutaway body.
- Slim, fast, low action neck with exclusive extra low frets—joins body at 22nd fret.
- One-piece mahogany neck with adjustable truss rod.
- Rosewood fingerboard, pearl inlays.
- Adjustable Tune-O-Matic bridge.
- Twin powerful humbucking pick-ups with separate tone and volume controls which can be pre-set.
- Three-position toggle switch to activate either or both pick-ups.

24¾" scale, 22 frets.
12¾" wide, 16" long, 1 5/16" thin.

No. 5432/02. Les Paul Standard Cherry .. 125 gns.
No. 5432/66. Plush-lined slim-line case for above .. £8 0 0

Bigsby True Vibrato Units can be supplied fitted to any Gibson Solid Guitar at a supplementary charge of 12 gns.

Cases, see page 16
4

SOLID HIT

the Les Paul guitars

by GIBSON

Les Paul and Mary Ford: two solid hits on the list of all-time guitar greats. With their own brand of sound, big and bright…with special stylings and effects–they reach listeners through every medium. Whether it's radio, night club, TV, a Columbia recording, or a dinner engagement…Les and Mary are always a solid hit–and it's always with their Gibson guitars.

Just out–and a solid success with guitar players–are the new Les Paul Model solid body Gibsons. Ultra thin, hand contoured, double cutaway…with new Gibson Vibrato and the famous "fretless wonder" neck (a low, fast action neck giving the ultimate in playing ease and mobility).

This dynamic Les Paul series is an exciting new approach to the solid body guitar. Beauty in gleaming white or cherry red that must be seen. Wonderfully clear bell-like tone that must be heard. Fast action that should be tried…soon. By Gibson, of course.

Gibson
KALAMAZOO, MICHIGAN

LEFT: **SG-shape Les Paul Standard entry, 1961 catalogue.**

CENTER: **SG-shape Les Paul Standard entry, 1963 UK catalogue.**

RIGHT: **Les Paul and Mary Ford endorsing the SG-shape Custom, 1961 ad.**

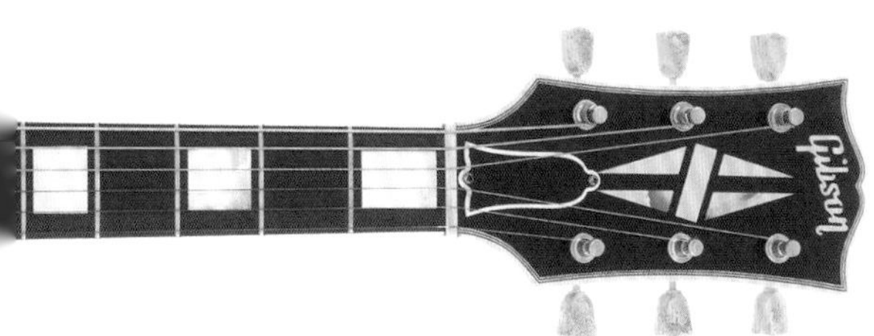

Solid Body ELECTRIC GUITARS

SG SPECIAL

Two ways new! A lovely new finish in white or Gibson's cherry red . . . an ultra-modern new sculptured shape. Outstanding for its tone, versatility, and low fast action at a modest price.

FEATURES: Ultra thin, contoured, double cutaway body, nickel-plated metal parts, enclosed individual machine heads. Slim, fast, low-action neck—with exclusive extra low frets—joins body at 22nd fret. Rosewood fingerboard, pearl dot inlays. One-piece mahogany neck, adjustable truss rod. Combination metal bridge and tailpiece, adjustable horizontally and vertically. Two powerful pickups with separate tone and volume controls which can be pre-set. Three-position toggle switch to activate either or both pickups. 12¾" wide, 16" long, 1 5/16" thin, 24¾" scale, 22 frets.

SG Special Cherry finish
SG Special White finish
0537 Faultless plush-lined case
316 Archcraft plush-lined case
116 Durabilt case
ZC-SGC Deluxe zipper case cover

SG Special entry in Gibson's 1963 catalogue.

ORIGINAL **GIBSON SG SPECIAL**
THIS EXAMPLE: ***1961***
This model did not have Les Paul markings like some of the other guitars in the new line of SG-shape models, and it was known from the start as the SG Special.

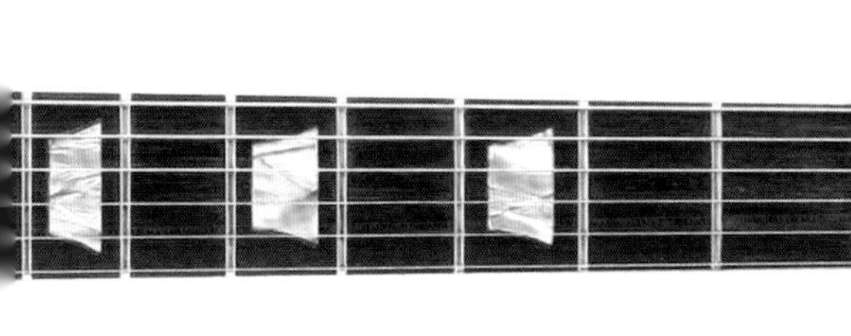

ORIGINAL **GIBSON (SG) LES PAUL STANDARD**
THIS EXAMPLE: ***1961***
The SG-shape Les Paul Standard was the first of Gibson's new SG models, and it remained marked as a Les Paul model until 1963. It replaced the sunburst-finish 1958–60 Standard that had the original Les Paul single-cutaway design.

SG Standards pictured in Gibson's 1983 catalogue.

First Editions

Only the most daring can transcend their own times to stand forever apart from the ordinary.

The SG, as well as the instruments shown on the following two pages are designs that shattered every visual and sonic stereotype of their day. Masterpieces of styling and sound innovation created in a supernova of design ingenuity.

The SG Standard. It's like no other guitar Gibson makes, an instrument that grew up in the 60's when Rock was reaching its zenith, versatile and powerful enough to project the rebellious tone which became the fabric of that classic era. Today the SG is continuing to prove its stamina as a workhorse instrument in a number of musical arenas.

The Futura. An uncommonly graceful shape, contoured to fit the player firmly. Neck-through-the-body construction to allow unimpeded access to all 22 frets. Evolved from two decades of engineering excellence, the Futura is the shape of things to come.

The Flying V and Explorer. Two free spirits from beyond the outer reaches of rock 'n roll. Together they created a sonic boom still being heard, often in the faint echo of imitators.

The EDS-1275. A two-horned dragon of almost mythical proportions. This double-necked cousin of the SG enables the player to produce both the soft-ringing tone of a 6-string and the silvery, translucent aura of a 12-string.

While radically different from other instruments of their time, and from each other as well, these Gibson legends share a common ancestry of materials, craftsmanship and electronic sophistication.

As distinctive now as when they were first conceived, these time machines have achieved a kind of immortality among fret aficionados.

Like fine wines, these first editions have only improved with age. Unlike fine wines, however, when you "open up" one of these guitars – the music pours forever.

SG Standard

BODY Contoured solid mahogany construction ☐ Double cutaway design ☐ Adjustable, chrome-plated Tune-O-Matic™ bridge and Stop Bar™ tailpiece ☐ Black fingerrest with white revealed edge ☐ Two chrome-plated Gibson Super Humbucking pickups with individual volume and tone controls ☐ Three-position toggle switch for pickup selection (individual or both pickups simultaneously) ☐ The new ultra-safe Gibson "Posi-Lok"™ strap button.
Body Size: Length 16", Width 13 9/32", Depth 1 9/16".

NECK Mahogany neck construction with 17 degree pitched peghead ☐ Width at first fret 1 11/16" ☐ Bound rosewood fingerboard with block inlays and corresponding side dots ☐ Distinctive peghead inlay ☐ Chrome-plated, individual machine heads with traditional keystone shaped buttons ☐ Gibson truss rod system with traditional truss rod cover. 22 frets ☐ 24 3/4" scale length.

22 23

GIBSON SG CUSTOM
THIS EXAMPLE: ***1978***
A late-70s example of the high-end SG model, which retains some of the features if not the flair of the original design. The model came as standard at this time without a vibrato.

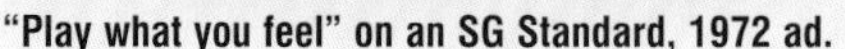

"Play what you feel" on an SG Standard, 1972 ad.

The early 70s were turbulent times for Gibson and for most of the other big US guitar makers. Japanese brands such as Ibanez were busily copying the American icons and selling them relatively cheaply (and successfully) to beginners, while Gibson itself had been taken over in 1969 by a brewing firm to form Norlin and was suffering as a result.

The SG line hit an odd blip in '71, replacing the Standard and Special with the Deluxe and Pro, two models of questionable design that did not last too long: the Pro was gone from the pricelist by 1972 and the Deluxe by '73. Ibanez, meanwhile, added the SG Pro to its catalogue of copy guitars—instruments that copied famous US originals—and called this one the 2377 model.

The SG Standard and Special were reinstated in the Gibson catalogue in 1973, and the company's prime SG models meanwhile continued through the decade with the Standard and the Custom, which at the time came as standard with a stopbar tailpiece. Into the 80s, and the SG Standard still had small-block fingerboard markers, first seen in 1972. In its 1983 catalogue, Gibson said the SG Standard continued "to prove its stamina as a workhorse instrument in a number of musical arenas."

It was at this time that the company had started to become more serious about its past. The first sign was an SG Standard made in the style of a 60s original (including period-correct crown inlays), and at first Gibson called this the SG-62 Reissue, introduced in 1986. The company has since continued to produce many more reissues and remakes based on the original SG Standard, Custom, Special, and Junior that pay tribute to this sometimes undervalued Gibson solidbody design.

GIBSON SG-62 REISSUE
THIS EXAMPLE: ***1989***
This was the first attempt at a proper reissue of a 60s original Standard, introduced in 1986. Next came a reissue of the original-style SG Custom, which Gibson added to its catalogue the following year.

SG fan Angus Young and the SG-62 reissue, 1986 ad.

IBANEZ 2377
THIS EXAMPLE: ***1973***
Ibanez and other Japanese brands made copies in the 70s of many of the best US originals, although this one copied Gibson's SG Pro, which is now considered to be one of the company's less impressive efforts.

Gibson's first signature SG was a Tony Iommi model—despite the fact that the Black Sabbath's favorite SG, "Old Boy," was made not by Gibson but was built for him by the British guitar maker John Diggins, better known as Jaydee. More SG signature models have followed the Iommi guitars, which were introduced by Gibson's Custom Shop in 1999 and then by the US factory in 2002.

The signature SGs have included instruments named for Pete Townshend (Special, 2000, 2011), Angus Young (Standard, 2000, 2009), Gary Rossington (Standard, 2003), Elliot Easton (Custom, 2006), Robby Krieger (Standard, 2009), Dickey Betts (Standard, 2011), Derek Trucks (Standard, 2012), Jeff Tweedy (Standard, 2012), Frank Zappa ("Roxy" Standard, 2013), and Brian Ray (Standard, 2015).

Into the 2000s, and Gibson's Custom Shop got into its stride with re-creations of classic-period SGs, which began with a Standard reissue in 2001, with Special and Custom models soon following. The Shop's output appeared alongside the US factory's regular models as well as some newer takes that developed the old design. For example, the SG Supreme (1999) was a sort of higher-end Custom for the new decade, coming with fancy split-diamond makers and a pretty figured maple top; the SG Voodoo (2002), which had a suitable red voodoo skull inlay at the fifth fret, a red headstock logo, and (naturally) a solid black finish; and one of the 50th Anniversary models (2012) provided a rare showing for a twelve-string SG-style guitar outside of a double-neck guitar.

GIBSON 50th ANNIVERSARY SG TWELVE-STRING
THIS EXAMPLE: ***2012***
Gibson celebrated the SG's 50th anniversary around 2011, and several models, including this twelve-string SG, were marked with a special "50 Years" inlay on the headstock.

SG Supreme, Standard, Special, Junior, 2001 catalogue.

GIBSON SG SPECIAL
THIS EXAMPLE: ***2001***
The SG Special had since 1991 been offered with two coverless humbuckers and a regular control layout, which replaced the three-knob layout used for most of the 80s. This particular Special has a handsome emerald finish.

TONY IOMMI SIGNATURE LES PAUL SG

- 1961 SG body construction with original style neck joint
- Beveled mahogany body, one piece mahogany "slim-taper" neck
- White binding on neck
- Sterling silver cross inlays
- 24 fret ebony fingerboard
- 24 ¾" scale, 1 11/16" nut width
- Two volume controls, two tone controls, selector switch
- Two Tony Iommi signature humbucker pickups
- Graphite Nut
- Sperzel Tuners
- ABR-1 bridge / stopbar tailpiece
- Chrome hardware
- Available in Ebony or Wine Red

As founding member and lead guitarist for Black Sabbath, Tony Iommi is renowned for his high-powered playing style and driving riffs. Undoubtedly one of heavy metal music's greatest influences, Iommi has deeply inspired succeeding generations of guitarists.

Gibson's Tony Iommi Signature model is constructed using the patented ultra-thin, double-cutaway 1961 Les Paul SG Custom body style which features the "slim taper" neck. The sculpted mahogany body is accented with distinctive chrome hardware. The 24-fret ebony fingerboard provides a two-octave range and is inlaid with stunning sterling silver accents echoing Iommi's trademark cross insignia. Finally, the musician's signature is emblazoned on the peghead, capping off the razor-sharp looks of this impressive instrument.

This sleek, high-profile guitar features two sets of volume and tone controls, a selector switch and concealed rim jack, a fully adjustable ABR-1 bridge, stop bar tailpiece, and two Tony Iommi Signature pickups.

Available in left and right-handed models, the Tony Iommi Signature Les Paul SG is designed and made by Gibson's Custom, Art and Historic Division, makers of the world's most sought after guitars. Call 1-800-4-GIBSON for more information.

Custom · Art · Gibson · Since 1894 · Historic

Gibson Musical Instruments • Custom, Art and Historic Division • 657 Massman Drive, Nashville, TN 37210 • (615) 871-4500 • www.gibson.com

Promo sheet for the Tony Iommi signature SG, 1999.

GIBSON SG ZOOT SUIT
THIS EXAMPLE: ***2009***
The wildly adorned Zoot Suit model had a dish-carved body that was made with multi-colored laminated birch strips, and necessitated a simpler control layout moved nearer to the edge of the body carve.

GIBSON SG ORIGINAL
THIS EXAMPLE: ***2014***
New for 2013, the SG Original in all but name and shipping date had the vibe of an early-to-mid-60s SG Standard.

GIBSON SG STANDARD HEAVY AGED
THIS EXAMPLE: ***2017***
At the time of writing, the latest Custom Shop take on an aged finish for an SG Standard was this "heavy aged" look, here on an instrument with a custom pelham blue finish, a Gibson color first seen in the mid 60s.

SG Deluxe, three mini-humbuckers, 1998 catalogue.

During the first few years of the 60s, Gretsch was making some significant changes to the shape and construction of its hollowbody electrics. As we've seen, the first move, from around 1960, was to make some of them thinner. Gretsch had found with the thinline Country Gentleman, introduced in 1958, that many players preferred the easier feel of a slimmer guitar.

The team at Gretsch set about slimming down the bodies of the White Falcon and the Country Club in the first years of the 60s, the single-cut 6120 was trimmed twice, and the Tennessean was thinned down, too. In 1961, the Tennessean gained the sealed body of the Country Gentleman with accompanying "fake" f-holes, while its single Filter'Tron humbucker was swapped for a couple of single-coil HiLo'Trons. This transformation would ensure a new popularity for the good-value Tennessean as the 60s progressed.

The White Falcon had been the first Gretsch hollowbody electric to go double-cutaway, in 1960, and the model retained its open-f-holes body. Gibson was, as ever, the primary inspiration for this shapely decision: since 1958, the Kalamazoo factory had been using double-cutaways to successful effect. Players could more easily reach the higher frets of the fingerboard with this kind of body design and make fuller use of the upper register when soloing.

The Tennessean, meanwhile, stayed as a single-cut guitar. Gretsch moved its Chet Atkins Country Gentleman and 6120 to a double-cutaway body in 1961, and the 6120 also gained the sealed body of the Gent, as usual with fake f-holes painted on for a reasonably traditional look. As with most things Gretsch during this fabulous period, with Jimmie Webster in charge of the look and substance of the guitar models, the company could not resist giving its new sealed double-cutaway body a grand name: Electrotone.

The double-cutaway Gent entry, '65 catalogue.

Resolutely single-cut: Tennessean, '65 catalogue.

Solid Body Electric Guitars

Double Cutaway • Twin pickup

"Out of this world"—these great Gretsch "jet stream" electromatic guitars. Play one and you find yourself soaring through musical space and time with confidence and ease. Each instrument is a revelation of electronic perfection . . . unlimited tonal coloring . . . ultra-fine projection and sustaining power . . . truly brilliant highs.

Exclusive Gretsch Filter'Tron electronic heads eliminate absolutely *all* electronic hum. You get pure guitar sound. Gretsch adjustable rod—Actionflo neck. Smooth, unobstructed Neo-Classic fingerboard. Compact, solid body is only 13½" wide. Individual machines with slip-proof metal buttons. Exclusive Space Control bridge for split-hair string adjustment. Flatwound Gretsch Electromatic strings (see page 13). Solid leather shoulder strap.

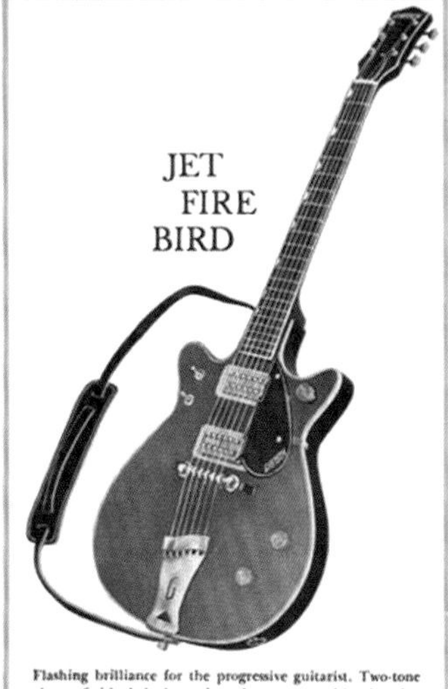

Flashing brilliance for the progressive guitarist. Two-tone ebony finished body and neck contrast with gleaming Oriental red top. Chrome-plated metal parts.

PX6131 Gretsch "Jet Fire Bird" Solid Body Electric Guitar $325.00

DUO-JET

A beauty with gleaming black top and mahogany sides and back. Polished chrome metal parts.

PX6128 Gretsch "Duo-Jet" Solid Body Electric Guitar $310.00

SILVER JET (Not illustrated)

Spotlight-catching silver sparkle top combined with rich mahogany body and neck. Chrome-plated metal parts.

PX6129 Gretsch "Silver Jet" Solid Body Electric Guitar $330.00

Double-cut semi-solids, Gretsch catalogue 1961.

ORIGINAL **GRETSCH DUO (SILVER) JET 6129**
THIS EXAMPLE: ***1969***
Gretsch applied the double-cutaway look to some of its semi-solid electrics, too, such as this late-60s Silver Jet. In fact, this is officially a Duo Jet, because Gretsch offered the sparkle colors as finish options of the Duo Jet from about 1963.

THE FRED. GRETSCH MFG. CO. CATALOG NO. 32

Country Gentleman, cover star of a 1965 catalogue.

ORIGINAL **GRETSCH CHET ATKINS COUNTRY GENTLEMAN 6122**
THIS EXAMPLE: ***1962***
The Country Gent goes double-cutaway, following the trend under way at Gretsch in the early 60s. The two knobs either side of the bridge control the (rarely used) mute system, and soon the knobs were changed to a pair of angled "flip-up" controls.

ORIGINAL **GRETSCH JET FIRE BIRD 6131**
THIS EXAMPLE: ***1965***
The Jet Fire Bird semi-solid went double-cutaway in 1961, too. This one has typical features of the period: "thumbnail" fingerboard markers, three volume knobs and three switches (standby, tone, pickups), and gold-plated metalwork.

GRETSCH VINTAGE SELECT EDITION '62 CHET ATKINS COUNTRY GENTLEMAN HOLLOW BODY 6122T-62

THIS EXAMPLE: ***2016***

Gretsch was able once again to call the Country Gentleman by its original name from 2007, and this one comes from what, at the time time of writing, was Gretsch's latest period-correct reproduction of a vintage-style double-cut Gent.

Gretsch Country Gentleman catalogue page, 2007.

GRETSCH ELECTROMATIC CENTER BLOCK DOUBLE JET 5655T-CB

THIS EXAMPLE: ***2014***

Center Block models first appeared in 2013, in both the main Gretsch brand and the budget Gretsch-Electromatic brand. They have a central wooden block inside the otherwise hollow body, in the style of Gibson's ES-335.

Malcolm Young of AC/DC powered his band's growing fame through the mid and late 70s with a '63 double-cutaway Gretsch Jet Fire Bird, which had been given to him by his elder brother George Young and Harry Vanda, who'd both been members of the 60s Australian band The Easybeats.

Malcolm bashed the Jet Fire Bird around to suit his driving rhythm-guitar stylings for AC/DC. Soon he stripped the red paint to reveal the natural wood underneath, and he left just the bridge pickup in place, alongside the results of some other reckless handiwork. Gretsch would issue a couple of Young reissue Jets in 1996, in single or double-pickup form, and in 2017 the company went further and produced a nit-picking re-creation of the battered guitar. Young himself died later that year, and the re-creation originally announced as a "Tribute" was issued as a "Salute" instrument.

Gretsch has drawn consistently in recent decades from its original double-cutaway models, both hollowbody and semi-solid, which it had first introduced back in the early 60s.

A new development for Gretsch came in 2013 with the introduction of its Center Block models, in the company's regular Professional series as well as among the second-tier Electromatic-brand models. The Center Blocks have a solid spruce block running the entire length of the body—although it's chambered at the lower bout to reduce weight—in a similar fashion to Gibson's influential ES-335 design.

GRETSCH COUNTRY CLASSIC II 6122-1962
THIS EXAMPLE: ***1993***
The Country Classic was the name Gretsch had to use for the Country Gentleman from 1989 until 2007, because the original name was associated with Gibson after Chet Atkins had moved to that company in the 80s.

GRETSCH CUSTOM SHOP MALCOLM YOUNG "SALUTE" JET 6131MY-CS
THIS EXAMPLE: ***2017***
A re-creation of Malcolm Young's battered Gretsch, which had started out as a red-finish two-pickup '63 Jet Fire Bird. Young had other ideas, and all his homespun modifications were lovingly duplicated in this Custom Shop edition.

GRETSCH DUO JET 6128T-1962
THIS EXAMPLE: ***2013***
Gretsch's reissue of the double-cutaway Duo Jet was introduced in 2001, with a pair of Filter'Tron pickups, and the model has been in the company's catalogue ever since.

SAINT PIERRE ET MIQUELON
POSTE AERIENNE
PLEUMEUR-BODOU
ANDOVER
TELSTAR
RF 50F
11-12 JUILLET 1962
1re LIAISON .T.V. PAR SATELLITE EUROPE-AMERIQUE

AMAZING FANTASY
APPROVED BY THE COMICS CODE AUTHORITY
12¢
15 AUG.
INTRODUCING SPIDER MAN
THOUGH THE WORLD MAY MOCK PETER PARKER, THE TIMID TEEN-AGER...
...IT WILL SOON MARVEL AT THE AWESOME MIGHT OF... SPIDER-MAN!
ALSO IN THIS ISSUE: AN IMPORTANT MESSAGE TO YOU, FROM THE EDITOR--ABOUT THE NEW AMAZING!

HARRY SALTZMAN and ALBERT R. BROCCOLI PRESENT
THE FIRST JAMES BOND FILM!
IAN FLEMING'S
DR. NO
TECHNICOLOR
SEAN CONNERY
URSULA ANDRESS · JOSEPH WISEMAN · JACK LORD
DAWSON · MARSHALL
KITZMILLER · GAYSON
BERNARD LEE
MAIBAUM HARWOOD MATHER YOUNG SALTZMAN BROCCOLI...EON PRODUCTIONS

- **NELSON MANDELA** is jailed in South Africa. In 1964, the leader of the banned African National Congress gets a life sentence for "sabotage" resulting in his internment until 1990.

- **SPIDER-MAN** appears in Marvel comics for the first time and becomes their most famous hero. The Beatles appear on Parlophone Records for the first time as 'Love Me Do' is released in October. They will become quite famous, too.

- **TELSTAR**, a communications satellite, is launched. It enables the first live TV transmissions between Europe and the US.

1962

- **ANDY WARHOL** is among the pop artists in the New Realists exhibition in the US. Warhol, who turns packaging into art, says, "In the future, everybody will be world-famous for fifteen minutes."

- **JAMES BOND** appears on film for the first time in *Dr. No*. The British secret service agent is portrayed by Sean Connery; the twangy guitar of the Bond theme tune is played by Vic Flick of The John Barry Seven.

- **JAMES MEREDITH** enrolls as the first black student at the University of Mississippi, despite riots by some white students.

1962

In 1962, Fender introduced a new top-of-the-line model, the Jaguar. It had the exaggerated offset-waist body first seen on the earlier Jazzmaster, a shape that would become widely influential. The Jaguar on its launch in 1962 listed in sunburst finish at $379.50, a notch above the $329.50 Jazzmaster. One of Fender's gleaming custom color finishes—Lake Placid blue, say, or surf green—would inch up a Jag to $398.49.

The new model had a separate bridge and vibrato unit, with a spring-loaded string-mute incorporated into the bridge. Fender optimistically figured players might prefer a mechanical string mute to the regular method of muting with the edge of the picking hand. Fender offered the Jaguar from the start in four different neck widths, one a size narrower and two wider than normal (coded A, B, C or D, from narrowest to widest, with "normal" B the most common). These width options were offered from 1962 on the Jazzmaster and the Strat as well. The Jag was the first Fender with 22 frets rather than 21, and its 24-inch scale (which Fender said was "faster, more comfortable") was shorter than the company's standard, adding to the Jag's easier playing feel compared to other Fenders.

The Jaguar's pickups were similar to a Strat's but sat in metal cradles, visible as a toothed metal panel each side, aimed to focus the magnetic field. The controls were elaborate, with a set on the lower body for the lead circuit: a volume and tone knob, plus a panel with a trio of slide-switches, two for selecting the pickups and one for engaging a "strangle" low-pass filter. There was a set of three further controls on the upper body: two small wheels for rhythm circuit tone and volume, and a slide-switch to choose between the lead circuit or rhythm circuit.

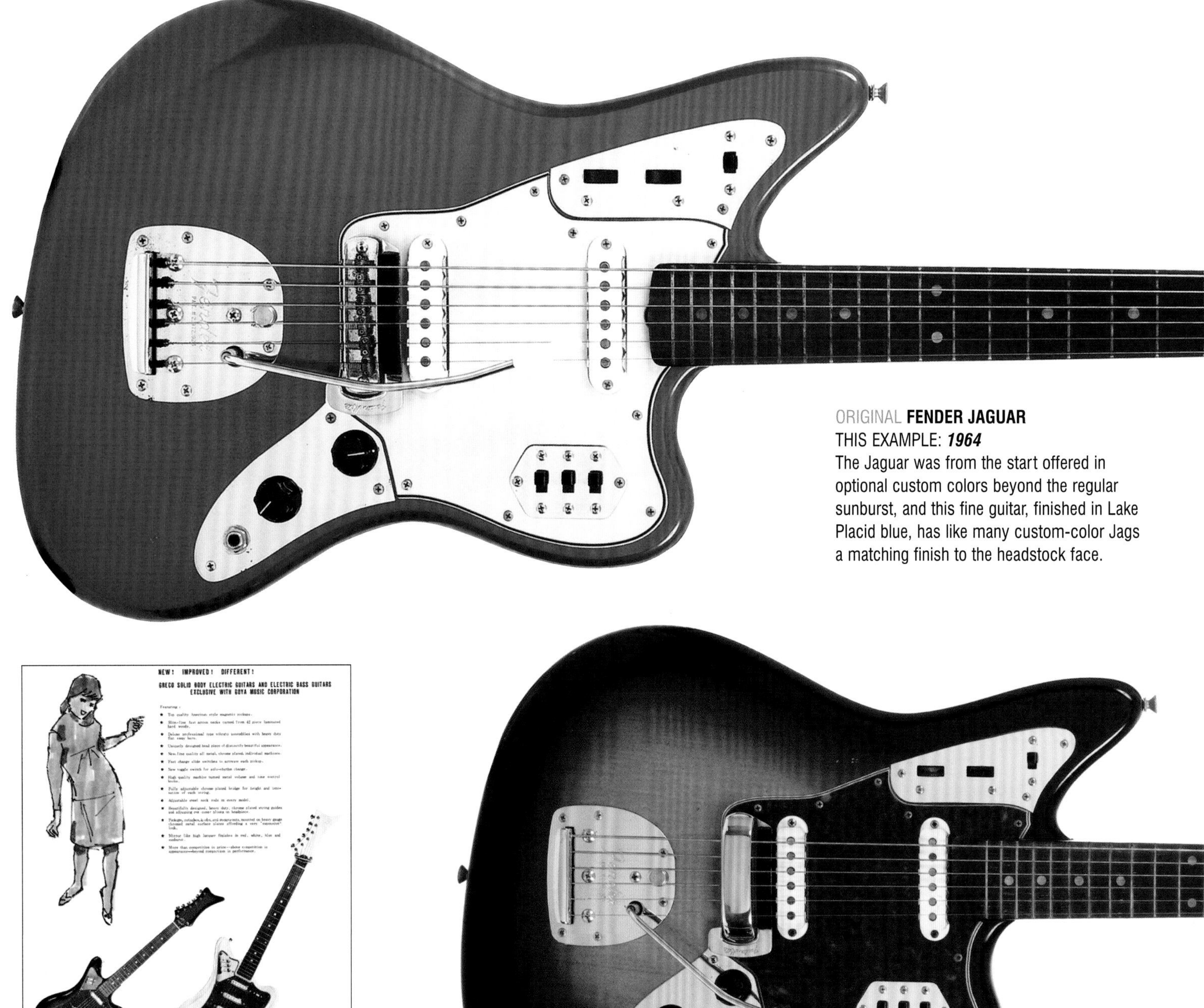

ORIGINAL **FENDER JAGUAR**
THIS EXAMPLE: ***1964***
The Jaguar was from the start offered in optional custom colors beyond the regular sunburst, and this fine guitar, finished in Lake Placid blue, has like many custom-color Jags a matching finish to the headstock face.

Offset-body influence, Greco catalogue, 1966.

ORIGINAL **FENDER JAGUAR**
THIS EXAMPLE: ***1965***
The fingerboard markers Fender used from the late 50s to the mid 60s are known as "clay dots" for their color. This Jaguar's body and matching headstock are finished in a black custom color that Fender called charcoal frost.

Candy apple red Jaguar on the '63 catalogue cover.

Surfing with a Jag, 1963 ad.

ORIGINAL **FENDER JAGUAR**
THIS EXAMPLE: ***1962***
A first-year sunburst Jaguar, boasting Fender's offset-waist body, a mechanical string-mute, 22 frets on a shorter-scale neck, floating vibrato, new pickups, and separate control panels with lead and rhythm-circuit knobs and switches.

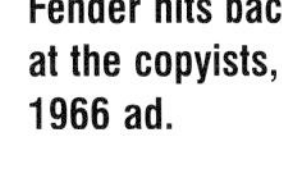

Fender hits back at the copyists, 1966 ad.

Kurt Cobain, Jag-Stang reissue, 2003 Japanese ad.

Squier has been Fender's secondary brand since 1982, when it was introduced on a line of Japanese-made reissues made for the company's European distributors. Soon Fender used it more widely, and it has become an important second-strand brand for good-value reissues as well as more experimental models. In the 90s, for example, Squier introduced its shortlived Vista series, with Jagmaster, Venus, and Super-Sonic models that mashed up Jaguars, Jazzmasters, and more.

At the same time, Kurt Cobain was a mashup fan, too. The left-hander's favored guitars for Nirvana were a 60s Jaguar and Mustang, and when he worked with Fender's Custom Shop to create a new instrument, he cut up some pictures and pasted them back together, coming up with his design. Following Cobain's untimely death in 1994, his family collaborated with Fender to release a production model, which on its release in 1996 was called the Fender Jag-Stang. A more recent adaptation of elements of the Jaguar design came in the early 2010s with Fender's Jaguarillo, a kind of three-pickup Jag, and the Offset Special, something like a Stratocaster meets Jazzmaster meets Jaguar … with f-hole and P-90s.

Individual players continue to be drawn to Jaguars, as much for their idiosyncrasies as for their lower visibility on the vintage radar and, consequently, some relatively attractive secondhand prices. A mark in the Jag's favor came in 2012 with the introduction of a Johnny Marr signature model, complete with his tweaks and improvements, notably to a simpler control circuit.

The glory of an undisturbed and original-style Jaguar is evident today in the company's modern lines. This was the case in the American Original series, where the unmistakable constituents of cradle pickups, shapely control panels, bridge string-mute, and 22-fret short-scale neck continued to make the Jaguar one of the secret weapons in the Fender arsenal.

FENDER JAGUARILLO
THIS EXAMPLE: ***2012***
The shortlived Jaguarillo was introduced in 2012 as a member of Fender's Pawn Shop series, with a pair of Strat-style pickups plus bridge humbucker, and a Gibson-like bridge. This one is finished in candy apple red.

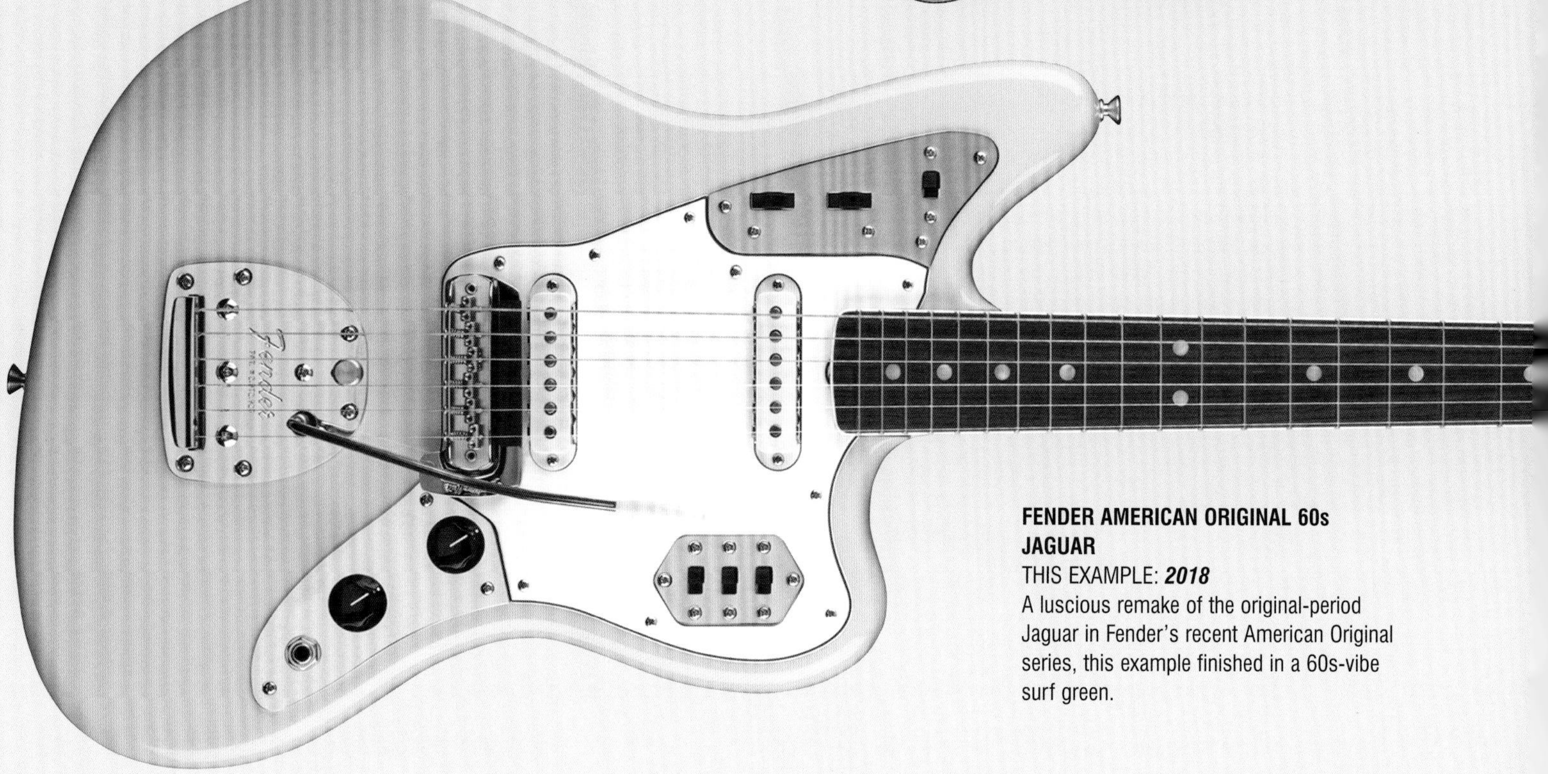

FENDER AMERICAN ORIGINAL 60s JAGUAR
THIS EXAMPLE: ***2018***
A luscious remake of the original-period Jaguar in Fender's recent American Original series, this example finished in a 60s-vibe surf green.

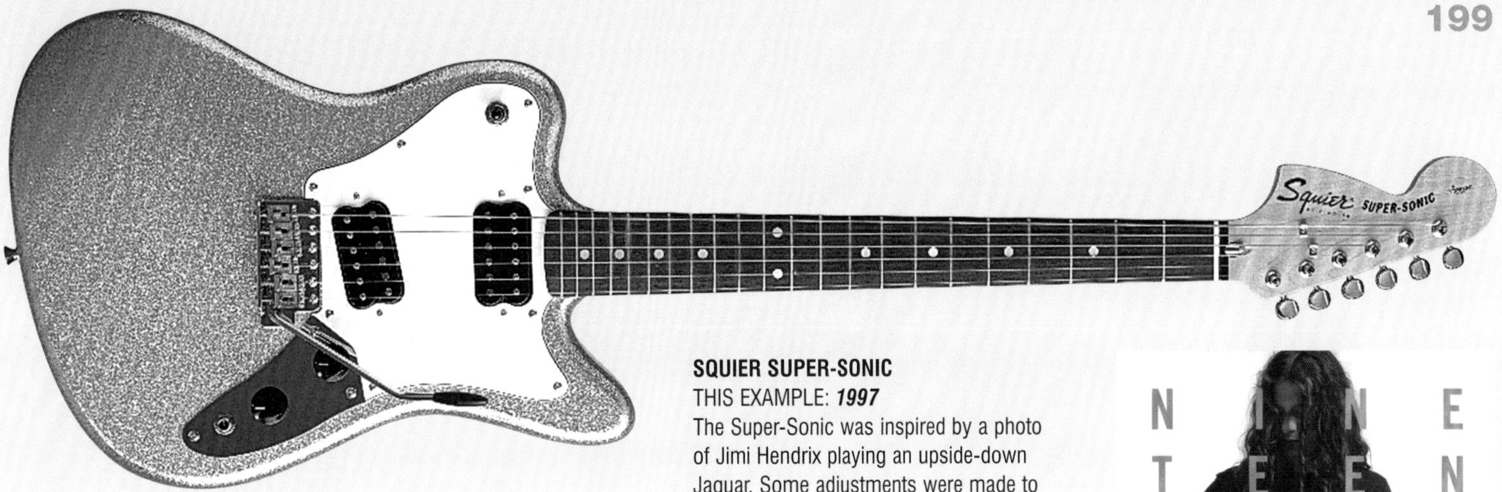

SQUIER SUPER-SONIC
THIS EXAMPLE: ***1997***
The Super-Sonic was inspired by a photo of Jimi Hendrix playing an upside-down Jaguar. Some adjustments were made to the size and shape, and a pair of humbuckers were added, the bridge unit tilted to improve tone.

Fender remembers Nineteen-Sixty-Next, 2018 Jaguar ad.

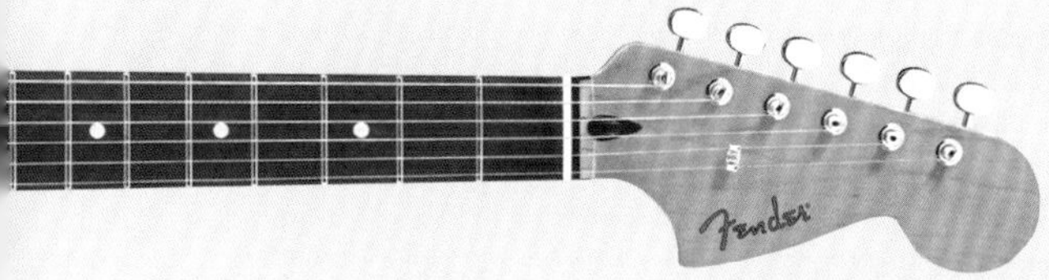

FENDER JAG-STANG
THIS EXAMPLE: ***1997***
Left-hander Kurt Cobain devised this model by mashing up photos of his favorite Jaguar and Mustang, but he did not live to see this production model's introduction in 1996.

Cult-status Jag and Jazz, 1995 ad.

1962

ORIGINAL **NATIONAL NEWPORT 84**
THIS EXAMPLE: ***1964***
The Newport models made up the second tier of National's new-for-'62 fiberglass-body lines. This Newport 84 is finished in sea foam green. The unusual body design was later nicknamed the map shape.

National's 1962 catalogue page for wood-body Westwoods.

ORIGINAL **NATIONAL GLENWOOD 98**
THIS EXAMPLE: ***1964***
A high-end fiberglass National, the Glenwood 98 has "butterfly pearl" fingerboard inlays and a bridge-mounted third pickup. This beautiful guitar, finished in pearl white, once belonged to Randy Bachman.

ORIGINAL **SUPRO CORONADO II**
THIS EXAMPLE: ***1962***
National's owner, Valco, also used fiberglass bodies for some models with its Supro brand, including this raven black Coronado II, introduced in 1962.

In 1962, National's owner Valco introduced a line of electrics with molded fiberglass bodies, the first time the material had been used for a production electric guitar. The Chicago-based company called its fiberglass material Res-O-Glas and used it for National Glenwood, Val-Pro (later Newport), and Studio models. The bodies of the Glenwoods and Newports had unusual shapes, while the Studio looked something like a plastic Les Paul.

Combined with the gleaming look of the fiberglass with some strong color choices—pepper red, sea foam green, and so on—the guitars looked like nothing else available at the time. The outline of these striking instruments was later nicknamed the map shape, supposedly because it resembled a map of the United States, although National never said so, and a comparison seems fanciful.

Most had one or two regular pickups, but some also featured a bridge-mounted "Silver-Sound Unit," a modified electro-magnetic pickup with polepieces inserted into the single-saddle bridge and connected to coils in the base. Valco had first used it on models introduced in the late 50s, including the Supro Rhythm Master and the National Val-Trol.

Valco used the new material for some models with its less fancy Supro brand, including the '62-style Belmont and Dual-Tone, the Tremo-Lectric, the Coronado II, and the Supersonic. There were also models that came in the unusual shapes but were made with conventional wooden construction, such as the National Westwoods. The experiment did not last, because the bodies had a tendency to develop cracks and the process was messier and more time consuming than Valco expected. By 1968, Valco would go out of business, taken down by the unwise purchase of the ailing Kay company, but the look and style of these models has inspired a number of re-creations in more recent decades.

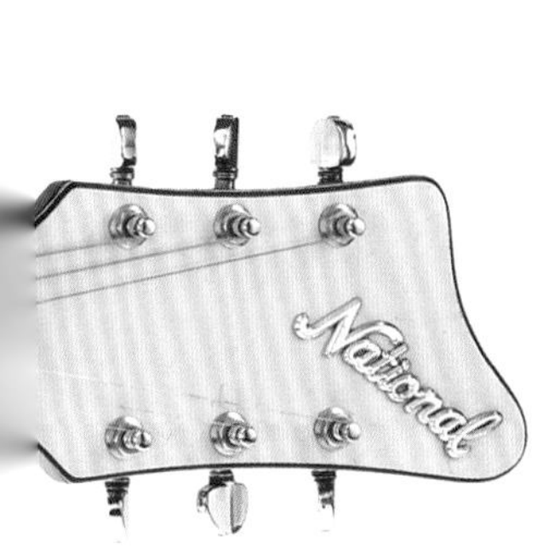

The Kim Sisters promote National Glenwoods, 1966 ad.

SUPRO CORONADO II
THIS EXAMPLE: ***2017***
The modern Supro brand's remake of the original 60s Coronado II is a dead-on looker, although owners Absara Audio made the body with a plastic top half and wooden lower half.

AIRLINE MAP DLX
THIS EXAMPLE: ***2018***
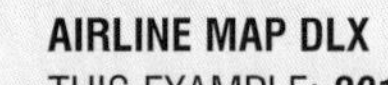
A revised and updated version of the so-called "map shape" Nationals of the 60s, this modern Airline-brand guitar has a wooden body and a pair of humbuckers.

Gibson first offered electric double-necks in 1958, which were thinline hollowbodys without f-holes. In 1962, a redesigned line of three SG-style solidbody double-necks replaced them. Like the hollowbodys, they were made only to special order. There were three variations. The EDS-1275 Double 12 mixed a six-string and a twelve-string neck, the EMS-1235 Double Mandolin a regular six-string neck and a short-scale neck with eight strings in four courses, like a mandolin. There was also the EBSF or EBS-1250 Double Bass, pairing a regular six-string with a four-string bass neck.

Jimmy Page used a Fender Electric XII to record the rhythm part on 'Stairway To Heaven' with Led Zeppelin around the turn of 1970 into '71, and his bandmates teased him about how to reproduce on stage the track's "guitar army." A double-neck seemed the perfect solution, and Page was soon seen at Zep live dates with his new Gibson EDS-1275 six-and-twelve. Subsequently, the popularity of the double-neck soared. Page's guitar was re-created by the Custom Shop in 2007 for a Gibson limited edition.

Also in 1962, Gibson introduced a signature model for the jazz guitarist Tal Farlow. It joined some other jazz-oriented signature hollowbodys that Gibson had launched the previous year. There were two Barney Kessel models, which had double pointed cutaways and, on the Custom, fancy bow-tie inlays, and a model for the jazz stylist Johnny Smith, with a mini-humbucker and single control floating on the pickguard (and later a two-pickup version).

Tal Farlow's Gibson was distinguished visually by extra binding that created a scroll-like shape in the cutaway, a shifted pickup selector, and a necessarily revised-shape pickguard, as well as a double crown inlay on the headstock. The Farlow in its original form lasted in the line until 1970, the Kessels until the early 70s, and the Smith until the late 80s.

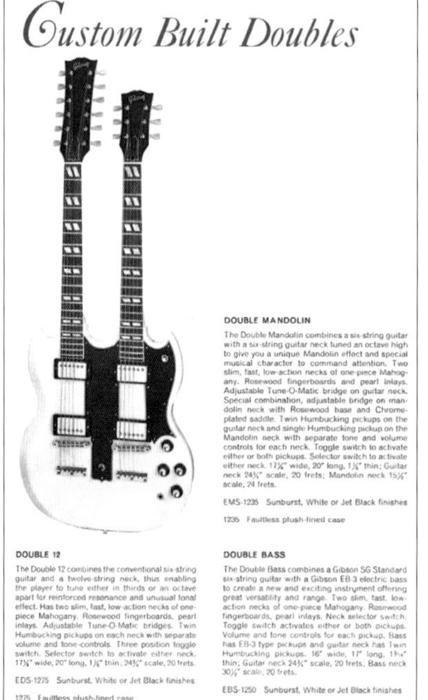

Custom Built Doubles

DOUBLE MANDOLIN

The Double Mandolin combines a six-string guitar with a six-string guitar neck tuned an octave high to give you a unique Mandolin effect and special musical character to command attention. Two slim, fast, low-action necks of one-piece Mahogany. Rosewood fingerboards and pearl inlays. Adjustable Tune-O-Matic bridge on guitar neck. Special combination, adjustable bridge on mandolin neck with Rosewood base and Chrome-plated saddle. Twin Humbucking pickups on the guitar neck and single Humbucking pickup on the Mandolin neck with separate tone and volume controls for each neck. Toggle switch to activate either or both pickups. Selector switch to activate either neck. 17¼" wide, 20" long, 1⅛" thin; Guitar neck 24¾" scale, 20 frets; Mandolin neck 15½" scale, 24 frets.

EMS-1235 Sunburst, White or Jet Black finishes

1235 Faultless plush-lined case

DOUBLE 12

The Double 12 combines the conventional six-string guitar and a twelve-string neck, thus enabling the player to tune either in thirds or an octave apart for reinforced resonance and unusual tonal effect. Has two slim, fast, low-action necks of one-piece Mahogany. Rosewood fingerboards, pearl inlays. Adjustable Tune-O-Matic bridges. Twin Humbucking pickups on each neck with separate volume and tone-controls. Three position toggle switch. Selector switch to activate either neck. 17¼" wide, 20" long, 1⅛" thin; 24¾" scale, 20 frets.

EDS-1275 Sunburst, White or Jet Black finishes

1275 Faultless plush-lined case

DOUBLE BASS

The Double Bass combines a Gibson SG Standard six-string guitar with a Gibson EB-3 electric bass to create a new and exciting instrument offering great versatility and range. Two slim, fast, low-action necks of one-piece Mahogany. Rosewood fingerboards, pearl inlays. Neck selector switch. Toggle switch activates either or both pickups. Volume and tone controls for each pickup. Bass has EB-3 type pickups and guitar neck has Twin Humbucking pickups. 16" wide, 17" long, 1 15/16" thin; Guitar neck 24¾" scale, 20 frets; Bass neck 30½" scale, 20 frets.

EBS-1250 Sunburst, White or Jet Black finishes

1250 Faultless plush-lined case

EDS-1275 in white, 1966 catalogue.

ORIGINAL **GIBSON EDS-1275 DOUBLE 12**

THIS EXAMPLE: ***1964***

Steve Howe used this six-and-twelve-string double-neck extensively on the road with Yes throughout the 70s. Like many other players, Howe replaced the guitar's period tuners with sturdier Grover units.

Six-string and bass EBSF double-neck, 1963 catalogue.

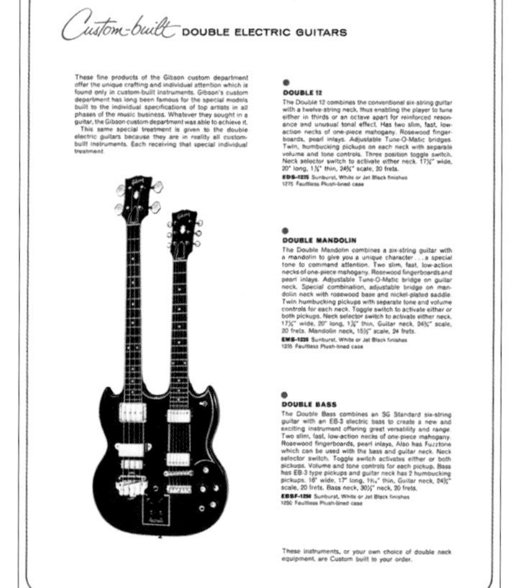

Custom-built DOUBLE ELECTRIC GUITARS

These fine products of the Gibson custom department offer the unique crafting and individual attention which is found only in custom-built instruments. Gibson's custom department has long been famous for the special models built to the individual specifications of top artists in all phases of the music business. Whatever they sought in a guitar, the Gibson custom department was able to achieve it.

This same special treatment is given to the double electric guitars because they are in reality all custom-built instruments. Each receiving that special individual treatment.

DOUBLE 12

The Double 12 combines the conventional six-string guitar with a twelve-string neck, thus enabling the player to tune either in thirds or an octave apart for reinforced resonance and unusual tonal effect. Has two slim, fast, low-action necks of one-piece mahogany. Rosewood fingerboards, pearl inlays. Adjustable Tune-O-Matic bridges. Twin, humbucking pickups on each neck with separate volume and tone controls. Three position toggle switch. Neck selector switch to activate either neck. 17½" wide, 20" long, 1⅛" thin, 24¾" scale, 20 frets.

EDS-1275 Sunburst, White or Jet Black finishes
1275 Faultless Plush-lined case

DOUBLE MANDOLIN

The Double Mandolin combines a six-string guitar with a mandolin to give you a unique character . . . a special tone to command attention. Two slim, fast, low-action necks of one-piece mahogany. Rosewood fingerboards and pearl inlays. Adjustable Tune-O-Matic bridge on guitar neck. Special combination, adjustable bridge on mandolin neck with rosewood base and nickel-plated saddle. Twin humbucking pickups with separate tone and volume controls for each neck. Toggle switch to activate either or both pickups. Neck selector switch to activate either neck. 17½" wide, 20" long, 1⅛" thin, Guitar neck, 24¾" scale, 20 frets. Mandolin neck, 15½" scale, 24 frets.

EMS-1235 Sunburst, White or Jet Black finishes
1235 Faultless Plush-lined case

DOUBLE BASS

The Double Bass combines an SG Standard six-string guitar with an EB-3 electric bass to create a new and exciting instrument offering great versatility and range. Two slim, fast, low-action necks of one-piece mahogany. Rosewood fingerboards, pearl inlays. Also has Fuzztone which can be used with the bass and guitar neck. Neck selector switch. Toggle switch activates either or both pickups. Volume and tone controls for each pickup. Bass has EB-3 type pickups and guitar neck has 2 humbucking pickups. 16" wide, 17" long, 1 15/16" thin, Guitar neck, 24¾" scale, 20 frets. Bass neck, 30½" neck, 20 frets.

EBSF-1250 Sunburst, White or Jet Black finishes
1250 Faultless Plush-lined case

These instruments, or your own choice of double neck equipment, are Custom built to your order.

Rick Nielsen was keen to take the double-neck idea to its extremes, and this ad from 1998 shows him with his five-neck guitar (count them!) custom-built for him by Hamer. Nielsen did actually manage to use the instrument on stage.

Gibson's Custom Shop re-created Jimmy Page's EDS-1275 Double 12 double-neck in 2007, and each guitar from the limited edition came with a Certificate of Authenticity, signed by Page and the Custom Shop's boss Rick Gembar.

ORIGINAL **GIBSON TAL FARLOW**
THIS EXAMPLE: ***1964***
This signature model for the jazz guitarist Tal Farlow, with its distinctive cutaway "scroll," came in what Gibson called a viceroy brown finish.

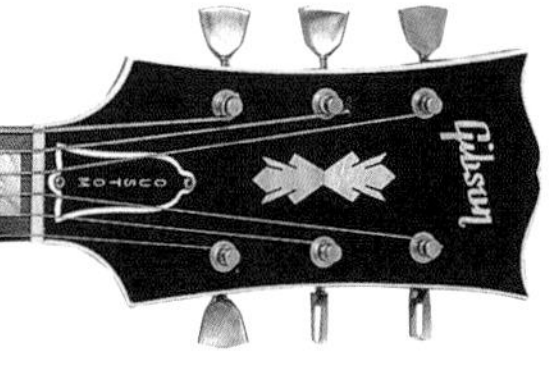

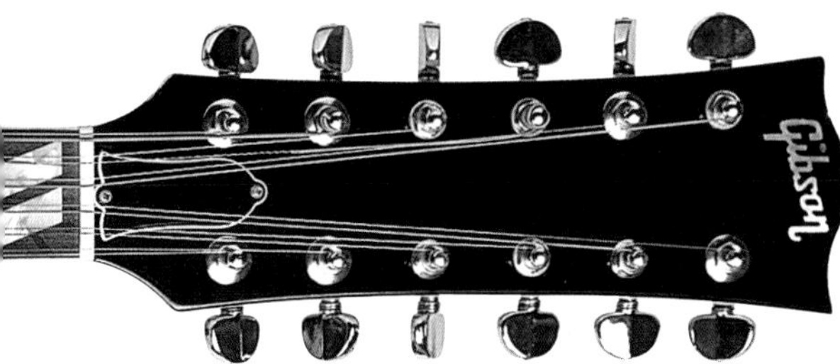

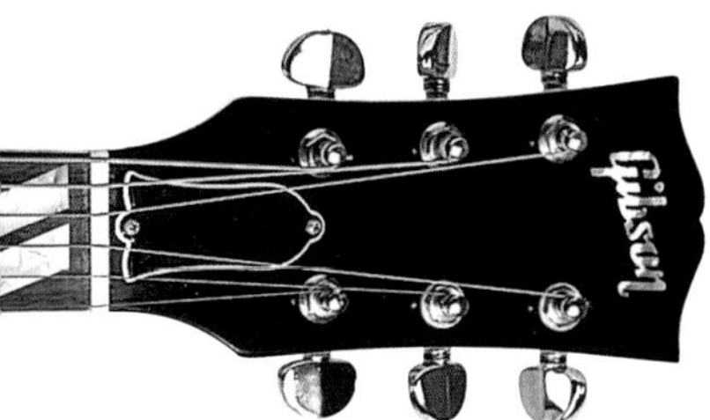

Farlow, Smith, and Kessel supergroup, 1964 ad.

THREE OF A KIND!

. . . all guitar greats . . . all perennial poll winners . . . and all agreed about their guitar: it's a Gibson, and it's the finest.

Each of these famous guitarists served as the inspiration for a special Gibson model—designed by him, for his kind of music, for his guitar technique, for his special sound. And they're very special sounds . . . lively, brilliant, poetic . . . unique with each artist on his special Gibson.

Gibson makes the world's widest selection of models. Jazz guitars, solid bodies, classics, flat tops, folk models, country and western, acoustic, amplified. All these instruments have their special properties—yet they're *all alike* in one important respect: their Gibson quality. Quality that has made Gibson the most sought-after guitar in the world for over half-a-century.

In every model, Gibson enhances the performance of the player. Its action is fast and easy, encouraging to the beginner. Its tone is pure and brilliant, challenging to the artist. Its response is perfect, a boon to anyone.

Today . . . there's a great and growing interest in guitar playing. You find it everywhere. The campus. The coffee house. The home. Every gathering place. And this makes Gibson doubly important, for Gibson is the world's most complete line of guitars, for every type of music.

Johnny Smith signature model, 1963 catalogue.

JOHNNY SMITH GUITAR

This new artist's guitar offers the most perfect combination of acoustic response and electronic amplification ever produced. An entirely new humbucking pickup and new method of mounting were designed to produce the purest tone amplification without restricting the acoustic response of the carved top.

FEATURES: Carved spruce top with bound "f" sound holes and matched figured maple rim, neck, and carved back. Slim, fast, low-action neck joins body at 14th fret. Three-piece curly maple neck with adjustable truss rod. Ebony fingerboard with pearl block inlays and nickel silver frets. Special ebony bridge with slanted ebony saddle. Special balanced tone humbucking pickups mounted free of body. Volume control and instrument jack mounted on pickguard, free of body, completely shielded. Gold-plated metal parts. Sealfast machine heads with keytone metal buttons. 17" wide, 20½" long, 3⅛" deep, 25" scale, 21 frets.

Double Pickup Model
JS-DN Natural finish
JS-D Sunburst finish

Single Pickup Model
JS-N Natural finish
JS Sunburst finish

Complete with special Faultless gold plush-lined case and zipper case cover

Princess guitar and amp, Gretsch catalogue 1962.

ORIGINAL **GRETSCH CORVETTE 6132**
THIS EXAMPLE: ***1962***
The Corvette was Gretsch's first true solidbody guitar, introduced in 1961 and then redesigned in '62 with a Gibson SG-like beveled-edge body. This one has Gretsch's Tone Twister fitted, a largely unsuccessful clip-on vibrato.

Gretsch had first used the Corvette name for a hollowbody electric introduced in the early 50s alongside the Country Club, and it lasted in the line until 1956. In 1961, the company revived the Corvette name for its cheapest solidbody electric, launched as a double-cutaway competitor for Gibson's budget Les Paul Junior. It was Gretsch's first true solidbody guitar, too, without the routed-out semi-solid construction of the Jets.

That '61-style Corvette came with a HiLo'Tron single-coil pickup and started life with a simple slab-style body similar to the old Gibson Junior. In 1962, Gretsch redesigned the Corvette with beveled-edge body contours, influenced by Gibson's new SG design, available with one pickup and no vibrato or two pickups and vibrato.

A variation on the new contoured Corvette was the colorful Princess model of 1962. "For the first time in guitar manufacturing history an instrument has been selectively constructed only for girls," Gretsch said in its promo material. "This is the unique adaptable Gretsch Princess Guitar, engineered with identical Gretsch precision to meet the needs and standards of young women all over the world." Gretsch had simply finished the Corvette in special pastel color combinations that it thought would attract female guitarists. It offered white body with grape pickguard, blue body with white pickguard, pink body with white pickguard, or white body with gold pickguard. The girls failed to respond to such charms, however, and the Princess retired from public view.

Another opportunist variant of the '62-style Corvette was Gretsch's Twist model. Chubby Checker's single 'The Twist' topped the US chart for the second time in January that year and set off a dance fad. This colored Corvette had a pickguard bearing a twisting red and white "peppermint" design—and this guitar, too, did not last long in the Gretsch lines.

ORIGINAL **GRETSCH PRINCESS 6106**
THIS EXAMPLE: ***1963***
The Princess was a pastel-finished Corvette that Gretsch hoped might attract female guitarists. This one is in white with gold pickguard, one of four restrained finish options for the shortlived model.

THERE'S ONLY ONE THING AS COMFORTABLE AS THE BACK OF THIS GUITAR.....

AND THAT'S THE FRONT OF THIS GUITAR.
The magic touch of Gretsch now brings you two exclusive refinements on the back and front of the Gretsch guitar to add comfort and ease to your playing. ☐ On the back . . . low on the body, we've shaped a springy pad of foam rubber. It's placed to cushion playing pressure . . . makes the guitar easy to hold, protects the back from scratches. ☐ On the front . . . Gretsch places a felt muffler pad between the bridge and pickup. It allows you to "muffle" your strings at the instant touch of an off-on switch. It gives you a completely free hand — takes cramp out of your style. ☐ More than ever you'll thrill to the ultimate experience at the touch of a Gretsch guitar — a feeling that you could play it forever. ☐ Gretsch — where hands for detail make the difference. See your dealer today!

GRETSCH THE FRED. GRETSCH MANUFACTURING CO.
60 Broadway, Brooklyn 11, N.Y. Dept. A-28
Please send me a copy of the new
GRETSCH GUITAR CATALOG

Name________

Address________

City____ Zone___ State____

Gretsch's padded back, 1963 ad.

GRETSCH GUITARS

NO ONE CAN COMPARE WITH CHET ATKINS...

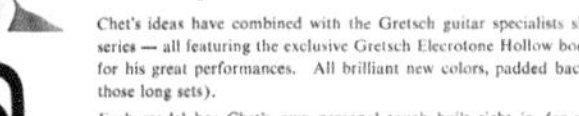

His name is famous all over the world . . . so is his unique playing style. Every year adds to his tremendous number of admirers through personal engagements and the ever increasing number of his RCA Victor Albums.

. . . No other guitars can match the exclusive new Gretsch Chet Atkins Guitars.

Chet's ideas have combined with the Gretsch guitar specialists skill to produce a spectacular new series — all featuring the exclusive Gretsch Elecrotone Hollow body for the resonance Chet requires for his great performances. All brilliant new colors, padded backs (cushioned for comfort during those long sets).

Each model has Chet's own personal touch built right in, for real modern tone and styling . . . exceptional playing ease . . . distinctive good looks that are hard to beat!

CHET ATKINS' GUITARS *(from left to right)* PX 6122 Country Gentleman PX 6119 Tennessean PX 6120 Hollow Body

Hollowbody lineup, 1963 catalogue.

ORIGINAL **GRETSCH CHET ATKINS HOLLOW BODY 6120**
THIS EXAMPLE: ***1962***
Following the move to a double-cutaway body for the White Falcon (1960) and the Country Gentleman (1961), the 6120 gained the new shape in '62, as well as the Gent's sealed body with fake f-holes.

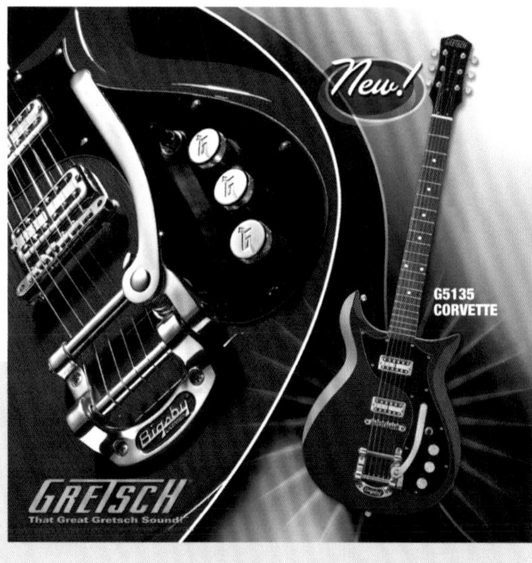

Gretsch Electromatic Corvette reissue, 2006 ad.

GRETSCH PLAYERS EDITION NASHVILLE CENTER BLOCK DOUBLE-CUT 6620TFM
THIS EXAMPLE: ***2017***
Gretsch renamed the Hollow Body 6120 as the Nashville in 1966, and this recent model has the company's new Center Block construction, with a 335-like wooden block running inside the otherwise hollow body.

1962

The distinctive E-for-Epiphone logo, 1962 ad.

EPIPHONE, inc.
KALAMAZOO, MICHIGAN

Epiphone continued to produce new models during the 60s with its new owner, Gibson, in charge of development and production at the factory in Kalamazoo, Michigan. A catalogue from the time sums up well the view that all the big American makers were taking of the market that was continuing to open up and expand all around them. "Today, the electric guitar Spanish guitar is found everywhere," ran the blurb, "in orchestras, combos, jazz bands, and as a featured solo instrument. Epiphone offers electric Spanish guitars to suit the need of every player from the top professional, to the semi-pro, to the amateur who wants an instrument for his own amusement or to join the gang on weekends."

A couple of new models launched in 1962 sat firmly at the professional end of that market. We've seen how some new Epiphones were similar to existing Gibson models, but with different pickups and varied feature sets, such as the 355-like Sheraton, introduced in 1959. Now Epiphone added the new Riviera alongside the Sheraton, and this semi-solid model with its "royal tan" finish and pair of mini-humbuckers broadly corresponded to Gibson's ES-335. Another new-for-'62 model was the Professional, which had controls for a companion amplifier on the guitar itself. It was sold with either the larger EA8P 35-watt amp, with 15-inch speaker, or the EA7P 15-watt amp, with 12-inch speaker.

Meanwhile, Kay was churning out guitars from its factory in Chicago, rivaling Harmony, the other big maker in the city, for the scale and range of its offerings. Each year, Kay revised its lines and added some new models, for example in 1962 introducing the hollowbody electric Jazz II model, with its flavor-of-the-moment thinline double-cutaway body and a Bigsby vibrato as standard.

ORIGINAL **EPIPHONE RIVIERA E360TD**
THIS EXAMPLE: ***1964***
Introduced in 1962, the Riviera was like an Epiphone equivalent of Gibson's ES-335, with a similar semi-solid double-cutaway body but its own typical Epi features of the period, including mini-humbuckers and Frequensator tailpiece.

Epi catalogue cover, 1962.

EPIPHONE NICK VALENSI SIGNATURE RIVIERA
THIS EXAMPLE: ***2007***
A signature model for the guitarist in The Strokes was introduced in 2007, with Gibson P-94 pickups, at a time when Epiphone's Riviera was available only in an Elitist version.

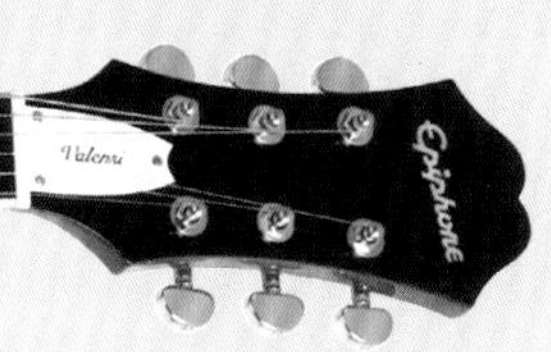

KAY JAZZ II
THIS EXAMPLE: ***2016***
Following the demise of Kay in the late 60s, the brand was used fitfully in the following decades, and then AR Musical Enterprises revived it in 1980. This Jazz II comes from a select line of reissues that AR began in 2010.

Sunburst Jazz II on Kay's 1962 catalogue cover.

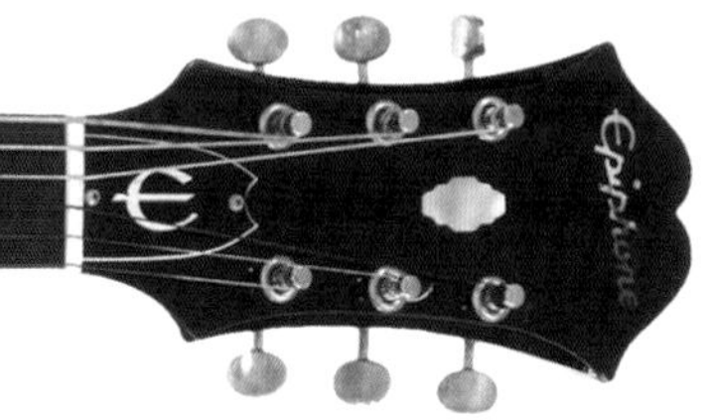

ORIGINAL **EPIPHONE PROFESSIONAL**
THIS EXAMPLE: ***1964***
Seven switches and five knobs? The Professional was sold as a set with an amplifier, which had one knob: all the rest of the amplifier's controls were on the guitar. The idea was ahead of its time, and the Professional was gone by 1966.

NEW "THIN-LITE" NECK
WITH ADJUSTABLE TRUSS ROD

Engineered for dependability and fast action. Gives positive adjustment to withstand the stress of terrific string tension. Avoids twisting or warping. This tried-and-proven truss rod support employs a sturdy steel member tightened in seconds by turning the adjusting nut. All top Kay models now incorporate this feature; and remember—every Kay guitar, even through the economical Student Model, has the steel reinforcing rod which assures permanent straightness to eliminate any chance of warping.*

A—Adjusting Nut B—Truss Rod Collar
C—Steel Truss Rod D—Truss Rod Anchor

*Every Kay neck is GUARANTEED not to warp or slip out of alignment.

$275.00
"JAZZ II"

Stunning Modern Arched Thinline Silhouette by Kay

THE "JAZZ II". This Gold-K electric spotlights the Bigsby Vibrato tailpiece. This handsome double cutaway Thinline guitar is 2" thin and super auditorium size—41" x 15½". Superior select curly maple top, back and sides, laminated throughout. Hard maple **Thin-Lite** adjustable neck. Oval rosewood fingerboard with hand inlaid genuine pearl markers, nickel silver frets, celluloid binding. Extra heavy celluloid binding on top and back edges with extra inlay on top. Flat wound professional electric guitar strings. Two incomparable Gold "K" pickup units with individual adjustable posts. Separate controls and selector switch. Cremona violin brown, golden sunburst, elegantly hand rubbed and polished.

K775 ARCHED THINLINE GUITAR............$275.00
K776 Same as above but blonde finish............$275.00
K9613 Hard shell 3-ply case for K775 and K776...$ 49.50

Kay Jazz II entry, 1962 catalogue.

ORIGINAL **KAY JAZZ II K776**
THIS EXAMPLE: ***1962***
The Jazz II came in sunburst (K775) and this natural finish (K776). A similar model was used by a young Eric Clapton in his early band The Roosters.

1962

Danelectro made a series of ingenious amp-in-case sets for Silvertone, the brand that the Sears, Roebuck company used in the United States for the instruments it sold through its popular mail-order catalogues. The idea was simple and effective: a budget-price electric guitar in a hard case that had a small amplifier and speaker fixed inside, making for a mobile guitar-and-amp set.

The Sears catalogues offered three types of Silvertone amp-in-case guitars during the 60s. The first, introduced in 1962, was a double-cutaway black model (1448 one pickup, 1449 two pickups), followed in 1964 by the red-sunburst 1457 (two pickups), and finally, in 1966, a black shallow-cutaway guitar (1451 one pickup, 1452 two pickups). All were gone by 1968.

In Sweden, Hagstrom launched a new model in '62, the PB-24-G, called the F-11 model by the American distributor. The body had an acrylic plastic top bolted to a vinyl-covered laminated-wood back, and the complex-looking control panel offered switches for L ("low," neck pickup on/off), H ("high," bridge pickup on/off), tone, and mute, plus a detented 11-position volume control. As well as Hagstrom's own versions, branded Hagstrom or Kent (not to be confused with the US brand Kent), around 1963 it made some for Selmer in Britain (with the Futurama brand) and for Guild (with the Cromwell brand).

Guild, meanwhile, introduced in 1962 a signature hollowbody electric named for Duane Eddy, although he was better known for playing a Gretsch 6120. And in Germany, also in '62, Framus replaced its earlier Hollywood solidbodys with a new line of Strato models. A number of different Strato variations followed. Framus produced a full range of guitars through later decades, and in the 80s it morphed into the Warwick brand, better known for basses. In 1995, Warwick revived the Framus brandname, which continues to appear on instruments today.

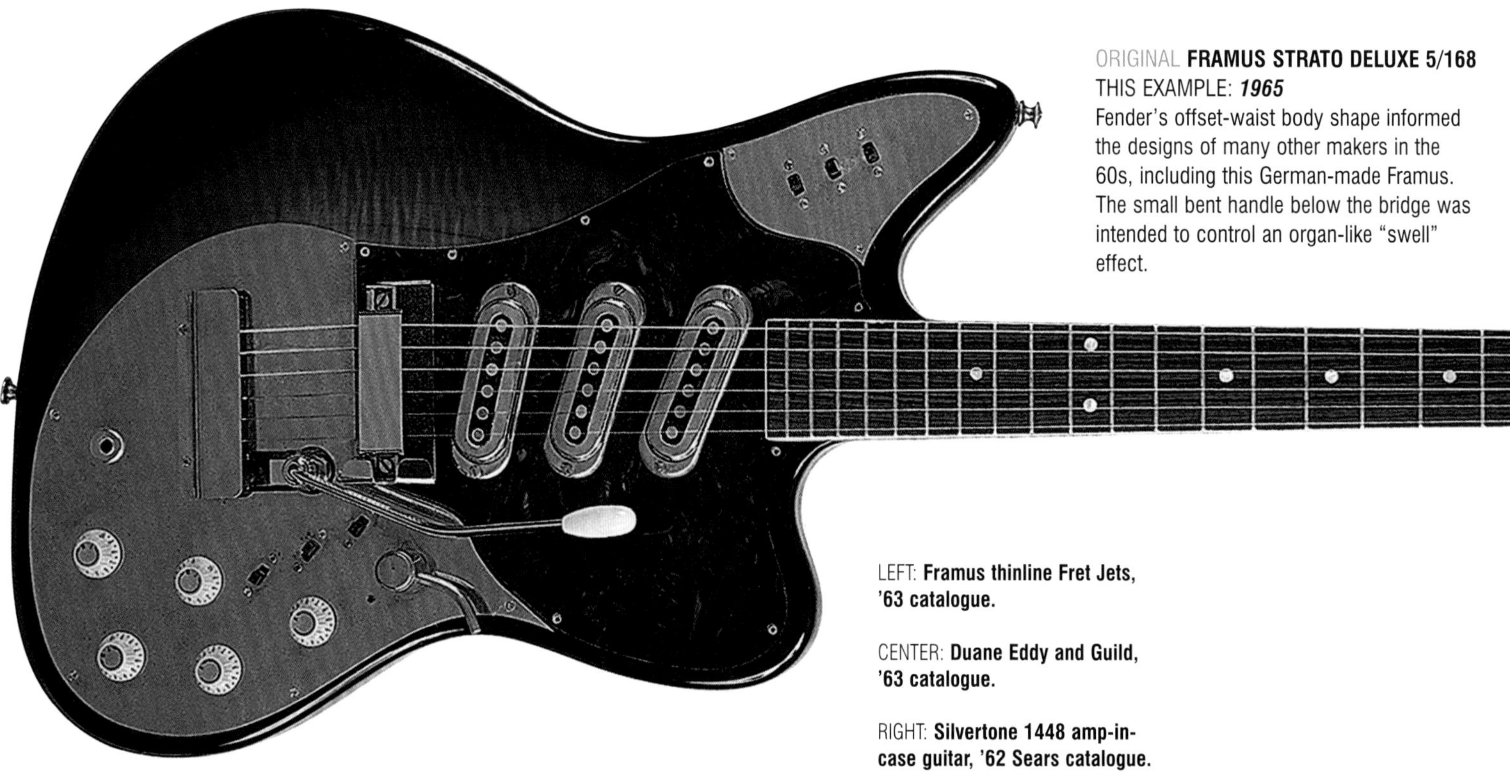

ORIGINAL **FRAMUS STRATO DELUXE 5/168**
THIS EXAMPLE: ***1965***
Fender's offset-waist body shape informed the designs of many other makers in the 60s, including this German-made Framus. The small bent handle below the bridge was intended to control an organ-like "swell" effect.

LEFT: **Framus thinline Fret Jets, '63 catalogue.**

CENTER: **Duane Eddy and Guild, '63 catalogue.**

RIGHT: **Silvertone 1448 amp-in-case guitar, '62 Sears catalogue.**

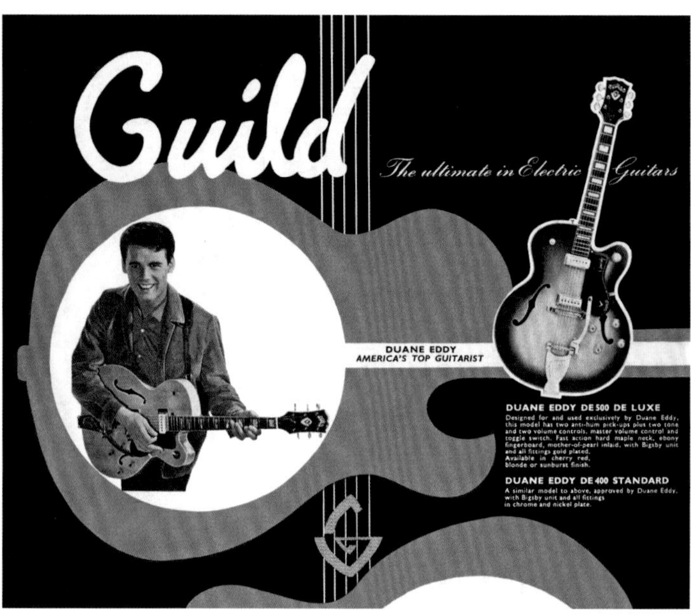

ORIGINAL **GUILD DUANE EDDY DELUXE DE500**
THIS EXAMPLE: ***1962***
Guild, renowned in the 60s for flattop acoustics, made this electric hollowbody named for the king of twang, Duane Eddy—and the one shown here is Eddy's own. Better known for playing Gretsch, he used it for a while on-stage in the 60s.

ORIGINAL **HAGSTROM PB-24-G**
THIS EXAMPLE: ***1963***
Hagstrom, the leading guitar maker in Sweden, introduced this model with a plastic-topped body in 1962. Some had the Hagstrom or Kent brand, while others were branded Futurama (for Selmer in the UK) or Cromwell (for Guild).

ORIGINAL **SILVERTONE 1457**
THIS EXAMPLE: ***1964***
Silvertone's ingenious budget-price all-in-one outfit, made by Danelectro, offered a guitar in a case that had a built-in amp and speaker. Silvertone was the brand used by Sears, Roebuck for the guitars sold through its mail-order catalogues.

Largest Daily Circulation In Texas

The Dallas Morning News

John F. Kennedy Life History, Pages 4 and 5

VOL. 115—NO. 54 — DALLAS, TEXAS, SATURDAY, NOVEMBER 23, 1963—46 PAGES IN 4 SECTIONS ★★ PRICE 5 CENTS

KENNEDY SLAIN ON DALLAS STREET

★ ★ ★ ★ ★ ★ ★ ★ ★ ★ ★ ★ ★ ★ ★ ★

Johnson Becomes 36th President

- **PRESIDENT KENNEDY** is assassinated in Dallas, Texas, and Lyndon B. Johnson becomes president the same day. Forty-eight hours later Lee Harvey Oswald, accused of Kennedy's murder, is shot and killed by Jack Ruby, a nightclub owner.

- **DR TIMOTHY LEARY** and a colleague are fired from Harvard for experimenting on students with LSD. "Drugs," Norman Mailer writes, "are a spiritual form of gambling."

- **CHEVROLET'S** Corvette Sting Ray is the chic new US sports car. Designed by Bill Mitchell, the coupe has split windows on a boat-tail rear and pivoting headlights.

1963

- **BRITAIN** is rocked by scandal and crime. Conservative minister John Profumo resigns after disclosure of his affair with Christine Keeler, who was also involved with a Soviet naval attaché. A gang steals an unprecedented £2.5 million from a mail train by hiding a green signal light with an old glove and lighting the red stop signal with torch batteries.

- **MARTIN LUTHER KING** delivers a speech to a gathering in Washington: "I have a dream that one day this nation will rise up and live out the true meaning of its creed: We hold these truths to be self-evident, that all men are created equal." Meanwhile, Governor George Wallace fails in his attempt to stop black students enrolling at the University of Alabama.

In 1963, Gibson added a new line of solidbody electrics, the Firebirds, with strong links back to its failed Explorer model. The motivation again seems to have been to compete with Fender's growing dominance of the solidbody market. Gibson hired an outside designer, Ray Dietrich, who had worked in the car industry for fifty years, to concoct something new and remarkable.

There were four Firebirds, the I, III, V, and VII, each with different appointments but following the same overall design and build. They were the first Gibson solidbody electrics to make use of a through-neck construction—all Gibsons had a glued-in set neck, while Fender used a screwed-on neck joint. For the Firebirds, a central multi-laminate mahogany-and-walnut section ran the entire length of the guitar, from headstock to strap button, providing the neck and the mid portion of the body in a single unit.

Standard finish for the Firebirds was sunburst, but Gibson went further than simply adopting Fender-like shapes for the new line and borrowed Fender's custom finishes idea. Gibson, too, issued its own color chart for the Firebird models, including cardinal red, frost blue, Inverness green poly, Polaris white, and Pelham blue poly ("poly" meant a metallic finish).

Danelectro and New York sessionman Vinnie Bell designed the first single-neck electric twelve-string, the Bellzouki, introduced in 1962. It was inspired by the Greek bouzouki, the modern version of which was often electric, usually featured four paired strings, and sounded not unlike a metallic twelve-string guitar. Danelectro's one-pickup Bellzouki 7010 had the look of a bouzouki, with its large-mandolin-like rounded body, while the two-pickup 7020 and 7021 were more ornate. "They evoke the mysterious charm and flavor of remote times and places, yet are easily played using familiar guitar technique," Danelectro claimed. The last Bellzouki was made in 1969.

Gibson Firebird catalogue with custom colors, 1963.

ORIGINAL **GIBSON FIREBIRD VII**
THIS EXAMPLE: ***1964***
This VII, finished in cardinal red and owned today by Phil Manzanera, has three pickups, and gold-plated metalwork, plus a Tune-o-matic bridge and Deluxe Gibson–Maestro Vibrola with tubular arm and decorated cover.

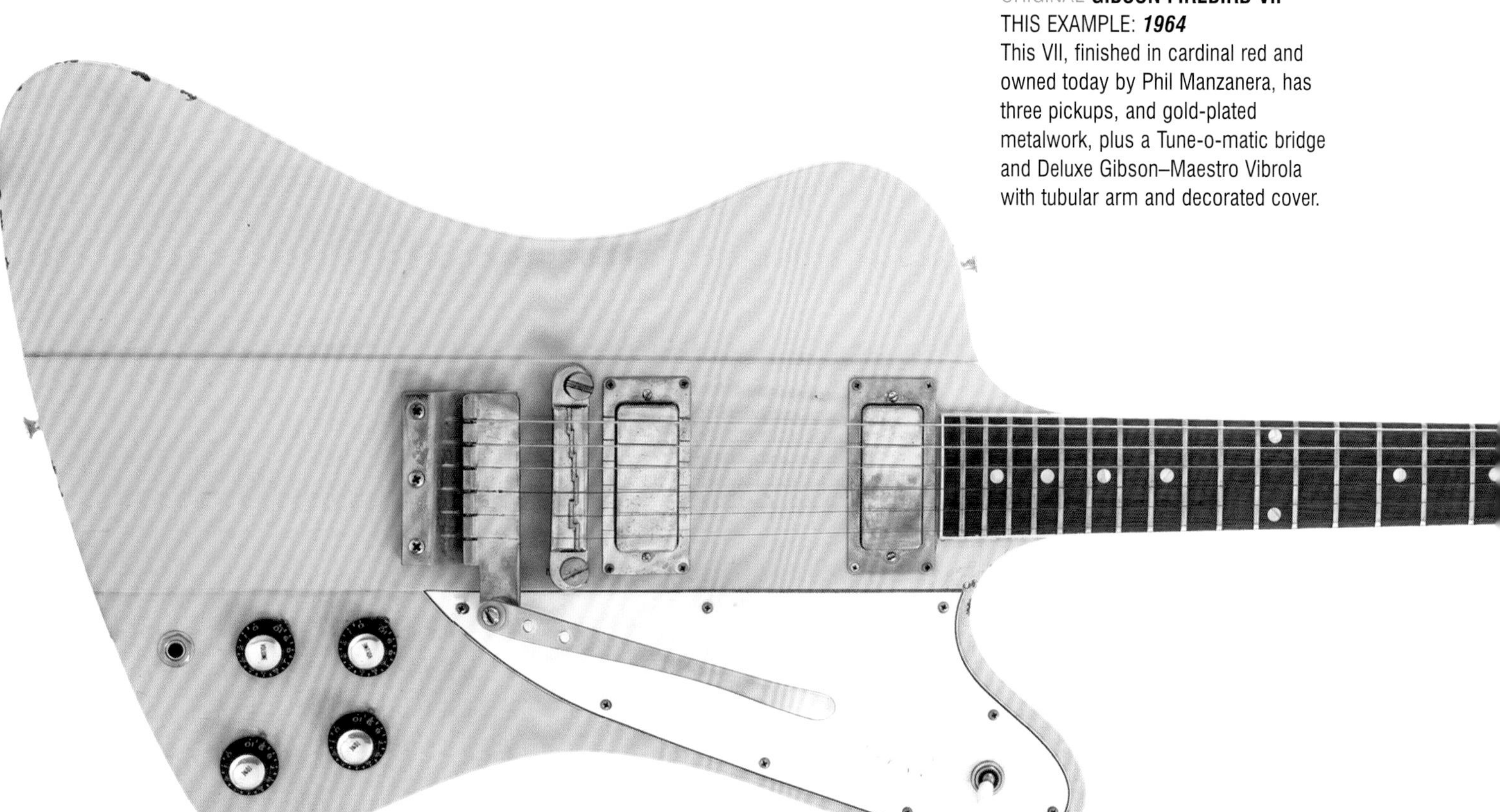

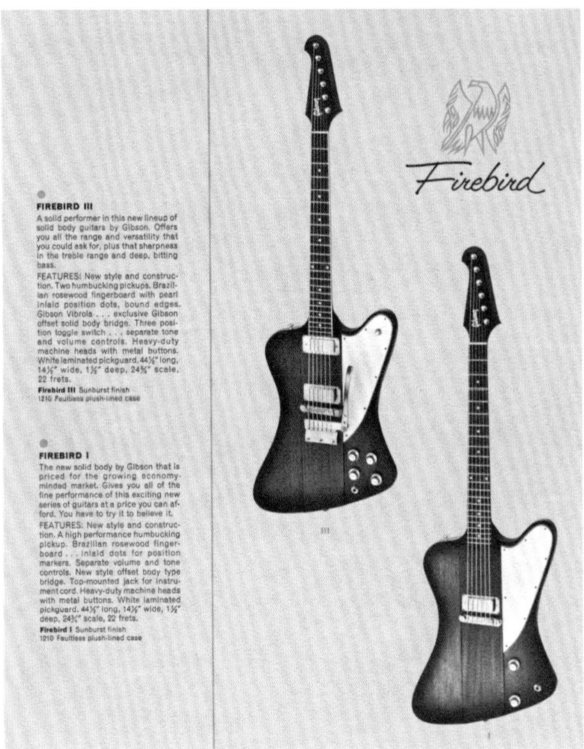

Single-pickup Firebird I alongside a III, 1963 catalogue.

Vinnie Bell with Bellzouki and D'Angelico, 1970 album.

ORIGINAL **DANELECTRO BELLZOUKI 7020**
THIS EXAMPLE: ***1963***
An early electric twelve-string was launched after a collaboration between Danelectro and the session guitarist Vinnie Bell, and they based their new instrument on the traditional Greek bouzouki.

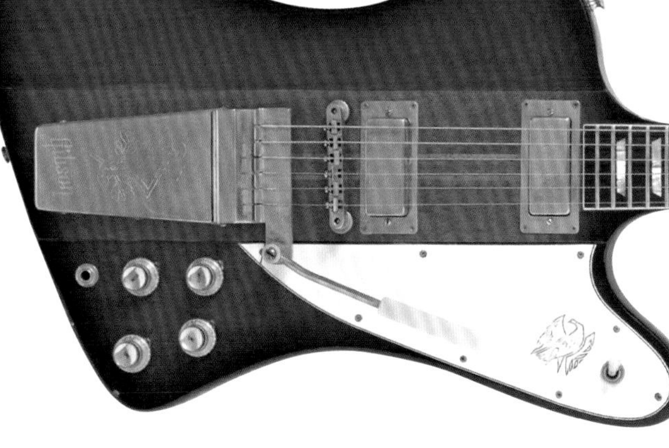

ORIGINAL **GIBSON FIREBIRD V**
THIS EXAMPLE: ***1964***
Gibson's new Firebirds debuted in 1963 alongside a pair of matching Thunderbird basses. This V has the original Firebird's "reverse body" shape, rear-facing "banjo" tuners, and (visible here) through-neck construction.

ORIGINAL **GIBSON FIREBIRD III**
THIS EXAMPLE: ***1963***
This is finished in frost blue, one of Gibson's ten Firebird custom colors. The III had dot fingerboard markers, and it featured a stud-style bridge and a simple Gibson–Maestro Vibrola with flat arm.

Announcing the Firebirds, 1963 ad.

Gibson's original Firebird guitars, launched in 1963, are known today as reverse models because of the body's asymmetrical shape, which drew on the earlier Explorer. As we'll see, in 1965 Gibson would redesign the Firebird line with a rather more conventional body shape, and as a result, players and collectors now distinguish those later types by describing them as non-reverse Firebirds, in contrast to that earlier reverse body.

The first reverse reissue came in 1972, with a limited run of Firebird V models that had an identifying medallion on the body. Four years later, the shortlived Firebird 76 appeared, sold to coincide with the USA's bicentennial celebrations, with a suitably transformed red-white-and-blue bird logo on the pickguard. Gibson has reissued and reinterpreted the original reverse Firebirds many times more in the decades since their first brief run from 1963 to 1965.

In 1977, Gibson took a fresh look at the way the electronics of a guitar could work, containing its experiments in the modified-Firebird shape of the new RD series. Active circuitry was popularized by Alembic in the 70s, designed to boost the signal and widen the tonal range of an electric guitar. This kind of hi-fidelity approach was prompted by the apparent competition from synthesizers, which had become big business during the late 70s. Gibson figured a hook-up with Moog, one of the synthesizer field's most famous names, might re-capture ground that guitars seemed to be losing to the new keyboards.

One of the RD models, the Standard, was a regular electric, without the active circuit, which was reserved for the Custom and Artist models. But the line was not popular, and many guitarists disliked what they considered the "unnatural" sounds of active circuitry, a major factor in the downfall of the series. The various RD models were gone from the catalogue by 1981.

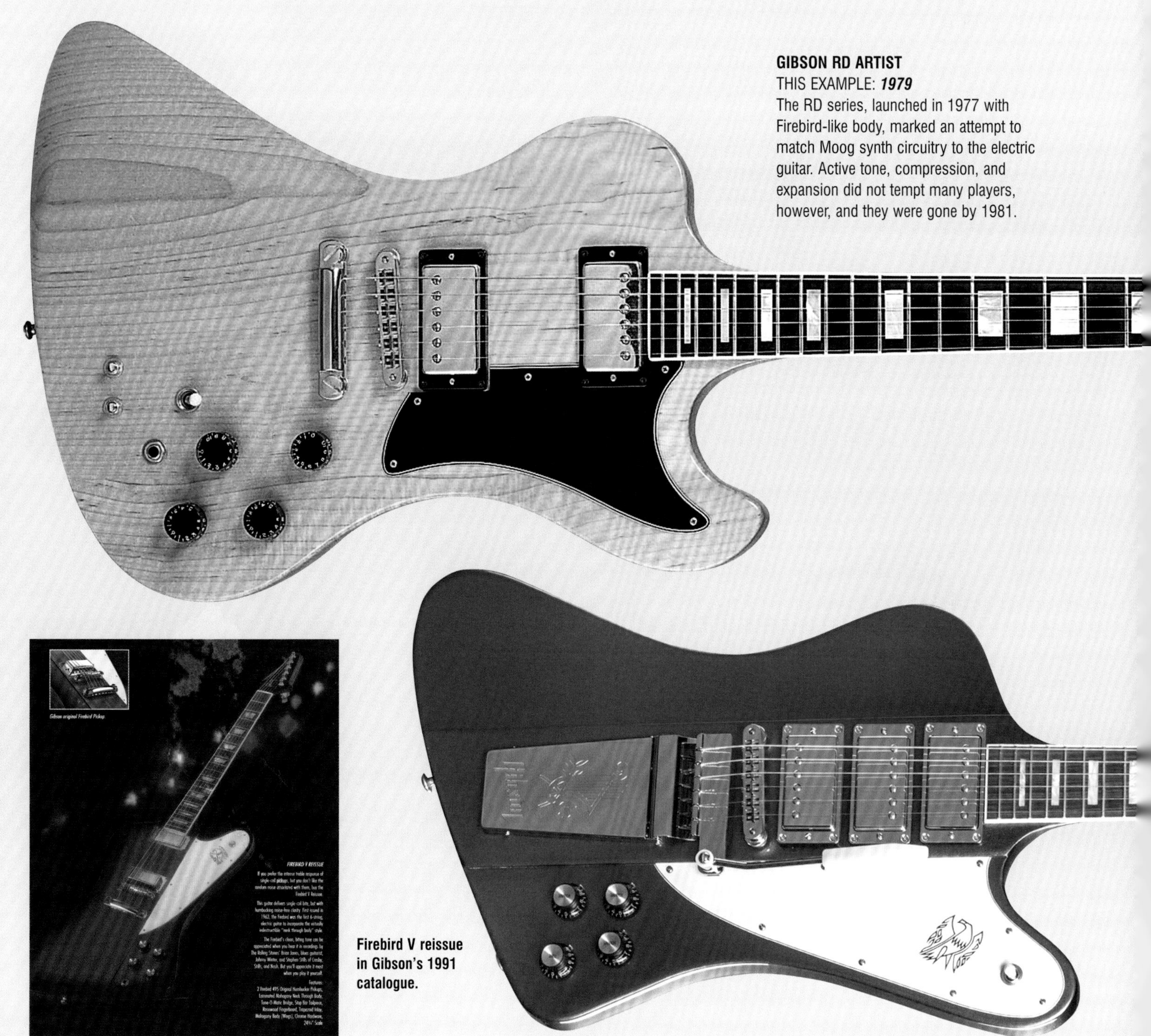

GIBSON RD ARTIST
THIS EXAMPLE: ***1979***
The RD series, launched in 1977 with Firebird-like body, marked an attempt to match Moog synth circuitry to the electric guitar. Active tone, compression, and expansion did not tempt many players, however, and they were gone by 1981.

Firebird V reissue in Gibson's 1991 catalogue.

GIBSON 1965 FIREBIRD V
THIS EXAMPLE: ***1999***
A re-creation of an original-style reverse Firebird V, introduced by Gibson's Custom Shop in 1999. It has a pair of mini-humbuckers and crown inlays, two features that together distinguish a Firebird V from the other reverse models.

Gibson ad for the active-circuit RD models, 1979.

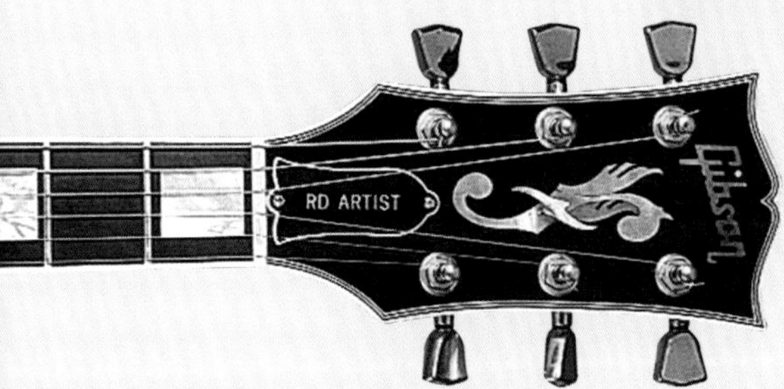

GIBSON 50th ANNIVERSARY FIREBIRD
THIS EXAMPLE: ***2013***
Gibson called this a "glorious gold-on-gold tribute to the revolutionary original 'Bird," dressing up a Firebird V-style guitar to mark 50 years since the introduction of the first Firebirds in 1963.

GIBSON FIREBIRD 7
THIS EXAMPLE: ***2014***
The Gibson USA factory's recent reinterpretation of the original Firebird VII has that model's distinguishing block fingerboard markers, but adds full-size humbuckers and chrome-plated metalwork. This one is finished in blue mist.

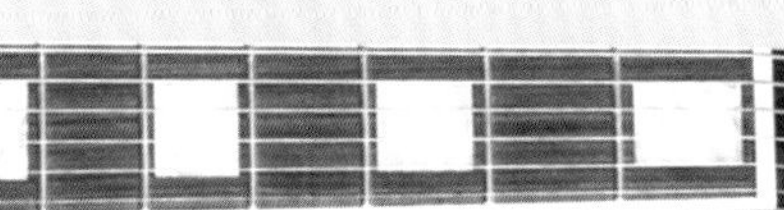

1963

Guitar makers in Europe were competing for the busy guitar market that seemed to be growing every year, as young hopeful guitarists followed the success of the new beat groups and decided an electric guitar was just the thing to set them on a similar path.

Established instrument-making firms in Germany were among the leading European makers of electric guitars. We've already met Hofner, and in 1963 the company introduced its newest solidbody model, the Galaxie, which had strong stylistic hints of the Fender Stratocaster, but with Hofner's flair for detailed control systems. The Galaxie had a Solo/Rhythm boost switch, three individual pickup tone wheels, a master volume wheel, and three pickup on/off switches marked Bass On, "Discant" On, and Treble On.

Hopf was a relatively ancient name that went back to German instrument making in the 17th century, although the modern company was founded in the early years of the 20th century. Dieter Hopf established the brand's first electric guitars in the late 50s and introduced the hollowbody Saturn 63 model early in the following decade. The elegant Saturn's main claim to fame came when it was clearly visible in a silhouette-like logo for the Star Club in Hamburg, famous as an early haunt of The Beatles and other fledgling beat groups of the era.

Italian guitar companies, too, were producing stylish electrics during the 60s, and many of the companies who became involved in guitar production at this time drew on their experience as accordion makers, in the process giving their instruments a distinctive quality—sometimes a sparkle finish, here the use of plastic components, there an intricate-looking control layout. Brands included Bartolini, Crucianelli, Eko, Galanti, Gemelli, Wandrè, and Welson, and many of them were made in the area around Castelfidardo and Recanati in the Marche region of eastern Italy.

Gemelli "twins" guitar, 1963 catalogue cover.

ORIGINAL **BARTOLINI 20V**
THIS EXAMPLE: ***1964***
This early-60s creation from Italy is a wonderful four-pickup example of the accordion-influenced guitars made during the 60s. It has a sparkle-finish body, pearl-plastic fingerboard, and multiple pushbuttons.

Selmer catalogue cover, 1963, with Hofner Galaxie.

MODEL 702V

MODEL 702B

MODEL 40V

MODEL 702
Semi-Acoustic Electric Guitar – Thin hollow body - can be played with or without amplifier. Available with or without Vibrato. Features Sunburst finish in red or brown, adjustable neck, bridge, 2 pickups, tone and volume controls. Heavy plexiglass guardplate, with cord.
Price.......... $200.00
MODEL 702V – Same as above with Vibrato.
Price.......... $225.00
Standard Case.......... 12.00
Deluxe Hard Shell Case.......... 40.00

MODEL 702B
Semi-Acoustic Electric Bass – Beautiful Sunburst finish, Brown or Red. Two pickups, tone and volume controls, chrome plated with adjustable pickups, bridge and steel-reinforced neck. Equipped with cord.
Price.......... $225.00
Deluxe Hard Shell Case.......... 40.00

MODEL 40V
Imperial Tonemaster Guitar – with 4 pickups and 6 switches which provide a variety of tone changes; tone and volume controls; with vibrato.
Price.......... $210.00
MODEL 40 (as above) without vibrato.
Price.......... $187.00
Deluxe Case.......... 35.00
Deluxe, Bound Case.......... 40.00

Crucianelli guitars in US Imperial catalogue, 1965.

ORIGINAL **HOFNER GALAXIE**
THIS EXAMPLE: ***1963***
Hofner's Strat-like three-pickup Galaxie model was especially popular in Britain, where it was sold by Hofner's distributor Selmer, whose catalogue claimed it was "backed by the craftsmanship that's made Hofner a name to be reckoned with."

ORIGINAL **HOPF SATURN 63**
THIS EXAMPLE: ***1963***
The Saturn's hollow body, with its Fender-like offset waist, had a couple of stylish teardrop-shape soundholes with metal binding, as well as similar binding to the top of the body, and it had an unusual non-standard jack.

Star Club single, 1964, with Hopf Saturn 63.

ORIGINAL **GRETSCH ASTRO-JET 6126**
THIS EXAMPLE: ***1967***
This weird-looking solidbody was introduced by Gretsch in 1963 but, not surprisingly, it lasted only a few years in the catalogue. At this time, Gretsch was using a Burns vibrato on some models.

ORIGINAL **EPIPHONE CAIOLA CUSTOM**
THIS EXAMPLE: ***1964***
Studio guitarist Al Caiola wanted fuller tone controls on his signature Epiphone model, resulting in the five "tone expressor" switches on its curved panel. He specified a zero fret at the nut, a feature not seen on any other Epiphone at the time.

The Ventures with their Mosrites, 1964 single.

ORIGINAL **MOSRITE VENTURES MODEL**
THIS EXAMPLE: ***1964***
Semie Moseley launched this distinctive model in 1963 in collaboration with The Ventures. It had a body like a flipped Strat, a stylish vibrato system, an angled neck pickup, and an M-cutout headstock. It survived with modifications until 1967.

The New York sessionman Al Caiola is best known for his prominent guitar on the themes for *Bonanza* and *The Magnificent Seven*, but he was a busy studio guitarist working for all kinds of artists and on a wide range of material. Epiphone introduced a signature model for him in 1963, which was more or less a long-scale Sheraton with multiple tone controls. Epiphone made some changes in its solidbody line at this time, too, introducing the high-end Crestwood Deluxe, a three-pickup companion to the Crestwood Custom, and the budget Olympic Junior and Special.

The new Gretsch solidbody for 1963 was the Astro-Jet, a strange looking guitar with a big misshapen body. It featured the new Super'Tron humbucking pickup, visually characterized by the absence of polepieces; instead it had two long bar-shaped laminated poles on the top. The intention was a hotter humbucker than the regular Filter'Tron, but the Super was never as popular. As for the peculiar Astro-Jet, it did not last long.

Mosrite began business in California in the late 50s, founded by Semie Moseley, who had worked as an assistant to Roger Rossmeisl at Rickenbacker. The brand's big break came in the early 60s with the Ventures Model. The Ventures were the biggest US instrumental guitar band, with hits such as 'Perfidia' and 'Walk—Don't Run.' Moseley lent a guitar to Ventures guitarist Nokie Edwards, and the group and the guitar firm soon collaborated to design a signature model. A credit line for Mosrite on one of the group's album covers alone created an enormous demand for the new instrument, launched in 1963. This first style of Ventures model is known as the Mark I; a slightly later version, with simpler design, is known as the Mark II and was the type that Johnny Ramone would play in the 70s.

Built-in Mosrite soul, 1966 ad.

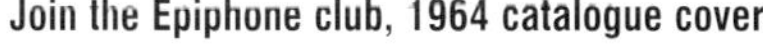

Join the Epiphone club, 1964 catalogue cover.

ORIGINAL **EPIPHONE CRESTWOOD DELUXE SB232**
THIS EXAMPLE: ***1966***
An addition to the solidbody line in '63 was the Crestwood Deluxe, with suitably high-end features: three mini-humbucking pickups, block-shape fingerboard markers, a bound ebony fingerboard, and bound headstock.

Jet-Star and Thunderbird, 1964 ad.

Guild was turning out popular flattops from its factory in New Jersey during the 60s but also found time to develop the electric side of its business, with several new models in reaction to the boom in demand. Following the Duane Eddy hollowbody we saw earlier, the company added a double-cutaway signature model for Bert Weedon in 1963. Weedon was a guitar star in Britain, appearing regularly on TV and playing on many studio sessions. He had a solo career making guitar instrumental records, including a top ten hit with his cover of 'Guitar Boogie Shuffle.' Many young guitarists knew him best as the author of *Play In A Day*, a basic tutor that started many a future star with C, F, and G.

Guild had discovered the thinline hollowbody electric style in 1958 when it introduced an aptly-named model, the Slim Jim T-100. In 1963, the company gave in to the trend toward double cutaways, launching the Starfire IV, V, and VI, which bolstered the line begun with three single-cutaway Starfires in 1960, the I, II, and III. But where many other makers simply absorbed the look of the Gibson-originated trend, Guild went further and matched the Gibson 335's semi-solid construction, using a centre-block in the body of the three new Starfire models.

The first solidbody models from Guild were launched in 1963, the single-pickup Jet-Star S-50 and the two-pickup Polara S-100 and Thunderbird S-200, all with an unusual body shape with a curved cut-out at the base. One ingenious feature of the 100 and 200 was a stand built into the back of the body, which could be folded out to support the instrument. Guild described the Thunderbird in a 60s catalogue as "an instrument for the hard-driving guitarist who searches continually for new horizons of sound."

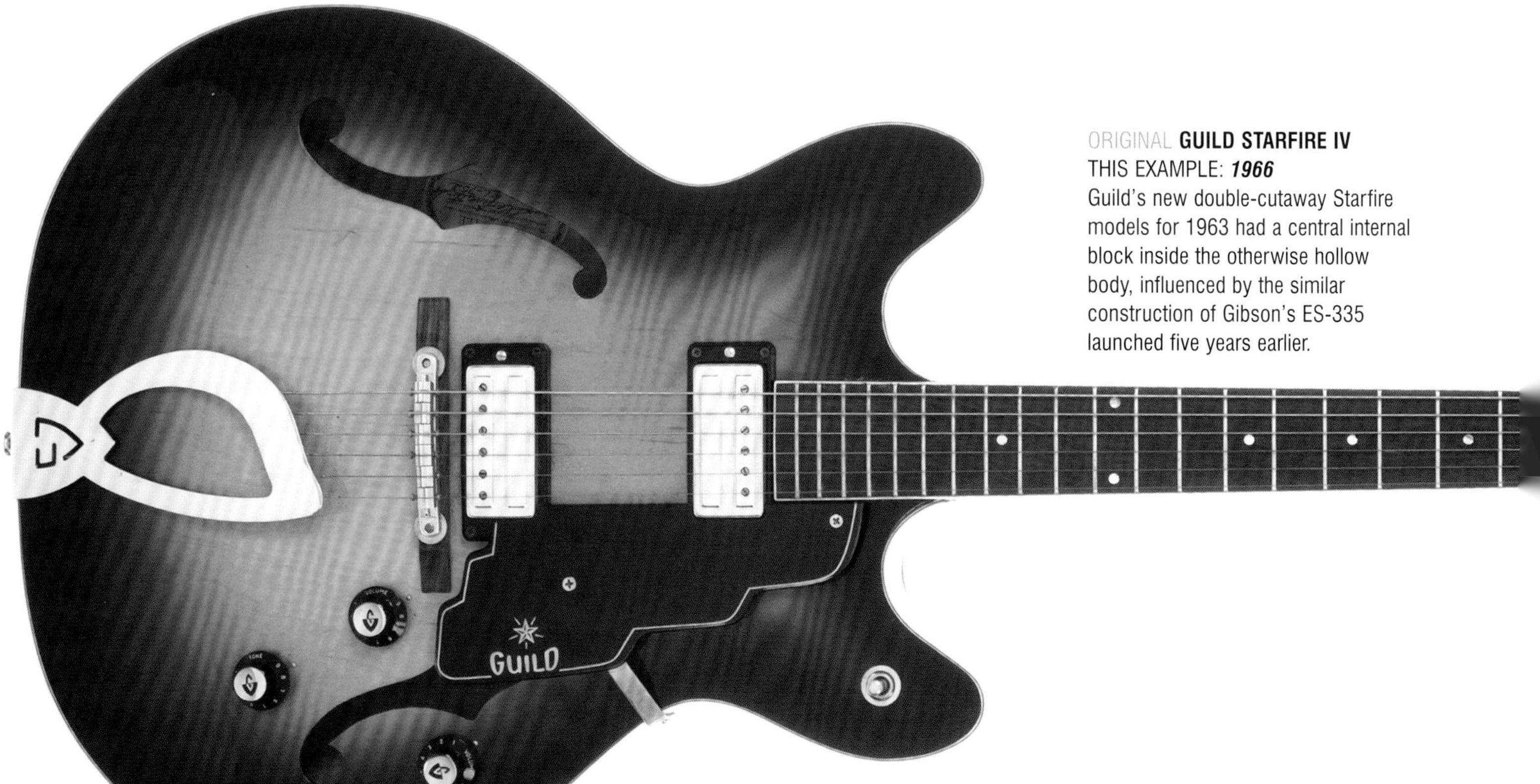

ORIGINAL **GUILD STARFIRE IV**
THIS EXAMPLE: ***1966***
Guild's new double-cutaway Starfire models for 1963 had a central internal block inside the otherwise hollow body, influenced by the similar construction of Gibson's ES-335 launched five years earlier.

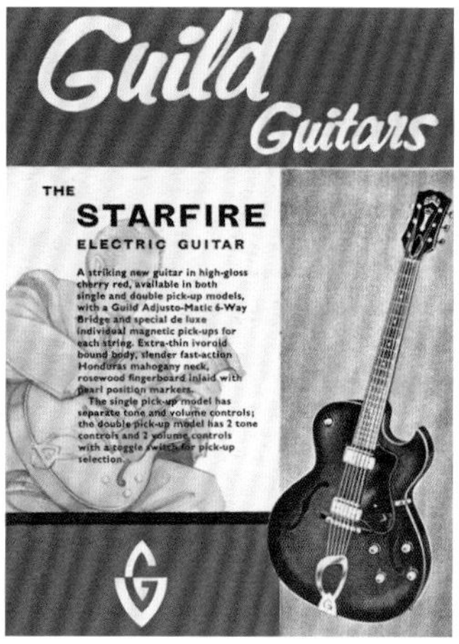

Earlier single-cut Starfire II, 1963 catalogue cover.

Bert Weedon with Guild signature model, 1963 UK catalogue.

Doors open for Guild players, 1963 catalogue cover.

ORIGINAL **GUILD BERT WEEDON**
THIS EXAMPLE: ***1963***
This was Weedon's own example of his Guild signature model, created for the British guitar star in collaboration with Guild's UK distributor, Boosey & Hawkes.

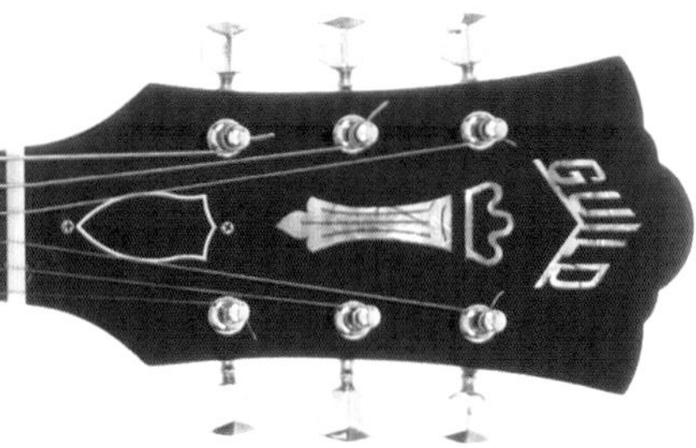

ORIGINAL **GUILD THUNDERBIRD S-200**
THIS EXAMPLE: ***1967***
The Thunderbird was one of three Guild models that marked the company's entry into the crowded market for solidbody electrics. It sat above the Polara S-100 and Jet-Star S-50, and had a novel stand built into the rear of the body.

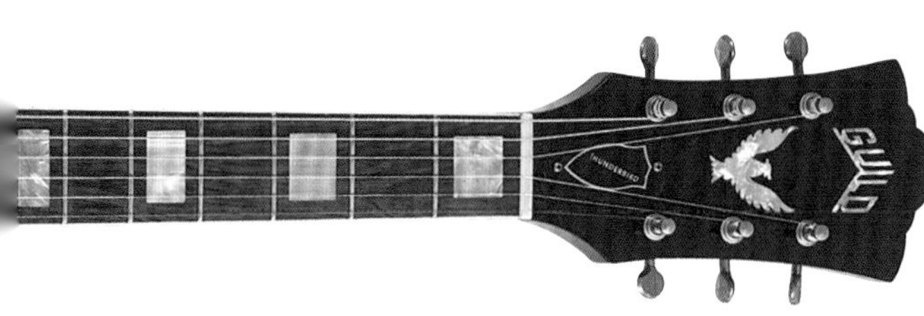

Guild was bought by Avnet in 1966, an electronics firm that acquired Hershman and its Goya brandname the same year, and Guild production began to shift to a new factory in Rhode Island, from where the brand continued to appear on instruments through the 70s and 80s. In the mid 80s, Avnet sold Guild to an investment group, and for a while the future of the brand seemed uncertain, ending in bankruptcy in 1988. A year later, it was sold to Fass of Wisconsin, which became the US Music Corporation, and Guild electrics began to reappear in the early 90s.

In 1995, Guild's woes appeared to be over when the brand was sold to Fender. The new owner decided also to bring Guild designs to a wider market with an additional line of less expensive equivalents, which were marketed with the DeArmond name, named for Harry DeArmond (whose Rowe company made many of Guild's early pickups). In 2001, Guild production was moved from the long-standing Rhode Island premises to Fender's factory in Corona, California. Three years later came a further move to Tacoma, Washington, but shortly after that, production of the company's electric models stopped.

Guild opened a Custom Shop in 2013 and launched the Orpheum series, which aimed to reissue a number of Guild's classic electrics of the 50s and 60s, but in 2014, Fender sold Guild to the Cordoba Music Group, and production of US-made Guild electrics was reinstated in California. The reinvigorated Cordoba operation has since offered a number of Guild electric models, and these have included a Thunderbird, renamed as the T-Bird, a Jetstar and Polara, the Bluesbird, and a swarm of Starfires, including the III, IV, V, and VI variants. Recently revived Guild hollowbody electrics included the M-75 Aristocrat, A-150 Savoy, X-175 Manhattan, C-100D Capri, and T-50 Slim.

GUILD T-BIRD ST P90
THIS EXAMPLE: ***2018***
This revised reissue of a Thunderbird came with the modern stability of an adjustable bridge and stopbar and simplified controls, and featured a pair of the new Guild operation's Franz P90 single-coil pickups. This T-Bird is finished in Pelham blue.

Kim Thayil with Polara S-100, 1996 ad.

GUILD S-200 T-BIRD
THIS EXAMPLE: ***2018***
The Thunderbird reissue has a two-way mode switch—neck-pickup-only, or neck-or-bridge—and separate volume and tone controls for each. The panel of three switches works only in neck-or-bridge mode, two for selecting pickups and one for tone.

GUILD STARFIRE VI
THIS EXAMPLE: ***2018***
The top-of-the-line Starfire reissue is the VI, and the blonde finish of this example highlights the figured maple top. The fancy fingerboard inlays have traditional Guild-style abalone V inserts in the pearl blocks.

Guild's comeback with Fender, 1997 ad.

GUILD STARFIRE IV
THIS EXAMPLE: ***2017***
Cordoba's reissue of the semi-solid Starfire IV model has a hollow maple body with a spruce centre block, and it's fitted with LB-1 Little Bucker replicas of the original smaller-size pickups. This one is finished in antique sunburst.

GUILD STARFIRE V
THIS EXAMPLE: ***2018***
A further Starfire semi-solid reissue, this white V has a mahogany body, with master volume control and pickup selector on the treble cutaway.

DUNDEE - MacDONALD ENTERPRISES, INC.
Presents
THE GREATEST FIGHT IN HISTORY
WORLD'S HEAVYWEIGHT CHAMPION-SHIP
SONNY
LISTON
Champion
CASSIUS
CLAY
Challenger
NO HOME THEATRE TV
MIAMI BEACH CONVENTION HALL
TUES. FEB. 25th
8:30 P.M.
ALL SEATS RESERVED STARTING AT $20
PHONE JE 2-3329 FOR TICKETS

- **A US DESTROYER** is attacked by North Vietnamese torpedo boats. President Johnson orders retaliatory air strikes, backed by Congress which, in the Gulf Of Tonkin resolution, authorizes the president to take any steps necessary "to maintain peace."

- **THE MUNSTERS** and The Man From U.N.C.L.E. debut on TV. The Transylvanian Munster family has a simple motto: "Every cloud has a dark lining." Transcending the cold war, the United Network Command for Law and Enforcement agents Napoleon Solo (American) and Illya Kuryakin (Russian) report to Alexander Waverly (British), chiefly by talking into their pens.

1964

- **MODS & ROCKERS** go into battle at British seaside resorts. Fashionable mods take speed, drive scooters, and listen to soul music. Leather-jacketed rockers drink, drive motorcycles, and listen to rock'n'roll. Arbitration is not sought.

- **CASSIUS CLAY** takes the world heavyweight boxing title. He later changes his name to Muhammad Ali.

- **PRESIDENT** Johnson signs the Civil Rights Act, "ending" US racial discrimination. Three civil rights workers missing in Mississippi following their arrest are found murdered. Martin Luther King receives the Nobel peace prize.

ORIGINAL **RICKENBACKER 360/12**
THIS EXAMPLE: ***1965***
The California company gave its deluxe models a new look in 1964, as this twelve-string model 360/12 shows, its rounded body front without binding in contrast to the bound-top sharp-edged body of earlier models.

ORIGINAL **RICKENBACKER 1993 (330/12)**
THIS EXAMPLE: ***1964***
Rickenbacker's electric twelve-string guitars, like this export 1993 model, had a headstock that ingeniously arranged the 12 tuners in two planes, with one set of six in the conventional positions and the other six facing backward.

John Lennon and 325/1996 model, 1965 ad.

Rick twelve-string ad, 1967.

Rickenbacker introduced an electric twelve-string in 1964, and it proved to be the company's masterstroke. It was not the first electric 12, as we've already discovered, but it turned out to be the most popular. That popularity was boosted considerably when the model was chosen by George Harrison in The Beatles and Roger McGuinn in The Byrds, among many others who subsequently came upon the haunting tone of an electric twelve-string. The California company gave Harrison his Rick 12 during The Beatles' first US tour in 1964, and he used the guitar's big chiming sound on many of the group's live shows and several recordings, including 'A Hard Day's Night,' 'I Should Have Known Better,' and 'Ticket To Ride.' McGuinn got his first Rick 12 in 1964 after seeing Harrison with one in the *Hard Day's Night* movie, and he used its jingle-jangling sound on almost every Byrds cut that followed.

In 1964, Rickenbacker began exporting guitars to the Rose-Morris distribution company in Britain. For a number of years, Rickenbacker had produced some of its short-scale 300-series guitars with an f-hole, distinct from others that had a sealed top. Rose-Morris liked the f-hole and asked for it on the bigger-body guitars it bought, too, instead of Rickenbacker's regular slash-shape soundhole. Most of the semi-hollow guitars that Rickenbacker subsequently made for export had f-holes, on instruments sold to firms in Canada, Australia, and Italy, as well as the UK. Rose-Morris had its own model-number system, cataloguing its Rickenbacker line as the 1993 (Rickenbacker's 330/12), 1995 (615), 1996 (325), 1997 (335), and 1998 (345). Rose-Morris did well for a time with its American guitars, bolstered by The Beatles' use of a 325 six-string (John Lennon) and a twelve-string (George Harrison), but the distributor decided to drop the line around 1968.

An earlier build-your-own kit, British Vox ad 1960.

UK Rose-Morris Rickenbacker line, 1964 catalogue.

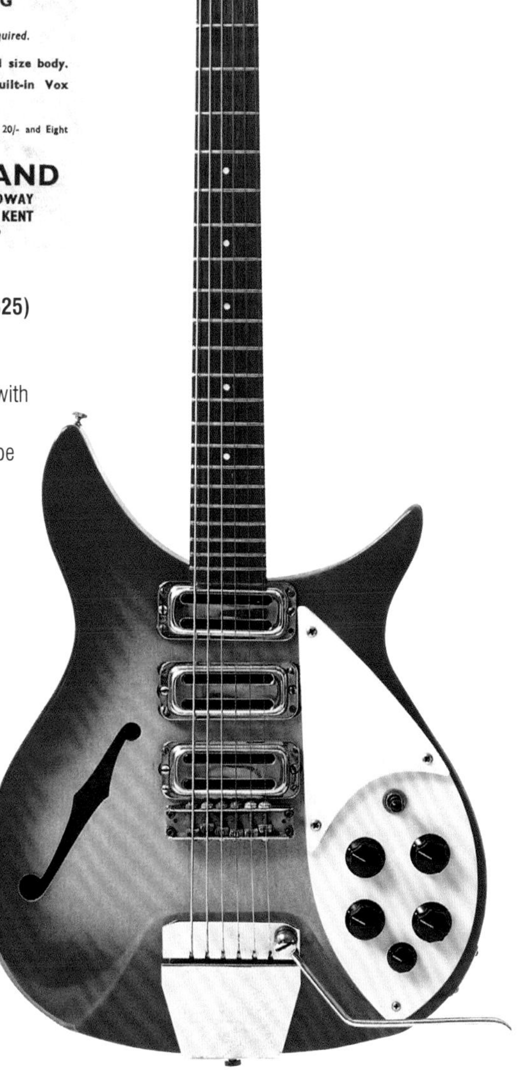

ORIGINAL **RICKENBACKER 1996 (325)**
THIS EXAMPLE: ***1964***
Another export model, sold by the British distributor Rose-Morris and with a distinctive f-hole rather than Rickenbacker's regular "slash"-shape soundhole. The 325 was a key six-string played by John Lennon in his Beatles days.

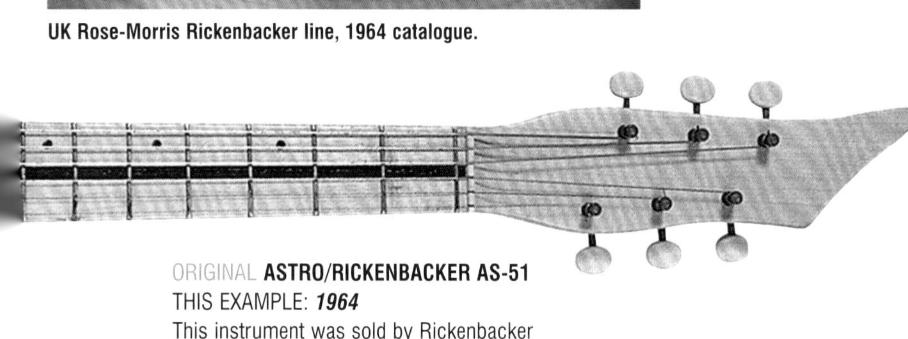

ORIGINAL **ASTRO/RICKENBACKER AS-51**
THIS EXAMPLE: ***1964***
This instrument was sold by Rickenbacker around Christmas 1964 as the Astro Kit, which arrived in a box of 25 parts—including unpainted body—ready for the brave recipient to build (with luck) his very own electric guitar.

Moody vintage vibe, 1984 catalogue cover.

In 1984, with the jangling, rhythmic thrust of Rickenbackers heard anew at the heart of some of pop's most vibrant offerings, the California company began a proper vintage reissue scheme. The first three models were the 325V59 Hamburg (because John Lennon used his original model 325 guitar there with The Beatles), the 325V63 Miami (because Lennon first tried out his new 325 in a Miami TV studio), and a twelve-string, the 360/12V64. The V suffixes linked to the vintage of the original, with V63 indicating 1963, V59 indicating 1959, and so on. Five years later, in 1989, Rickenbacker moved its factory from Kilson Drive after some 27 years, consolidating factory and offices at the corner of South Main and Stevens in Santa Ana.

Numbered limited-edition signature models first appeared from Rickenbacker in 1987 with a Pete Townshend model and, a year later, a twelve-string named for Roger McGuinn. Several more have followed since then. There has been some renaming of the vintage-style models at Rickenbacker in more recent years, with a C series introduced in 2001 alongside the V models. Beyond the company's rarely-changing model lineup, there is another unusual detail that marks out the company when compared to most other modern US guitar makers: Rickenbacker continues to make all of its instruments in the United States.

At the time of writing, alongside the specific reissues—325C64, 350V63, 360/12C63, 381V69, 381/12V69, 1996, and 5002V58—Rickenbacker offered instruments with strong roots in the best guitars of its past, with the heart of the Rick line remaining in its 300-series twelve-strings: the 330/12 (mono, two pickups, dot fingerboard markers), the 360/12 (stereo, two pickups, triangle markers), and the 370/12 (stereo, three pickups, triangle markers), with 330 and 360 six-strings to match.

RICKENBACKER 330/12
THIS EXAMPLE: ***1996***
Rickenbacker's best known guitars are the 330 and 360 models. The twelve-string here has the 330 style's typical dot fingerboard markers, in contrast to the "deluxe" triangle-shape markers used for the various 360 models.

Rickenbacker's C Series reissues, 2001 catalogue.

RICKENBACKER 350V63
THIS EXAMPLE: ***2014***
A problem with Rickenbacker's 325 models for some players is that it has a short-scale neck. This vintage-style 350 is a regular-scale version, which for some provides a more playable layout but with the required vintage vibe.

Rick color options, 1982 catalogue.

RICKENBACKER 325V63 MIAMI
THIS EXAMPLE: ***2000***
A vintage remake of the style of 325 model that Rickenbacker gave to John Lennon, which was the guitarist's second Rickenbacker and one that served him well through the rest of his time with The Beatles.

RICKENBACKER 360/12V64
THIS EXAMPLE: ***1998***
One of the first models in Rickenbacker's reissue program was the 360/12V64, introduced in 1984 and aimed to reproduce the charm, playability, and chiming sound of the original models that enticed many a 60s strummer.

RICKENBACKER 370/12 RME1 ROGER McGUINN
THIS EXAMPLE: ***1988***
This is a prototype for the guitar launched in 1988 as an artist-model twelve-string to celebrate the Byrds guitarist's use of the signature Rick twelve-string sound on so many of the band's hits and key recordings.

We've seen how Jennings Musical Industries (JMI), established in the UK in the early 50s, began to produce guitars in 1959, notably with the angular Phantom models introduced in 1961. As if somehow to make up for the five-sided shape of the Phantom's striking body, the next new Vox model had a notably curvaceous look to the instrument. Mick Bennett at JMI was tasked with designing what at first was called the Phantom Mark III—later, it was renamed simply as the Mark VI. This design was introduced into the Vox guitar lines in 1964, alongside the brand's better-known amplifier heads and combos.

The later nickname given to the Mark guitars, the "teardrop," describes well their rounded symmetrical body style. At first, the line consisted of the Mark VI three-pickup six-string, Mark XII twelve-string, and a bass, and a few years later Special versions were added, which had on-board active circuitry controlled by a row of six pushbuttons.

An odd variation of the earlier Phantom design was Vox's Guitar Organ, the brainchild of Dick Denney, who designed many of the brand's amps. The Guitar Organ was first marketed in 1964 but was not in full production until a few years later. Its frets had special contacts connected to part of the innards of a Vox organ built into the body, and the instrument was designed to create organ or guitar sounds, individually or simultaneously. However, it was difficult to play—not least because of a neck wider at the nut than the body—and did not last long, while the regular Phantom and Mark models survived until the late 60s. Vox added production in Italy and distribution in the US, but business problems led in 1969 to the demise of the guitar brand, which has been revived a number of times since.

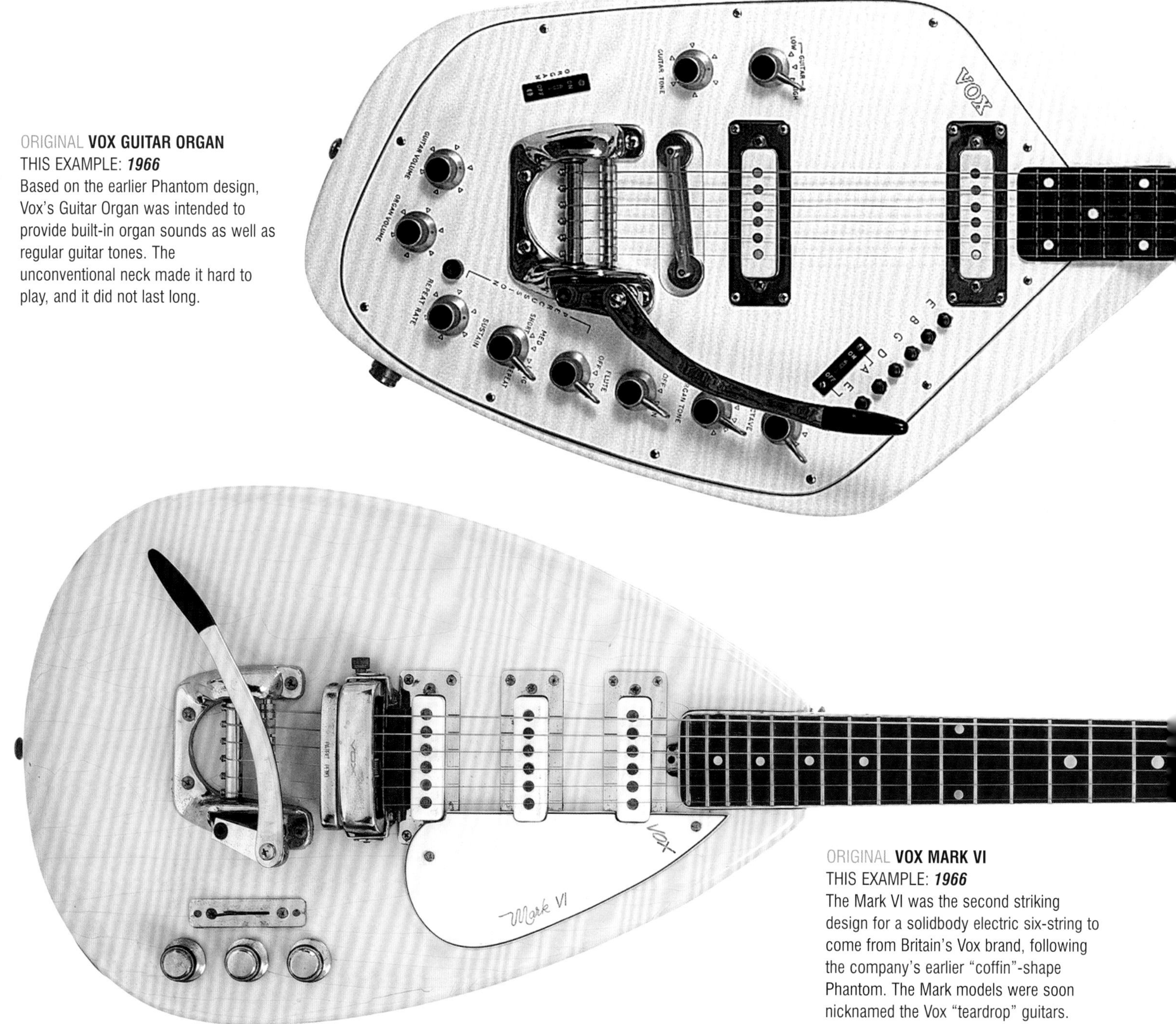

ORIGINAL **VOX GUITAR ORGAN**
THIS EXAMPLE: ***1966***
Based on the earlier Phantom design, Vox's Guitar Organ was intended to provide built-in organ sounds as well as regular guitar tones. The unconventional neck made it hard to play, and it did not last long.

ORIGINAL **VOX MARK VI**
THIS EXAMPLE: ***1966***
The Mark VI was the second striking design for a solidbody electric six-string to come from Britain's Vox brand, following the company's earlier "coffin"-shape Phantom. The Mark models were soon nicknamed the Vox "teardrop" guitars.

Vox HQ, Dartford, England, 1964 catalogue view.

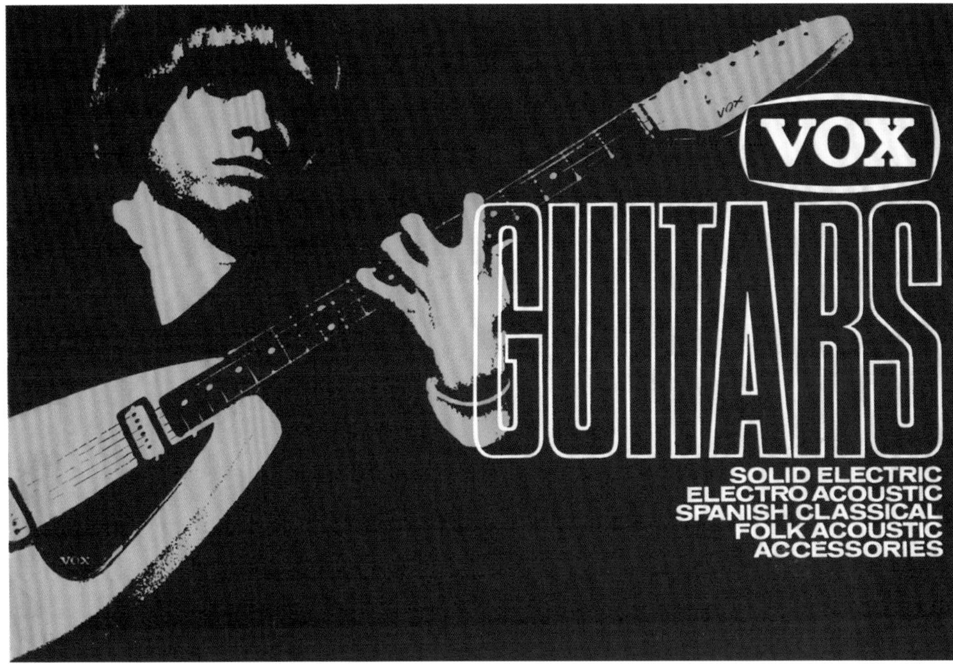

Brian Jones and two-pickup Mark VI, 1967 catalogue cover.

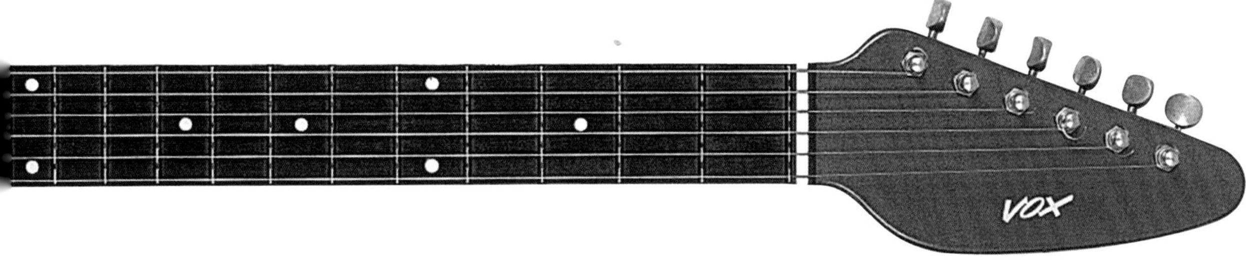

Vox US catalogue cover, 1965.

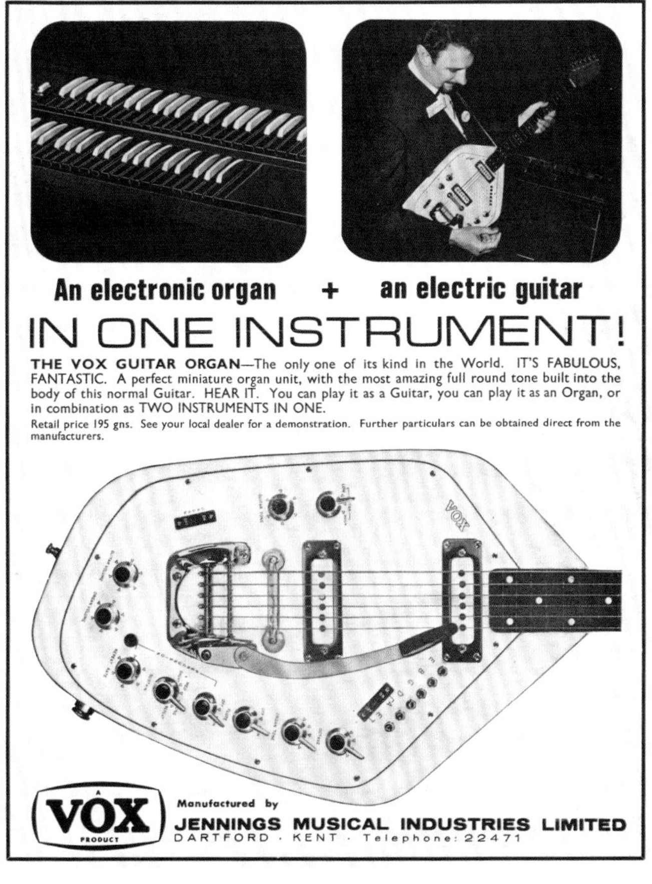

Two instruments in one, Vox Guitar Organ ad, 1966.

ORIGINAL **HARMONY H77**
THIS EXAMPLE: ***1964***
The cherry sunburst finish of this high-end model seemed fitting for such a stylish creation of the Chicago powerhouse that Harmony had become by the early 60s.

LEFT: **Mustang and friends, Fender '65 catalogue.**

CENTER: **Harmony catalogue cover, 1967, with H77.**

RIGHT: **Electric and acoustic in Harmony, 1967 ad.**

Harmony in Chicago produced several impressive new models in the early 60s, not least the H75/76/77/78 double-cutaway thinline models with their three pickups, six control knobs, and bank of three selector switches. Harmony's 1964 catalogue did not hold back when describing the virtues of what it called its "finest electric guitars": maple bodies, "ultra-slim" necks with dual truss rods, three DeArmond pickups with adjustable polepieces, and potential selection of all seven pickup permutations using those three on/off switches. The 75 was in sunburst, 76 the same with Bigsby vibrato, 77 was in cherry red, and the 78 the same but with Bigsby.

Fender, meanwhile, added a new model to the lower end of its catalogue, the Mustang, introduced in 1964 and effectively a Duo-Sonic with added vibrato. This time the California company used a simplified vibrato that was adjustable for height and length. "The new Floating Bridge," Fender explained, "works in conjunction with the [vibrato] and contains a master bridge channel with new barrel-type individual bridges for each string." Two three-position switches controlled each pickup, offering on, off, or reverse-phase, and there was an overall control knob each for volume and tone.

At first, the Mustang shared the slab-style body of the earlier Duo-Sonic, but Fender gradually introduced a contoured body to all of its student models of the time: the one-pickup Musicmaster, two-pickup Duo-Sonic, and vibrato-equipped Mustang. While the existing Duo-Sonic and Musicmaster had previously been available only with a short scale, from 1964 they were also offered in optional versions with longer 24-inch scales, and the new Mustang, too, was offered in either scale-length. Later, Fender offered a new finish option for the Mustang, in 1968, when it released the Competition Mustang with a contrasting body stripe, and these striking variants would last until 1973.

FENDER CLASSIC SERIES '65 MUSTANG
THIS EXAMPLE: ***2009***
Fender's original Mustang lasted until 1981, and it was first reissued a few years later in a Japanese-made version. This Classic Series reissue was available from 2006 to 2016, and this one is finished in daphne blue.

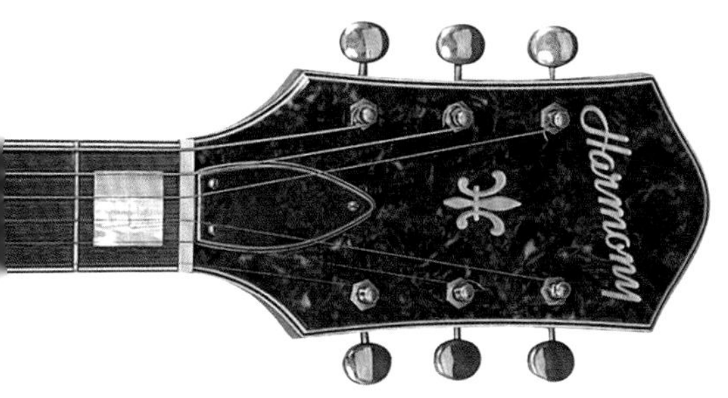

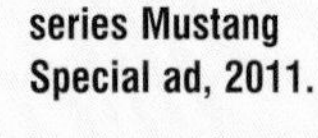

Pawn Shop series Mustang Special ad, 2011.

ORIGINAL **FENDER MUSTANG**
THIS EXAMPLE: ***1964***
Fender's Mustang, introduced in 1964, was like a Duo-Sonic with added vibrato. The guitar shown started life with a blue finish, but its top lacquer coat has yellowed with age, turning it into a pleasing pastel green.

AIRLINE H78
THIS EXAMPLE: ***2018***
Eastwood's Airline-brand re-creation of Harmony's classic H77-family models improves the bridge, matches the original control layout, and here offers a metallic blue finish to add a modern vibe.

Early Ibanez models, 1962 catalogue.

The most famous model made by the Burns company in the UK in the 60s was the Marvin. Hank Marvin of The Shadows was well known as a Stratocaster player, and he and the group had become role models for thousands of British youths who figured an electric guitar must be an easy route to unimaginable fortunes. Following discussions with the Shadows lead guitarist, Burns introduced the Marvin model in 1964, drawing heavily on the Strat but also adding new features of its own, such as a scrolled headstock design and a Rezo-tube vibrato, which had a knife-edge bearing and six individual tubes to anchor the strings, instead of Fender's metal block. Burns said proudly in its catalogue blurb that the new vibrato resulted in "singing strings."

The Ibanez brandname derives from a Spanish classical maker, but it was Hoshino in Japan who took it over and applied it to electric guitars, a little later on copies of American classics and later still to original designs. However, in the years from the late 50s to the late 60s, Ibanez offered several models that drew on multiple influences, primarily from Fender's Jazzmaster, Jaguar, and Stratocaster, from Burns guitars, and, in the hollowbody lines, from Gibson. The guitar shown on these pages, Ibanez's Model 2103, is a typical example of one of those early Burns-influenced models by Ibanez, notably in the body's exaggerated horns.

We've seen how several Italian makers drew on expertise as accordion makers in order to create individual-looking instruments, and Eko was one of the biggest and most successful in the 60s. The company had been established in 1959 by Oliviero Pigini in Recanati, in the instrument-making Marche region of eastern Italy, and the brand became well known for some distinctive instruments that boasted sparkle and pearl plastic coverings, multiple control layouts, and a number of angular shapes.

ORIGINAL **IBANEZ MODEL 2103**
THIS EXAMPLE: ***1964***
The Ibanez brand was established by the Japanese company Hoshino, which added electric guitars in the late 50s. This early model shows how Japanese makers absorbed and adapted foreign designs, here drawing on Burns style.

Hank Marvin with Burns Marvin, 1965 ad.

ORIGINAL **BURNS MARVIN**
THIS EXAMPLE: ***1964***
Designed in collaboration with Hank Marvin, lead guitarist in the popular British instrumental group The Shadows, the Burns Marvin drew on Hank's favored Stratocaster but added new features, including a redesigned vibrato.

Sitting with a 700, Eko catalogue 1964.

BURNS HANK MARVIN SIGNATURE
THIS EXAMPLE: ***2017***
The British company Burns in its original form lasted until 1970, and following a few revivals, the current Burns London firm has been in business since 1992. The guitar shown is a re-creation of the original Burns Marvin model of the 60s.

Burns Marvin-inspired Marquee model, 2005 ad.

Eko catalogue cover, 1963.

ORIGINAL **EKO 700/4V**
THIS EXAMPLE: ***1964***
The shapely 700 bore clear evidence of the Italian company Eko's accordion-making heritage, including a heat-molded plastic finish and a layout of multiple controls featuring switches, knobs, and pushbuttons.

ВПЕРВЫЕ
ОСУЩЕСТВЛЕН
ВЫХОД ЧЕЛОВЕКА
ИЗ КОРАБЛЯ
„ВОСХОД-2"
В КОСМИЧЕСКОЕ
ПРОСТРАНСТВО
18 марта
1965 года

ПОЧТА
СССР
10к

Twiggy brings swinging London to the beautiful Bahamas
In Freeport's authentic International Shopping Arcade, Twiggy styles are exclusive to:
The London Pacesetter Boutique
(a member of the Mundy Group)
E H MUNDY & CO LTD
are the only travel agents with offices in London, Nassau and Freeport.
London: Walsingham House Seething Lane, EC3; 87 Jermyn St, SW1
Also offices at Southampton, Manchester and Liverpool.

newport folk festival
july 22-25 1965

- US MARINES and Australian troops arrive in South Vietnam. American planes bomb North Vietnam targets in the first US retaliatory raids. President Johnson says he will continue "actions that are justified as necessary for the defense of South Vietnam." In June, US troops conduct their first Vietcong offensive; soon, there are 200,000 of them in Vietnam.

- BOB DYLAN goes electric at the Newport Folk Festival this summer, strapping on a sunburst Fender Stratocaster to announce his conversion to amplified folk-rock. Some conservative folkies in the audience may not have approved, but Dylan and the music never looked back.

1965

- RUSSIAN cosmonaut Alexei Leonov is the first man to "walk" in space, leaving his Voskhod 2 craft for twelve minutes during its twenty-six-hour flight.

- SPIKE JONES, founder of the wonderfully mad City Slickers group, dies in Los Angeles. Saul Hudson is born in England. In the 80s he will become Slash, guitarist of wonderfully riotous Guns N' Roses group.

- CARNABY STREET is the center of Swinging London, selling op-art mini dresses, PVC kinky boots, colored tights, and soft bras, as modeled by Jean Shrimpton and Twiggy.

- A SPEED LIMIT of 70mph is tested for the first time on UK motorways. Scottish driver Jim Clark becomes Formula One World Champion for the second time.

Gibson's factory managers were aware of problems with the Firebirds, introduced in 1963. They were difficult and expensive guitars to make. If a neck developed a fault, the through-neck design meant a good portion of the body, too, was lost. The laminated through-neck, the carving, and the tricky wiring added to production time and costs. And the Firebirds were prone to breakages where the head met the neck.

Gibson redesigned the line. The most obvious change to the brand new Firebirds that appeared in 1965 was a slightly more conventional body shape, known today as the "non-reverse" style, in contrast to the earlier "reverse" Firebirds. Gone was the through-neck and the body "shelf," replaced by Gibson's conventional glued-in neck. The pickups on the two cheaper models were regular P-90 single-coils, and the headstock was more Fender-like and came with regular tuners. However, a price cut and the design changes were not enough to stop a decline in sales of the non-reverse Firebird models during the 60s, and at the end of the decade they were finally dropped.

Trini Lopez strummed an electric guitar rather than the acoustic one might expect for his folk-based repertoire. His big hit was 'If I Had A Hammer' in 1963, and Gibson issued two Lopez models in '65. The Deluxe was a full-depth hollowbody electric that Lopez played for years, based on his Barney Kessel model, while the Standard was a thinline semi-solid, like a 335 but with soundholes and fingerboard markers in the shape of elongated diamonds, plus a Fender-style headstock with tuners all on one side, like the one on the new non-reverse Firebirds.

The Trini Lopez Standard lasted in the catalogue just beyond the end of the 60s, and it had some exposure later when Dave Grohl used one on stage and in the studio.

ORIGINAL **GIBSON TRINI LOPEZ STANDARD TL-S**
THIS EXAMPLE: ***1968***
Gibson issued two Lopez signature models in 1965. This semi-solid 335-like Standard, with diamond-shape markers and soundholes and a (new) Firebird-like head, was partnered by a full-body Deluxe model.

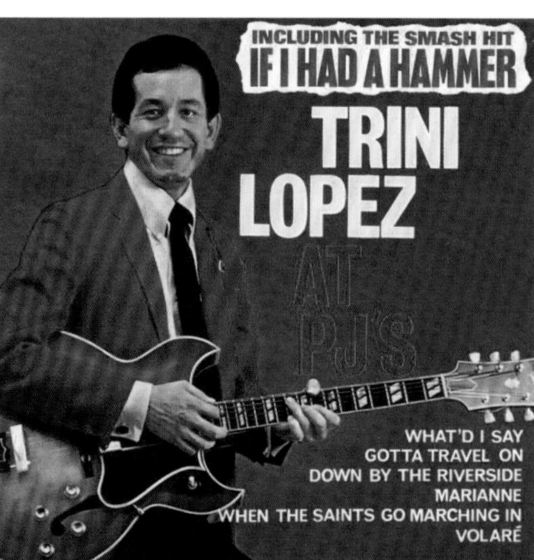

Trini Lopez with Gibson Barney Kessel, 1964 album.

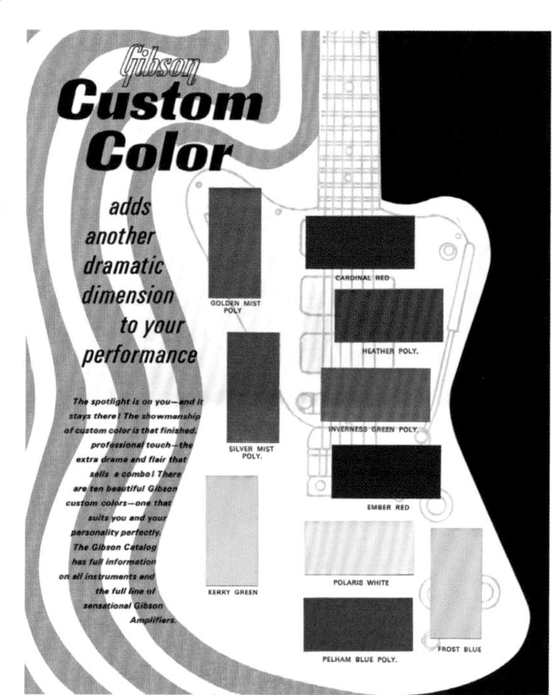

Color chart for non-reverse Firebirds, 1966.

GIBSON FIREBIRD ZERO
THIS EXAMPLE: ***2017***
Gibson has reissued fewer of the non-reverse Firebirds than the original and now well-regarded reverse-style models. One recent exception was this Firebird Zero from Gibson's "affordable" S Series introduced in 2017.

GIBSON DAVE GROHL ES-335
THIS EXAMPLE: ***2014***
Gibson's first Dave Grohl signature model appeared in 2007, designed in the style of his vintage Trini Lopez Standard. This second version, also a limited edition, was introduced in 2014.

ORIGINAL **GIBSON FIREBIRD III**
THIS EXAMPLE: ***1966***
Here was the new look for the Firebird models, introduced in 1965 to replace the earlier style, which had manufacturing problems. The new body design is known today as the "non-reverse," in contrast to the earlier reverse-body Firebirds.

Firebird

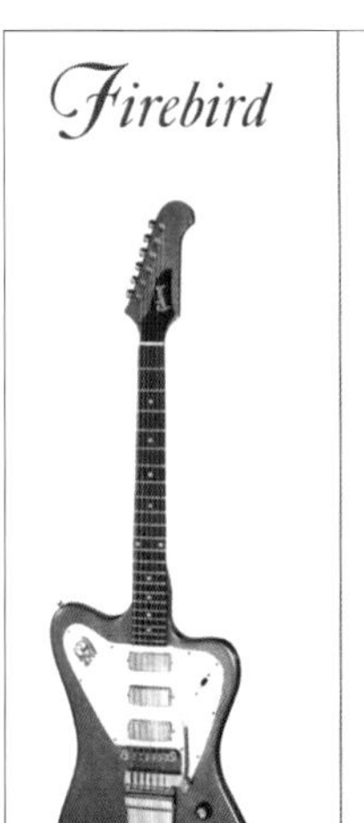

FIREBIRD VII

Here is the ultimate in a solid body guitar by Gibson. A completely new and exciting instrument that offers all the sound, response, fast action and wide range that could be desired.

FEATURES: New style solid Mahogany body and special construction. Three special design Humbucking pickups with Gold-plated covers. Rosewood fingerboard with white pearl inlays. New style Gibson Deluxe Vibrola. Gold-plated. Gold-plated machine heads. Top-mounted jack for instrument cord. Gold-plated Tune-O-Matic adjustable bridge. Three position toggle switch. Tone and volume controls for bass and treble pickups. White laminated pickguard. 13¾" wide, 19¾" long, 1½" thin; 24¾" scale, 22 frets.

Firebird VII Sunburst finish or Gibson Custom colors

1210 Faultless plush-lined case
310 Archcraft plush-lined case

FIREBIRD V

Another in the revolutionary new series of solid body guitars by Gibson. Exciting in concept, exciting to play. You find a whole new world of sound and performance on this fine instrument.

FEATURES: New style and construction. Twin Humbucking pickups. Brazilian Rosewood fingerboard—with bound edges and pearloid dots. New style Deluxe Vibrola—Chrome-plated. Exclusive Gibson Tune-O-Matic bridge. Three position toggle switch. Separate tone and volume controls for each pickup. White laminated pickguard. 13¾" wide, 19¾" long, 1½" thin; 24¾" scale, 22 frets.

Firebird V Sunburst finish or Gibson Custom colors

1210 Faultless plush-lined case
310 Archcraft plush-lined case

FIREBIRD III

A solid performer in the exciting lineup of solid body guitars by Gibson. Offers you all the range and versatility that you could ask for, plus that sharpness in the treble range and depth in the bass.

FEATURES: New style construction. Three powerful adjustable pickups. Brazilian Rosewood fingerboard with pearl inlaid position dots, bound edges. Gibson Vibrola. Exclusive Gibson offset solid body bridge. Three position toggle switch. Separate tone and volume controls. White laminated pickguard. 13¾" wide, 19¾" long, 1½" thin; 24¾" scale, 22 frets.

Firebird III Sunburst finish or Gibson Custom colors

1210 Faultless plush-lined case
310 Archcraft plush-lined case

FIREBIRD I

The new solid body by Gibson that is priced for the growing economy-minded market. Gives you all of the fine performance of this exciting new series of guitars at a price you can afford. You have to try it to appreciate it.

FEATURES: New style and construction. Twin high performance adjustable pickups. Brazilian Rosewood fingerboard. Inlaid dots for position markers. Separate volume and tone controls. Gibson Vibrola. New style offset solid body bridge. Top-mounted jack for instrument cord. White laminated pickguard. 13¾" wide, 19¾" long, 1½" thin; 24¾" scale, 22 frets.

Firebird I Sunburst finish or Gibson Custom Colors

1210 Faultless plush-lined case
310 Archcraft plush-lined case

Four new non-reverse Firebirds, 1966 catalogue.

Marauder, Jaguar, 1965–66 catalogue.

Electric XII, Telecaster, 1966–67 catalogue.

ORIGINAL **FENDER ELECTRIC XII**
THIS EXAMPLE: ***1966***
Fender's version of the fashionable electric twelve-string came with a necessarily elongated headstock that became known as the hockey stick. This one is finished in olympic white, which has yellowed with age.

ORIGINAL **FENDER MARAUDER**
THIS EXAMPLE: ***1966***
The doomed Marauder started life as a hidden-pickups experiment, but this later prototype had multiple control switches, angled frets, and conventional pickups. It, too, failed to go into production.

Electric XII at the game, 1965 ad.

In January 1965, the Fender companies were sold to the mighty Columbia Broadcasting System Inc, better known as CBS. The $13 million price was the highest ever paid in the instrument industry for a single manufacturer, and the event caused a stir, not only among business insiders, but gradually among some guitarists, who came to feel that Fenders made after the sale were less good than those made before.

Meanwhile, Fender made a design change to the Stratocaster that has come to distinguish Strats made after CBS's acquisition of Fender. In 1965, the Strat gained a broader headstock, matching that of the existing Jazzmaster and Jaguar. Also at this time, Fender began to add a stylized F-for-Fender logo to the small neck-fixing plate on the rear of the body.

A new model for 1965 was the Fender Electric XII. Rickenbacker had popularized the electric twelve-string, and now Fender joined in the battle with their own rather belated version. The body had the familiar offset-waist of Jazzmaster and Jaguar, and the XII's long headstock, necessary to carry the extra tuners, was finished in a distinctive curved end that earned it the nickname "hockey-stick." An innovation was the 12-saddle bridge that allowed for precise adjustments of individual string heights and intonation, a luxury hitherto unknown on any twelve-string guitar. But the twelve-string craze of the 60s was almost over, and Fender's Electric XII proved shortlived, lasting in the line until 1968.

Fender's Marauder appeared in the 1965–66 catalogue but never went to production. "It appears as though there are no pickups," said the blurb. "There are, in reality, however, four newly created pickups mounted underneath the pickguard." Prototypes were made, including a later revised version with regular pickups and multiple switching, but the model was shelved.

Big-head Strat, electric Mandolin, 1966–67 catalogue.

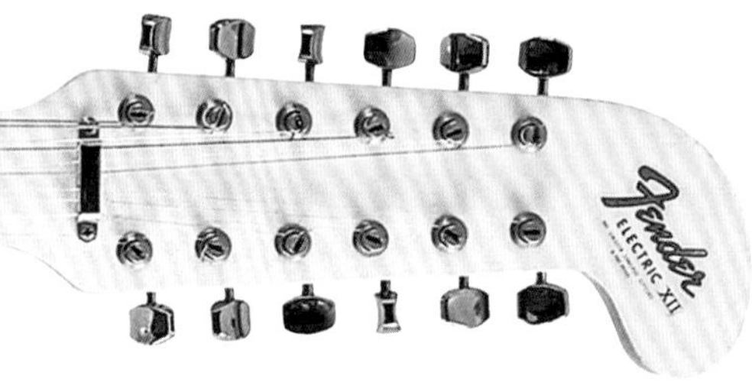

CBS, Fender's new owner, 1965.

ORIGINAL **FENDER STRATOCASTER**
THIS EXAMPLE: ***1965***
Fender changed the look of the Stratocaster toward the end of 1965 by enlarging the headstock to match the head already on its Jazzmaster and Jaguar models. This '65 Strat is finished in the 60s custom color known simply as black.

Fender's reissues of Stratocasters have tended to re-create the look and vibe and playability of guitars from the so-called pre-CBS period favored by vintage collectors, in other words before CBS took over Fender in 1965. But as guitarists at the time and since have discovered, Fender did manage to make quite a number of good guitars during the CBS period.

More recently, the "big head" Strat—the type with the enlarged headstock introduced in late 1965—has been the target of some reissues from the modern Fender company. One natural focus for this activity has been the association with Jimi Hendrix, who during his short career played mostly new Strats that he acquired in the mid to late 60s, and therefore all with the larger head.

In 1997, Fender introduced the Jimi Hendrix Stratocaster. Faced with the fact that Hendrix was a left-hander but that most players would want a right-handed guitar, the company decided to make a completely reversed version of one of Jimi's typical 60s big-head Strats. The result was a guitar that right-handed players needed to consider as a regular left-handed guitar turned upside down and re-strung, recreating Jimi's experience in reverse. Fender added a final flourish, applying the headstock logo in reverse. In the mirror, the owner could be Jimi Hendrix.

Following the shortlived Electric XII of the 60s, solidbody twelve-strings have been scarce in the Fender lines. A twelve-string Stratocaster was launched in 1988 and again in the mid 2000s, the Custom Shop briefly offered a twelve-string Telecaster in the late 90s, and Fender's budget Squier brand introduced another shortlived model, the not-so-budget Venus XII, in 1997. The Venus design was inspired by some custom guitars that a maker called Mercury had built for Courtney Love, and the twelve-string had split pickups like those on the original Electric XII.

FENDER AMERICAN SPECIAL STRATOCASTER
THIS EXAMPLE: ***2018***
Fender's latest update of the big-head Strat has the post-'65 look but adds contemporary touches such as a trio of punchy Texas Special pickups and a revised tone circuit, along with a modern neck profile and fingerboard radius.

FENDER STRAT XII
THIS EXAMPLE: ***2007***
The twelve-string take on the Strat first appeared in the late 80s, and on this later version the bridge has through-body stringing for six of the strings. This attractive example is finished in burgundy mist.

Billy Corgan's big-head signatures, 2008 ad.

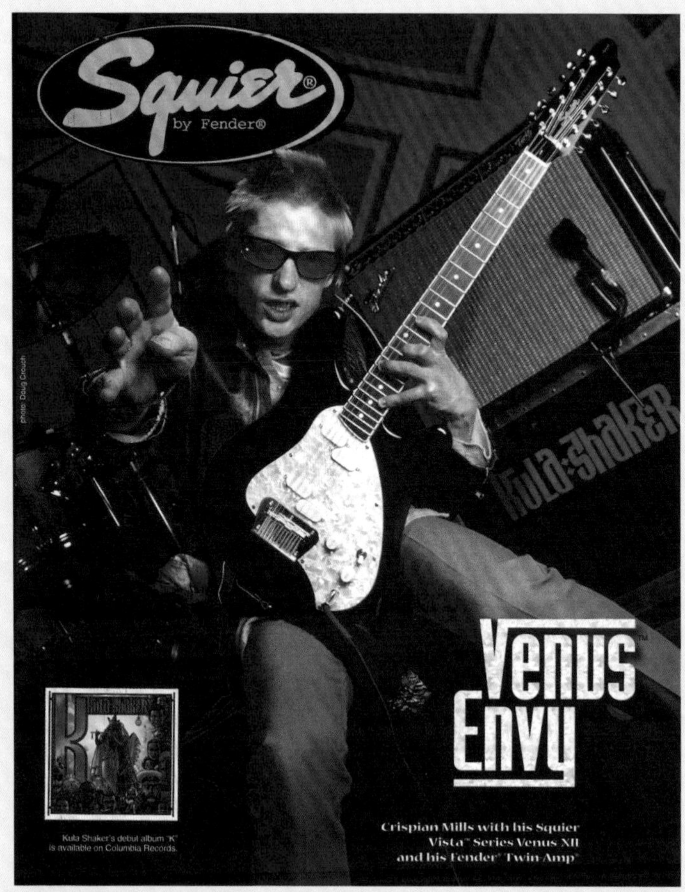

Crispian Mills and a Venus XII, 1997 ad.

SQUIER VENUS XII

THIS EXAMPLE: ***1997***

A guitar made by Mercury and played by Courtney Love was the inspiration for Squier's shortlived Venus models, which included this twelve-string model as well as a regular six-string.

Mixing left and right, Hendrix Strat, 1997 ad.

In Japan, the 60s guitar boom led to an array of often interrelated factories and distributors and brandnames. The Teisco company was one of the biggest and typically produced instruments for a large number of overseas customers, as well as developing models at home with its own brand. Teisco was founded in Tokyo in the 40s, and into the 60s it produced guitars for many American, British, European, and Australasian companies, with a large number of different brands, such as Audition, Gemtone, Jedson, Kent, Kingston, Mellowtone, Norma, and Top Twenty, as well as Teisco and (from 1965 in the US) Teisco Del Rey.

The Sears, Roebuck mail-order company in the US was another business that bought from Teisco, among a number of other suppliers, to build the line of instruments for its guitar brand, Silvertone. As with many of the other firms for whom Teisco made guitars, the Silvertone models were sometimes almost identical to Teisco-brand instrument—as with, for example, the Silvertone 1437 pictured on these pages.

Another American mail-order operation, Montgomery Ward, also bought instruments for its house brand, Airline, from a number of sources, at home and abroad. Valco in Chicago was one such supplier, and in the mid 60s it built a series of models for Ward, some of which used the molded fiberglass bodies it had developed for several of its own National and Supro-brand guitars.

Other domestic guitar distributors, too, devised a brandname and then simply bought in guitars from various suppliers to fill the still-growing demand for electric guitars. Hershman of New York City, for example, used its Goya brand on electrics made at first by Hagstrom in Sweden and then by Zerosette in Italy, such as the Rangemaster pictured here. In 1966, the Goya name was acquired by Avnet, the owners of Guild.

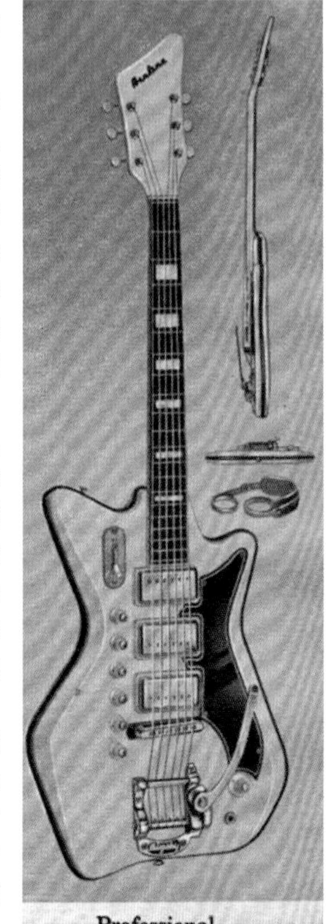

Fiberglass-body Airline Professional, Montgomery Ward catalogue 1965.

ORIGINAL **AIRLINE PROFESSIONAL 7244**
THIS EXAMPLE: ***1965***
This is one of several guitars made for the Montgomery Ward mail-order firm by Valco (owner of the National and Supro brands). This asymmetrical wooden-body version of the Professional was offered as the one-pickup 7243 and two-pickup 7244.

ORIGINAL **SILVERTONE 1437**
THIS EXAMPLE: ***1965***
Silvertone's model 1437 was supplied by Teisco to the American mail-order and retail chain Sears, Roebuck. It was virtually identical to the Japanese company's own-brand ET-440 model.

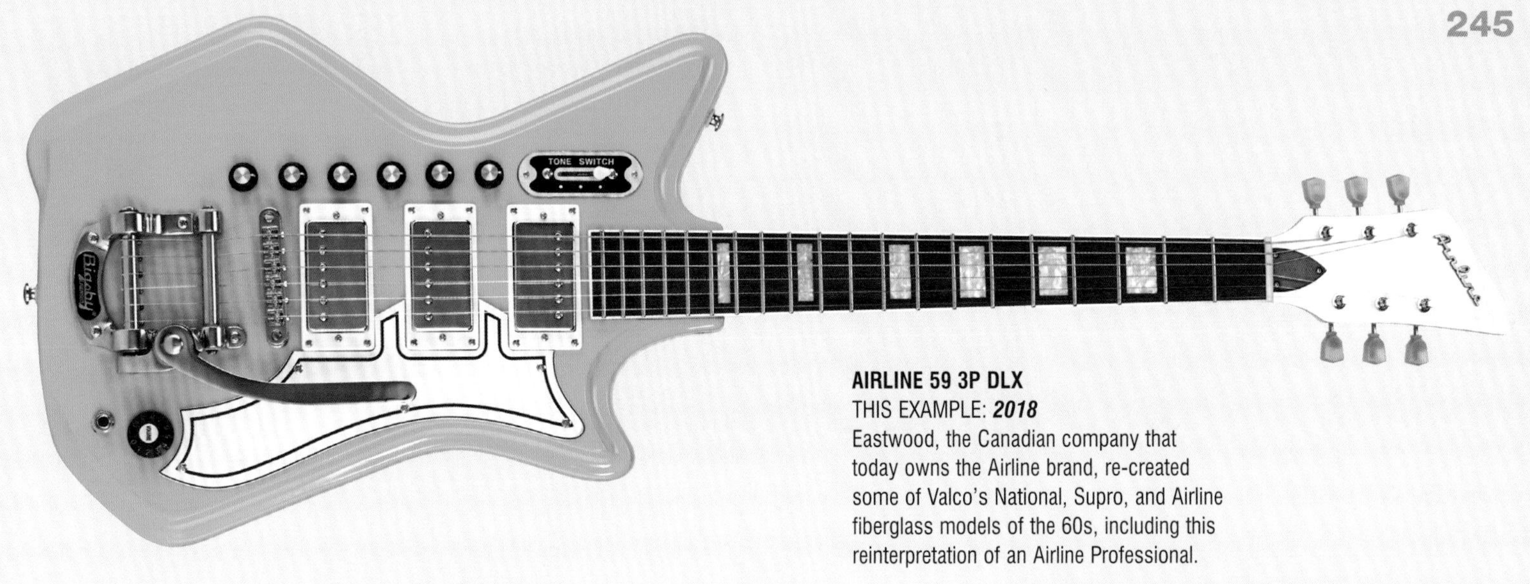

AIRLINE 59 3P DLX
THIS EXAMPLE: ***2018***
Eastwood, the Canadian company that today owns the Airline brand, re-created some of Valco's National, Supro, and Airline fiberglass models of the 60s, including this reinterpretation of an Airline Professional.

Teisco Del Rey ET-440, US catalogue cover, 1965.

Teisco TRE-100 amp-in-guitar ad, 1965.

ORIGINAL **GOYA RANGEMASTER 116**
THIS EXAMPLE: ***1968***
Goya was a brandname used by a US distributor for guitars imported to the US from various sources, and this example, with its multiple pushbutton controls and stylish touches, was made by Zerosette in Italy.

Italian-made Goya, catalogue cover, 1966.

DANCE
CONCERT
JIM KWESKIN JUG BAND
ELECTRIC TRAIN
BIG BROTHER & THE HOLDING COMPANY
OCTOBER 7
AVALON BALLROOM
SAN FRANCISCO
8 OCTOBER
TICKET OUTLETS:

Bill Graham Presents-In Concert
LENNY BRUCE
AND
IN DANCE
THE MOTHERS
ADMISSION 2.50
No Minors ADULTS ONLY
9 P.M.
FRIDAY
SATURDAY
FILLMORE AUDITORIUM
JUNE 24·25
at geary and fillmore streets .... san francisco

QUANT BY QUANT

- **SAN FRANCISCO** is the hippie capital of the world. The Psychedelic Shop opens on Haight Street, and the Avalon Ballroom is the grooviest rock venue. The Trips Festival at the Longshoreman's Hall features the Grateful Dead. "We learned to start improvising on just about anything," Dead guitarist Bob Weir explains. In October, LSD is outlawed in California and Nevada.

- **LONDON** is the fashion capital of the world. Stores such as Biba on Kensington Church Street, John Stephen in Carnaby Street, and Mary Quant on the Kings Road are the in places to shop. Labour wins the general election, England wins the World Cup, the first issue of *International Times* is out, and The Beatles release *Revolver*.

1966

- **LENNY BRUCE** dies from drug-related causes. America's most controversial comedian, variously busted for drugs or obscenity, assaulted the unmentionable subjects of sex, race, religion, and politics, all rolled up in a hip Jewish delivery.

- **WEEKLY WAGES** for average jobs are about £10 to £25 in Britain and $40 to $180 in America. A pint of British beer costs 1/3 (6p) while a US six-pack is 99c. A black-and-white TV goes for £90, or $150. A Fender Stratocaster is £172/14/- (£172.70) or $299.50. The exchange rate for £1 is $2.80.

- **AUSTRALIA GOES DECIMAL** with the introduction of the Australian dollar, valued at two old pounds and divided into 100 cents.

Coronado line, 1966–67 Fender catalogue.

Fender brought in Roger Rossmeisl from Rickenbacker in 1962 to design acoustic and hollowbody electrics. They were all manufactured at the firm's separate acoustic guitar plant on Missile Way in Fullerton. Rossmeisl, the son of a German guitar-maker, had come to the States in the 50s and at first worked for Gibson, soon moving to Rickenbacker where he made a number of one-off custom guitars and designed production models, which as we've seen included the classic 330/360 instruments.

Rossmeisl's Fender Coronado thinline guitars were launched in 1966, the first of his electric designs for Fender. Despite their double-cutaway bound bodies with large stylized f-holes, they still had the regular Fender bolt-on neck and headstock design. Options included a new vibrato tailpiece, and there was a twelve-string version that borrowed the Electric XII's "hockey-stick" headstock. Fender's first foray into thinline electric-acoustics was not a success, however, and the various versions were all dropped from the Fender catalogues by 1971. In 1965, meanwhile, Fender's Electric XII, Jaguar, and Jazzmaster gained binding at the edges of fingerboard, while in '66 the same trio had new block-shaped fingerboard inlays rather than the previous dot markers.

Over at Gretsch, despite George Harrison's enthusiasm for the company's guitars, there was never a Gretsch signature Beatles model in the 60s… but the brand did introduce an instrument endorsed by The Monkees. In 1966, Gretsch supplied instruments to the group, including the company's new twelve-string guitar, a bass, a White Falcon, and a drum set. That same year, Gretsch put its Monkees model on to the market, a red-finish double-cutaway thinline that was emblazoned with Monkees guitar-shaped logos on the truss-rod cover and on the pickguard. The model never appeared in an official catalogue or pricelist, and it did not last long in the line.

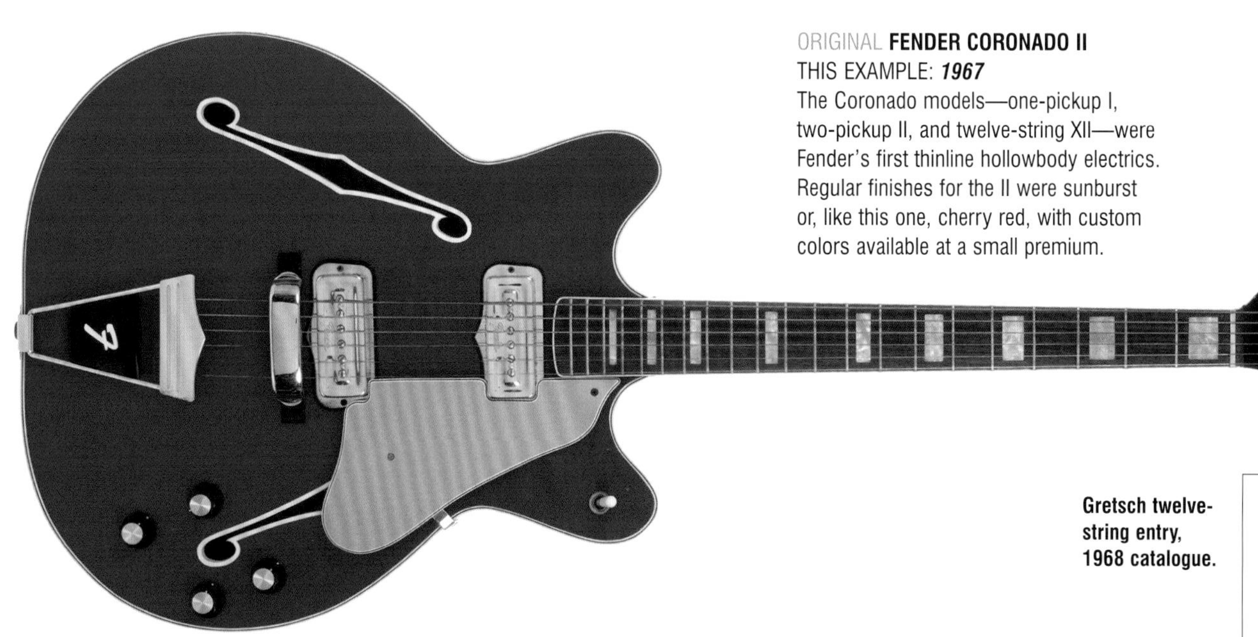

ORIGINAL **FENDER CORONADO II**
THIS EXAMPLE: ***1967***
The Coronado models—one-pickup I, two-pickup II, and twelve-string XII—were Fender's first thinline hollowbody electrics. Regular finishes for the II were sunburst or, like this one, cherry red, with custom colors available at a small premium.

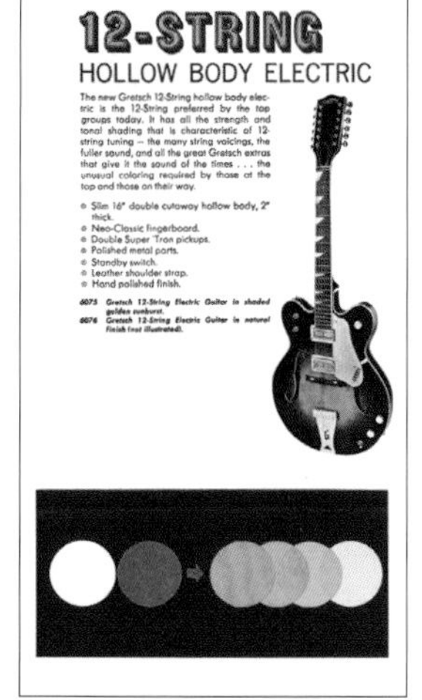

Gretsch twelve-string entry, 1968 catalogue.

ORIGINAL **GRETSCH MONKEES 6123**
THIS EXAMPLE: ***1967***
This shortlived model endorsed by the TV-created pop group The Monkees did not do as well as Gretsch hoped, and there were stories of owners writing in for replacement pickguards and truss-rod covers without the Monkees logo.

Jaguar and Jazzmaster, 1966–67 Fender catalogue.

Mustang, block-marker Jaguar, Fender 1975 Japanese catalogue.

FENDER TROY VAN LEEUWEN JAZZMASTER

THIS EXAMPLE: ***2015***

Introduced in 2014, this reissue of a Jazzmaster in late-60s style was named for the Queens Of The Stone Age guitarist. It had revised controls, a Mustang bridge with Jazzmaster vibrato, and the finish was known as oxblood.

ORIGINAL **FENDER JAZZMASTER**

THIS EXAMPLE: ***1966***

Fender's Jazzmaster model gained a bound fingerboard in 1965 and the following year the original dot fingerboard markers were replaced with block markers. This example is finished in blue ice metallic.

ORIGINAL **FENDER JAGUAR**

THIS EXAMPLE: ***1966***

The Jaguar, like its stablemate the Jazzmaster, was given a new set of block fingerboard markers in 1966, set off by the bound fingerboard which had been added to the model the previous year. Fender's Electric XII saw similar same changes, too.

D.H. Baldwin was an Ohio-based instrument company that specialized in the manufacture of pianos and organs. It was keen to buy a guitar-making operation, and in 1965 bid unsuccessfully for Fender. Baldwin then bought Jim Burns's British guitar company for £250,000 (about $700,000 at the time) and applied the Baldwin brandname to many existing Burns models.

Baldwin's annual report for 1966 described a rosy picture: for the first time in Baldwin's long history, overall sales exceeded $40 million, and for the fifth year running sales and profits were up. Keyboard instrument sales had declined, but since the firm introduced Burns guitars and amplifiers, it had seen substantial increases over the previous year. Hungry for more of this, Baldwin decided it could benefit further with a guitar brandname that had an existing high profile in the USA, and the bosses turned their attention to Gretsch. Baldwin's interest in Burns-style guitars then faded, and the line was dropped by 1970.

Later, Jim Burns made a few comebacks, in 1973 as Burns UK, best known for the angular Flyte, endorsed by Dave Hill and Marc Bolan, and in 1979 as Jim Burns, best known for the unusual Scorpion, but both ventures were shortlived. In 1992, the new Burns London company began producing authentic reproductions, updates of 60s classics, and new models, with Jim himself onboard until his death in 1998, and that firm continues successfully today.

St Louis Music in Missouri began in the 50s selling guitars by Kay, Harmony, and others. In the early 60s, the company created its own Custom Kraft brand, at first mostly applied to Japanese-made solidbody models and Kay-made hollowbodys. Later in the decade, Custom Krafts began to appear made by Valco, the parent company that produced various National, Supro, and Airline models. The Custom Kraft brand lasted until 1970.

Baldwin Vibraslim, 1967 catalogue cover.

ORIGINAL **CUSTOM KRAFT AMBASSADOR VIBRAMATIC 4271**

THIS EXAMPLE: ***1966***

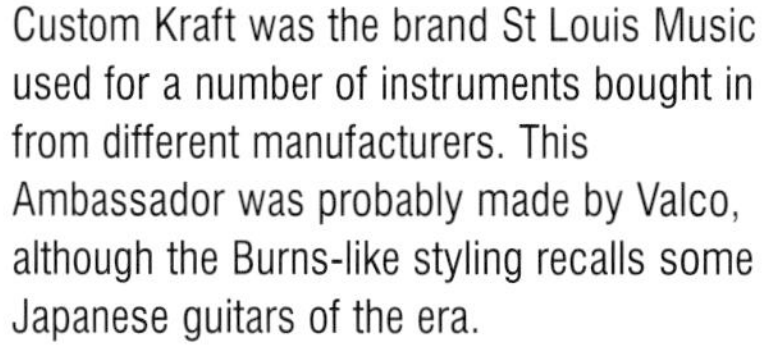

Custom Kraft was the brand St Louis Music used for a number of instruments bought in from different manufacturers. This Ambassador was probably made by Valco, although the Burns-like styling recalls some Japanese guitars of the era.

St Louis Music's Custom Kraft catalogue, 1969.

Custom Kraft catalogue cover, 1969.

Baldwin Marvin guitar, Shadows bass, 1967 catalogue.

ORIGINAL **BALDWIN DOUBLE SIX 525**
THIS EXAMPLE: ***1966***
Baldwin in the US bought the Burns company of England in the mid 60s. This Double Six twelve-string keeps much of the original Burns vibe but adds a Baldwin logo.

ORIGINAL **BALDWIN BABY BISON**
THIS EXAMPLE: ***1966***
One of the new models that Baldwin introduced following its acquisition of Burns was the Baby Bison, which had a presence control in addition to volume and tone, and came in red, black, sunburst, or white finishes.

Burns Steer and Double Six, 2007 ad.

BURNS APACHE DOUBLE SIX SPECIAL
THIS EXAMPLE: ***2017***
The current Burns company has been in operation since 1992, and this Apache Double Six is an example of its re-creations, with three Tri-Sonic pickups, Rez-o-tube vibrato, and a special "Limited Edition" inlay at the 12th fret.

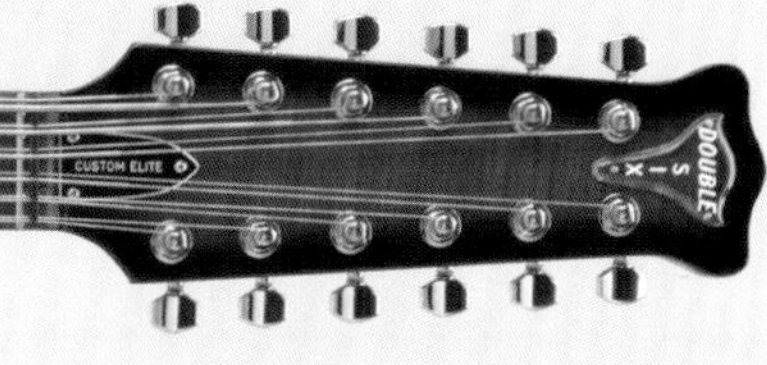

Teisco was one of the biggest guitar companies in Japan in the 60s, supplying instruments to many distributors and outlets abroad with their brandnames and also selling a line of models at home with its own brand. Young budding Japanese guitarists were just as keen to form groups and find stardom as anyone in America, Britain, or anywhere else that the 60s pop bug had bitten. In Japan, the scene was known as Eleki and then Group Sounds, and bands such as The Spacemen, The Blue Comets, and The Jacks found success at this time.

Teisco had success through its US distributors, at first Westheimer, who later bought from Kawai, and then W.M.I., and it was at this time that the Teisco Del Rey brandname appeared. One of the best-known of the Teisco Del Rey models was the solidbody Spectrum 5, introduced in 1966. It had a thin, curving, sculpted mahogany body, covered with what Teisco claimed as "seven coats of lacquer," parachute-shape fingerboard inlays, two jacks for mono or stereo output, and three pickups, split for the Spectrum 5's stereo feed when required. The model name derived from the "five different basic color tones which can be produced with this unusual guitar," indicating the colorful pickup and phase switches on the upper part of the pickguard.

The Japanese guitar companies competed for attention among this new homegrown market, and a notable new contender was Yamaha. It was an old name, founded in the 1880s as a keyboard manufacturer and diversifying as the decades went by into many other areas, notably motorcycles. The first Yamaha acoustics appeared after World War II, and budget electrics in 1964, and then the better SG series two years later. Among the early SGs were the conventionally shaped SG-2 and 3, and the reverse-body SG-5 and 7.

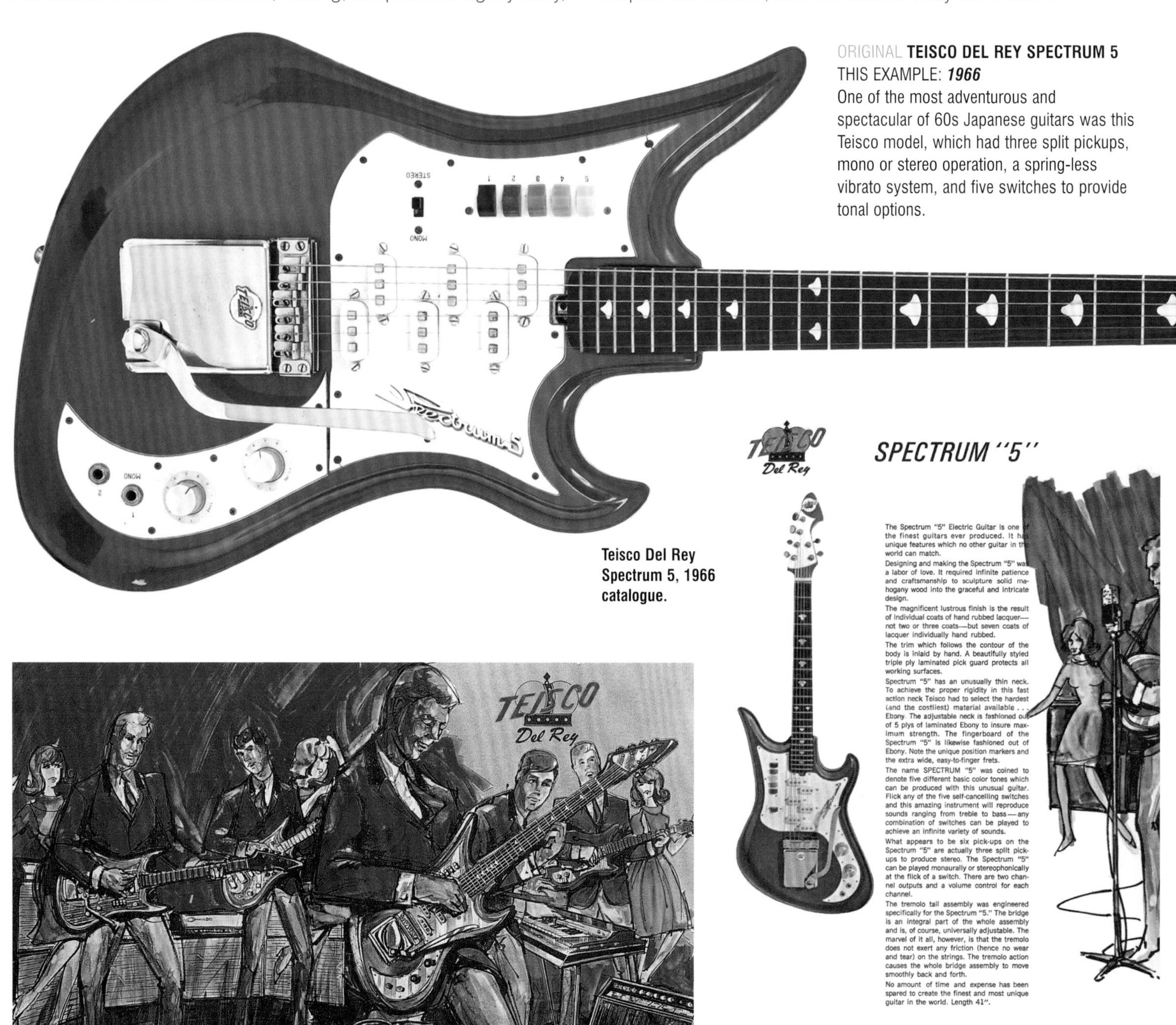

SPECTRUM "5"

The Spectrum "5" Electric Guitar is one of the finest guitars ever produced. It has unique features which no other guitar in the world can match.

Designing and making the Spectrum "5" was a labor of love. It required infinite patience and craftsmanship to sculpture solid mahogany wood into the graceful and intricate design.

The magnificent lustrous finish is the result of individual coats of hand rubbed lacquer—not two or three coats—but seven coats of lacquer individually hand rubbed.

The trim which follows the contour of the body is inlaid by hand. A beautifully styled triple ply laminated pick guard protects all working surfaces.

Spectrum "5" has an unusually thin neck. To achieve the proper rigidity in this fast action neck Teisco had to select the hardest (and the costliest) material available . . . Ebony. The adjustable neck is fashioned out of 5 plys of laminated Ebony to insure maximum strength. The fingerboard of the Spectrum "5" is likewise fashioned out of Ebony. Note the unique position markers and the extra wide, easy-to-finger frets.

The name SPECTRUM "5" was coined to denote five different basic color tones which can be produced with this unusual guitar. Flick any of the five self-cancelling switches and this amazing instrument will reproduce sounds ranging from treble to bass—any combination of switches can be played to achieve an infinite variety of sounds.

What appears to be six pick-ups on the Spectrum "5" are actually three split pick-ups to produce stereo. The Spectrum "5" can be played monaurally or stereophonically at the flick of a switch. There are two channel outputs and a volume control for each channel.

The tremolo tail assembly was engineered specifically for the Spectrum "5." The bridge is an integral part of the whole assembly and is, of course, universally adjustable. The marvel of it all, however, is that the tremolo does not exert any friction (hence no wear and tear) on the strings. The tremolo action causes the whole bridge assembly to move smoothly back and forth.

No amount of time and expense has been spared to create the finest and most unique guitar in the world. Length 41".

ORIGINAL **TEISCO DEL REY SPECTRUM 5**
THIS EXAMPLE: ***1966***
One of the most adventurous and spectacular of 60s Japanese guitars was this Teisco model, which had three split pickups, mono or stereo operation, a spring-less vibrato system, and five switches to provide tonal options.

Teisco Del Rey Spectrum 5, 1966 catalogue.

Teisco Del Rey catalogue cover, 1966.

The Jacks with Yamaha SG-12, 1968 single.

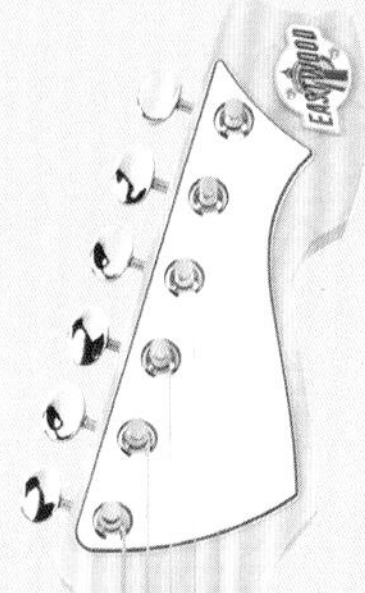

Yamaha SGV reissue, 2001 catalogue cover.

YAMAHA
YAMAHA GUITAR & BASS

ORIGINAL **YAMAHA SG-5A**
THIS EXAMPLE: ***1966***
Yamaha's first major solidbody models were the SGs, introduced in 1966 and including the Fender-inspired SG-2 and 3 and the Mosrite-influenced SG-5 and 7, with an extended lower horn to the body and a long, slim headstock.

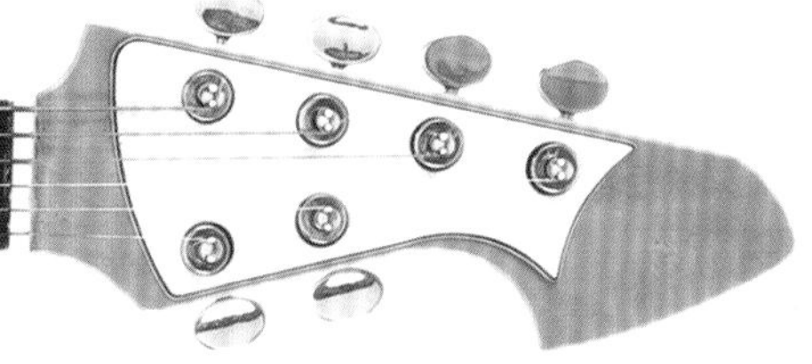

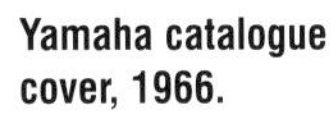

Yamaha catalogue cover, 1966.

EASTWOOD SPECTRUM 5 PRO
THIS EXAMPLE: ***2017***
Eastwood's modern interpretation of the classic Teisco Del Rey Spectrum 5 captures most of the features of the original, adding a roller-type vibrato, and it was offered in metallic blue or metallic red finishes.

alexis korner
alex harvey
creation
charlie browns
clowns
champion jack
dupree
denny laine
gary farr
graham bond
ginger johnson
jacobs ladder
construction co.
move
one one seven
pink floyd
poetry band
purple gang
pretty things
pete townshend
poison bellows
soft.machine
sun trolley
social deviants
stalkers
the utterly incredibl
too long ago
to remember
sometimes shouting
at people
marc sullivan
martin doughty
maureen pope
john pope
mike stocks
noel murphy
dave russell
christopher logue
barry fantoni
ron geeson
john fahey
mike horowitz
alex trocchi
mike kenshall
yoko ono
binder edwards
& vaughan
26 kingly street
the flies
robert randall
14
HOUR
international times
free speech benefit
alexandra palace N.22
8pm saturday
29 april-sun 30
tickets £1
in advance-only
indica better books colletts
dobells dave curtis 57 greek
st w.1 ger 1548 and main
it distributors
or your local agent
bus shuttle from wood green
highgate 8:12pm

2/6
OZ
BLOWIN' IN THE MIND
SHARP

JUNE 16·17·18
MONTEREY
INTERNATIONAL
POP FESTIVAL

- ***OZ*** magazine is launched in London by Richard Neville. *Rolling Stone* magazine is launched in San Francisco by Jann Wenner.

- **THE 14-HOUR TECHNICOLOR DREAM** takes place at London's Alexandra Palace, the largest gathering of the emerging UK underground scene. Thousands attending the all-night happening are entertained by Pink Floyd, The Creation, Tomorrow, and others, alongside a helter-skelter and a fiberglass igloo.

- **ISRAEL** defeats an Arab coalition in the Six-Day War.

1967

- **DONALD CAMPBELL** dies in his Bluebird craft on an English lake during an attempt to break his own world water-speed record of 276mph.

- **THE BBC** bans broadcasts of The Beatles 'A Day In The Life' because of the line "I'd love to turn you on... " which the Beeb fears is "much in vogue in the jargon of drug addicts." Meanwhile, the £ sterling is turned down; its new value is $2.40.

- **THE MONTEREY POP** festival in June boasts a line-up including The Who, The Byrds, Jefferson Airplane, Janis Joplin, Jimi Hendrix, and Otis Redding. Hendrix signs to Warner-Reprise for over $50,000; Redding dies in a plane crash in December.

Gibson introduced in 1967 a new version of the Flying V, a design last seen in the late 50s. The reworked model featured different hardware and materials compared to the original. It was without through-body stringing or body-edge rubber strip, but it gained a large white pickguard and truss-rod cover, a mahogany body and neck, a Tune-o-matic bridge plus Gibson–Maestro vibrato, and chrome-plated hardware. Gibson redesigned the control layout, too, now arranging the V's three knobs—two volumes and a tone—into a triangular group rather than the three-in-line style of the original, providing the new Flying Vs with a quickly identifiable look.

The revised Flying V was hardly featured in Gibson promotional material and seems to have been afforded little importance within the company. It was available in sunburst, cherry, or sparkling burgundy finish. One significant guitarist who did discover the new model was Jimi Hendrix, who acquired one in 1967, decorated it himself, and played it through to the start of 1969 as his main non-Stratocaster guitar. The revised Flying V was dropped by Gibson in 1970, save for a limited edition in '71 with a numbered medallion on the body.

A more compact guitar body came in the shape of the LaBaye 2-By-4, a shortlived instrument conceived by Dan Helland and made in Neodesha, Kansas. Helland's idea was that an electric guitar was really just pickups and strings, so a 2x4 wooden block should suffice as the body. Few people at the time agreed. In Italy, meanwhile, stylish pushbutton-crazy guitars flourished, with Galanti a typical maker. Galanti guitars had close stylistic links with Zerosette, a maker in the same eastern Italian region. Galanti was successful, too, as a maker of electronic organs, and some came with an alternative Galanti brandname, Gem, which it also used for guitars.

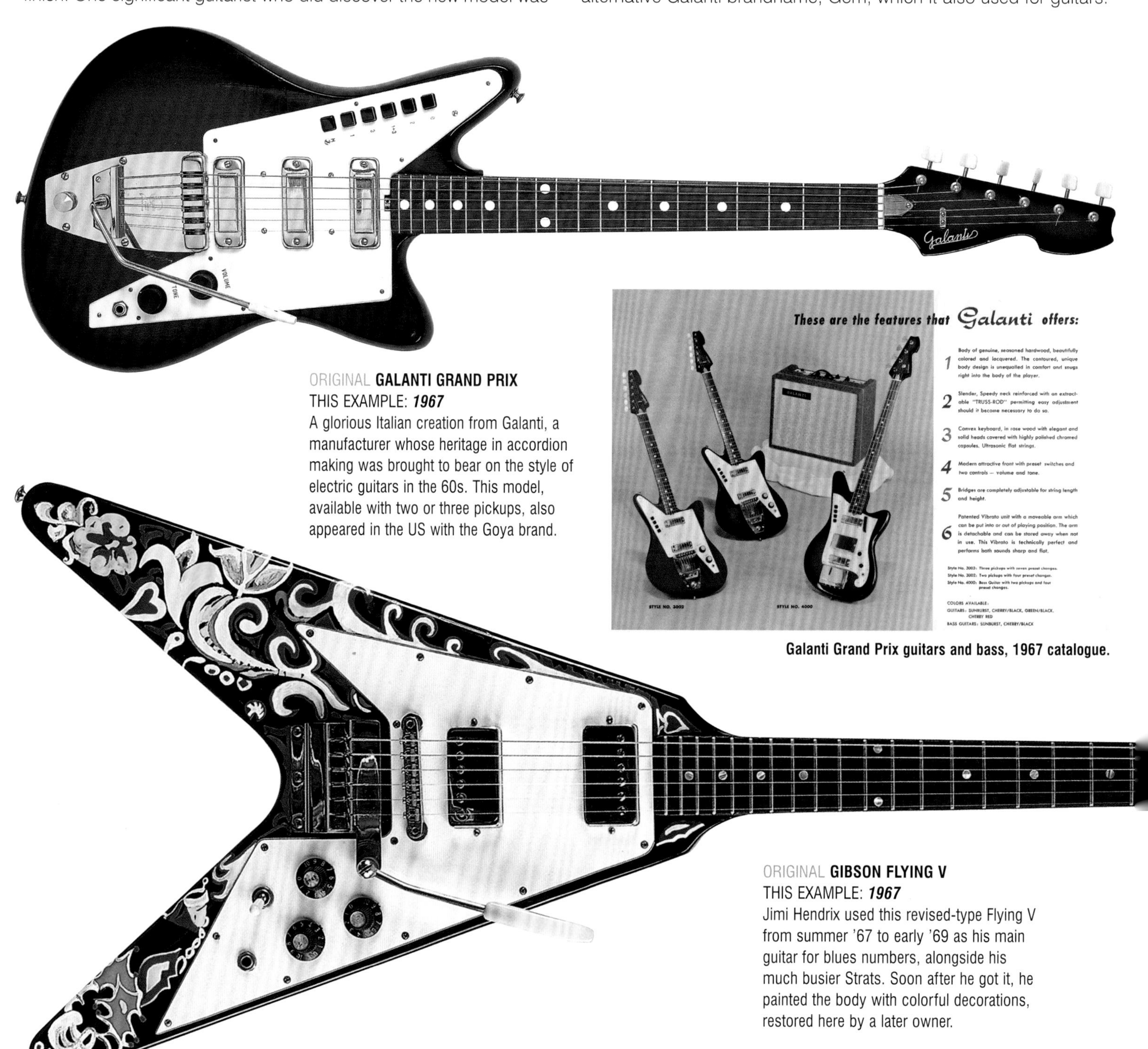

ORIGINAL **GALANTI GRAND PRIX**
THIS EXAMPLE: ***1967***
A glorious Italian creation from Galanti, a manufacturer whose heritage in accordion making was brought to bear on the style of electric guitars in the 60s. This model, available with two or three pickups, also appeared in the US with the Goya brand.

These are the features that Galanti offers:

1 Body of genuine, seasoned hardwood, beautifully colored and lacquered. The contoured, unique body design is unequalled in comfort and snugs right into the body of the player.

2 Slender, Speedy neck reinforced with an extractable "TRUSS-ROD" permitting easy adjustment should it become necessary to do so.

3 Convex keyboard, in rose wood with elegant and solid heads covered with highly polished chromed capsules. Ultrasonic flat strings.

4 Modern attractive front with preset switches and two controls — volume and tone.

5 Bridges are completely adjustable for string length and height.

6 Patented Vibrato unit with a moveable arm which can be put into or out of playing position. The arm is detachable and can be stored away when not in use. This Vibrato is technically perfect and performs both sounds sharp and flat.

Style No. 3003: Three pickups with seven preset changes.
Style No. 3002: Two pickups with four preset changes.
Style No. 4000: Bass Guitar with two pickups and four preset changes.

COLORS AVAILABLE:
GUITARS: SUNBURST, CHERRY/BLACK, GREEN/BLACK, CHERRY RED
BASS GUITARS: SUNBURST, CHERRY/BLACK

STYLE NO. 3002

STYLE NO. 4000

Galanti Grand Prix guitars and bass, 1967 catalogue.

ORIGINAL **GIBSON FLYING V**
THIS EXAMPLE: ***1967***
Jimi Hendrix used this revised-type Flying V from summer '67 to early '69 as his main guitar for blues numbers, alongside his much busier Strats. Soon after he got it, he painted the body with colorful decorations, restored here by a later owner.

The Robbs, rare fans of LaBaye's 2-by-4, 1967.

ORIGINAL **LABAYE 2-BY-4**

THIS EXAMPLE: ***1967***

A 60s oddity was the LaBaye, made in '67 with a bare minimum body, many years before Ned Steinberger created his more sophisticated (and more successful) take on the notion of minimalism in electric guitar design.

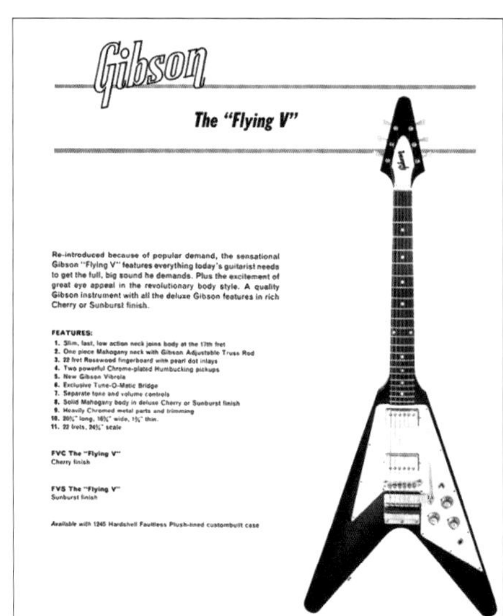
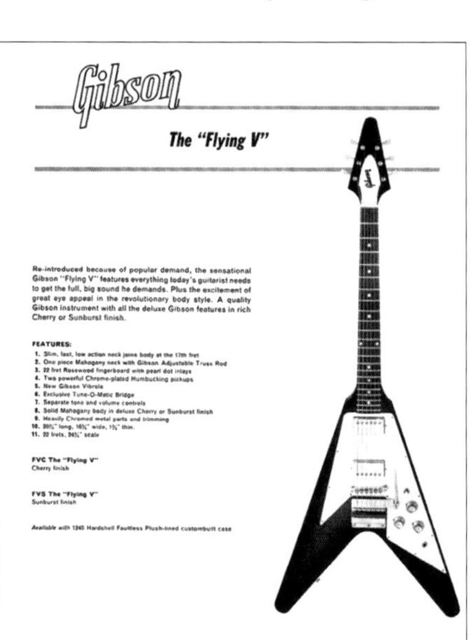

Gibson

The "Flying V"

Re-introduced because of popular demand, the sensational Gibson "Flying V" features everything today's guitarist needs to get the full, big sound he demands. Plus the excitement of great eye appeal in the revolutionary body style. A quality Gibson instrument with all the deluxe Gibson features in rich Cherry or Sunburst finish.

FEATURES:

1. Slim, fast, low action neck joins body at the 17th fret
2. One piece Mahogany neck with Gibson Adjustable Truss Rod
3. 22 fret Rosewood fingerboard with pearl dot inlays
4. Two powerful Chrome-plated Humbucking pickups
5. New Gibson Vibrola
6. Exclusive Tune-O-Matic Bridge
7. Separate tone and volume controls
8. Solid Mahogany body in deluxe Cherry or Sunburst finish
9. Heavily Chromed metal parts and trimming
10. 20[illegible]" long, 16[illegible]" wide, 1[illegible]" thin.
11. 22 frets, 24[illegible]" scale

FVC The "Flying V"
Cherry finish

FVS The "Flying V"
Sunburst finish

Available with 1245 Hardshell Faultless Plush-lined custombuilt case

Promo sheet for Gibson's revised Flying V, 1967.

Italia stresses cool, 1994 catalogue cover.

ITALIA IMOLA VARIO

THIS EXAMPLE: ***2016***

The Italia brand was founded in 1998, with early designs developed by Trev Wilkinson of Fret-King. Drawing on and mashing up classic 60s style elements, and not solely those of Italian makers, Italia's guitars are retro reinterpretations with modern twists.

Since the demise of the original Flying V in the late 50s and its brief revised appearance in the late 60s, the design has become a great influence on other makers and musicians. Some have worked directly with the V's individual shape, while others have absorbed the general idea that an electric guitar can be more or less any shape you want it to be. Makers from Jackson to Dean in the United States and from Ibanez to ESP in Japan have all found some inspiration in that old V-shaped configuration, in a way that Gibson could never have dreamed of when the model took its first tentative steps in 1958.

Gibson itself reintroduced the revised '67-style V—the type with the triangular control-knob formation—in 1975, and this design became the look of the regular Flying V models from that time on. The most unusual recent V was the Modern Flying V, with a reconfigured curving-shape body. Also, it featured a Richlite fingerboard. Richlite, made from recycled paper and phenolic resin, is one of the alternatives to rosewood and similar woods, which have become increasingly difficult to use following restrictions on cross-border trading.

Grover Jackson met Randy Rhoads in 1980 when Rhoads was the 20-something whiz-kid guitarist with Ozzy Osbourne. Together they designed a custom guitar based on the general look and feel of the classic Flying V. A year or so later, they collaborated again on a more radical variant with a notably offset body style. It was around this time that Grover, who had bought Wayne Charvel's guitar-parts business in 1978, began to use the Jackson brand for his guitars. With Rhoads's tragic death in an aircraft accident in 1982 and the subsequent interest in his unusual Jacksons, the first Jackson-brand production instrument appeared in 1983, the Randy Rhoads model.

GIBSON MODERN FLYING V
THIS EXAMPLE: ***2018***
Gibson called this new Custom Shop limited-edition Modern Flying V "a blast from the future." We'll have to see about that. It had a new-for-Gibson V-style shape, sparkle "prism" finishes, Richlite fingerboard, and plated pickguard.

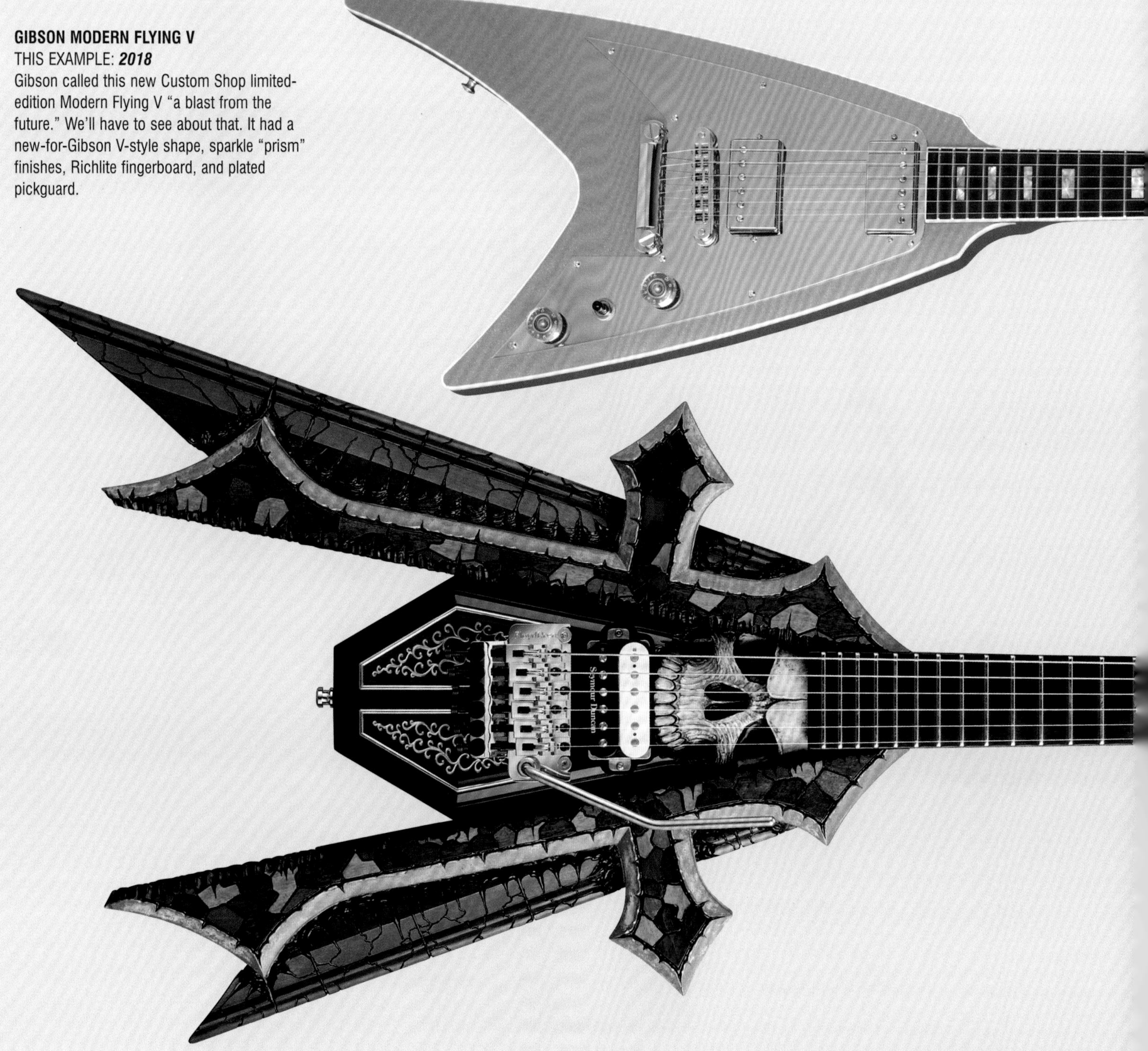

Mick Thomson with signature Ibanez MTM, 2012 ad.

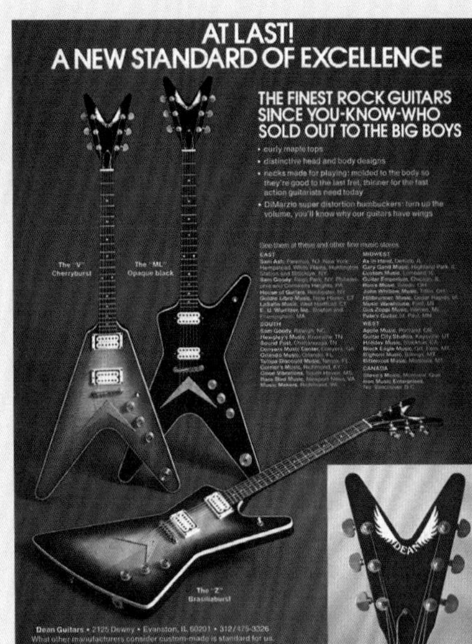

Dean's V, Z, and ML models, 1977 ad.

Alexi Laiho with signature ESP model, 2007 ad.

JACKSON RANDY RHOADS
THIS EXAMPLE: ***1983***
This was the first Jackson Rhoads model built, and the first equipped with a Floyd Rose vibrato, which in the 80s was quickly becoming the metal guitarist's dive-bombing trem system of choice.

ESP AMAKUSA
THIS EXAMPLE: ***2010***
ESP began in Tokyo in 1975, moving from early copies and superstrats to more original designs. This guitar was built for a trade exhibition as a showpiece to draw attention to ESP's high-end capabilities.

1967

When MCA bought Danelectro in 1966, it introduced a new Danelectro-made brand, Coral, named after one of MCA's record labels. The most unusual Coral instrument produced during the brand's short life was the electric sitar, the first of its kind. George Harrison had used a real sitar on 'Norwegian Wood' on The Beatles' *Rubber Soul* album in 1965, and guitarists lined up to try to play the Indian instrument amid a craze for music from the subcontinent. They quickly discovered that a real sitar is a very difficult instrument to get a decent sound from, let alone to master.

The Coral Sitar was a relatively successful attempt to provide a sitar-like sound from an instrument that offered the simpler playability of a regular electric guitar. The key to its sitar imitation was an almost-flat plastic bridge, designed by the US session guitarist Vinnie Bell (Bell also helped to design Danelectro's twelve-string Bellzouki model). The bridge did create a buzzy edge to the Coral Sitar's tone—but it also meant that the instrument was almost impossible to keep in tune. That did not stop the Coral's use on hits such as 'Green Tambourine' by The Lemon Pipers and 'Games People Play' by Joe South.

A Danelectro-brand electric sitar followed, forsaking the ornate shape of the Coral's body and opting instead for something a little closer to the teardrop style of a real sitar, which traditionally used a gourd for its body. The shape was reflected in the rounded headstock design. The Danelectro model also came with a metal leg-rest screwed to the lower edge of the body to assist any electric sitar players who favored the seated position when exploring their ragas. Both the Coral and the Dan'o sitars lasted only to the end of the 60s, but there have been revivals of the idea.

Coral catalogue cover, 1968.

ITALIA MODENA SITAR
THIS EXAMPLE: ***2013***
The Italia company's recent take on the electric sitar uses a Gotoh Buzz bridge to emulate the Coral/Dan'o original, as well as lipstick pickups and drone strings. This one has a finish called white crackling.

ORIGINAL **DANELECTRO SITAR**
THIS EXAMPLE: ***1968***
Danelectro introduced its own version of the Coral-brand electric sitar, and it was a simpler single-pickup take on the design, with a rounded body (complete with leg-rest) that hinted at the shape of the real Indian instrument.

Danelectro's sizzling sitar reissue, 2015 ad.

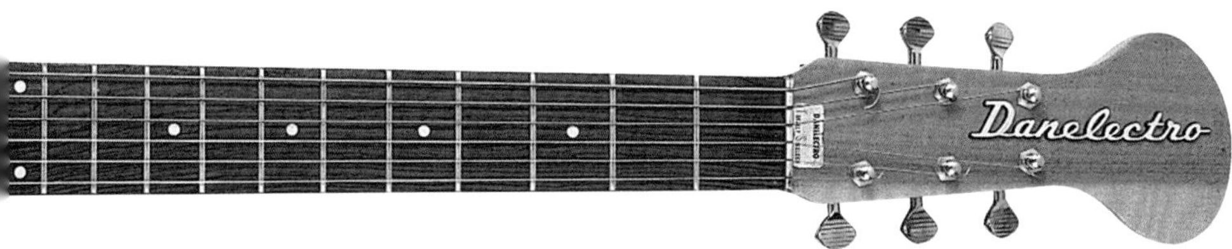

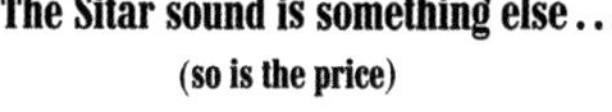

New DANELECTRO electric sitar . . . $139 list

Now you can create the hit recording sounds of the Lovin Spoonful, Strawberry Alarm Clock, Turtles, Richie Havens, Gabor Szabo and countless others with the Danelectro Electric Sitar. The action's so fluid. The sound so great. Any guitarist can play sitar in no time at all. Sitarmatic bridge (patents pending), fast action Danelectro neck and convenient chrome plated lap mount make this the outstanding new instrument for 1968. Now, at $139 shouldn't you be a sitarnick?

FREE! Write for complete details and color catalog today.

CORAL/DANELECTRO, A subsidiary of MCA Inc. 211 West Sylvania Avenue, Neptune City, New Jersey 07753

Danelectro sitar ad, 1968.

ORIGINAL **CORAL SITAR**
THIS EXAMPLE: ***1967***
The Danelectro-made Coral Sitar had a flat plastic bridge to induce sitar-like tones from an instrument playable by guitarists, plus 13 drone strings designed to resonate sympathetically with the regular strings. This example is owned by David Gilmour.

You don't have to be HINDU to play the CORAL® ELECTRIC SITAR

Danelectro CORPORATION
A SUBSIDIARY OF MCA INC.
211 West Sylvania Avenue, Neptune City, New Jersey 07753

Coral® PRESTIGE GUITARS AND AMPLIFIERS Vincent Bell SIGNATURE DESIGNS

© Copyright 1967 – Danelectro Corp., a subsidiary of MCA, Inc. Printed in U.S.A.

Vinnie Bell in Coral/Danelectro sitar ad, 1967.

Bronco guitar and matching amp, 1968 catalogue.

Fender had trouble with the body binding on some of the Coronado hollowbodys it had introduced in 1966. The problem arose when attempting to bond the binding material to the body, and often it would pop out of the groove cut for the purpose. When the company's workers tried to rebind the bodies, this would sometimes leave scorch marks on the body—so rather than dispose of the burnt carcasses, Fender devised a special white-to-brown shaded finish, which it called Antigua, to hide the damage. The finish was first used on some Coronado II and Coronado XII models in 1967, and this look lasted until 1971. The Antigua finish would be revived in the late 70s as an option on some Stratocasters, Telecasters, and Mustangs, and has seen other more recent appearances.

A further unusual finish was developed for the Coronados in 1967, this time called Wildwood. As pop culture immersed itself in the dazzling art of psychedelia, so Fender predictably announced the Coronado Wildwoods as "truly a happening in sight and sound" with "exciting rainbow hues of greens, blues, and golds." They certainly looked different. The effect was achieved by injecting dyes into beech trees during growth, which produced in the cut wood a unique colored pattern that followed the grain. These, too, were shortlived, and all Fender's thinline hollowbody Coronado electrics had disappeared from the line by 1971.

Fender had long ago indulged in the marketing scheme of a matching guitar and amplifier set aimed at beginners, with packages of steel-guitar and amp. In 1967, it launched another of its "student" solid electrics, the $150 Bronco, which had a single pickup, simple vibrato, misshapen pickguard, and a Dakota red finish. It was sold as a set with the Bronco five-watt amp.

ORIGINAL **FENDER CORONADO XII WILDWOOD**
THIS EXAMPLE: ***1967***
A twelve-string Coronado with Fender's new Wildwood finish, a streaked look achieved by using wood from color-injected beech trees. Each guitar with the finish was different, but there were three broad types, known as rainbow greens, blues, or (as here) golds.

ORIGINAL **FENDER BRONCO**
THIS EXAMPLE: ***1968***
The Bronco came as a set with a matching amplifier, aimed as a budget-price package to start the beginner guitarist on their road to rock'n'roll stardom. This basic guitar had a surprisingly long life in the Fender line, lasting until 1980.

Stylized Coronado on 1966–67 catalogue rear cover.

Antigua and Wildwood Coronados, 1969 catalogue.

FENDER MODERN PLAYER CORONADO
THIS EXAMPLE: ***2013***
Fender revived the 60s Coronado style briefly in 2013 as part of its Chinese-made Modern Player series, adding a center-block to the body and opting for a pair of Gretsch-like humbucking pickups instead of the original single-coils.

ORIGINAL **FENDER CORONADO II ANTIGUA**
THIS EXAMPLE: ***1967***
Fender's Antigua finish, first used for some Coronado models, was developed as a way to cover scorch marks made when re-binding the body. It had a white-to-brown shaded effect, with the dark section usefully close to the troublesome binding area.

FENDER FSR ANTIGUA STRATOCASTER
THIS EXAMPLE: ***2012***
FSR in Fender-speak means Factory Special Run, a limited edition launched occasionally to offer something a little different from the catalogued lines. This one revives the original Antigua look, last seen on Strats in the 70s.

ORIGINAL **DOMINO BARON**
THIS EXAMPLE: ***1967***
Another striking Domino guitar was the Baron, also of Japanese manufacture, and seen here in impressive four-pickup form—although it was also available with one, two, or three pickups. Domino insisted it had a "super-speed short scale jazz neck."

Domino HAS A WINNER – FOR YOU!

Solidbody Californian models, Domino 1967 catalogue.

ORIGINAL **GUYATONE LG-350T SHARP 5**
THIS EXAMPLE: ***1967***
In 1967, the Japanese brand Guyatone launched this signature model for the Sharp 5 group, whose lead guitarist was Nobuhiro Mine. This example, with Guyatone's distinctive "G" logo on the headstock, has had its vibrato arm removed.

Guyatone Sharp 5 catalogue page, 1969.

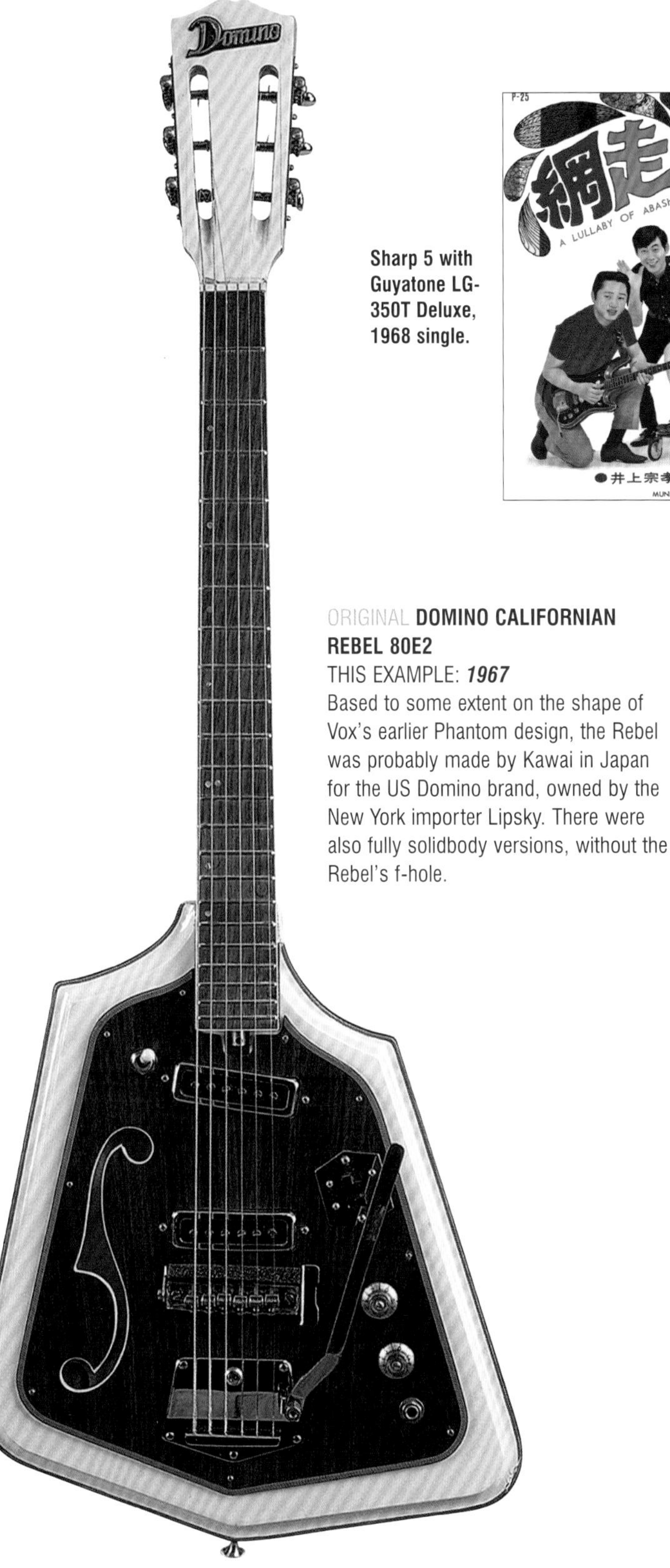

Sharp 5 with Guyatone LG-350T Deluxe, 1968 single.

Guyatone was founded by Mitsuo Matsuki in Tokyo in the 30s. The company introduced its first solidbody electric in the mid 50s, and we've seen how its LG models proved popular in Britain toward the end of that decade. Into the 60s, and the range and quality improved, with models such as the LG-160T, complete with handy body hole, a couple of SG and MG hollowbodys, and the LG-200T, which had four pickups and multiple pushbutton selectors. Guyatone sold some instruments at this time to the Canadian mail-order catalogue company Eaton's, including versions of its LG-65T and LG-130T.

Probably the best known Guyatone model is the Sharp 5, introduced in 1967 and named for the Japanese group of the same name. The Sharp 5, part of the Group Sounds trend that spread across Japan at this time, were led by Munetaka Inoue and guitarist Nobuhiro Mine, and their break came in 1967 when they signed to Columbia Records. Guyatone saw an opportunity for a liaison with the band, naming its LG-350T guitar and EB-9 bass the Sharp 5 models. Mine played the 350 Deluxe, with blue finish, three pickups, and gold-plated metalwork.

Meanwhile, other Japanese makers were busy exporting guitars, too. Maurice Lipsky, a distributor based in New York City, bought guitars for its Domino brand from several Japanese sources, including Fujigen, Matsumoku, and Kawai. One of the most striking series from Domino was the Californian, introduced in 1967 and probably made by Kawai. Some were fully solid, while others, including the Californian Rebel, had a single f-hole cut into the otherwise solid body, a classical-style slotted headstock, and edge "binding" actually painted on. All shared the five-sided body that reflected a little inspiration from Vox's earlier Phantom guitars. The Californians did not last, gone from the Lipsky lines by 1968.

ORIGINAL **DOMINO CALIFORNIAN REBEL 80E2**
THIS EXAMPLE: ***1967***
Based to some extent on the shape of Vox's earlier Phantom design, the Rebel was probably made by Kawai in Japan for the US Domino brand, owned by the New York importer Lipsky. There were also fully solidbody versions, without the Rebel's f-hole.

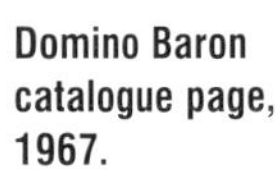

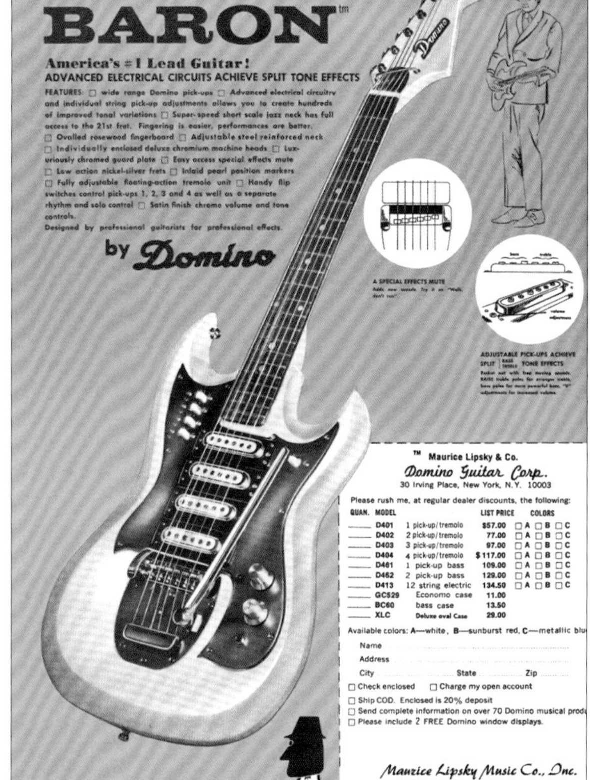

Domino Baron catalogue page, 1967.

GOOD MORNING
Although the area skies will clear today, the weather will be clouded by a chilly spell.

MORNING ADVOCATE

THE INDEX

Amusements	9-D	Financial	10-B
Classified	3-E	Society	2-B
Comics	2-E	Sports	2-C
Deaths	10-A	Television	10-B

43rd Year, No. 279 ★ Baton Rouge, La., Friday Morning, April 5, 1968 Associated Press, United Press International 66 Pages Ten Cents

King Shot to Death in Memphis

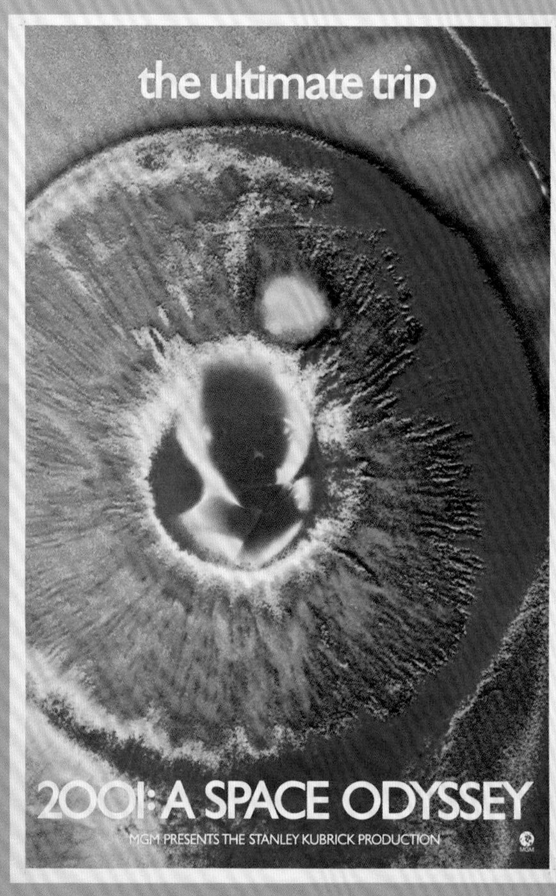

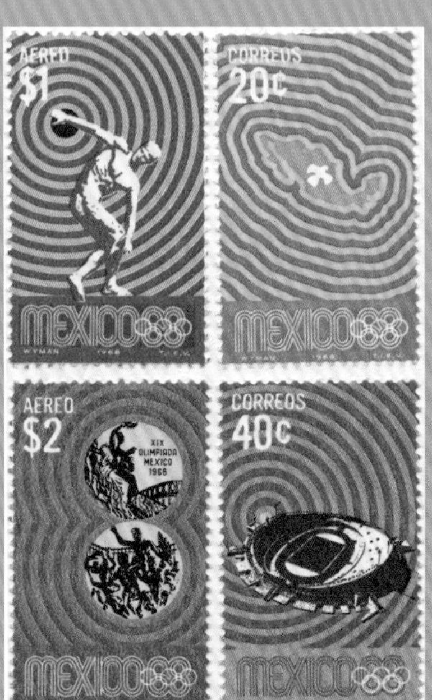

- **MARTIN LUTHER KING** is shot dead in Memphis, and Senator Robert Kennedy is assassinated in Los Angeles.
- **2001: A SPACE ODYSSEY** has 60s audiences enthralled by its sweeping tale from ape-man to space station, its trip-like visuals, and its enigmatic message. One review describes the two-hours-plus movie as "somewhere between hypnotic and immensely boring."
- **THE VIETCONG** mount the Tet Offensive, a series of continued attacks on the South Vietnamese capital, Saigon. This calls into question the ability of South Vietnamese and US forces to win the war.

1968

- **FRENCH STUDENTS** riot and heavy street fighting ensues. Workers call a general strike in support and the country comes to a halt. Elections are called amid new riots, but the Gaullists hold power, defeating the Communists in a landslide.
- **BLACK ATHLETES** give controversial black-power salutes at a Mexico Olympics awards ceremony.
- **SOVIET** and other Warsaw Pact forces invade increasingly liberal Czechoslovakia, re-imposing totalitarianism. A treaty is signed providing for Soviet troops to be stationed in Czechoslovakia, which becomes a two-state federation.

Roger Rossmeisl and Virgilio "Babe" Simoni at Fender devised a new lightweight version of the Telecaster in 1968. The Thinline Telecaster had three hollowed-out cavities inside the body, offering a different tonality, and there was a single f-hole over one of the chambers. The Thinline Tele at first came in what Fender called "groovy natural" finishes—in ash or mahogany—and the model lasted in the line until 1971. In that year, it would be modified with two of Fender's new humbucking pickups, designed by Seth Lover, whom the company had poached from Gibson. A number of other humbucker-equipped Teles would appear in the 70s, including the Custom and Deluxe models, although their popularity did not grow until more recent times.

Rossmeisl's speciality was the German carve, which gives a distinctive indented lip around the top edge of a guitar body, following its outline. He adopted this feature for two new models, the Montego and LTD, the first Fender full-depth hollowbody electrics, both firmly traditional but still obstinately using Fender's bolt-on neck. Very few were made and they were soon dropped. Rossmeisl did not last much longer at Fender, and after returning to Germany he died there in 1979 at the age of 52.

In 1968, psychedelia hit Fender. The company's designers applied self-adhesive wallpaper with a paisley or floral pattern to a couple of Telecaster models, and the results, the Paisley Red and Blue Flower Teles, were dramatic. The Paisley Red quickly became identified with James Burton, who played as a sessionman with many artists, but in 1969 he became the regular guitarist with Elvis Presley, and he and his Paisley Tele would remain at Presley's side until the singer's death in 1977. Much as it suited Burton, Fender's dazzling wallpaper experiment with the Paisley Red and Blue Flower Telecasters did not last long in its original run.

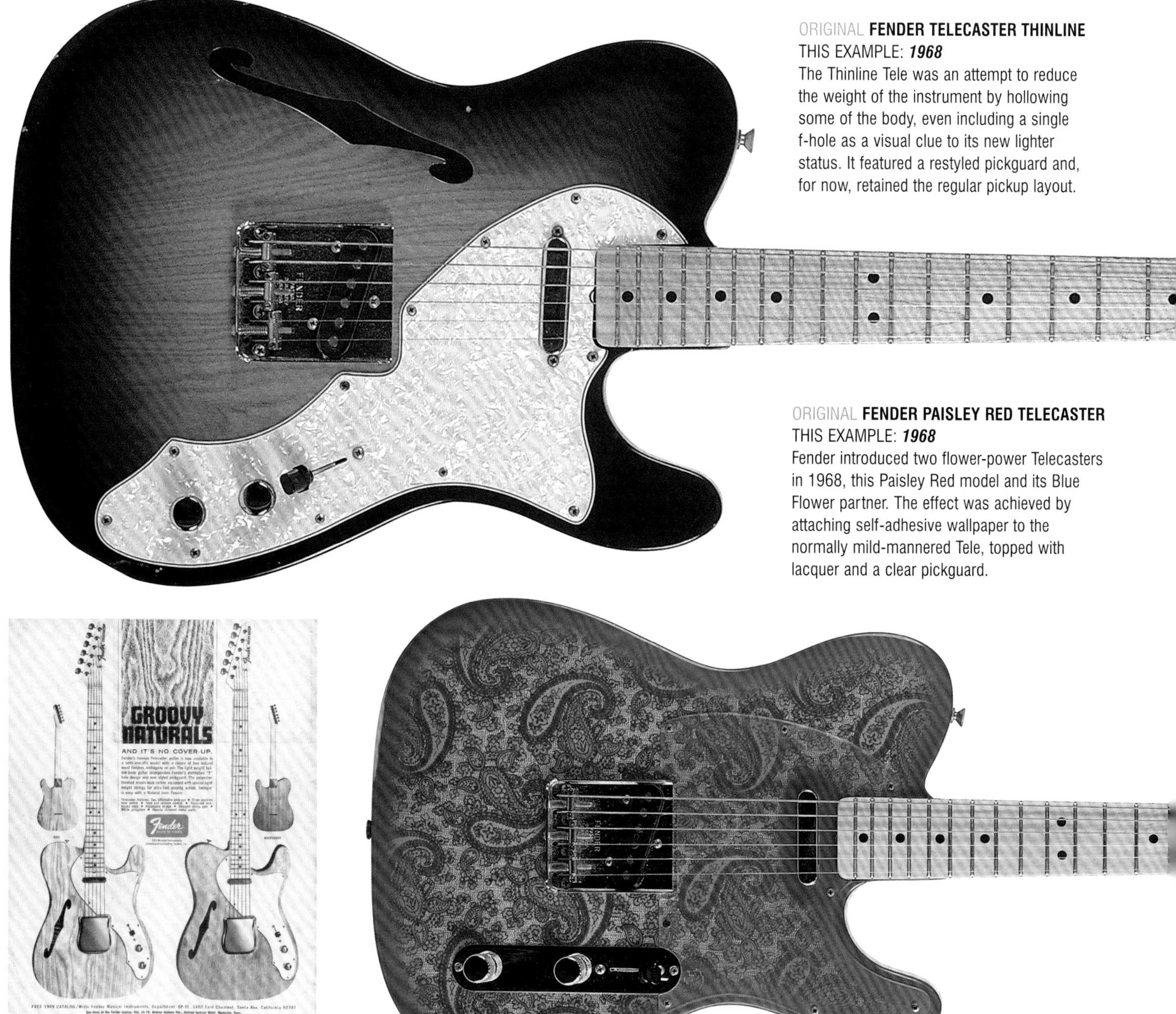

ORIGINAL **FENDER TELECASTER THINLINE**
THIS EXAMPLE: ***1968***
The Thinline Tele was an attempt to reduce the weight of the instrument by hollowing some of the body, even including a single f-hole as a visual clue to its new lighter status. It featured a restyled pickguard and, for now, retained the regular pickup layout.

ORIGINAL **FENDER PAISLEY RED TELECASTER**
THIS EXAMPLE: ***1968***
Fender introduced two flower-power Telecasters in 1968, this Paisley Red model and its Blue Flower partner. The effect was achieved by attaching self-adhesive wallpaper to the normally mild-mannered Tele, topped with lacquer and a clear pickguard.

Fender's groovy Telecaster Thinline ad, 1968.

FENDER'S **Blue Flower**

Blue Flower bursts forth in a dazzling array of subtle purple and green patterns. Never before has such an exciting profusion of color been offered.

Telecaster $279.50, Telecaster Bass $289.50

(These finishes are available on the Telecaster and Telecaster Bass only.)

CBS Musical Instruments
Columbia Broadcasting System, Inc.

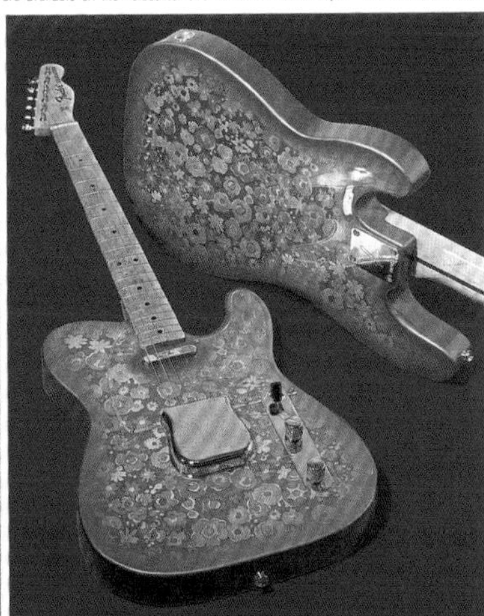

Fender's even groovier Blue Flower Tele promo, 1968.

ORIGINAL **FENDER MONTEGO II**

THIS EXAMPLE: ***1968***

A rare example of the Montego, one of two full-depth hollowbody models designed by Roger Rossmeisl and introduced briefly by Fender in 1968. The accompanying LTD had a floating pickup, where the Montego (with one or two pickups) had its electrics built-in.

Two Montegos and an LTD, Fender catalogue 1969.

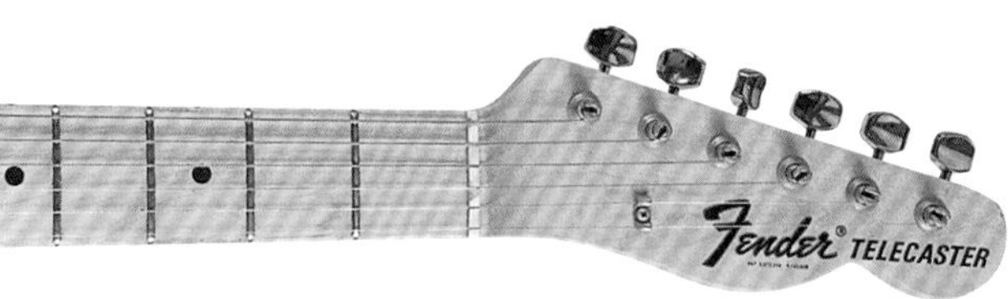

Tele Thinline influence, James Trussart ad, 2013.

FENDER JAMES BURTON TELECASTER
THIS EXAMPLE: ***2017***
Fender's first Burton signature model had a lurid paisley pattern covering the whole of the front of the body, in gold or red. A newer version, introduced in 2006, came either in this red paisley flames or a blue paisley flames finish.

FENDER BLUE FLOWER TELECASTER
THIS EXAMPLE: ***2008***
Fender has revived the look of the original Paisley Red and Blue Flower Telecasters several times since their brief run in the late 60s, and this Fender Japan model is typical of the modern take on the period style.

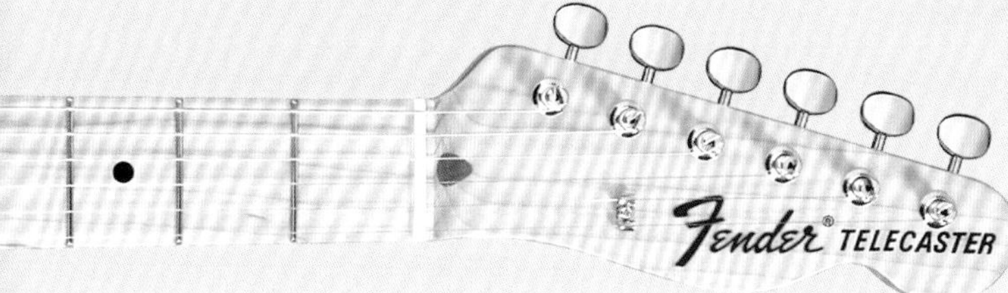

Fender's original Paisley Red and Blue Flower Telecasters had brief lives in the catalogue—they were introduced in 1968 and dropped the following year. However, the unusual look of this pair has since inspired a number of reissues and reinterpretations through the years, starting with some copycat re-creations that were produced by Fender Japan in the mid 80s.

We've seen how James Burton was the best-known 60s player of the original Paisley Red version—not surprisingly, because he was seen with it regularly on stage with Elvis Presley. Burton had first come to notice with a regular 50s Tele when he was seen almost every week playing alongside pop'n'roller Ricky Nelson on the TV show *The Adventures Of Ozzie & Harriet*. Burton may well have had the first Telecaster-fueled Top 40 hit when his guitar lick set the tone for Dale Hawkins's raw 'Suzie Q,' a song that crashed into the chart in July '57, bursting with Burton's earthy playing. But in 1969 he landed that gig with Elvis, and with Paisley Red Tele in tow, Burton was the king's guitarist until Presley died in '77. He continued to play sessions, too, and used the guitar for work with Emmylou Harris, Gram Parsons, and many others.

In the 80s, Fender talked to Burton about the possibility of a signature model, but the prize of first artist-named Fender model went to Eric Clapton, whose signature Strat went on sale in 1988. Burton had to wait another two years for his signature Tele to appear. It had three single-coil pickups in a Strat layout, and some examples were finished in a paisley pattern more vivid than his original Paisley Red model. A revised version in 2006 offered a blue or red paisley "flames" finish, and there was also a two-pickup option in plain old candy apple red.

FENDER FSR BLACK PAISLEY STRATOCASTER HSS
THIS EXAMPLE: ***2012***
Another of Fender's limited-edition Factory Special Runs, this Strat had a muted black version of the paisley pattern, and it features the modern HSS pickup style, indicating a layout of humbucker, single-coil, single-coil.

Fender Japan catalogue, paisley Tele reissues, 1989.

FENDER AMERICAN ELITE TELECASTER THINLINE
THIS EXAMPLE: ***2018***
This latest take on the Thinline Tele is part of Fender's recent high-end American Elite series, claimed by the company as "the pinnacle of innovation" and including Fender's fourth generation Noiseless pickups, a cutaway neck heel, and locking tuners.

Gibson Les Paul reissue catalogue cover, 1968

In 1968, Gibson finally bowed to the popularity of old-style Les Paul models with players such as Eric Clapton and Michael Bloomfield, reissuing two guitars: the relatively rare two-pickup Les Paul Custom; and the Les Paul Standard (Goldtop) with P-90 pickups and six-saddle bridge. Les Paul himself was at the trade-show launch to promote the new guitars for Gibson.

The press ad publicizing the revived guitars, headlined "Daddy Of 'Em All," admitted that Gibson had been forced to reintroduce the guitars. "The demand for them just won't quit," it said. "And the pressure to make more has never let up. OK, you win. We are pleased to announce that more of the original Les Paul Gibsons are available. Line forms at your Gibson dealer." A spokesman told a magazine reporter: "The revival of these instruments answers a pressing need. It will soon be no longer necessary to search for used models that sell in auction for $700 to $1,000 in the United States." Gibson had a success in the making, and soon the idea of reissuing classic models would become an important part of many a guitar maker's business plan. For now, though, the mystery as far as many guitarists were concerned was why Gibson had waited so long—and why it reissued the "wrong" Les Pauls. Where was the sunburst model with humbuckers that everyone wanted?

Meanwhile, smaller makers continued to try their luck in the flourishing electric guitar business. Kustom was begun by Bud Ross in Kansas in the mid 60s and became known for its amps, but the firm introduced a shortlived line of semi-solid electrics in 1968. Micro-Frets in Maryland produced models with an unusual side-join body construction, and some had an intonated nut and a built-in wireless transmitter, but the brand was gone by the mid 70s.

ORIGINAL **MICRO-FRETS THE ORBITER**
THIS EXAMPLE: ***1968***
Today it's common to see wireless systems on stage, but this innovative instrument from Micro-Frets was the first wireless guitar, well ahead if its time. The antenna for the on-board FM transmitter can be seen on the upper horn of the body.

ORIGINAL **KUSTOM K200C**
THIS EXAMPLE: ***1968***
Kustom's shortlived guitar line was designed by Doyle Reading, who had worked with other small-scale makers such as Holman and Alray. Kustom was better known for amplifiers, and its semi-solid guitars like this K200C were soon dropped.

Bigsby-equipped Kustom guitars, 1968 catalogue.

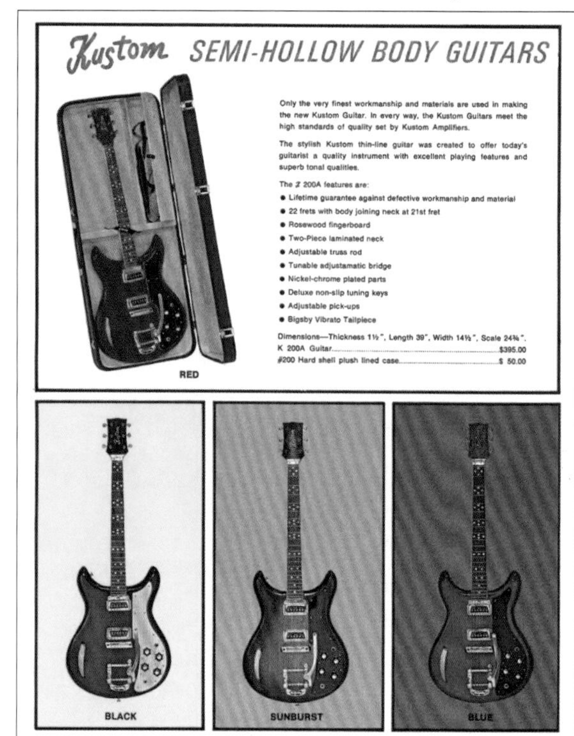

Kustom SEMI-HOLLOW BODY GUITARS

Only the very finest workmanship and materials are used in making the new Kustom Guitar. In every way, the Kustom Guitars meet the high standards of quality set by Kustom Amplifiers.

The stylish Kustom thin-line guitar was created to offer today's guitarist a quality instrument with excellent playing features and superb tonal qualities.

The K 200A features are:

- Lifetime guarantee against defective workmanship and material
- 22 frets with body joining neck at 21st fret
- Rosewood fingerboard
- Two-Piece laminated neck
- Adjustable truss rod
- Tunable adjustamatic bridge
- Nickel-chrome plated parts
- Deluxe non-slip tuning keys
- Adjustable pick-ups
- Bigsby Vibrato Tailpiece

Dimensions—Thickness 1½", Length 39", Width 14½", Scale 24¾".
K 200A Guitar........ $395.00
#200 Hard shell plush lined case........ $ 50.00

RED

BLACK

SUNBURST

BLUE

ORIGINAL **GIBSON LES PAUL STANDARD**
THIS EXAMPLE: ***1969***
The Goldtop was one of two Les Pauls that Gibson reissued in 1968 in original 50s single-cut form. The specific style is of the Goldtop made originally between 1955 and 1957, with P-90 pickups alongside a Tune-o-matic bridge and separate "stud" tailpiece.

ORIGINAL **GIBSON LES PAUL CUSTOM**
THIS EXAMPLE: ***1971***
Gibson reissued two single-cutaway Les Pauls in 1968, including this Custom. It planned to finish the Custom in white, like the contemporary SG Custom, but sensibly reverted to the original black after problems with contaminated white paint.

Reissued duo, 1968 Gibson catalogue page.

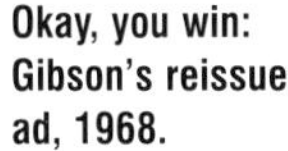

Okay, you win: Gibson's reissue ad, 1968.

EASTWOOD CUSTOM K-200 DLX
THIS EXAMPLE: ***2018***
Eastwood notes that the original Kustom 200 model of the 60s, on which this remake is based, looks something like the lovechild of a secret liaison between Rickenbacker and Mosrite.

EASTWOOD MICRO-FRETS SPACETONE
THIS EXAMPLE: ***2016***
The original Micro-Frets Spacetone was introduced by the Maryland company in 1967, and this reissue was produced in recent years by Eastwood, which specializes in re-creations of 60s retro classics.

Aria Diamond catalogue cover, 1968.

In the mid 60s, Teisco was one of the leading Japanese guitar makers, alongside Guyatone and Kawai. In 1965, the company had even sponsored a movie, *Eleki No Wakadaisho* ("The Young Electric Guitar Wizard"). It starred guitarist Yuzo Kayama as a member of the fictional Young Beats group, who entered a battle-of-the-bands competition—and they all played Teisco guitars through Teisco amps, of course.

Despite such cultural breakthroughs, as well as the opening of a new factory in Okegawa and the export of instruments to Britain, Finland, Germany, the Netherlands, Norway, Sweden, the US, and elsewhere, Teisco battled with financial problems, and it declared bankruptcy at the start of 1967. The company was bought that year by Kawai, which continued to offer Teisco guitars until about 1970.

Kawai dates back to the 20s, when Koichi Kawai started a keyboard company in Hamamatsu. The firm began making guitars in the 50s, and into the 60s expanded the Kawai-brand lines and, like many Japanese firms, exported widely to customers who used their own brandnames, including Domino, Kent, Kimberly, and TeleStar in the US.

The Arai company was founded in Nagoya by the classical guitarist Shiro Arai in 1956. At first Arai made only classicals, but it added electrics in the early 60s, soon using the Aria and Aria Diamond brands (and in the 70s and later the company would become better known for its Aria Pro II brand). Aria had been the Japanese distributor of Fender guitars in the late 50s, so it's not surprising that some of its own solidbody models were Fender-like in appearance, although there were also a number of Aria hollowbody electrics. The company has survived many ups and downs in the guitar business and continues successfully today with a large and impressive line of electrics alongside acoustic guitars and, of course, classical guitars.

ORIGINAL **ARIA DIAMOND ADSG-12T**
THIS EXAMPLE: ***1968***
The Arai company used two main brands in the 60s, Aria and Aria Diamond. This twelve-string Aria Diamond guitar has an offset-waist body shape inspired by the Fender design that appealed to many makers in Japan and elsewhere.

Teisco thinline electrics, 1967 catalogue.

ORIGINAL **TEISCO MAY QUEEN**
THIS EXAMPLE: ***1968***
After Kawai bought a bankrupt Teisco in 1967, the revived brand offered new models, including this May Queen, which followed a Japanese trend at the time for hollowbody instruments. The body shape was influenced by Vox's earlier Mando Guitar.

Beach fun 60s-style with Kent guitars, 1969 ad.

ORIGINAL **KENT 742**
THIS EXAMPLE: ***1968***
Kent was a brandname applied by the New York distributor Buegeleisen & Jacobson to its imported lines of Japanese-made guitars. At first, Kents were made by Guyatone, but this magnificent four-pickup model was probably made by Kawai.

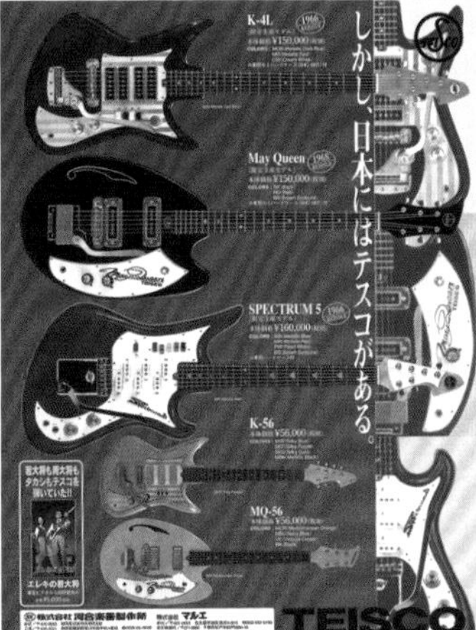

Teisco reissues, including Spectrum and May Queen, 2000 ad.

ARIA RETRO 1532
THIS EXAMPLE: ***2015***
Introduced in 2010, this reissue of Aria's late-60s offset-waist 1532 has several modern improvements to please today's guitarists, including a back-angled headstock, upgraded pickups, and a closer take on a Jaguar/Jazzmaster-style vibrato.

ORIGINAL **KAWAI CONCERT**
THIS EXAMPLE: ***1968***
By the late 60s, Kawai was one of the biggest guitar makers in Japan, producing guitars for the domestic market as well as many export customers in Europe and the US. This distinctive weapon-like Concert model drew on Hofner's violin-shape body style.

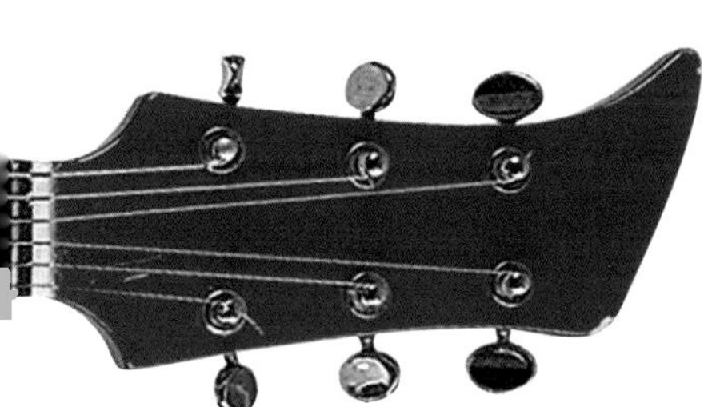

9d
GENTLEMAN
Concorde
HARRISON

WOODSTOCK
MUSIC & ART FAIR
presents
AN
AQUARIAN
EXPOSITION
in
WHITE LAKE, N.Y.
WITH
AUGUST
15, 16, 17.
3 DAYS
of PEACE
& MUSIC

BBC records
MONTY PYTHON'S
FLYING CIRCUS
With John Cleese, Michael Palin, Graham Chapman, Eric Idle, Terry Jones, Carol Cleveland

- **IN VIETNAM** the first major contingent of US troops is withdrawn. The war will continue into the mid 70s, leaving dead well over a million people. Journalist Michael Herr speaks for a generation of participants when he writes: "Vietnam was what we had instead of happy childhoods."

- **NEIL ARMSTRONG** is the first man to step on to the moon. Understandably nervous, he seems to fluff his words, apparently saying (nonsensically): "That's one small step for man, one giant leap for mankind." But the script remains word-perfect: "That's one small step for *a man*, one giant leap for mankind."

1969

- **WOODSTOCK** in upstate New York hosts 400,000 music lovers cast in a sea of mud and entertained by Jimi Hendrix, Sly & The Family Stone, Richie Havens, Crosby Stills Nash & Young, Santana, Joe Cocker, The Who, Ten Years After, and others.

- **MONTY PYTHON** debuts on British TV. "I took the liberty of examining that parrot when I got it home, and I discovered the only reason that it had been sitting on its perch in the first place was that it had been nailed there."

- **BRITISH TROOPS** begin patrolling Catholic areas of Belfast as unrest and violence erupt in Northern Ireland.

- **CONCORDE** supersonic airliners make maiden flights in France and Britain. The aircraft will enter full service in 1976.

1969

Les Paul himself had ideas on guitar design that did not necessarily coincide with what Gibson thought commercially viable, and one of his unusual preferences was for low-impedance pickups. An advantage of low-impedance pickups is wide-ranging tone; a disadvantage is that they need their power boosted before the signal reaches the amplifier.

When Les Paul went to Gibson in 1967 to discuss the reissue of Les Paul guitars, he convinced the company to go ahead with the Les Paul Professional and the Les Paul Personal, introduced in 1969. They had a complex array of controls, and the Personal even provided a volume control for a handy on-board microphone input. Both guitars required connection using the special cord supplied, which had a built-in transformer that boosted the output from the low-impedance stacked-coil humbucking pickups to a level suitable for use with normal high-impedance amplifiers. The guitars were not successful and they made only a brief appearance in the Gibson lines. Meanwhile, Gibson changed the style and name of the recently reissued Les Paul Standard model, introducing in its place the Les Paul Deluxe in 1969. It was an attempt to give players the reissued Les Paul with sunburst finish and humbuckers that they wanted. However, Gibson's managers wanted to do this without new costs and decided to fit Epiphone mini-humbuckers into the spaces already routed for smaller P-90s. At first, the Deluxe came in Goldtop finish, but sunbursts and other colors were added.

At the time of writing in 2018, Gibson had just filed for bankruptcy, and the precise nature of its future was unclear. This book has shown that in the history of the guitar business, nothing is certain and, with a few honorable exceptions, nothing lasts forever. Let's hope that the Gibson brand continues to be one of those honorable exceptions.

ORIGINAL **GIBSON LES PAUL PROFESSIONAL**
THIS EXAMPLE: ***1969***
The Professional was one of two shortlived Les Pauls with low-impedance pickups introduced in 1969, both of which came with multiple controls and a special cord with a built-in transformer to boost the output for use with a regular amplifier.

ELECTRO-ACOUSTIC SOLID AND FLAT-TOP GUITARS

Selmer UK Gibson catalogue cover, 1967.

ORIGINAL **GIBSON LES PAUL PERSONAL**
THIS EXAMPLE: ***1969***
On the original 50s models, Gibson put Les Paul's name on its own design. In 1969, the roles were reversed, and Gibson put its name on a couple of models that had Les's favored low-impedance pickups. This aptly-named Personal was one of them.

Gibson Les Paul catalogue cover, 1970.

Gibson electric-acoustics catalogue cover, 1970.

ORIGINAL **GIBSON CREST**
THIS EXAMPLE: ***1971***
Gibson's Crest, new for 1969, was a sort of high-end ES-330, with a rosewood body, often figured like this example, and with luxury features, including gold-plated metalwork. It lasted just a couple of years in the Gibson catalogue.

ORIGINAL **GIBSON LES PAUL DELUXE**
THIS EXAMPLE: ***1970***
Gibson's second Les Paul reissue came in 1969 with the Deluxe, and this '70 example had the desirable benefit of a sunburst finish and two humbuckers—although these were Epiphone mini-humbuckers rather than the full-size pickups players wanted.

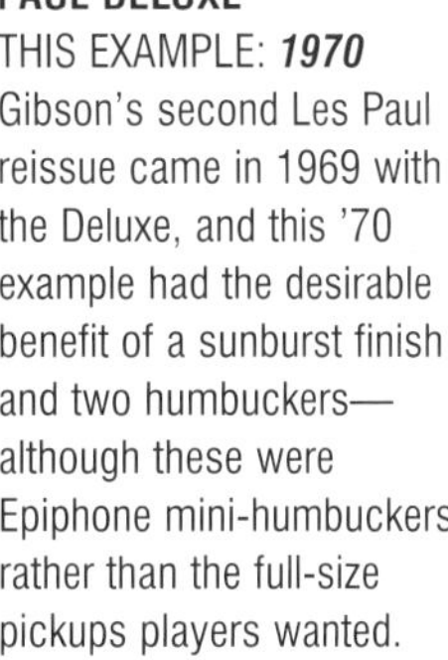

Feature-crazy low-impedance models, 1969 catalogue.

Jimi certainly plays a Strat, 1969 ad.

In summer 1968, Fender's Don Randall managed to secure a meeting with The Beatles, and the result was the band scoring a VI six-string bass, a Jazz Bass, a number of amplifiers, including a PA system, and a prototype Telecaster Rosewood. The Beatles famously played their last ever concert on the rooftop of their Apple HQ in London in January 1969, and George Harrison played the Telecaster Rosewood, as featured in the subsequent movie *Let It Be*. A production model appeared that year but lasted only a couple of years. Its body was made with a thin layer of maple between a solid rosewood top and back. Fender tried to lighten the heavy guitar a little later by adding hollowed chambers, but the weight and unusual tonality meant the model was never popular. It has been revived a number of times in recent years.

Toward the end of the 60s came evidence of Fender wringing every last drop of potential income from unused factory stock that would otherwise have been written off. Two shortlived guitars, the Custom and the Swinger, were assembled from leftover components of other models. Both were made in necessarily limited numbers and did not last.

Everett Hull set up Ampeg in New York in the 40s to make amplifiers and double-bass pickups. In the late 60s, Ampeg hired a local repairman, Dan Armstrong, to design a new line of electric guitars. Armstrong carved bodies from blocks of clear plastic, intending to make the result distinctive as much as to exploit the sonic potential of the material. The See-Through guitar was offered with six slide-in pickups labelled Rock, Country, and Jazz, with a Treble and Bass variety of each. It lasted little more than a year in production, brought down by conservative guitarists (Keith Richards excepted) and an expensive production process.

ORIGINAL **FENDER TELECASTER ROSEWOOD**
THIS EXAMPLE: ***1969***
George Harrison used a prototype of this guitar in the *Let It Be* movie, and Fender produced a shortlived production model, first sold between 1969 and 1972. Its weight and unusual tonality reduced its popularity at the time, despite the Beatles connection.

Keef transparently plays an Ampeg, 1970 ad.

ORIGINAL **AMPEG DAN ARMSTRONG SEE THROUGH**
THIS EXAMPLE: ***1969***
The See-Through model was designed by Dan Armstrong with a body of acrylic plastic known as Lucite or Plexiglas. Ampeg's instructions suggested that if the body became scratched, the best way to repair it was to polish it with toothpaste.

FENDER GEORGE HARRISON TELECASTER
THIS EXAMPLE: ***2017***
A re-creation of the Rosewood Tele that George Harrison used briefly in the late 60s brings this book almost full circle, from the original Telecaster that Fender introduced in the early 50s as the world's first commercially-sold solidbody electric guitar.

Ampeg's See-Through reissues, 1998 catalogue.

Custom

6-STRING SOLID BODY ELECTRIC GUITAR

A versatile Fender with two split pickups for perfectly balanced string sound

- 2 wide-range high-fidelity split pickups give perfectly balanced sound between all six strings
- 4 position pickup selector switch permits special phase reversal tone effects
- Exclusive Fender floating bridge assures perfect intonation and custom string adjustment
- Patented Fender dynamic tremolo has smooth action—returns strings to exact tuned pitch
- Exclusive Fender contoured waist design for maximum playing comfort

SPECIFICATIONS
Size: 41¾"L, 13"W, 1¾"D

BODY
Cutaway design
Exclusive Fender "off set" contoured waist body design
Fender thick-skin® high-gloss finish
Laminated pick guard
2 strap buttons
Heavily-chromed hardware throughout

NECK
Detachable hard rock maple
Fast-action design
Curved rosewood fingerboard
Completely adjustable truss rod
White neck binding
Molded nut with custom hand filed string notches
25½-inch scale
21 nickel-silver frets
9 rectangular simulated pearl inlaid position markers
10 side dot position markers
6 individual machine heads
Exclusive Fender head design

BRIDGE
Exclusive Fender floating bridge
2 way adjustable design
6 individually adjustable bridge sections
Removable bridge cover

PICKUPS
2 fully grounded wide-range high-fidelity split pickups individually adjustable
6 pole pieces on each pickup

SPECIAL EFFECTS AND CONTROLS
Patented Fender dynamic tremolo with removable arm
4-position pickup selector switch
Master volume control
Master tone control

STANDARD ACCESSORIES
Bridge wrench, guitar cord, polishing cloth
Black leather guitar strap

OPTIONAL ACCESSORIES
Hard shell plush lined case

Sunburst finish only

For prices and ordering information consult the Fender Price List under Numbers 11-5000 and 11-5020

Sunburst Finish

Fender Custom bitser in the 1970 catalogue.

ORIGINAL **FENDER CUSTOM**
THIS EXAMPLE: ***1969***
The Custom (also called the Maverick) was one of a couple of models devised by Fender in the late 60s to use up scrap material left over from other models. It was a necessarily shortlived experiment.

ORIGINAL **FENDER SWINGER**
THIS EXAMPLE: ***1969***
The Swinger was Fender's other bitser of the late 60s, signaling that the company's new owner, CBS, might be more interested in the balance sheet than a well-designed guitar. It was made using unwanted parts from Musicmasters, Bass Vs, and Mustangs.

Index

G

H

Index

R

S

T

U

V

W

Z

Acknowledgements

IMAGES

OWNERS KEY

The guitars illustrated in this book came from the collections of the following individuals and organisations, past and present, and we are very grateful for their help. The owners are listed here in the alphabetical order of the code we've used to identify their instruments in the Instruments Key that follows.

AA Absara Audio. **AB** Andy Babiuk. **AC** Anonymous collector. **AG** Aria Guitars Co. **AH** Adrian Hornbrook. **AL** Andrew Large. **AM** Albert Molinaro. **AO** Alex Osborne. **AR** Alan Rogan. **BB** Bruce Bowling. **BF** Brian Fischer. **BL** Burns London. **BM** Bill Marsh. **BW** Bert Weedon. **CA** Chet Atkins. **CB** Clive Brown. **CC** Chinery Collection. **CD** Chris DiPinto. **CK** Clive Kay. **CM** Country Music Hall Of Fame. **CN** Carl Nielsen. **DA** Dave Gregory. **DB** Dave Brewis. **DC** Doug Chandler. **DD** Doug Doppler. **DE** Duane Eddy. **DG** David Gilmour. **DN** David Noble. **DU** Duesenberg Guitars. **EC** Eric Clapton/Christie's. **EG** Eastwood Guitars. **ES** ESP Guitar Co. **FA** Fretted Americana. **FM** Fender Musical Instruments. **GD** Gary Dick. **GG** Gruhn Guitars. **GH** Gardiner Houlgate Guitar Auctions. **GI** Gibson Brands Inc. **GJ** Ged Johnson. **GR** Gretsch Guitars. **GU** Guild Guitars. **GW** Gary Winterflood. **HA** Heritage Auctions. **HK** Hiroshi Kato. **JH** John Hornby Skewes & Co. **JL** Jay Levin. **JR** John Reynolds. **JS** John Sheridan. **KG** Kay Guitar Company. **KH** Karl Höfner GmbH. **LA** Larry Wassgren. **LW** Lew Weston. **MD** Mark Duncan. **MK** Martin Kelly. **MS** Mike Slubowski. **MW** Michael Wright. **NC** Neville Crozier. **PA** Paul McCartney. **PD** Paul Day. **PG** PRS Guitars. **PH** Phil Manzanera. **PM** Paul Midgeley. **PU** Paul Unkert. **RB** Ron Brown. **RG** Robin Guthrie. **RI** Rickenbacker International Corp. **RM** Rose-Morris. **RR** Robin Baird. **RV** Rivolta Guitars. **RW** Robert Witte. **SA** Scot Arch. **SC** Simon Carlton. **SH** Steve Howe. **SM** Samick Music Group. **SO** Steve Ostromogilsky. **TB** Tony Bacon.

INSTRUMENTS KEY

This key identifies who owned which guitars at the time they were photographed. After the relevant bold-type page number(s) there is a model identifier, followed by an owner code (see the alphabetical list in the Owners Key above).

8–9 ES-150, HA. **9** Zephyr, CC; ES-300, CC. **10** Electro Spanish, CC. **11** Bigsby Merle Travis, CM; Ultratone, HA. **16–17** Broadcaster, SA. **17** Zephyr Emperor Regent, CC; Leo Fender Broadcaster, FM. **20–21** Tele, GG. **21** Esquire, DG; Nocaster, GG. **22–23** Tele 40th, PM; American Original Tele, FM. **23** 50s Tele, AO; '51 Nocaster, FM. **24–25** Super 400, CC. **25** ES-175, GG; L-5CES, BM. **26** Super 400, CC. **26–27** Wes Montgomery, GI. **27** L-5 Doublecut, GI; ES-175, GI. **30–31** '53 Les Paul, MS. **31** Les Paul Reissue, GI; '55 Les Paul, MS. **32–33** Double-Neck, CC. **33** ES-295, GG; 1952 ES-295, GI. **36–37** '56 Country Club, CC; '55 Country Club, CC. **37** Duo Jet, FA. **38–39** '95 Duo Jet, GR; '17 Duo Jet, GR. **39** '16 Country Club, GR; '79 Country Club, GG. **40** Guild, PU. **41** Kay, MW; Harmony, HA. **42–43** Guild, GU; Eastwood, EG. **43** Kay x3, KG. **46–47** '56 Strat, CC. **47** '58 Strat, CC. **48** '97 Strat, FM. **48–49** '04 Strat, FM. **49** '10 Strat, FM; '79 Strat, SC.

50–51 '88 Strat, PM. **51** '90 Strat, PM; '18 Strat FM; '96 Strat, MS. **52–53** Stratford, GG; '54 Custom, DN. **53** Aristocrat, GU; '08 Custom, GI. **54–55** '56 Junior, DN; '56 Silver Jet, SA. **55** '10 Junior, GI; '18 Silver Jet, GR. **58–59** ES-5, SA; Byrdland, SA. **59** ES-350T, SA.**60–61** '96 ES-5, HA. **61** '02 ES-5, GI; Byrdland, GI. **62** '55 Special, CB; TV, MS. **63** Junior, HA, '91 Special, HA. **64–65** Prototype, CA; Solid Body, FA. **65** 6120, LW. **66–67** Setzer, GR; Cochran, GR. **67** Solid Body, GR; 6120, GR. **68** Convertible, CC. **68–69** '59 Falcon, JR. **69** '56 Falcon, SA. **70** Stills, GR; '75 Falcon, JR. **71** Black Falcon, HA; White Falcon, GR. **72–73** Club 50, RB; Club 40, LA. **73** '99 Jet, HA; '56 Jet, HA. **74–75** Twin, PD; Single-Neck, HA. **75** Belmont, CC; Dual Tone, CC. **76–77** Wray, EG; Bowie, AA. **77** Jamesport, JH; Westbury, JH. **80–81** U-1, HA; U-2, HA. **81** Baritone, JH. **82** '56 Penguin, CC; '59 Duo-Sonic, RG; Musicmaster, RG. **83** '18 Duo-Sonic, FM; '17 Penguin, GR. **86–87** Kay, CC; Rickenbacker, RI. **87** '58 Les Paul, MS; '57 Les Paul, CC. **88–89** Rivolta, RV; Airline, EG. **89** Frampton, GI; Tribute, GI. **90–91** Committee, NC. **91** Grimshaw, GH; 457/12, KH. **92** Harmony, MW. **92–93** 1323, MD; Mark III, MW. **93** 1303/U2, SM; Mark V, MW. **96** Prototype, GG. **96–97** Flying V, CC. **97** Explorer, EC. **98–99** Gothic, GI; Custom, GI. **99** V2, NC.

100 Designer, HA. **100–101** '18 Explorer, GI. **101** X-Plorer, GI; Moderne, DC. **102** Dean, AL. **102–103** B.C. Rich, HA. **103** Ibanez, MW. **104** Bikini, PD. **104–105** Rock Oval, CN. **105** Kay, MW; Duesenberg, DU. **106** EDS-1275, FA. **107** TV, HA; Junior, CB; Armstrong, GI. **108–109** '59 335, SA. **109** '58 335, HA. **110–111** Studio, HA. **111** Figured, GI; Carlton, GI; Dot, GI. **112** '58 Standard, AR. **112–113** '60 right-hander, GW; '60 left-hander PA. **113** '59 Standard, GJ. **114** Allman, MS. **114–115** Reissue, MS. **115** Clapton, GI. **116–117** Gibbons, GI. **117** Page, GI; Ralphs, GI. **118–119** Reissue, DN; Wallace, MS. **119** Classic RM; Heritage, MS. **120–121** Anniversary, MS; Reissue, MS. **121** Reissue Aged, GI. **122** Daughtry, GI. **122–123** HP, GI. **123** Reissue, GI; Traditional, GI. **124–125** '60 355, CC; '59 355, HA. **125** Lucille, GI; Reissue, 355. **126–127** '59 Jazzmaster, CC. **127** '60 Jazzmaster CC. **128–129** Costello, FM. **129** Anniversary, FM; Mascis, FM. **130–131** Country Club, AR. **131** '59 Gent, AC; Falcon, SA; '17 Gent, GR. **132–133** Anniversary, AH; Double Anniversary, GG. **133** Tennessean, GG. **134–135** Rose, GR. **135** Anniversary, GR. **136** Guitarlin, PD. **136–137** Standard, MD. **137** Double-Neck, HA. **138** Longhorn, JH. **138–139** Convertible, JH. **139** 59X, JH; 12S, JH. **140** Stratotone, MW. **140–141** Guyatone, DB. **141** Meteor, CD; Silvertone, SM. **144** Strat, MS. **144–145** Futurama, LW. **145** Tele, SA. **146–147** Cray, FM. **147** Vaughan, FM. **148** '82 Strat, PM. **148–149** '80 Strat, PM. **149** '83 Strat, PM; Strat XII, FM.

150–151 HH, FM; VG, FM; 60s, FM. **152–153** Deluxe, HA; '52, DA. **153** White, FM; Elite, PD. **154** Classic, FM. **154–155** Original, FM. **155** Relic, FM. **156** Crestwood, AR; Vega, CC. **157** '59 Emperor, AR; '11 Emperor, GI. **158–159** Hagstrom, PD; Framus, PD. **159** Hofner, BW. **160–161** 345, MS. **161** 330, MS; Melody Maker, CB; Special, PU. **162** PRS, PG. **162–163** DC Pro, MS. **163** 330, GI; Melody Maker, GI; Special, GI. **168** L-5CES, SA. **168–169** Falcon, JR. **169** Electromatic, GR; L-4XES, HA; Super 400, CC. **170** Verithin, BW; Harmony, MW. **170–171** Kay, CC. **171** Verythin, KH; Airline, EG. **174–175** Vox, NC. **175** Watkins, MW; Burns, PD. **176** Vox, HA. **176–177** Burns, BL. **178–179** Esquire, BF; Strat, SA. **179** Tele, SO; Jazzmaster, CC. **180–181** Tele, BF; Jazzmaster, FM. **181** Strat, FM. **182** Sheraton, CC. **182–183** Casino, HA. **183** Rickenbacker, AM; Gallagher, GI. **184–185** Custom, HA; Standard, HA. **185** Special, MS. **186–187** Custom, HA; Ibanez, DD. **187** Reissue, HA. **188** Anniversary, GI. **188–189** Special, HA. **189** Original, GI; Aged, GI; Zoot Suit, GI. **190–191** Gent, GD. **191** '69 Jet, SA; '65 Jet, HA. **192** Gent, GR; Electromatic, GR. **192–193** Classic, GR. **193** Duo Jet, GR; Young, GR. **196–197** '64 Jag, HA; '62 Jag, HA. **197** '65 Jag, HA. **198–199** Jaguarillo, FM; Jag-Stang, FM; 60s, FM. **199** Squier, FM.

200 Newport, CC; '62 Supro, HA. **200–201** Glenwood, HA. **201** '17 Supro, JH; Airline, EG. **202–203** EDS-1275, SH. **203** Farlow, DC. **204–205** Princess, JL; Corvette, HA. **205** 6120, CC; Nashville, GR. **206–207** Riviera, HA; Professional, HA. **207** '16 Kay, KG; Valensi, GI; '62 Kay, CC. **208–209** Framus, MW. **209** Guild, DE; Hagstrom, MW; Silvertone, MW. **212–213** VII, PH; III, HA. **213** Bellzouki, MW; Firebird V, MS. **214–215** RD Artist, PD;

Firebird 7, GI. **215** Firebird V, GI; Anniversary, GI. **216–217** Hofner, PD; Bartolini, TB. **217** Hopf, TB. **218** Caiola, SH. **218–219** Mosrite, CK; Gretsch, PD. **219** Crestwood, PD. **220–221** Starfire, HA; Thunderbird, MW. **221** Weedon, BW. **222** S-200, GU. **222–223** ST P90, GU. **223** VI, GU; IV, GU. **226** 360/12, AB. **226–227** 1993, ML; Astro, RI. **227** 1996, DA. **228** 350, RI. **228–229** 330/12, HA. **229** 325, HA; 360/12, HA. **230–231** Guitar Organ, PD; Mark VI, HA. **232–233** Harmony, PD. **233** '64 Mustang, RR; '09 Mustang, FM; Airline, EG. **234** Ibanez, PD. **234–235** '64 Burns, PM. **235** Eko, PD; '17 Burns, BL. **238–239** Lopez, MS. **239** Grohl, GI; Zero, GI; Firebird III, DA. **240–241** Electric XII, SO; Marauder, GG. **241** Strat, PM. **242** '18 Strat, FM. **242–243** Strat XII, FM. **243** Venus XII, FM. **244** '65 Airline, HA. **244–245** Silvertone, PD. **245** '18 Airline, EG; Goya, MW. **248** Coronado, HA; Gretsch, JS. **249** '66 Jazzmaster, CC; Jag, MS; Leeuwen, FM.

250 Custom Kraft, MW. **251** Baldwin Double Six, PD; Baby Bison, PD; Burns Double Six, BL. **252–253** Teisco, HA. **253** Yamaha, PD; Eastwood, EG. **256** Galanti, PD. **256–257** Flying V, DB. **257** LaBaye, MW; Italia, JH. **258–259** Gibson, GI; ESP, ES. **259** Jackson, RW. **260–261** Danelectro, PD; Coral, DG. **261** Italia, JH. **262** Bronco, HA. **262–263** XII, MW. **263** II, HA; Modern Player, FM; Strat, FM. **264** Baron, MW. **264–265** Guyatone, AC. **265** Californian, MW. **268–269** Thinline, BF; Paisley, AH. **269** Montego, RR. **270** Burton, FM. **270–271** Blue Flower, FM; Strat, FM. **271** Elite, FM. **272** Kustom, MW. **272–273** Micro-Frets, CC. **273** Standard, HA; Custom, HA, Eastwood Custom, EG; Eastwood Micro-Frets, EG. **274** '68 Aria, PD. **274–275** Teisco, MW. **275** Kent, MW; Kawai, MW; '15 Aria, AG. **278** Personal, HK. **278–279** Professional, HA. **279** Crest, MS; Deluxe, BB. **280** '69 Tele, AH. **280–281** Ampeg, DG. **281** Harrison, FM; Swinger, PD; Custom, RR.

Original advertisements and catalogues reproduced here came from the collections of: Tony Bacon; John Cooke; Paul Day; Gary Deacon; Martin Kelly; *The Music Trades*; National Jazz Archive; Alan Rogan; Vintaxe.com; and from various manufacturers' online and physical resources.

THANKS

In addition to those thanked in the picture credits, the author would like to thank: Julie Bowie; David Brass (Fretted Americana); Steve Brown (vintaxe.com); John Cooke (guitar-yard.com); Paul Cooper; Joe Cutoni (Wizard Design Studios); Gary Deacon; Barry Gibson (Burns London); Ben Green (WD Music); Mike Gutierrez (Heritage Auctions); Christopher Hjort; Luke Hobbs (Gardiner Houlgate Guitar Auctions); Dustin Jack; Martin Kelly; David Koltai (Supro Pigtronix); Michael McDivitt (Gibson); Nao (Paradise Records); Justin Norvell (Fender); Jason Padgitt (Gibson); Heinz Rebellius (Duesenberg Guitars); Mike Robinson (Eastwood Guitars); Vince Schaljo (Eastwood Guitars); Stu Suchit (Supro Pigtronix); Scott Tsai (Retrofret Guitars); Simon Turnbull (JHS); Ron Wood; Andrew You (Samick Music Group).

"This old guitar ain't mine to keep,/It's only mine for a while."
Neil Young 'This Old Guitar'